MEDICAL SEXISM

MEDICAL SEXISM

Contraception Access, Reproductive Medicine, and Health Care

Jill B. Delston

LEXINGTON BOOKS
Lanham • Boulder • New York • London

Published by Lexington Books
An imprint of The Rowman & Littlefield Publishing Group, Inc.
4501 Forbes Boulevard, Suite 200, Lanham, Maryland 20706
www.rowman.com

6 Tinworth Street, London SE11 5AL

British Library Cataloguing in Publication Information Available

Library of Congress Cataloging-in-Publication Data

ISBN 978-1-4985-5821-1 (cloth)
ISBN 978-1-4985-5822-8 (electronic)

For Eleanor and Beatrix

TABLE OF CONTENTS

ACKNOWLEDGMENTS

Thank you to Jana Hodges-Kluck, who gave me the opportunity to write this book in the first place, as well as Trevor F. Crowell, Sydney Wedbush, Jon Wisniewski, all those who contributed at Lexington Books, and an anonymous reviewer.

Thank you to my writing groups near and far for the many needed boosts, work sessions, helpful comments on drafts, and conversations about the argument. In the writing groups near, thank you especially to Taffy Ross, Rebecca Schuman, and Jason Gardner. In the writing groups far, thank you especially to Emily Crookston, Lynn Niizawa, Lavender McKittrick-Sweitzer, Ramona Ilea, and Krista K. Thomason. I am grateful for these and all the other friends who helped make writing social instead of solitary.

Thank you to the friends and mentors who gave me many and great comments on chapters, including especially: Brit Brogaard, Larry May, Marilyn Friedman, Eric Brown, the great and also good doctor Amy Ravin, Liz Sepper, Rabbi Randy Fleisher, Michelle Ciurria, Katherine Sweet, Frank Lovett, and everyone who came to my session at WPES.

Thank you to UMSL for support that made this book possible, to my students, and to my department and my colleagues, especially Sally Ebest, Jon McGinnis, Kathleen Nigro, Gualtiero Piccinini, Waldemar Rohloff, and Eric Wiland.

I used content from a previously published article for this book: "When Doctors Deny Drugs: Sexism and Contraception Access in the Medical Field." *Bioethics* 31, no. 9 (November 2017): 703–10. Thank you to *Bioethics* and John Wiley & Sons, Inc. for permission to use that article, and to those who gave me comments on drafts of that paper.

Thank you to those who helped me track down obscure information, especially Mary A. Hyde at the Resource Center for the American College of Obstetricians and Gynecologists, Julia Kaye at the ACLU, and Iain Milne at the Royal College of Physicians of Edinburgh for permission to use the image for the cover.

To simply thank my family for the moral, emotional, and unconditional support they gave me does not sufficiently capture their significance to the completion of this book. My parents, my sister, and my husband gave me the love and encouragement and confidence I needed to write this book, acted as a sounding board for my ideas, gave me perspective, and also read chapters and gave me feedback.

Thank you to my children, whose love for all things medical I share. Maybe you can add this to your collection of "doctor books" even though there are no pictures of shots. Your joy, your spirit, your empathy, your focus, your hard work, your witticisms, your intelligence, your sisterhood, and your love teach me, inspire me, and give meaning to my life every day. I hope you grow up in a more just and peaceful world. To Eleanor, who told me when I was having trouble finishing to write one word at a time and if I could not do that, to write one letter at a time, thank you for the sage advice. I hope I helped you write your books on Thursdays as much as you helped me write my book. And I much prefer the deadlines of the books you write, which are "due when they're done." To Trixie, who describes herself as the author of every book she encounters, you once declared a book of Shakespeare to be your masterpiece and brought your sister a board book version of *Oliver Twist* because she was sad. Your growth marks the time I have been working on this book from birth, days after I signed the book contract, weaning just as I finished the draft, until now as I finish the revisions and you are learning your letters and numbers. Both of you contributed more than you know.

Thank you to Jeff. I am so grateful I found you and I am so lucky I have spent half my life with you. Your pep talks, your suggestions, your love, and your inspiration, as well as your reminders to take a break, make me better and happier.

Rachel, thank you for your scientific expertise and your common sense, your humor and your laughter, your reassurance and your encouragement, your breakfasts and lunches, your snacks and dinners. Talking to you makes the week better. Thank you to Matt, all of whose suggested titles I love, especially “Fallopian Rhapsody.” Thank you to Andy and Charlie for your creative energy, your love, and support.

Thanks to my far-flung family: Uncle Rick and Sam, Kate and Lyle, Chris and Sherry, Lyle and Emory, and Gramma Joan Sweet.

Thank you to Bridget, who gave me the gifts of time and peace of mind while she cared for my children.

Some influential people in my life are no longer with us. Thank you to my grandparents: Irma Baker, Walter Baker, Ethel Schoenberg Delston, and Vernon Delston. Thank you to GG, Granddad Sweet and Aunt Bertha.

Everyone should have parents as wonderful and supportive and feminist as my mom and dad. Thank you for long talks over popcorn after the kids go to bed and short talks between patients and billable hours. To my dad, thank you for your legal expertise, your jokes, the articles you send, and for improving the title immeasurably. To my mom, you have my eternal gratitude for your psychological expertise, your incredible insight, for reading the whole damn thing and giving me such great comments, and for your confidence in me. I cannot thank you enough for what you did to help me, but I will keep trying.

INTRODUCTION

Paternalism, Pap Tests, and the Pill

Medical sexism exists. Medical sexism is also insidious, pervasive, and grave. It is insidious because it often persists unacknowledged, it is pervasive because it systemically reaches far-reaching and disparate components of medical care, and it is grave because it can often be a matter of life and death. These are serious charges, so a defense of these claims requires treading carefully. In this book, I use a close examination of a case study to build up the argument for medical sexism as a systemic problem impacting large populations with serious harms and rights violations. The role of the case study is first, to defend the view that medical sexism exists; second, to demonstrate why that designation is the best explanation of current practices; and third, to use that analysis to investigate common themes and patterns in other areas of medicine, making it possible to designate medical sexism as comprising a broad range of phenomena.

To achieve this goal, I need to use a case study that has certain features. It should be a case that is very common so that the systemic nature of the problem is evident. It should have large impacts on health outcomes, making it difficult to minimize. It should be an area of medicine central to the lives of those it impacts so that the attribution of medical sexism is a significant one. It should be a case that is not so politicized that prior commitments bias us against the analysis. And, it should be a case that is not already accepted as medical sexism, so that I can use a deliberate and methodical demonstration of medical sexism in that case to evaluate other, more egregious or politicized cases.

I argue that a particular instance of hormonal contraception prescription refills has these features to a sufficient degree that it serves my purposes in this investigation. In the case I consider, doctors decline to refill contraception prescriptions until patients undergo a Pap test or other test like a pelvic examination unrelated to the medical safety of the prescribed hormones themselves. Why think that this case has the above features to make it a relevant case for my purposes?

The majority of people who are eligible to use hormonal contraception do choose to use it, making contraception access an issue that affects most women. Contraception also has significant impacts on health outcomes, since pregnancy as well as the other conditions hormonal contraception addresses are central to an individual's health. In her book, *Outrageous Acts and Everyday Rebellions*, Gloria Steinem points out that, "Obviously, reproductive freedom is simply a way of stating what feminism has been advancing for thousands of years."[1] Reproductive care is a linchpin in broader issues of health, not only as necessary preventative care and essential protection of autonomy, but also as a treatment for a broad range of issues. And, although contraception itself is politicized in the United States, the specific issue of doctors creating obstacles for patients seeking prescription refills is not currently politicized. Similarly, most doctors and patients view this case as one having a medical basis, meaning it is not yet viewed through the lens of sexism.[2] Contraception is of central importance to a full discussion on sexism in the medical field, but also provides an avenue to discuss other forms of sexist treatment in medicine.

BROADER IMPLICATIONS AND SIGNIFICANCE IN APPLIED ETHICS

According to feminists like Charlotte Bunch, the fight over gender inequality often takes place on the territory of women's bodies. Controlling women's bodies, then, would connect patriarchal power hierarchies like gender and sexuality oppression to abortion (chapter 6), breastfeeding (chapter 7) and heart disease (chapter 8). And, if women's bodies are the political territory on which a fight over gendered power structures plays out, then medical sexism is of primary significance when addressing sexism more broadly. Investigating the difficulties patients face in seeking contraception refill access without addressing sexism would then be incomplete, but so would addressing a single instance of medical sexism out of context from its instantiation of a broader systemic societal problem.

This unity of purpose in understanding unjust power relations, then, shows how medical sexism is central in a debate on sexism and how reproductive health is central in a debate on medical sexism.

Reproductive health is of real and immediate interest to those concerned with feminism and biomedical ethics. Furthermore, reproductive rights play an essential role in autonomy and self-control and also, by extension, in women's rights and outcomes generally. When such restrictions are used to control some groups or keep them subjugated, reproductive control becomes a central feature in feminist debates.

This argument works both ways: not only do protections for reproductive rights support rights, but rights also have an impact on reproduction. For example, some studies show that supporting women's rights leads to a reduction in the numbers of births per individual and by extension the overall population rate.[3] That is, when women have the opportunity and means to do anything other than have children, they often choose those options. In contrast, when their sole value to society and their sole ability to contribute to the household is through childbirth, when they lack the ability to make decisions about their own reproductive choices, and when health outcomes are such that mortality rates among children are high, women have more children. I discuss the role sexism plays in contraception access in more detail in chapter 5, but for now it suffices to point out that family planning, and by extension contraception access, is a feminist issue.

These questions also play a central role in the fundamental questions posed in biomedical ethics: questions of informed consent, autonomy, physician-patient relationships, health care and health-care allocation, reproductive rights, technology use, the boundaries of life, and the right to refuse medical care. Historically, the ethical controversy surrounding abortion has played a dominant role when such issues arise, crowding out other related issues like contraception, pregnancy, and childbirth. In the remainder of this book, I argue that contraception is just as central a feature of biomedical ethics concerns as abortion and is a rich area of philosophical interest.

However, perhaps these arguments only serve to show that contraception access is a niche category of relatively narrow interest. If one has a focus on "women's health," informed consent, or questions of doctor-patient relationships, then one will see the significance of physician restrictions on contraception access. Otherwise, one may be inclined toward apathy or disinterest. Is such a stance justified? How broad is the significance of these questions? Why might people have reason to take these issues seriously if their pursuits lie outside the scope of feminism and biomedical ethics?

In fact, lack of contraception plays a causal role in a variety of current issues in applied ethics. As a result, this issue has broad interest beyond the areas of feminism and biomedical ethics. In the remainder of this section, I explain why contraception access is relevant to a range of other areas in applied ethics. No matter what your area of moral concern, you have good reason to take contraception access seriously, and by extension, look critically at the role physicians play in restricting contraception access.

The belief that having too many children causes poverty could potentially lead physicians and public health officials to deny the poor their reproductive rights, ostensibly for their own good.[4] It is therefore dangerous to focus excessively on whether there might be a connection. In analyzing the racist history of the birth control movement, Annette Dula points out that racism is central to a full understanding, saying,

> While blacks perceive birth control per se as beneficial, blacks have historically objected to birth control as a method of dealing with poverty. Rather, most blacks believe that poverty can be remedied only by creating meaningful jobs, raising the minimum wage so that a worker can support a family, providing health care to working and nonworking people through their jobs or through universal coverage, instituting a high-quality day care system for low- or no-income people, and improving educational opportunities.[5]

Dula points out that much more complex factors contribute to poverty and therefore much more complex solutions are required.

While birth control is not a method for dealing with poverty, it can exacerbate difficult conditions for families and contribute to existing obstacles. When people are denied the opportunity of family planning—choosing a time to have a child that is right for them—they are harmed in their ability to pursue their goals.[6] Having a child earlier than individuals wish can cause them to make career sacrifices or lose the possibility of raising the child with sufficient support, which can affect individuals emotionally.[7] For example, lower birth weight, infant and maternal mortality, and medical complications are all more likely in unintended births than intended ones.[8] Studies show a negative outcome in terms of psychological impacts like positive affect starting very early in life.[9]

For related reasons, birth control restrictions can lead to major obstacles to educational outcomes for parents.[10] For example, legal restrictions on access to the pill leads to lower rates of postsecondary attainment, among other negative effects on women.[11] Studies also show that pregnancy can impact a teen's ability to graduate from high school, enroll in college, and graduate from college.[12] However, timing the births leads to better outcomes in both education and income from the perspective of individual choice.[13] These results should not be surprising. A birth is a major life event and the more individuals are in control of when it happens, the more they are able to ensure they can devote the necessary time, meet their other goals, and prepare adequately for the event. Education is a social good and contributes to financial and psychological well-being.[14] Being deprived of educational opportunities is a serious wrong. The question of contraception access connects not only to poverty, since patients who are already poor have fewer resources with which to handle provider obstacles, but also educational attainment, since control over the direction of one's life allows individuals to plan their lives accordingly.

However, I need not rely on this argument to make the case that such actions are wrong because such actions are wrong whether or not they are in the interest of society or the individual's own good. As I will discuss throughout the book, and especially in chapter 4, paternalism is not justified in the medical context and never justified in overriding patient rights. It is not within the purview of doctors to determine that because patients may be more financially secure if they do not have children, it is therefore permissible to sterilize them or otherwise deny them reproductive rights. Patients must make these decisions for themselves and protecting their choice should be a doctor's top priority.

A variety of reasons contribute to individuals having unwanted children, but lack of contraception access is a significant contributor. When doctors deny their patients birth control, they can have large impacts on unwanted fertility. For example, the birthrate among minors drops when provided access to the birth control pill.[15] In addition, while wealth and privilege allow patients to absorb the costs of extra restrictions on birth control without significant impact, lower socio-economic status can influence a patient's ability to accommodate these obstacles. Thus, restricting access can have differential impacts on the rich and the poor, leading to greater inequity in autonomous control over individual fertility.[16] Having children does not cause poverty, but poverty can pose problems in achieving reproductive autonomy.

Fear of overpopulation has a history of xenophobia and racism, and has a history of being overblown and exaggerated.[17] In both food access and environmental depletion, overpopulation is not the main concern. As Amartya Sen has argued, the major famines in history are due to problems in food distribution and not inadequate food production, which is why he argues democracy protects against famines.[18] Similarly, when it comes to environmental depletion, the way individuals choose to live their lives is more significant than the number of people in the world. Americans use orders of magnitude more resources, goods, services, and energy than people born in Brazil, China, or India.[19] Human beings are not the enemy, and achieving social justice is a more efficient way of helping the environment, not to mention a better approach to overpopulation.[20]

Nevertheless, social justice is connected to bodily autonomy. Those who purport to care about overpopulation want to put limits on individuals who sincerely desire more children. In other words, they use overpopulation to deny individuals their own reproductive control. All the while, people who do not want to become pregnant are ignored, denying them the bodily autonomy to protect their preferences. Margaret P. Battin thus proposes universal and reversible long-acting contraception, such as universal intrauterine devices (IUDs) to address this problem.[21] Respecting autonomy, not ignoring it, is the best way to achieve these goals.

Empirical facts provide evidence for Battin's thesis. Access to contraception leads to lower birthrates, especially among minors, and independent of legalized abortion.[22] Family planning clinics like

Planned Parenthood are associated with lower rates of teen pregnancies (and STDs).[23] Giving individuals control over their own bodies requires no sacrifice, requires no coercion, and it in fact enhances autonomy. Thus, attempting to limit population growth on the one hand while denying people choice in their own fertility on the other is a double attack on autonomy.

The same is true of medical decisions more generally. When some face differential treatment, their moral standing is doubly undermined because their choice is devalued and their health is impacted. Similarly, when doctors treat some patients differently from other patients, they are recreating societal injustices in the medical health context, meaning that analysis from the perspective of sexism is required to understand and address the issue.

OVERVIEW

In this section, I provide an overarching discussion of the main topics and questions covered in this book.

In the next chapter, I show the existence of the phenomenon that doctors deny patients access to birth control at very high rates. I then analyze its prevalence, arguing that it is incredibly common and widespread. In this chapter, I also compare different methods of birth control to analyze their role in human health.

In the next several chapters, I consider the practice in more detail. Do medical reasons support this practice? Does the practice lead to better outcomes for patients? What justification do doctors have for engaging in this practice regularly? By looking at the practice directly, my goal is to offer a more thorough analysis leading to new results on informed consent and reproductive health and to questions of sexism in the medical field generally.

In chapter 2, I argue that current practices violate the precept to "do no harm." By focusing on the medical and scientific evidence against denying patients birth control, I show how it leads to direct and real harm. I identify what harms are possible or likely as a result of these practices and what side effects those harms are likely to have on patients long term. Understanding the medical consequences of denying patients birth control helps us understand why doctors may or may not engage in the practice and also evaluate the moral permissibility of the position.

I also investigate the standards in the field of obstetrics and gynecology (OB/GYN) to determine first, whether doctors may be justified in denying contraception access due to professional recommendations, and second, whether reasonable doctors would justifiably engage in the practice. By looking at major institutions in the medical field and their recommendations, I offer an understanding of the practice and the potential motivations behind it. I use these standards to explore first, whether these standards are likely to influence doctors; second, whether they should influence doctors; and third, whether doctors are likely to know of the potential harms to patients that attend the practice.

In chapter 3, I focus specifically on the legal ramifications of denying patients birth control in favor of prerequisite testing in a U.S. context. I explore the legal definitions of medical malpractice and negligence to determine whether they apply to the practice I establish in chapter 1. Using the results from chapter 2, I am able to better investigate the implications for doctors and the legal field. By using the law to evaluate the practice, I provide not only a more concrete analysis than can be provided by the first two chapters, but also a stronger reason for doctors to pay attention to the issue and stay educated on the relevant guidelines. I argue that imposing added tests on patients before refilling a prescription is an instance of medical malpractice.

Understanding the potential medical and physical harms done to patients is a valuable contributor to my evaluation of the practice. However, too much emphasis is placed on these medical harms to the exclusion of the moral implications. In chapter 4, I put aside the medical and legal ramifications of denying patients birth control for the purpose of getting patients to engage in more testing. The physical and legal effects of the practice cannot tell the entire story since they are by nature descriptive and not normative evaluations. They can only tell us how the practice does play out and not how it should. In chapter 4, I move toward evaluating the morality of the practice independent of law and medicine. By considering autonomy, paternalism, and informed consent, I offer a more complete understanding of doctors withholding patients' contraception. In addition to applying norms like informed consent on the medical practice to determine its moral permissibility, I also apply the medical practice to the moral norms to better understand what is required of doctors and why. By understanding the interplay between these two fields, I employ applied ethics—applying theory to practice—and engage in practical ethics more generally—showing how individual medical case studies can influence theory.

Why is this practice so prevalent and why has it persisted for so many decades despite the lack of scientific evidence justifying it as well as its ostensible illegality? In chapter 5, I move to a possible explanation for doctors routinely denying their patients contraception. Identifying why doctors are likely to engage in such a practice so frequently is a key component in evaluating the practice successfully, understanding how to treat it going forward, and understanding the obstetrics/gynecology field generally. I propose sexism as a primary consideration in this context. Using the arguments from chapter 4, I examine why this issue is such an outlier in the medical field and how to perceive that fact. If sexism is a key contributor in a practice, then overlooking it would be a grave mistake and lead to wrongly characterizing the practice, its causes, and its effects.[24]

Once I defend a fuller understanding of why doctors deny their patients contraception on a routine basis, a better picture of medicine beyond the practice of contraception access emerges. Having argued medical sexism is at stake in the case of contraception access in chapters 1–5, I am able to use the work developed there to first, identify medical sexism in other cases; and second, show how our discussions of those cases can be reframed in more helpful ways. In chapter 6, I tackle the controversial case of abortion. Abortion is highly politicized and therefore not helpful in my initial claims that medical sexism exists and is problematic. Armed with the analysis from hormonal contraception refills, however, I defend a fuller understanding of the case of abortion, demonstrating how rape and incest exceptions, treatment in religious hospitals, and even the focus on the moral status of the fetus are all miscast. In this chapter, I argue that insofar as they attempt to discuss abortion without tackling the inextricable nature of sexism in abortion restrictions, they address only the symptoms and not the cause of the problem. Thus, correctly diagnosing sexism without correctly identifying why and how sexism pertains can lead to incoherent positions or failures to address the underlying problem.

In chapter 7, I investigate reproductive health more broadly. In this chapter, I explore other areas of patient preference, such as the morning after pill, Caesarean sections, vaginal birth after Caesarean sections (VBAC), birthing decisions, and in vitro fertilization. I also consider other areas of pregnancy prevention like sterilization, IUDs, and eugenics. What greater insight does the understanding of contraception from chapters 4, 5, and 6 bring into these areas of reproductive health? Why are doctors' decisions in reproductive care at odds with comparable decisions in other areas of health care? How can the revised concept of informed consent from chapter 4 help to evaluate practices in these areas? I take up these questions in chapter 7.

Next, I apply my analysis to the treatment of patients in other areas of medicine beyond reproductive health, such as breast cancer treatment, stroke treatment, treatment of pain, and autoimmune disorders. In chapter 8, I make a broader case for my thesis, showing how it has a much wider significance than even the OB/GYN field. Considering these cases requires first considering the role sexism plays in diagnosis, treatment, and outcomes for patients.

In the concluding chapter I consider potential solutions for the problems I raise in the first eight chapters of the book. I consider education, training, and awareness as components of a potential solution to the myriad of problems raised already. I also propose a new standard of care for contraception access and evaluate the alternative possibilities. Defending specific proposals to solve the problems I raise in this book has the goal of changing physicians' behavior, empowering patients, and redirecting scholarly work toward real cases of social justice.

NOTES

1. Steinem, *Outrageous Acts and Everyday Rebellions*, 165.
2. Though I argue for this point in Delston, "When Doctors Deny Drugs."
3. United Nations Population Fund, *State of World Population 2019*.
4. Roberts, *Killing the Black Body*, 4; Roberts, "Reproductive Justice, Not Just Rights," 80.
5. Dula, "Bioethics: The Need for a Dialogue with African Americans."
6. Sonfield et al., *The Social and Economic Benefits of Women's Ability to Determine Whether and When to Have Children*.
7. Institute of Medicine (US) Committee on Unintended Pregnancy; Brown and Eisenberg, eds. *Consequences of Unintended Pregnancy*.

8. Brown and Eisenberg.
9. Brown and Eisenberg.
10. Brennan, "Recent Work in Feminist Ethics," 883.
11. Sonfield et al., *The Social and Economic Benefits of Women's Ability to Determine Whether and When to Have Children*.
12. Sonfield et al.
13. Sonfield et al.
14. Gutmann, "Distributing Public Education in a Democracy"; Gutmann, *Democratic Education*, 42; Delston, "Gutmann, Amy."
15. Guldi, "Fertility Effects of Abortion and Birth Control Pill Access for Minors."
16. Gillespie et al., "Unwanted Fertility among the Poor."
17. Roberts, *Killing the Black Body*, xx; Steinem, *Outrageous Acts and Everyday Rebellions*, 5; Collins, "It's All In the Family," 77.
18. Sen, "Democracy as a Universal Value."
19. Scheer and Moss, "Use It and Lose It."
20. Purdy, *Reproducing Persons*, 100.
21. Battin, *Sex & Consequences*.
22. Guldi, "Fertility Effects of Abortion and Birth Control Pill Access for Minors," 825.
23. Packham, "Family Planning Funding Cuts and Teen Childbearing"; Yaver, "Analysis: States with More Planned Parenthood Clinics Have Fewer Teen Births and Sexually Transmitted Diseases."
24. Delston, "When Doctors Deny Drugs."

1

DOCTORS DENYING DRUGS

The Role of Physicians in Contraception Access and Why It Matters

The debate surrounding birth control traditionally centers on health-care distribution, religion, and basic freedoms.[1] These moral and legal issues are paramount to basic decisions individuals must address on a daily basis. Politicians, employers, courts, and health-care companies have each worked toward restricting contraception access. Politicians have waged an unprecedented attack on reproductive rights and contraception access in the past 5–10 years.[2] From 2011 to today, legislatures have enacted hundreds of new restrictions on reproductive rights.[3] In 2015, 11 states worked to defund Planned Parenthood and other family planning providers, often resulting in a significant impact on contraception access; 28 states and counting introduced abortion bans in 2019.[4] Two-thirds of Planned Parenthood locations serve half of all women seeking contraceptive care and they are the only family planning centers in another fifth.[5]

Employers have also sought to limit reproductive care in the same time period, usually relying on religious objections.[6] Large groups of people are now denied access due to working at institutions with religious objections to birth control.[7] Courts have often supported these employer goals. While the Supreme Court struck down Texas abortion restrictions in 2016, it also supported corporations in denying contraception access[8] or avoided making some decisions on the matter altogether.[9] Despite advances the Affordable Care Act has made in expanding birth control coverage, health insurance companies have also made significant efforts to limit or eliminate access to contraception, making birth control either more expensive for some, or much harder to obtain.[10] These actions are noteworthy in an effort to protect contraception access.

However, another group with arguably more direct control over patients has quietly been much more effective at preventing access to contraception than legislatures, courts, or private companies. This group has the power not just to increase costs and barriers to gaining contraceptive access, but also to deny access altogether. Furthermore, this group is often overlooked in discussions of biomedical ethics and contraceptive access generally, meaning that insufficient debate has attended their role in the status quo. This group, the majority of which routinely deny patients access to birth control is, of course, physicians.

Rather than counteracting the barrier other major American institutions pose by working to expand access, most doctors simply add to the obstacles patients already face by requiring they undergo unnecessary, irrelevant, and costly tests and appointments. The significance of this phenomenon is broad, and interfaces with a number of seemingly distinct issues in applied ethics. A real debate and an in-depth philosophical analysis are required to understand the role and impact of physician attitudes toward contraceptives. I aim to fill that gap.

In this chapter, I first provide an overview of the medical differences among different types of contraceptives with the goal of uncovering why hormonal birth control methods are so prevalent and whether this prevalence is justified. Pregnancy prevention enjoys significant popularity in the United States and understanding the different contraceptive options gives us the necessary background to explore questions of why it is sometimes denied.

I next turn to the medical field and evaluate the empirical facts surrounding the issue of physicians denying contraception to patients. I establish the problem which serves as the main focus of the first half of the book: doctors routinely deny patients access to hormonal birth control in service of their other aims and values. Specifically, a large proportion of doctors require yearly Pap tests or pelvic exams before providing contraceptive prescriptions and renewals. I review the evidence, identify its limitations, and show how common it is that doctors use this model.

In the last section, I review the significance of contraception in health. Denying patients access to contraception has wide-reaching implications: it plays a causal role in a variety of current issues in applied ethics, including racism and sexism.[11] As a result, this issue has broad interest beyond the biomedical field and biomedical ethics.

WHY HORMONAL BIRTH CONTROL?

The use of birth control is prevalent in the United States by any measure. Recent studies suggest that almost all women[12] capable of reproduction who have had sexual intercourse have also relied on contraception at some point in their lives.[13] That is, more than 99% of women between the ages of 15 and 44—roughly 53 million American women—have used birth control in their lifetimes.[14] Variations occur by age, race and ethnicity, education level, and religious affiliation, but in all groupings, remarkably high rates of women have used contraception during their lifetimes. Women are also extremely likely to rely on the most effective forms of birth control: "Additionally, nearly 9 out of 10 sexually experienced women reported ever having used a highly effective, reversible method of birth control."[15] In other words, the majority of people who need birth control to avoid becoming pregnant use it, and the majority of people who use it use reliable methods.

By several measures, long-acting reversible contraceptives (LARCs) are the best option for most people. Intrauterine devices (IUDs) and implants are generally less expensive than hormonal birth control. They can last for up to 12 years, meaning the upfront cost does not reflect the yearly cost, especially if patients choose to use them for the full duration of their effectiveness. For example, if an IUD costs $400, it has a considerably larger upfront cost than $30 for a month of hormonal birth control. However, an IUD is effective for up to 12 years while a pack of hormonal birth control only lasts 1 month. Thus, when spread out over the course of its effective lifetime, the yearly cost of an IUD, just over $30, approaches the monthly cost of hormonal birth control. Even a patient who desires contraceptive protection for less than the full length an IUD lasts would be better off choosing it. That is, a person seeking birth control for 5 years instead of 12 still would have an estimated fivefold savings by choosing an IUD over hormonal birth control. From a financial perspective, IUDs offer a greater cost savings over alternatives.

How relevant are these financial savings for individuals choosing birth control? Insurance companies have a real incentive to cover IUDs due to the financial savings. Since the passage of the Affordable Care Act (ACA), insurance companies must cover all FDA-approved contraceptives with no copay. Therefore, even if insurance companies have such an incentive, they cannot coerce patients to use IUDs over other methods by covering one and not the rest. So, the cost differentials are only applicable to those without insurance coverage. However, over 10% of the U.S. population still remains uninsured after the passage of the ACA, so the costs of varying options may still be influential in individual decision-making for some.[16] Furthermore, insurance companies could choose to educate consumers on the benefits of an IUD to achieve these cost savings.[17]

In addition, IUDs and implants are more effective than the alternatives. "Time of need" contraceptives like condoms are unreliable primarily due to user error. As a result, IUDs and implants are between 90 and 360 times more effective than male condoms in typical use.[18] Some methods like withdrawal or fertility awareness-based methods are so ineffective as to have a failure rate of almost one in four. When compared to implants and IUDs, these numbers are stark. In fact, reversible implants and IUDs can be even more effective than permanent contraception such as a vasectomy or abdominal, laparoscopic, or hysteroscopic sterilization.[19] Additionally, these permanent forms of sterilization can often be costly, require a longer recovery time, require patients' use of general anesthesia, and require patients use a backup method of contraception for at least three months after surgery.[20]

Lastly, in addition to financial benefits and effectiveness, IUDs and implants are often associated with fewer side effects than the alternatives. The IUD does have risks of some serious side effects, such as perforation of the uterus (for both the hormonal and the copper IUD) and menstrual problems (for the copper IUD). The hormonal IUD can also cause temporary side effects like benign cysts, mood swings, and acne. However, beneficial side effects also accrue to users beyond contraceptive efficacy, such as reducing menstrual bleeding, cramps, or menstruation altogether, an effect many women seek out; reduced rates of endometrial cancer; reducing endometriosis; and reducing ectopic pregnancy. By contrast, oral contraceptives pose risks of many more side effects and side effects that last longer, including blood clots, depression, reduced libido, headaches, visual changes, spotting, nausea, and weight gain.

Nevertheless, patients do not choose long-acting, reversible contraception to the same degree as the alternatives. For a variety of reasons, which may include physician influence, upfront cost, perceived invasiveness, and general fears, many often choose other methods. According to some studies, counseling about the alternatives combined with defraying the cost, moved participants significantly toward LARC methods, with 75% of participants choosing the IUD or implant over shots, pills, rings, or patches.[21] Since these conditions are not met in standard cases, IUDs and implants remain relatively rare. About 10% of women using contraceptives choose IUDs.[22]

Thus, despite the availability of more effective forms of contraception,[23] a large proportion of people in the U.S. rely on oral contraceptive pills and other hormonal methods. More than a third of contraception users rely on oral contraceptive methods, more than any other form of contraception.[24] Twice as many women rely on oral contraceptive pills than the male condom as their method of birth control and four out of five women with sexual experience have used the pill at some point in their lives.[25] Monthly hormonal birth control like pills are still the method of choice for most women.

Hormonal birth control, while not the best form of birth control by most measures, is still extremely highly valued for a variety of reasons. First, the upfront cost is relatively low, meaning that no accumulated wealth is required to choose this method. Second, hormonal birth control is extremely effective. It boasts over a 90% success rate over a given year and is twice as effective as a male condom. When used in combination with male or female condoms, which are required for STD protection, its users experience added gains in pregnancy protection. Third, the side effects are relatively minimal because hormonal birth control is extremely safe. To the extent that it does have side effects, these last only for the duration of use and most are reversible. Fourth, a significant degree of choice is involved. In addition to a variety of different brands and types of pills, users can choose patches, rings, or injectable shots for their method of delivery. This choice allows patients to tailor their contraception to their particular needs. Fifth, hormonal birth control offers users options not available with other methods of contraception, such as eliminating periods, which is a side effect only some experience with LARCs. Many patients may find such possibilities an added benefit over and above the contraceptive function. Sixth, hormonal birth control can treat a variety of medical conditions unrelated to pregnancy prevention. For example, while contraceptives like sterilization and condoms may be effective, they do not treat the range of health issues that hormonal birth control treats, such as polycystic ovary syndrome or endometriosis, whereas hormonal birth control does. Seventh, it offers users a form of birth control that is not time sensitive, which is helpful not only for effectiveness, but also because it puts control in the hands of the user. That is, a partner need not be aware of a user's reliance on hormonal pills to protect against pregnancy, which gives users added protection from potentially controlling partners. Other forms of birth control offer the same protection, but male and female condoms as well as patches do not, so the pill and injectable shots are preferred forms of birth control for this purpose. Thus, for some people, hormonal birth control is the best option regardless of how effective or inexpensive the alternatives are by comparison.

Despite its prevalence, high demand, effectiveness, and safety, significant parties aim to limit patient access to birth control. Even if individuals live in a state with minimal restrictions, have health insurance, work for an employer who will cover it, and live near a family planning center that can provide it, when doctors refuse to prescribe it, individuals will still be denied access.

PHYSICIANS POSE PREGNANCY PREVENTION PROBLEMS

Both LARCs like intrauterine devices (IUDs) and implants as well as hormonal birth control[26] require reliance on medical providers in the United States. LARCs require doctors to both insert and remove the device, whereas hormonal birth control methods require doctors to write both prescriptions and renewals. In both instances, this reliance leads to obstacles for patient choice. When patients rely on doctors for access to medicine, doctors can pose obstacles to patients gaining access to needed medical care.

Obstetricians and gynecologists routinely deny their patients access to hormonal contraception, ostensibly in the name of health, by withholding birth control until patients undergo certain exams.[27] That is, obstetricians/gynecologists generally require pelvic exams and Pap tests before offering or renewing prescriptions for birth control.[28] Exam requirements for prescriptions are often taken as standard, despite acknowledgment that they are not medically necessary.[29] In fact, even when patients need emergency contraception, some doctors deny access in order to obtain Pap tests.[30]

The exact percentage of doctors whose patients miss doses due to obstacles is hard to ascertain, as it relies on physician surveys.[31] What evidence is there that this practice is occurring, let alone that it is happening at a high frequency? Some put the percentage of doctors generally requiring these examinations for birth control at nearly 50%.[32] Other studies show 65–85% of doctors recommend Pap tests every year.[33] According to one study, 97% of doctors required Pap tests before refilling an oral contraceptive prescription.[34]

These studies suggest a very high percentage of patients face obstacles to obtaining birth control. When 97% of doctors are engaging in a practice, it is unlikely any patient can avoid it. Another study showed about three-quarters of doctors require annual Pap tests for patients starting at age 18, regardless of sexual activity.[35] That study did not specify whether Pap tests were tied to birth control, so it is unknown whether 75% of doctors limited patient access to birth control, but several reasons suggest that they did. While it is possible that patients in those contexts were choosing to go in for examinations for an STD without ever having had sex, the more likely explanation is that they agree to undergo exams to attain some further goal like getting a birth control prescription.

In another study of 1,551 doctors that focuses on pelvic exams, about one-third of OB/GYNs reported "always" requiring the exam before prescribing birth control and another 50% reported "usually" requiring it.[36] Less than 5% never required it.[37] Among all clinicians in this study, which included family practitioners and nurses, the numbers were not much better. About two-thirds always or usually required pelvic examinations for contraception refills while less than 5% never required it.[38]

The clinicians least likely to provide obstacles for patients were family medicine advanced practice nurses, but even among this group, less than 10% separated pelvic exams from contraception prescriptions. That means in the best-case scenario, patients are facing over 90% of their clinicians always, usually, or sometimes requiring exams for prescriptions.

In that study, the most significant indicators as to whether physicians required the test were the characteristics of the physicians and the patients they serve:

> Providers in private practice were more than twice as likely as those working in family-planning or community clinics to require pelvic examinations (OR 2.30, $P<.01$). Clinicians from the South (OR 1.70; 95% CI 1.10–2.62) and those reporting that half or more of their patients are insured by Medicaid (OR 1.62; 95% CI 1.11–2.37) were also more likely to always require pelvic examinations for oral contraception.[39]

Multiple studies found older physicians were less likely than their younger counterparts to prescribe birth control without a Pap test or pelvic exam.[40] However, both groups required the tests at extremely high rates.[41]

The description of the doctors in the above study sheds light on which patients are most affected by these industry practices. For example, if doctors in the South are more likely to impose restrictions, Southern patients are more likely to face problems, though significant restrictions apply to all patients.[42] In addition, since doctors who serve communities insured by Medicaid are more likely to require exams for contraception prescriptions, poorer patients likely face greater obstacles in gaining access to birth control than wealthier ones. Since poorer patients are also the least likely to be able to easily overcome such obstacles to birth control access, it is possible to assume that at least some poor patients who want birth control and have access to doctors through insurance are not receiving it.[43] Furthermore rejecting "two of the most perverse tenets of eugenic thinking: that social problems are caused by reproduction of the socially disadvantaged and that their childbearing should therefore be deterred"[44] is possible while still advocating that the socially disadvantaged should have as much reproductive control as their counterparts in wealthier communities.

Studies like these include several significant limitations that should lead us to believe that the situation is much worse than it seems. For example, this practice currently flouts the standard of care, as discussed in the next chapter, so doctors may not be forthcoming in such surveys. As stark as these numbers are, showing a significant proportion of doctors posing unnecessary obstacles to patient access to contraceptives, they likely present a more positive picture than reality would indicate. Studies tend to acknowledge these limitations: "Social desirability bias could affect responses, with clinicians indicating idealized or professionally normative practices."[45] In other words, the disparity between theory and practice is likely to lead to doctors inflating their own compliance with guidelines. Especially in the context of a survey in which doctors are self-reporting and communicating with agencies they can presume are evaluating their behavior, doctors may be incentivized to exaggerate how often they follow guidelines.

In addition, the surveys rely on vignettes of patient scenarios with attached questionnaires rather than requesting clinical data on what proportion of patients face these obstacles. As a result, doctors may be more likely to see themselves as following guidelines in hypothetical scenarios while contradicting guidelines in actual practice. Thus, the combined effect of relying on self-reports and relying on questionnaires about hypothetical scenarios means that, even if over 90% of doctors place at least some restrictions on their patients' access to birth control, the numbers actually may be even higher than reported.

Surveys of patients confirm the data on physicians.[46] For example, one survey found that a significant percentage of women and girls under the age of 25 reported having undergone a Pap test in the previous 12-month period despite never being sexually active.[47] That result suggests that millions of patients are undergoing what is essentially a test for a sexually transmitted disease despite never having had sex. In fact, even after becoming sexually active, medical indicators do not suggest a value in Pap testing for several years, since HPV has a long latency period even when it does lead to cervical cancer and since cervical cancer rates among young women and girls under the age of 25 are rare.[48] In addition, since that survey only asked whether individuals had received Pap tests in the previous 12-month period, it is very likely that a much larger percentage had received these unnecessary tests.

Some studies also do not show a trend away from the practice over time.[49] Studies in the early 2000s and well into the 2010s all show similar evidence of doctors requiring extra unnecessary exams before they write or refill birth control prescriptions.[50] The fact that this practice has been occurring for decades suggests a significant oversight on the part of doctors and a serious systemic problem.

The prevalence of practitioners individually implementing the same obstacles to patients without any coordination and against professional standards suggests an incredibly unlikely and therefore significant phenomenon. In other words, the frequency of the practice supports the idea that the practice is systemic in the field and therefore worthy of investigation. Therefore, it raises the sort of serious questions I aim to answer in the remainder of this book.

In fact, even if the percentages were significantly lower, there would still be reason to believe that the requirements were systemic. We have reason to believe that currently, less than 5% of doctors follow professional guidelines. However, even if 80% of doctors placed no exam requirements on patient access to contraception, that would still be concerning. If only one in five doctors placed these restrictions on patients, there would still be reason to identify the practice as a systemic problem affecting the medical profession generally and OB/GYNs specifically.

This practice inevitably leads to reduced access to birth control for many patients.[51] Assuming about 20,000 OB/GYNs in the country,[52] and, taking the lower end of the study's numbers, if about 50% always require exams before offering birth control prescriptions, that translates to about 10,000 doctors. Most OB/GYN physicians see between 50 and 124 patients a week.[53] Again, taking the lower end of the numbers, and assuming doctors work around 48 weeks a year, then doctors typically see around 2,400 patients a year. These numbers suggest that around 24 million patients are affected by these policies at the lower end. In other words, millions of people are impacted even if not every doctor deters contraception access.

In addition, even small numbers of doctors engaging in the practice would have a large impact on patients. Most patients are unable to change doctors when they face problems, make immediate changes in times of crises, or search for a doctor who best suits their needs. Given restrictions on patient access to a large number of potential doctors, patients are likely at the mercy of the doctors available to them. For example, about 50% of U.S. counties have no OB/GYN at all, so many patients have severely limited options.[54] Even in counties that do have OB/GYN doctors, geographical distance limits the number of doctors a patient could realistically see. Patients who rely on public transportation will also find extra appointments or switching doctors particularly burdensome. Limitations from insurance coverage also pose problems. Patients are subject to the restrictions placed on them through their health insurance companies, meaning that they may not be able to see a doctor they like if that doctor is not covered through their plans.

Other reasons suggest that this phenomenon has a large impact on patients. The examination poses a cost in time and planning, just as any mandated waiting period imposes costs. A search for a doctor requires research and possibly multiple appointments, which may not be feasible for patients with limited time or money. Thus, if even a small percentage of doctors require these tests, that would mean that some patients would not have access to doctors who give unfettered access to birth control at all. A doctor's appointment is a considerable time investment, especially for patients with certain characteristics. For example, patients who travel often or who commute long distances will find the extra appointments burdensome, as scheduling in the appropriate time frame becomes difficult.

Hourly workers suffer a loss of income when they attend doctors' appointments, so waiting periods and extra appointments are especially problematic. About 48% of women make under $15 an hour.[55] Furthermore, a disproportionate number of minimum wage earners are women. Women make up 47% of the workforce but as high as 62% are minimum wage earners.[56] Minimum wage earners not only have among the lowest incomes, but also are hourly workers. Thus, women are disproportionately affected by extra appointments.

Other patients uniquely affected by such policies are patients with dependents. Providing care for dependents is often expensive and time-consuming, exacerbating the kinds of problems patients face in securing appointments. When patients have to find childcare or elder care, they may have to delay or indefinitely postpone these extra appointments, and their access to contraception will be compromised.

Another reason these requirements may impact patient access to birth control is that busy doctors may be unable to offer appointments in the allotted time frame. In addition, many doctors work limited hours, complicating scheduling for patients. If patients forget how many prescription refills they have left; are menstruating at the time of the appointment; switch jobs; lose a job; or have other changes in insurance, this requirement could lead to a lapse in coverage. Such patients will have to go off their medication, either for days or for weeks, until such time as they can undergo an examination.

In the case of LARCs, the obstacles doctors impose are relatively less influential because the rate of patient reliance on LARCs is much less. Nevertheless, these obstacles constitute significant restrictions for patients. Doctors are sometimes unwilling to recommend or comply with the patient's choice to receive IUDs, especially in the case of patients who have not yet had children. Some doctors are also unwilling to give IUDs to unmarried patients or patients who are non-monogamous due to concerns about the impact of certain STDs on patients with IUDs. However, for reasons discussed later in the book, this reluctance on the part of doctors more closely aligns with doctor values and not patient concerns.

CONCLUSION

In this chapter, I argued that the phenomenon of requiring added tests and appointments exists and is systemic. This practice can impact patient access to health care, patient choice, and patient outcomes. Is it legally or morally permissible for doctors to withhold prescriptions for yearly pelvic exams or Pap tests either due to protection of patient interests, physician principles, or to improve health outcomes for patients? In the remainder of the book, I argue that such practices are never justified.

NOTES

1. Elizabeth Sepper and Alisha Johnson, "Rhetoric Versus Reality: The Contraception Benefit and Religious Freedom," *Religion and Politics*, April 9, 2013, http://religionandpolitics.org/2013/04/09/rhetoric-versus-reality-the-contraception-benefit-and-religious-freedom/.

2. Steve Benen, "Senate Republicans Return to Controversial Contraception Posture," MSNBC, May 26, 2015, http://www.msnbc.com/rachel-maddow-show/senate-republicans-return-controversial-contraception-posture.

3. Elizabeth Nash, Rachel Benson Gold, Gwendolyn Rathbun, and Zohra Ansari-Thomas, "Laws Affecting Reproductive Health and Rights: 2015 State Policy Review," Guttmacher Institute, January 1, 2016, https://www.guttmacher.org/laws-affecting-reproductive-health-and-rights-2015-state-policy-review; "Radical Attempts to Ban Abortion Dominate State Policy Trends in the First Quarter of 2019," Guttmacher Institute, April 2, 2019, https://www.guttmacher.org/article/2019/04/radical-attempts-ban-abortion-dominate-state-policy-trends-first-quarter-2019; Elizabeth Nash, Rachel Benson Gold, Lizamarie Mohammed, Zohra Ansari-Thomas, and Olivia Cappello, "Laws Affecting Reproductive Health and Rights: State Policy Trends at Midyear, 2018," Guttmacher Institute, July 31, 2018, https://www.guttmacher.org/article/2018/07/laws-affecting-reproductive-health-and-rights-state-policy-trends-midyear-2018.

4. "Radical Attempts to Ban Abortion Dominate State Policy Trends in the First Quarter of 2019."

5. "Laws Affecting Reproductive Health and Rights," January 1, 2016.

6. Mary Agnes Carey, "Hobby Lobby Ruling Cuts Into Contraceptive Mandate," NPR.org, June 30, 2014, sec. Shots Health News, http://www.npr.org/sections/health-shots/2014/06/30/327065968/hobby-lobby-ruling-cuts-into-contraceptive-mandate.

7. Sepper and Johnson, "Rhetoric Versus Reality."

8. Caldwell, "The Supreme Court Just Made the Hobby Lobby Ruling Even Worse," *Mother Jones*, July 3, 2014, http://www.motherjones.com/politics/2014/07/supreme-court-scotus-hobby-lobby-all-forms-contraception.

9. United States Supreme Court, Zubik v. Burwell, No. No. 14-1418 (May 16, 2016).

10. Leonard, "Obama Administration: Insurance Companies Must Cover Birth Control," *US News & World Report*, May 11, 2015, http://www.usnews.com/news/articles/2015/05/11/obama-administration-insurance-companies-must-cover-birth-control.

11. Gloria Steinem, *Outrageous Acts and Everyday Rebellions: Second Edition*, (New York: Holt Paperbacks, 1995), 9.

12. I aim to use inclusive terminology when discussing reproductive issues. Wherever possible, I use the term "people" to discuss the affected parties in decisions pertaining to contraception and reproductive health. Since not all women require contraception and not all people who require contraception are women, this term is meant to most accurately reflect the correct groupings. In addition, while I often discuss "patients" instead of people to signify a medical

context, I do not wish to reduce people to their role in a doctor-patient relationship nor to overly medicalize the question of reproductive health. Two exceptions are relevant to this terminology. First, in most studies discussing reproductive health and contraceptive access, data pertains to women specifically. Where such studies specify that their data relied on women, I use the term "women" so as not to inaccurately generalize the results. For example, if the article discusses pregnant women, it would be wrong to generalize the conclusions of the study to trans men, nonbinary people, and others not included in the sample. Second, where medical sexism arises, I sometimes use the term "women" so as to signify and highlight the ways in which doctors perceive and categorize their patients, as well as the way the public understands these issues, even if those categorizations are unhelpful and even if people who are not women can be subject to sexism. Lauren Freeman and Saray Ayala López, "Sex Categorization in Medical Contexts: A Cautionary Tale," *Kennedy Institute of Ethics Journal* 28, no. 3 (October 25, 2018): 243–80, https://doi.org/10.1353/ken.2018.0017. Still, as I hope to show in several chapters, women are not the only affected parties of medical sexism.

13. Kimberly Daniels, William Mosher, and Jo Jones, "Contraceptive Methods Women Have Ever Used: United States, 1982-2010" (National Health Statistics Reports, February 14, 2013), http://www.cdc.gov/nchs/data/nhsr/nhsr062.pdf.

14. Daniels, Mosher, and Jones.

15. Daniels, Mosher, and Jones.

16. Nader Nekvasil, "Uninsured Down Since Obamacare; Cost, Quality Still Concerns," Gallup.com, Agust 29, 2016, http://www.gallup.com/poll/195086/uninsured-down-obamacare-cost-quality-concerns.aspx.

17. Of course, prior to the ACA, insurance companies also had incentives for covering IUDs. Due to the large upfront costs, patients found greater financial obstacles in affording IUDs. This fact, combined with evidence discussed below that IUDs are orders of magnitude more effective than the alternatives, should have incentivized insurance companies to provide IUDs so consumers would not rely on monthly hormonal pills instead. Pregnancy and childbirth are comparatively much more expensive. Taking into account that 50% of all pregnancies and about 33% of all births are unwanted, paying for an expensive pregnancy that the consumer does not want instead of paying for inexpensive and highly effective birth control seems counterintuitive. However, a fair number of insurance companies did not offer coverage of any alternatives, leading precisely to the ACA mandate.

18. Centers for Disease Control and Prevention, "Effectiveness of Family Planning Methods," 2014, http://www.cdc.gov/reproductivehealth/contraception/unintendedpregnancy/pdf/family-planning-methods-2014.pdf.

19. Jeanette Ferrara, "The Top Five Most Effective Methods of Birth Control," *Scienceline*, January 30, 2016, http://scienceline.org/2016/01/the-top-five-most-effective-methods-of-birth-control/.

20. Centers for Disease Control and Prevention, "Effectiveness of Family Planning Methods."

21. "The Choice Project," accessed October 17, 2016, http://www.choiceproject.wustl.edu/#MISSION.

22. "Contraceptive Use in the United States," Guttmacher Institute, July 2018, https://www.guttmacher.org/fact-sheet/contraceptive-use-united-states.

23. Margaret P. Battin, *Sex & Consequences: World Population Growth vs. Reproductive Rights*, 54th Annual Frederick William Reynolds Lecture (Salt Lake City, Utah: Frederick William Reynolds Association, 1994), http://catalog.hathitrust.org/Record/002958488.

24. Jo Jones, William Mosher, and Kimberly Daniels, "Current Contraceptive Use in the United States, 2006–2010, and Changes in Patterns of Use Since 1995," *National Health Statistics Reports* 60 (October 18, 2012).

25. Ibid.

26. I contrast LARCs with hormonal birth control even though implants and some IUDs make use of hormones. By "hormonal birth control" I include not only oral contraceptives like the pill but also shots, patches, and rings, all of which require a physician prescription and are shorter-term forms of birth control.

27. Jen Gunter, "Do You Need a Pap Smear to Get Birth Control?," *The New York Times*, October 18, 2018, sec. Well, https://www.nytimes.com/2018/10/18/well/do-you-need-a-pap-smear-to-get-birth-control.html.

28. Meredith Melnick, "Are Doctors' Exams a Barrier to Birth Control?," *Time*, December 6, 2010, http://healthland.time.com/2010/12/06/why-annual-exams-shouldnt-be-required-to-get-birth-control-pills/.

29. Felicia H. Stewart et al., "Clinical Breast and Pelvic Examination Requirements for Hormonal Contraception: Current Practice vs Evidence," *JAMA* 285, no. 17 (May 2, 2001): 2232, https://doi.org/10.1001/jama.285.17.2232.

30. Eleanor Bimla Schwarz et al., "Cervical Cancer Screening Continues to Limit Provision of Contraception," *Contraception* 72, no. 3 (September 2005): 179–81, https://doi.org/10.1016/j.contraception.2005.04.009.

31. Amir Qaseem et al., "Screening Pelvic Examination in Adult Women: A Clinical Practice Guideline From the American College of Physicians." *Annals of Internal Medicine* 161, no. 1 (July 1, 2014): 67–72, https://doi.org/10.7326/M14-0701.

32. Melnick, "Are Doctors' Exams a Barrier to Birth Control?"

33. Debbie Saslow, "American Cancer Society Expert Voices Blog: Is a Pap Test Necessary Every Year?," Cancer.org, March 14, 2012, http://www.cancer.org/Cancer/News/ExpertVoices/.

34. Schwarz et al., "Cervical Cancer Screening Continues to Limit Provision of Contraception."

35. Mona Saint, Ginny Gildengorin, and George F. Sawaya, "Current Cervical Neoplasia Screening Practices of Obstetrician/Gynecologists in the US," *American Journal of Obstetrics and Gynecology* 192, no. 2 (February 2005): 414–21, https://doi.org/10.1016/j.ajog.2004.09.026.

36. Jillian T. Henderson et al., "Pelvic Examinations and Access to Oral Hormonal Contraception:," *Obstetrics & Gynecology* 116, no. 6 (December 2010): 1257–64, https://doi.org/10.1097/AOG.0b013e3181fb540f.

37. Ibid.

38. Qaseem et al., "Screening Pelvic Examination in Adult Women."

39. Henderson et al., "Pelvic Examinations and Access to Oral Hormonal Contraception."

40. Ibid.; Jean M. Yu et al., "Obstetrician-gynecologists' beliefs on the importance of pelvic examinations in assessing hormonal contraception eligibility," *Contraception* 90, no. 6 (December 2014) 612–614, https://doi.org/10.1016/j.contraception.2014.06.038.

41. Ibid.

42. Other studies found no difference by location.

43. A presumably larger population of patients that includes those without insurance or access to doctors also cannot get contraception.

44. Dorothy Roberts, *Killing the Black Body: Race, Reproduction, and the Meaning of Liberty* (Vintage, 2014), 81.

45. Henderson et al., "Pelvic Examinations and Access to Oral Hormonal Contraception."

46. Juliana M. Kling et al., "Routine Pelvic Examinations: A Descriptive Cross-Sectional Survey of Women's Attitudes and Beliefs after New Guidelines," *Preventive Medicine* 94 (January 1, 2017): 60–64, https://doi.org/10.1016/j.ypmed.2016.11.007; George F. Sawaya et al., "Effect of Professional Society Recommendations on Women's Desire for a Routine Pelvic Examination," *American Journal of Obstetrics and Gynecology* 217, no. 3 (September 1, 2017): 338.e1-338.e7, https://doi.org/10.1016/j.ajog.2017.05.003; Laura L. Norrell et al., "Women's Beliefs about the Purpose and Value of Routine Pelvic Examinations," *American Journal of Obstetrics and Gynecology* 217, no. 1 (July 1, 2017): 86.e1-86.e6, https://doi.org/10.1016/j.ajog.2016.12.031; Kavita S. Vinekar et al., "Cervical Cancer Screening, Pelvic Examinations, and Contraceptive Use Among Adolescent and Young Adult Females," *Journal of*

Adolescent Health 57, no. 2 (August 1, 2015): 169–73, https://doi.org/10.1016/j.jadohealth.2015.04.001.

47. Mona Saraiya et al., "Pap Testing and Sexual Activity Among Young Women in the United States:," *Obstetrics & Gynecology* 114, no. 6 (December 2009): 1213–19, https://doi.org/10.1097/AOG.0b013e3181be3db4.

48. Saraiya et al.

49. Though note Kate Grindlay and Daniel Grossman, "Prescription Birth Control Access Among U.S. Women at Risk of Unintended Pregnancy," *Journal of Women's Health* 25, no. 3 (December 14, 2015): 249–54, https://doi.org/10.1089/jwh.2015.5312; Heather P. Eastman-Mueller and Sara B. Oswalt, "Trends in Pap Test Practices and Results: An 11-Year Review of the Annual ACHA Pap Test and STI Survey," *Journal of American College Health* 65, no. 7 (October 3, 2017): 474–81, https://doi.org/10.1080/07448481.2017.1341898.

50. Sirovich and Welch (2004), Stewart et al (2001), Melnick (2015), Henderson et al (2014).

51. While for many years, this examination imposed a financial burden, the Affordable Care Act moved to require free preventative health care for insurance companies.

52. Bureau of Labor Statistics, "Obstetricians and Gynecologists," May 2018, http://www.bls.gov/oes/current/oes291064.htm.

53. "Medscape OB/GYN Compensation Report: 2011 Results," 2011, http://www.medscape.com/features/slideshow/compensation/2011/womenshealth; "Obstetrician/Gynecologist Average Salary: Medscape Compensation Report 2014," 2014, http://www.medscape.com/features/slideshow/compensation/2014/womenshealth#17.

54. Maureen Salamon, "Half of U.S. Counties Have No Ob-Gyn: Study," Consumer HealthDay, May 8, 2012, https://consumer.healthday.com/sexual-health-information-32/childbirth-health-news-126/half-of-u-s-counties-have-no-ob-gyn-study-664462.html.

55. Claire Zillman, "Who Makes Less than $15 per Hour, in 3 Charts," *Fortune* (blog), April 13, 2015, http://fortune.com/2015/04/13/who-makes-15-per-hour/.

56. Jens Manuel Krogstad, "More Women than Men Earn the Federal Minimum Wage," *Pew Research Center* (blog), May 5, 2014, http://www.pewresearch.org/fact-tank/2014/05/05/more-women-than-men-earn-the-federal-minimum-wage/.

2

CONTRACEPTION CARE CORRUPTED

Negative Health Outcomes of Limited Access to Birth Control

When doctors deny necessary medical care to their patients or require unnecessary medical care of their patients, physical harms can follow. In this chapter, I catalog the medical harms that can arise as a result of withholding yearly contraception prescriptions so as to achieve compliance with pelvic exams and Pap tests.

This exercise is valuable for a number of reasons. First, while I go on to argue that medical harms are not the only or even the primary concern when evaluating these policies, it is instructive to understand what they are. In fact, leaving them out could imply that no medical injuries ensue. Second, standard recommendations follow evidence on just these types of patient outcomes, so explaining these standard recommendations and their justification requires familiarity with the evidence. Third, it is essential for doctors to understand the consequences of their actions. This understanding can help inform doctors' decisions and shed light on patient choices. Fourth, the medical harms will come into play particularly in chapter 3, when I consider the legal ramifications of these policies. For example, recognition of the existence or gravity of injuries is central to an attribution of medical malpractice. Fifth, showing these policies violate the most basic tenets of bioethics and the role of doctors itself helps to advance an understanding of the value and ethics of the policies. Sixth, moral evaluation from a consequentialist standpoint requires analysis of these types of harms. Thus, for a variety of reasons, the discussion in this chapter contributes to a full moral analysis.

PRIMUM NON NOCERE

Current practices of withholding contraception prescriptions until such time as patients undergo pelvic exams or Pap tests violate the principle of primum non nocere, or "first, do no harm," in which harm causes physical injury or sets back one's rights or interests. This principle plays an especially large role in bioethics.[1] Doctors take themselves to be subject to this principle and are held to it in part due to the grave hazards of medical intervention. All interventions pose risks to the patient and physicians must take into account these potential dangers when discussing options with their patients. In fact, admonitions not to cause harm are found not only in the earliest versions of the Hippocratic Oath, dating back to the fifth century BCE, but also in its modern version used in contemporary medical schools, highlighting its importance for the medical profession. The principle, then, is not only a valuable moral dictum for the populace generally and a common oath for doctors specifically, but it is also wrapped up with the role of a doctor itself such that it shapes the public's understanding of doctors and the understanding doctors have of themselves. Medical professionalism demands it.

The "do no harm" maxim prohibits at least three types of actions: intentional harm (the principle of nonmaleficence), needless or avoidable harm, and unnecessary risk.[2] The first type of harm, which is intentional, clearly rules out malicious actions that doctors perpetrate on unwitting patients looking for medical care. However, not all intentional harm is necessarily malicious. Deliberately inflicting injury on patients might be done as a trade-off for other gains or to protect their overall best interests.

The next category of action is harm done to a patient accidentally. Doctors may harm their patients unintentionally, but it is still necessary to highlight and reduce these injuries. Because avoidable or needless harm has a high likelihood of attending medical interventions, doctors have a special duty to reduce these accidents and to ensure the safety of their patients.

The last type of action excluded by the principle is the exposure of patients to risk that they need not face. For example, a doctor may come to work with a contagious illness and expose patients to the possibility of becoming sick themselves. Even if no patient falls ill, the doctor needlessly exposed patients to risk and therefore harmed them. Calling the exposure to risk a harm is imperative because it allows us to recognize the ways in which doctors can go astray and perform the wrong action, even if no concrete negative consequences arise as the result of the action.

Requiring a pelvic exam or other intervention like a Pap test before prescribing birth control pills is an example of withholding medical care. But withholding medical care, even to achieve a beneficial result, is a prime example of the type of action the "do no harm" principle should rule out. Since in such cases birth control has already been established by the doctor and patient as a needed medical intervention, any disruption of this need counts as a harm to the patient. This harm applies whether or not evidence shows value in yearly tests. Thus, the principle of nonmaleficence should prohibit the kind of behavior doctors engage in when they impose prerequisites for birth control prescriptions.

However, even the principle of nonmaleficence does not prohibit doctors withholding treatment and allowing harm does not meet the same moral requirements of doing harm, allowing preventable medical harm to a patient under one's care is morally problematic. For example, doing and allowing harm do not need to be equal, as James Rachels alleges in order for allowing harm to be a morally impermissible act.[3]

And, to evaluate the impermissibility of allowing harm by tying birth control prescriptions to unnecessary exams, it is useful to catalog the exact dangers that this practice involves. By focusing on the medical and scientific evidence against denying patients birth control, I can show how it leads to real and direct physical harm.

THE HISTORY OF PAP TESTS

The advent of Pap tests has been a boon for millions of patients and has led to decreased mortality rates from cervical cancer across the board. Furthermore, some groups of patients continue to suffer at higher rates of cervical cancer. For example, African American women are at higher risk for cervical cancer and face higher mortality rates from it when they are diagnosed.[4] Protecting access and coverage is a demonstrable good for society.

George Papanicolaou first started research on cervical cancer in the 1920s, when cervical cancer was one of the most lethal cancers in the United States, and the most lethal cancer for women, killing more women than lung cancer or breast cancer. By the 1940s, Papanicolaou had developed and popularized the Pap smear, later named for him. At the time, nobody knew what caused cervical cancer or whether all cancerous cells found on the cervix were equally deadly. By detecting abnormalities and precancerous cells early, the Pap smear served as a huge advance in preventative care. While roughly 4,000 women in the United States still die from cervical cancer every year, it is not even in the top 10 cancers that kill women, let alone the number one cause of cancer deaths among women.[5] These advances had real benefits for patients across the country.

Ten years later, in 1951, Henrietta Lacks, a 30-year-old black woman living in Jim Crow Virginia changed the landscape again with cells Dr. Richard TeLinde removed from a cancerous tumor in her cervix.[6] TeLinde took the sample without Lacks's knowledge—in fact, she was never informed she suffered from cancerous tumors.[7] He then sent the cell sample to George Gey, who collected cells in hopes of creating a replicable cell line, again, without Lacks's knowledge. Because scientists like Gey were able to grow the cells from Lacks's cancerous tumor in a lab, they represented the first instance of the development of a human cell line that could be indefinitely cultured because they do not die after a set number of cell divisions. This advance allowed for vast new areas of scientific and medical research.[8]

Only much later, in the late 1970s, would Harald zur Hausen discover the cause of nearly all cervical cancers in just two strains of human papillomavirus, or HPV, using the cells from Lacks's original tumor. This breakthrough essentially reclassified cervical cancer as a type of sexually transmitted disease. The scientific advance led to great strides in preventative care and targeting at-risk populations. In the 1990s, further refining of cervical cancer screenings became standard, with more efficient liquid-based cytology tests superseding conventional Pap smears as the test of choice. Screening is now a standard component of health care for all susceptible patients.

Pap tests yield either negative results for abnormalities, or positive results for abnormalities in at least five different categories. The first two types are not classified as likely to signify cancerous or even precancerous cells. The most common positive Pap test result is for atypical squamous cells of undetermined significance (ASC-US).[9] Squamous cells are found on the external cervix, and this diagnosis suggests changes in cervical cells. While this result merits further testing, depending on the patient's age and HPV status,[10] often a repeat Pap test a year after the result is all that is required. The next possible diagnosis is a low-grade squamous intraepithelial lesion (LSIL). LSIL suggests abnormalities in cervical cells, but is also not necessarily a dangerous result. For many patients, such as those in their early twenties or who test negative for HPV, a repeat Pap test in one year is deemed sufficient.

Other abnormal Pap tests generally indicate the need for more invasive procedures. A high-grade squamous intraepithelial lesion (HSIL) is a more serious result that merits further testing for precancerous and cancerous cells immediately.[11] For most patients getting an HSIL result, a colposcopy is done, in which the colposcope is used as a magnifying device to better examine the cells. During the procedure, the doctor may also take a biopsy of unusual areas in the cervix. In some cases of HSIL, doctors may instead recommend excisional treatments in which the abnormal area of the cervix is immediately removed. A commonly used excisional treatment is a loop electrosurgical excision procedure (LEEP) in which doctors use an electrified loop to remove abnormal cells. Since the Pap test also looks at other cells in the reproductive system, the last possible Pap test result is that of atypical glandular cells (AGC). In this case, it is the glandular cells that indicate possible precancerous or cancerous cells. In addition to colposcopy, endocervical or endometrial sampling may be recommended as follow up tests.[12]

For decades after the introduction of the Pap test, it was recommended to be done yearly. The recommendations for screening intervals have changed based on evidence without any loss of efficacy. Yet, to this day, some doctors still recommend yearly screenings. Pap tests and other exams undoubtedly help patients across the board, and that doctors should continue to use them. Denial of such tests would be extremely harmful to a variety of patients. However, the fact that these tests help patients and prevent deaths should not lead us to believe that they should therefore be used at any frequency or in any manner.

The range of possible abnormal Pap test results and the acceptable treatments associated with those results show just how invasive a regular yearly Pap test is when used as a universal approach to every patient. Follow-up Pap tests after 12 months are an acceptable treatment for abnormal results—not suitable for routine screenings of patients with normal results. Treating all patients as if they received a LSIL result from their Pap test suggests a misunderstanding of both the possible dangers of abnormal results and a misunderstanding of how Pap tests ought to be used. And, since more testing is more likely to lead to more false positives, it is easy to see how too many Pap tests can lead to unnecessary colposcopies or even excisional treatments.

STANDARD RECOMMENDATIONS

Before I discuss the ways in which doctors harm patients when they limit access to birth control, I first explain the standard medical recommendations in the field. If doctors are merely following medical guidelines when they require Pap tests for birth control prescriptions, then they may be more justified in imposing such obstacles on patients. However, first, guidelines can be wrong, and thus merit scrutiny. Second, as I argue in later chapters, they would not be justified in following such guidelines, because the problem is not merely one of medical indicators but also of deeper ethical concerns. Third, given the harms I catalog below, I would still argue in this instance that such behavior would be unwarranted even if guidelines allowed or recommended them. Guidelines are a key indicator of the permissibility of a practice as well as the evidence supporting it, and when doctors go against guidelines, they ought to have good reasons. However, it would be understandable and a clear explanation of the phenomenon would be forthcoming in such conditions. Nevertheless, industry guidelines in no way support the practice. In other words, guidelines are not a possible excuse.

Although a very high percentage of doctors and health providers tie contraception to pelvic exams, requiring visits before writing yearly prescriptions, this practice violates standards in the field. In fact, the high numbers of doctors who put up barriers to prescriptions look even starker in light of these standard recommendations.[13] Every major medical organization recommends against added tests and barriers for contraception access. In this section, I review the professional medical organizations that serve as the standard-bearers and look at the evidence for their recommendations. I conclude that requiring yearly Pap tests or pelvic exams as well as tying these exams to birth control prescriptions have no evidential basis and violate what reasonable doctors would recommend. This argument will come into play in chapter 3, where I argue for a legal standard and show how doctors fall short of it.

The practice at stake here has two components, each of which separately violates standard practices: first, requiring yearly exams, and second, tying these exams to birth control prescriptions. One way to understand standard practices is to look at communities of doctors, reputable medical organizations, and what these organizations recommend. In the case of tying birth control to added tests, the major organizations recommend against it.

The Center for Disease Control and Prevention (CDC),[14] the American College of Physicians,[15] and the American College of Obstetricians and Gynecologists (ACOG),[16] among others, all recommend against added tests for contraception access. In the United States, these organizations comprise the major governing institutions for reproductive health and cancer treatment. They are made up of scientists and physicians who use evidence-based research to determine guidelines away from the pull of political, financial, or corporate aims. That there is such a wide consensus on the phenomenon is a key indicator and crucial guideline for individual doctors when determining treatments and policies for their patients.

Another way to understand standard practices is to look at the scientific data that informs these organizations and evaluate the research independently. In this instance, the scientific data also recommends against the practice for reasons I discuss below. Thus, linking contraception to exams and tests is problematic.

The second component of the practice is requiring pelvic exams on a yearly basis. The Center for Disease Control,[17] The American Congress of Obstetricians and Gynecologists,[18] the American College of Physicians,[19] the U.S. Preventative Services Task force,[20] The American Cancer Society,[21] The American Society for Colposcopy and Cervical Pathology,[22] and the American Society for Clinical Pathology[23] are among the many organizations that recommend against screening every year as the default practice and recommend against routine pelvic examinations.[24] Particular features of individual patients may justify yearly screenings, such as an abnormal test, immunosuppression from illness or medications, or negative cytology with a positive test for the high-risk forms of HPV. Nonetheless, this yearly interval of tests as the default for all patients flouts the recommendations of major medical health organizations. In fact, major medical societies and doctors working on this research published recommendations not to engage in yearly screenings in 1995 because frequent screening causes more harm than good, but the practice continues today.[25]

Similar problems attend doctors withholding LARC methods.[26] As discussed in chapter 1, LARC methods are more effective, less expensive, and contribute many of the same benefits as oral contraceptives, such as effectively treating PCOS and preventing a host of cancers. Additionally, LARC methods are a particularly good choice for younger patients like teens because they require less effort on the part of the patient. Younger patients are less likely to effectively use other treatments,[27] more likely to suffer greater consequences for unintended pregnancies, and more likely to get the financial benefit of using the LARC for its full duration of effectiveness (5–10 years). For this reason, major organizations such as the American College of Obstetricians and Gynecologists (ACOG)[28] and the American Academy of Pediatrics (AAP)[29] recommend LARC methods for adolescents. Nevertheless, doctors routinely counsel young patients away from LARC options, fail to advocate effectively for them, or put up obstacles to access. As a result, while LARC methods are extremely popular abroad, they are comparatively uncommon in the United States[30] and many young patients remain unaware of IUD options in practice.[31] In fact, doctors are also known to deny young patients access to LARC methods, making them inaccessible even when patients are educated on their benefits.

The first major obstacle for young patients gaining access to LARC options is lack of provider education and training.[32] Doctors are often misinformed about the risks of LARC methods, overestimating them on the whole. The second major obstacle is that doctors, insurance companies, or ineffective scheduling processes impose extra appointments for the insertion of an IUD or implant, imposing the same costs and harms that arise when waiting periods and delays attend prescriptions of oral contraception discussed above. Around 87% of doctors impose the requirement of extra visits for IUD insertion, and those doctors who do not require extra visits understandably see more patients use them.[33] The third obstacle for patients gaining access to LARC options is doctors outright denying them IUDs due to misconceptions about fertility problems[34] or the dangers of sexually transmitted diseases.[35]

HARMS

Clear evidence shows that testing saves lives meaning that regular screening is necessary for complete health care. However, screening also harms patients when used in the wrong way, at the wrong intervals, or with the wrong aims. In a Practice Guideline, ACOG points out that,

> Protection from cervical cancer is the primary goal of screening, but as the prevalence of the disease decreases, other considerations may become equally important in the decision-making process. For example, the effects of invasive diagnostic workups (eg, colposcopy and biopsy) and overtreatment of lesions likely to regress have adverse consequences related to costs and potentially to reproductive outcomes. In addition, the anxiety and stigma associated with HPV infection are significant concerns for women who participate in cervical cancer screening programs.[36]

Because I focus primarily on tying birth control prescriptions to pelvic exams and Pap tests, the ways in which this practice harms patients varies significantly. I categorize two groups of problems in this practice, which overlap in a variety of ways. The first set of harms result from the Pap tests themselves: harms from the administration of the test; harms from overtesting; harms from overdiagnosis; harms from overtreatment. The second set of harms results from withholding the contraceptive in question: lack of access to birth control; pregnancy; multiple births; harms from eliminating long-term use; lack of treatment for underlying conditions; and harms from short hiatuses of contraception.

The first category of harms caused by the practice in question is the constellation of harms that result from testing itself. The administration of the test itself can harm patients for a variety of reasons. For example, pain is a relevant harm in this context. Both Pap tests and pelvic exams are invasive and can be painful for some patients. Although many patients report feeling only a mild pressure during the exam, a significant subset report pain during the procedure.[37] A test being painful is not necessarily a reason to avoid it, especially if the pain is minor and the test prevents against deadly diseases one is likely to be exposed to, as is the case in much routine testing. But if the test is unlikely to bring any benefits or is performed at more frequent intervals than needed, this pain should not be discounted. New research adds further concern to this component of the test, since evidence shows doctors consistently ignore or downplay the reported pain of women.[38]

Additional side effects can occur after the exam. Painful cramping is a very common side effect, as is bleeding due to scraping sensitive vaginal and cervical cells. Again, these side effects are relatively minor and usually temporary. However, I focus here on the harm of overtesting, not of testing in a manner prescribed by medical institutions and evidence. When evaluating the harm of testing too much, any side effect is unnecessary and any risk outweighs the likely benefits by definition.

The next related harm is the harm of yearly Pap tests and pelvic exams when they are not medically indicated. Pelvic exams are not indicated as a routine test.[39] Requiring these tests at more frequent intervals than they are medically indicated results in overtesting. Overtesting can cause problems for patients for a variety of reasons. Falling under this category are the costs in time, money, and stress as well as the harm from the exam itself.

Overtesting is a significant harm to patients in part due to indirect costs. Tests themselves can be costly, either for patients themselves or for insurance companies, who pass the cost onto consumers. Patients without insurance may be charged out-of-pocket for the expensive tests, which can be a significant sacrifice for those with limited income. It can even be prohibitive for patients who either cannot afford the test or who cannot get access to a doctor who will prescribe birth control to a patient without insurance. Even for patients with insurance, the tests can be costly, and not just due to copays. For decades, female patients were charged higher insurance premiums than male patients.[40] This cost differential was justified in part by the sort of added tests women face like Pap tests. In the last chapter, I also looked at the burden patients face in opportunity costs and time spent in having extra doctors' visits to add to busy schedules.

The psychological burden of the tests is also non-negligible. Waiting for the results can be harmful to patients because they worry about their health. The results from a Pap test can take anywhere from three days to two weeks.[41] Added to this concern is the fact that doctors' offices often do not inform patients of test results unless they test positive for a disease.[42] Thus, patients endure a waiting game that can be stressful. Although no particular feature of Pap tests specifically or of doctors' offices generally require that patients wait a long time for their results, in practice, patients often do not find out that they are healthy and merely deduce it from an absence of contact from their doctors. This avoidable fact unfortunately means that more tests can sometimes mean more stress.

The next category of harms includes the risk of overdiagnosis. Although overdiagnosis is always a risk when undergoing a medical test, these risks increase when the tests are performed more often than is medically indicated. The false positive rate for Pap tests is between 1% and 10%.[43] Thus, the more often you receive the test, the more likely you are to get a false positive result. For example, "if you get a yearly PAP between the ages of 18 to 78, and one assumes a 5% incidence of false positives, you would have a 95% chance of getting a false positive report during that time."[44] A 95% likelihood of receiving an abnormal test result over the course of a lifetime is no small matter. According to these numbers, most women will face a positive diagnosis for a disease and cancer they do not have. The overuse of the test threatens to make it meaningless. And, the fact of overdiagnosis is a serious threat to health.

The risks of overdiagnosis are myriad because overdiagnosis often leads to overtreatment. The most common treatments for cervical cancer are surgery, radiation therapy, chemotherapy, and targeted drugs such as angiogenesis inhibitors. These treatments are lifesavers for the numerous people afflicted with cervical cancer. The side effects and risks of these interventions are well worth the benefit they bring. Cervical cancer is highly treatable and can often be cured with high quality care.

However, for those people who receive treatment due to a false positive, the treatments are not such a boon.[45] The more invasive the surgery, the less probable it is that a patient is subjected to it for a false positive. Chemotherapy is an unlikely treatment for a patient with a false positive, since it is only preferred in cases where the cervical cancer has spread beyond the cervix, which requires further tests. However, even the threat of chemotherapy can be particularly frightening to patients. And, less invasive treatments can still be harmful to patients. Treatments even for precancerous cells can cause problems with fertility or preterm labor in future pregnancies because of long-term damage to the cervix. More testing itself can be invasive and damaging. For example, colposcopy, a common follow-up procedure used for diagnosis, carries risks of bleeding and infection, as do cervical biopsies, another common follow-up diagnostic procedure after a positive Pap test. Colposcopy and other treatments may also have a negative influence on sexual functioning as well as cause psychological distress.[46]

These threats of further testing and treatment are particularly worrisome for young women. For women under the age of 25, most abnormal Pap results, like Pap tests showing atypical squamous cells, low-grade squamous intraepithelial lesions (LSIL) are not necessarily indicative of a patient needing treatment.[47] For young women, the body clears the infection with HPV and the abnormal cells over time.[48] But if precancerous cells and lesions can regress over time with no intervention, then treatment poses more of a threat because its relatively higher risks are less justified. Young women who have never been pregnant and want to be pregnant someday are also at the highest risk for adverse side effects because risks to fertility have the greatest impact on them. Thus, more tests do not just mean more false positives for those who have no abnormal cells to treat, but may also mean more treatment, stress, and worry for those who have abnormal cells but do not need treatment. One wonders then, how valuable testing is that can lead to such a high number of false positives and for whom a positive test may not require treatment in the first place. Patients given a true choice about whether to undergo Pap tests and who are informed that a positive result would require no treatment may justifiably choose to delay or reduce testing.

The next category of harms has to do not with the Pap test itself, but with the decision to withhold birth control until the patient receives the required exam. The first set of harms in suspending treatment includes the body's direct response to stopping birth control. The most immediate response is the lapse in contraceptive coverage. Missing a pill, taking a pill at a different time of day, and interactions with other medications may influence effectiveness of hormonal contraceptives. Thus, it is no surprise that missing many consecutive days when a prescription runs out, as opposed to just one missed pill accidentally, can lead to a failure in pregnancy protection.

Keeping in mind our earlier definition of harm, lack of contraception access itself is a problem, even if a patient never gets pregnant during the lapse. In fact, pregnancy is much more dangerous than many other medical conditions, meaning that the threat of pregnancy alone should be sufficient to rule out the practice. Because lack of contraception access imposes a risk of a pregnancy on the user, and because that risk is unnecessary, lack of birth control constitutes a harm to the patient. Pap test waiting periods and antibiotics could have similar impacts on birth control. For example, if a course of antibiotics like rifampin to combat tuberculosis leads to a reduction in contraceptive efficacy, the patient faces risks from both.[49] However, given that tuberculosis is painful and dangerous, the trade-off would likely be justified. A yearly Pap test provides no such benefits and unlike the antibiotics, is completely unrelated to the use of birth control except by the doctor's own decision to link the two.

Because a lapse in an individual's preferred birth control method can lead to accidental pregnancy, one risk in withholding birth control is an unintended pregnancy. In the last chapter, I discussed the problems associated with people not being able to time and plan their births, such as financial and emotional burdens. However, pregnancy is also a medical condition and has medical consequences. For example, the United States is among the worst for maternal mortality rates in the developed world[50] due to reasons which may include obesity, lack of health care, diabetes, racial discrimination, and even domestic abuse, which often increases with pregnancy.

Even when pregnancy falls short of these fatal complications, it can still cause pain, suffering, and disability. For example, pregnancy can lead to or increase the likelihood of carpal tunnel syndrome, gestational diabetes, back pain, hypertension, depression, and strokes.[51] Rarely, pregnancy causes lifelong disabilities. But much more commonly, pregnancy can cause short-term disability, such as recovery from a Caesarean section or episiotomies, and these conditions are covered under the Americans with Disabilities Act (ADA). Significantly, both C-sections and episiotomies also occur at higher rates than medically indicated.[52] Perineal trauma or tearing is another significant risk factor, since upwards of 85% of patients experience tears in labor and the rates are going up.[53] Not every pregnancy has these dangerous complications—some pregnant people even find childbirth to be only minimally painful. But again, exposure to the risk of pregnancy, even if no complications occur, is problematic. To the extent that withholding birth control exposes patients to these physical risks unnecessarily, it is unjustified from a medical perspective.

That stopping birth control would lead to a failure in contraception and therefore to unintended pregnancy is a concrete and expected result. But perhaps more worrisome is the fact that directly after stopping birth control pills, fertility actually increases. In fact, the likelihood of having twins may go up just after stopping birth control.[54] One possibility for why this effect occurs is that after ovulation suppression, the body responds with hyperovulation, or releasing more than one egg during a single cycle. Hyperovulation in turn may increase the likelihood of fraternal twins. The irony of being more fertile at a time when patients most want to be covered with protection against pregnancy, but are denied it by their doctors, is telling.

Furthermore, carrying twins itself is associated with risks. Multiple pregnancies are more likely to lead to Caesarean sections, a painful and serious surgery; preterm babies; babies with low birth weights; preeclampsia; and gestational diabetes, among other conditions. That is, the life and health of both the mother and the babies are at greater risk in the multiple pregnancies that occur as the result of withholding birth control. Most of the time, multiple pregnancies are outside the scope of doctor or patient action, such as maternal age or genetic predisposition. In this case, however, if multiple pregnancies occur as the result of a doctor withholding needed access to birth control are clearly both preventable and unnecessary.

Other side effects of going off birth control for nonmedical reasons are also significant. Hormonal contraceptives offer a host of benefits unrelated to pregnancy prevention.[55] In long-term use, hormonal birth control can prevent or limit ovarian cysts, lower the risks of some cancers, and treat endometriosis.[56] Some such benefits increase with long-term use.[57] Thus, the temporary cessation of oral contraceptives can lead to other medical problems that patients may not even be aware their birth control is protecting them from, such as ovarian cysts.

The fact that birth control may help protect against endometrial, colorectal, and ovarian cancer to a very significant degree is particularly noteworthy.[58] Doctors and health-care professionals are ostensibly protecting their patients from untreated cervical cancer by tying Pap tests to birth control prescriptions. However, if birth control helps prevent other forms of cancer, and they are denying their patients birth control, they may actually be contributing to their patients contracting cancer through their actions. Whereas doctors cannot prevent cervical cancer through the act of cervical screening unless some subsequent treatment of abnormalities takes place, they can help patients prevent ovarian and endometrial cancer by prescribing birth control. In addition, while some studies show a slight, temporary increased risk from long-term use of hormonal birth control,[59] other studies show no added risk.[60]

Next, some problems arise as the result of a temporary hiatus in birth control due to the associated conditions that go temporarily untreated. Many patients rely on birth control to treat conditions unrelated to pregnancy. Hormonal pills are an effective treatment for a variety of conditions, including: endometriosis, a painful disorder which can cause problems in fertility; polycystic ovary syndrome (PCOS), a hormonal imbalance that can lead to diabetes and heart disease; premenstrual syndrome (PMS), a syndrome linked to more than 150 symptoms including physical and psychological problems; premenstrual dysphoric disorder (PMDD), a more severe type of PMS; primary ovarian insufficiency (POI), an estrogen imbalance that can affect bone health; irregular periods; and acne.[61] When these conditions go untreated due to lack of access to birth control, they can lead to immediate problems such as pain and suffering or long-term problems associated with failure of treatment. More than half of contraceptive users—58%—rely on hormonal contraception in part for conditions unrelated to birth control.[62] Since 11.2 million women are estimated to use oral contraceptive pills, the inability to treat severe medical problems besides birth control would also affect millions.[63]

Lastly, even when patients are unaffected by the lack of access to birth control or the lack of access to treatment of unrelated medical conditions, going on and off the pill itself constitutes a harm for many patients. Going on and off the pill causes significant changes to the body's hormones, which in turn lead to undesirable side effects. Headaches, nausea, worsening cramps, and other problems can arise during the adjustment period when patients start and stop using pills. These side effects are completely preventable by the continued use of birth control without a temporary hiatus.

The harms of withholding birth control itself are myriad. Many patients will not face these harms because, despite requiring the exams to give a yearly prescription, some doctors will offer a single refill to tide a patient over while waiting for the needed appointment. However, not all doctors offer this relief, while other doctors who engage in this practice will likely only prescribe this stop-gap measure once. Thus, some subset of patients may face breaks in continuity of treatment.

Other patients will not face these harms because the dangers may not manifest themselves. For example, patients only have a 95% chance of receiving a false positive in their lifetime; 5% of patients will not. These patients will not face the harms of follow-up tests or overdiagnosis. These patients may not get nausea from brief hiatuses in birth control coverage, and may not be at risk for pregnancy either because they use a backup method like condoms or because they are not sexually active during the hiatus. If these patients are not relying on birth control for the treatment of other conditions like endometriosis, then they will not suffer the harms from that untreated condition. Patients meeting these criteria may never see the negative side effects from the practice in question. Nevertheless, at the outset of the chapter, I defined harm as including not just intentional or unintentional harm, but also the exposure to unnecessary risk. Even though some patients may successfully avoid the side effects catalogued in this chapter, they are still exposed to the risks of these harms unnecessarily. That risk, even if they are not aware of it, is a significant threat to their health and other personal resources.

UTILITARIANISM

In chapter 4, I argue that perhaps too much emphasis is placed on the physical harms of withholding birth control; these denials would matter even if they caused no medical impacts. However, for a consequentialist or utilitarian evaluation, harm is of primary moral significance because acts or policies are evaluated based on whether they produce good or bad consequences.[64] One of the reasons that the medical establishment does not recommend tying birth control prescription refills to Pap tests is that in the cost benefit analysis, doing so is not conducive or protective of long-term health. On the contrary, I argue above that the policy is extremely harmful overall. This empirical evaluation is of central importance to utilitarian approaches in which the predicted, likely, or actual impacts of an act or policy determines its moral worth. Thus, from an impartial, maximizing, and consequentialist perspective, I argue the practice is morally impermissible.[65]

INTENT

Many, if not most doctors do not actually want patients to stop using birth control, even when they refuse requests to extend prescriptions or require extra tests to refill those prescriptions. The goals for such incentives are not for patients to lose access to birth control but rather for patients to comply with valued Pap testing. Thus, the harms imposed are likely not malicious. In fact, by some definitions, they may not even be intended. Of course, doctors are aware of the possibility that their patients may lose birth control access when they refuse the same. But the fact that the side effect is foreseen is not necessarily evidence that it is intended.

The Doctrine of Double Effect is a philosophical position that recognizes that one can have a single action with two effects: one aimed at and one foreseen but not desired.[66] According to the Doctrine of Double Effect, "it is sometimes permissible to bring about by oblique intention something that you cannot permissibly directly intend."[67] For an action to pass the test on common understandings, it may not be immoral in its own right.[68] Whether or not making birth control hinge on unrelated testing is morally permissible is a subject I take up in later chapters. The next requirement to pass the Doctrine of Double Effect is that the agent must intend the good effect and not the bad one. That doctors do not intend for their patients be noncompliant and suffer the consequences I have argued above. The third condition covers the relationship between the good and bad effect: the good effect must not be produced by the bad one. If that were allowed, then the principle would reduce to the good ends justifying the means, and it aims to rule such actions out. For example, unemployed gravediggers may not sell poisonous oil to kill more people and get more work, because the unintended foreseen consequence (the death of many) is required to achieve the good effect (more work).[69] One way to assess this condition is to consider whether you would aim at the bad effect even if by some stroke of luck you did not have to so as to achieve the good effect. For example, if by some stroke of luck the gravediggers' poisonous oil did not kill anyone, they would have failed in their actions. By contrast, if one aims to save the life of a patient by performing a hysterectomy, even though the patient is pregnant and the fetus is likely to die as a result, and by some stroke of luck the fetus does not in fact die, one does not then kill the fetus. The last condition is that the good effect outweighs the bad one (proportionality).

In the case of the doctor withholding a prescription, are the above conditions met? A doctor does not require the bad effect of a patient getting pregnant or having a recurrence of ovarian cysts to successfully get the good effect of the patient undergoing a Pap test. And the doctor would not aim to cause those bad effects if by some stroke of luck they did not occur when the medicine is withheld. Thus, even though the doctor foresees the bad effect, and even though the doctor uses the bad effect as a threat, it may seem as though the doctor does not intend the bad effect.

However, the doctor arguably violates at least three of the above conditions. First, as I argue later in chapter 4, the act itself is impermissible, not morally good or morally neutral, ruling out the action as eligible for the doctrine. But more significantly for our purposes here, the act fails if the good effect is produced by means of the bad one. Recalling the earlier discussion of harm as including imposing unnecessary risk, if the bad effect is understood here not as the patient getting pregnant or suffering from endometriosis but as being exposed to the risk of those possibilities, then the third condition gets activated. The doctor needs the imposition of risk on the patient to make sense of the act at all. Without the risk of those results, the patient would not be sufficiently motivated to comply with the doctor's recommendation. In other words, if the patient does not see unintended pregnancy or untreated medical conditions as a risk of withholding birth control, then the withholding of birth control will not be a successful measure to ensure the patient comes in for testing. The patient will merely ignore the need for more birth control as well as avoid the sought-for Pap test. Thus, the bad effect looks to be too closely causally related to the good effect.

The fourth condition is also at stake. The desire for patients to comply with Pap tests is an admirable one, but the decision to withhold needed medication to achieve the result is disproportionate to the goal. Keeping in mind that birth control can successfully prevent cancer while Pap tests can merely serve as early warnings and need separate treatments to prevent cancer, and keeping in mind that pregnancy, just as cervical cancer, can lead to death, the good of testing does not outweigh the potential harms that may ensue. Birth control is a treatment while cervical cancer screenings are a test; they have different goals and purposes. To be sure, the mortality rate of pregnancy is much lower than the mortality rate of cervical cancer. But taking into account that testing yearly does not prevent cancer more often than testing at longer intervals and in fact leads to the greater harms of false positives, the point is relevant. Doctors arguably cannot meet the proportionality criterion when they withhold needed medical care for ill-advised testing. On one understanding, then, the bad result is, at least in some sense, intended.

Intentional harm is not necessarily malicious. Malice is notoriously difficult to identify and track. It requires insight into doctors' motives often opaque to the doctors themselves, the outside world, or both. A doctor needlessly cutting open a patient so as to cause that patient pain acts maliciously. But a doctor cutting open a patient so as to perform a lifesaving surgery may foresee pain but nevertheless act in the patient's overall best interests. Most medical interventions impose some risks on patients, and doctors and patients together must weigh these risks with the potential benefits the interventions can bring. In addition, forgoing medical interventions also brings its own set of risks. What sets apart the practice in question from standard medical procedures aiming at the patient's best interest is first, that the test is unnecessary, meaning that it is done at too frequent an interval; second, that the test is needlessly risky, meaning that the potential benefits are not sufficient to outweigh the known risks; and third, that the doctor withholds other, unrelated medical care to achieve compliance from the patient. Because doctors know and aim at these results, I argue that they act intentionally and that they act harmfully, even if they do not necessarily act maliciously.

As I argued in the discussion of harm at the outset of the chapter however, the principle of "do no harm" does not require that the harm be intended. The discussion of intention is instructive, but not conclusive on the question of violating the "do no harm" principle. Thus, even if, contra the above discussion, the Doctrine of Double Effect clears the doctor of intentional harm, the practice would still be unwarranted in this case because the doctor caused harm unnecessarily.

CONCLUSION

That doctors hurt patients when they withhold medical care is not new or surprising. What is significant to point out in this instance is that doctors are not merely refusing to continue treatment on established patients but also aiming to act in the patient's overall best interests. That is, by using birth control as a bargaining chip to incent patients to engage in other tests for their help, doctors may think they are justified, and therefore overlook or minimize the harm being done. Is it permissible for doctors to withhold prescriptions either due to protection of patient interests, physician principles, or to improve health outcomes for patients? In the remainder of this book, I argue that such practices are never permissible. Specifically, I use the discussion in this chapter to argue in chapter 3 that doctors actually engage in medical malpractice when they deny their patients birth control. Before I move to those arguments, however, I first aim to identify the practice for what it is and understand its significance.

More often than not, patients know and understand the potential harms of testing—if not of too-frequent pelvic exams, then certainly of being denied birth control. So, worry, stress, and psychological burdens play a role in the health outcomes of patients denied access to birth control in addition to the physical and medical harms discussed above.

Doctors have long known that withholding birth control is harmful to their patients. Most practitioners, even those who engage in the practice, would likely acknowledge the arguments discussed in this chapter. As discussed, virtually every reputable health organization recommends against it. In fact, I can go further than just to say that doctors know they harm their patients when they withhold birth control for unrelated purposes. I argue these doctors are counting on that harm, and counting on their patients to know that they are being harmed in this context. According to this view, these facts are central to the practice itself. Doctors know that withholding birth control harms patients; otherwise, it would not be an effective means to ensure compliance with otherwise unrelated tests.

The only possible justification for withholding an established treatment that the doctor and patient have both agreed on and that the doctor and patient both agree the patient needs is the second part of the practice: tying it to pelvic exams or Pap tests. If doctors want to do what is in their patients' best interests, and the exams help protect patients' long-term health, then incentivizing patients to undergo these tests will also be in the patient's best interests, according to this logic. In other words, doctors think that these tests are so critical that they can go to great lengths to ensure their patients undergo them. So, doctors accept what they consider to be a smaller harm to prevent what they consider to be a larger one. Armed with this charitable interpretation of the doctors' actions—after all, I am not attributing maliciousness to the majority of the health profession—I argue for a better understanding of why doctors are not merely aware of the potential harm of withholding birth control, but actually rely on it.

It is the need for birth control and the pain and stress that attends not having access to it that doctors rely on when they require Pap tests for prescriptions. If they did not choose to withhold medical care desired by their patients, their goals at increasing Pap tests would not be very effective. Doctors know that patients need their medication urgently. It is precisely for this reason that they choose to withhold it. Preventing access to something that patients neither need nor want would not be an effective way of gaining compliance with a test doctors (and not patients) think is valuable. To get patients to comply with tests, doctors need to use something they know their patients rely on. Doctors know that birth control is the biggest bargaining chip they have because it would cause the greatest harm to their patients if they were to deny it. Thus, doctors fully understand the harm of withholding birth control when they engage in this practice, and in fact openly depend on that harm to achieve their goals.

One way to understand this point is to see how ineffective doctors would be if they flipped around the practice. Since they acknowledge how helpful pelvic exams and Pap tests are for the long-term health of their patients, would they withhold these tests until they ensure patients successfully follow their birth control regimen? For example, would they ask patients who want testing to take birth control and document regular compliance over time before allowing patients to come in for a Pap test? A couple of reasons suggest why this practice would not work. First, withholding tests only increases the risk of long-term harm while not necessarily leading to the type of immediate harm that may incent patients to act. And second, patients do not want and desire these tests as much as they want and desire birth control. Instead, doctors capitalize on their patients' wants and needs to successfully gain compliance with tests they cannot successfully convince their patients are equally necessary. If patients wanted Pap tests so much that they were willing to take birth control to get them, then this hypothetical practice would be at least as successful as current practices today. However, such a policy would be deemed unethical because it relies on the desperation or medical need of patients to achieve an unrelated goal.

Understanding and quantifying the physical harm done by the practice helps make salient the fact that this practice is not just an office policy like requiring 24 hours' notice for cancellations or hiring extra support staff. By focusing on the fact that the practice is harmful, doctors cannot hide behind these potential excuses. And, by focusing on the physical harm and not just the emotional or financial harm, I aim to present a stronger case to a clinician likely focused primarily on the science.

However, recognizing that doctors are aware of the way they hurt their patients when engaging in the practice, and indeed count on hurting their patients in this way, explains first, why too much emphasis has been placed on the physical detriments covered in this chapter, and second, why establishing the harm would not be effective in reducing the incidence of the practice. These two points are connected. It is for this reason that I go on to discuss the legal and moral harms done in this case.

The discussions outlined in this chapter are gaining more traction in the literature, prompting discussion of the practice.[70] A consensus has emerged that the negative health outcomes are significant and thus that doctors should not require the tests.[71] However, that consensus has not always acknowledged an ensuing violation of medical professionalism and the role of the doctor. And, arguably too much emphasis is placed on these physical problems with the practice and not the deeper moral harms, discussed later in the book. The physical injury and damages are not required, I argue, for the practice to be unjustified.

There is a related reason why the physical damages doctors cause when they require exams to give birth control prescriptions may not be enough to deter the practice: explaining the harm is not effective because doctors rely on that harm in the first place. If doctors did not know they were causing harm or exposing their patients to unnecessary risk, then educating them about that fact might be sufficient to stop the practice. But because they know what they are doing, reminding them of this point will not likely alter their behavior. Instead, more explanation is required to show why the practice should end.

In the next chapter, I argue that this practice goes beyond exposure to harm and actually constitutes medical malpractice. Using a legal framework, I show that the practice constitutes illegal measures. I go on to argue that the moral harms doctors impose on patients are greater still. In chapter 4, I look at the moral wrongs done to patients in cases like these. If "first, do no harm" is an exhortation not to hurt the patient physically, as I have interpreted it here, then physical explanations alone can answer the question. But if harms are broad enough to include violations of rights, denial of patient interests, or the violation of legal protections, then evaluating the morality of the act is necessary to answer the question of whether doctors do patients harm when they engage in this practice. I take up these moral and legal issues next.

NOTES

1. Cedric M. Smith, "Origin and Uses of Primum Non Nocere—Above All, Do No Harm!," *The Journal of Clinical Pharmacology* 45, no. 4 (2005): 371–77, https://doi.org/10.1177/0091270004273680.

2. Tom L. Beauchamp and James F. Childress, *Principles of Biomedical Ethics* (Oxford University Press, 2001), 117; Ronald Munson, *Intervention and Reflection*, 8th ed. (Belmont, California: Thomas Wadsworth, 2008), 770.

3. James Rachels, "Active and Passive Euthanasia," *Bioethics: An Introduction to the History, Methods, and Practice*, 1975, 77–82.

4. Arvizo, Cynthia, and Haider Mahdi. "Disparities in Cervical Cancer in African American Women: What Primary Care Physicians Can Do." *Cleveland Clinica Journal of Medicine* 84, no. 10 (Ocrober 2017): 788–94.

5. Otis Brawley, "No More Annual Pap Smear: New Cervical Cancer Screening Guidelines," CNN, March 15, 2012, http://www.cnn.com/2012/03/14/health/brawley-cervical-cancer-screenings/index.html.

6. Rebecca Skloot, *The Immortal Life of Henrietta Lacks* (New York: Broadway Books, 2011), 27.

7. Skloot, 66.

8. American Cancer Society, "Can Cervical Cancer Be Prevented?," http://www.cancer.org/cancer/cervicalcancer/detailedguide/cervical-cancerprevention.

9. The American College of Obstetricians and Gynecologists, "Abnormal Cervical Cancer Screening Test Results: FAQ187," January 2016, http://www.acog.org/Patients/FAQs/Abnormal-Cervical-Cancer-Screening-Test-Results#difference.

10. George Koliopoulos et al., "Cytology versus HPV Testing for Cervical Cancer Screening in the General Population," *Cochrane Database of Systematic Reviews*, no. 8 (2017), https://doi.org/10.1002/14651858.CD008587.pub2.

11. Pushp Lata Sachan et al., "A Study on Cervical Cancer Screening Using Pap Smear Test and Clinical Correlation," *Asia-Pacific Journal of Oncology Nursing* 5, no. 3 (September 2018): 337–41, https://doi.org/10.4103/apjon.apjon_15_18.

12. The American College of Obstetricians and Gynecologists, "Abnormal Cervical Cancer Screening Test Results: FAQ187."

13. "American Cancer Society Expert Voices Blog," Cancer.org, accessed May 28, 2015, http://www.cancer.org/Cancer/News/ExpertVoices/; Schwarz et al., "Cervical Cancer Screening Continues to Limit Provision of Contraception."

14. Center for Disease Control, "US Selected Practice Recommendations for Contraceptive Use, 2016 Appendix C: Examinations and Tests Needed

Before Initiation of Contraceptive Methods," December 25, 2017, https://www.cdc.gov/reproductivehealth/contraception/mmwr/spr/appendixc.html.

15. Amir Qaseem et al., "Screening Pelvic Examination in Adult Women: A Clinical Practice Guideline From the American College of Physicians Screening Pelvic Examination in Adult Women," *Annals of Internal Medicine* 161, no. 1 (July 1, 2014): 67–72, https://doi.org/10.7326/M14-0701.

16. The American College of Obstetricians and Gynecologists, "Committee Opinion, Number 544 Over-the-Counter Access to Oral Contraceptives," *Committee on Gynecologic Practice*, December 2012, https://www.acog.org/-/media/Committee-Opinions/Committee-on-Gynecologic-Practice/co544.pdf?dmc=1&ts=20150125T0334021611.

17. Center for Disease Control, "What Should I Know about Screening?," Centers for Disease Control and Prevention, August 23, 2018, http://www.cdc.gov/cancer/cervical/basic_info/screening.htm.

18. "Cervical Cancer: Screening," uspreventiveservicetaskforce.org, March 2012, http://www.uspreventiveservicestaskforce.org/Page/Document/Update-SummaryFinal/cervical-cancer-screening; US Preventative Services Task Force, "Final Update Summary: Cervical Cancer: Screening," August 2018, https://www.uspreventiveservicestaskforce.org/Page/Document/UpdateSummaryFinal/cervical-cancer-screening2.

19. "American College of Physicians Recommends against Screening Pelvic Examination in Adult, Asymptomatic, Average Risk, Non-Pregnant Women," acponline.org, July 1, 2014, https://www.acponline.org/acp-newsroom/american-college-of-physicians-recommends-against-screening-pelvic-examination-in-adult-asymptomatic.

20. "Cervical Cancer: Screening."

21. Debbie Saslow, "American Cancer Society Expert Voices Blog: Is a Pap Test Necessary Every Year?," Cancer.org, March 14, 2012, http://www.cancer.org/Cancer/News/ExpertVoices/.

22. "Screening Guidelines," asccp.org, 2012, http://www.asccp.org/guidelines/screening-guidelines.

23. "To Pap or Not to Pap: What the New Cervical Cancer Screening Guidelines Mean for Women," ascp.org, March 14, 2012, http://www.ascp.org/Newsroom/To-Pap-or-Not-to-Pap-What-the-New-Cervical-Cancer-Screening-Guidelines-Mean-for-Women.html.

24. Debbie Saslow et al., "American Cancer Society, American Society for Colposcopy and Cervical Pathology, and American Society for Clinical Pathology Screening Guidelines for the Prevention and Early Detection of Cervical Cancer," *CA: A Cancer Journal for Clinicians* 62, no. 3 (2012): 147–72, https://doi.org/10.3322/caac.21139.

25. Brenda E. Sirovich and H. Gilbert Welch, "The Frequency of Pap Smear Screening in the United States," *Journal of General Internal Medicine* 19, no. 3 (March 2004): 243–50, https://doi.org/10.1111/j.1525-1497.2004.21107.x; "ACOG Committee Opinion. Recommendations on Frequency of Pap Test Screening. Number 152--March 1995. Committee on Gynecologic Practice. American College of Obstetricians and Gynecologists," *International Journal of Gynaecology and Obstetrics: The Official Organ of the International Federation of Gynaecology and Obstetrics* 49, no. 2 (May 1995): 210–11.

26. Timothy Canavan, "Appropriate Use of the Intrauterine Device," American Family Physician 58, no. 9 (December 1, 1998): 2077–84.

27. Donna Shoupe, "LARC Methods: Entering a New Age of Contraception and Reproductive Health," *Contraception and Reproductive Medicine* 1 (2016): 4, https://doi.org/10.1186/s40834-016-0011-8.

28. Committee on Adolescent Care: Long-Acting Reversible Contraception Working Group, "Adolescents and Long-Acting Reversible Contraception: Implants and Intrauterine Devices," *The American College of Obstetricians and Gynecologists* 539 (October 2012), http://www.acog.org/-/media/Committee-Opinions/Committee-on-Adolescent-Health-Care/co539.pdf?dmc=1&ts=20170330T1452030170.

29. Mary A. Ott, Gina S. Sucato, and Committee On Adolescence, "Contraception for Adolescents," *Pediatrics* 134, no. 4 (October 1, 2014): e1257–81, https://doi.org/10.1542/peds.2014-2300.

30. Canavan, "Appropriate Use of the Intrauterine Device - American Family Physician."

31. Stephanie B. Teal and S. Elizabeth Romer, "Awareness of Long-Acting Reversible Contraception among Teens and Young Adults," *The Journal of Adolescent Health: Official Publication of the Society for Adolescent Medicine* 52, no. 4 Suppl (April 2013): S35-39, https://doi.org/10.1016/j.jadohealth.2013.01.013.

32. Sally Rafie et al., "Roles of the Pharmacist in the Use of Safe and Highly Effective Long-Acting Reversible Contraception: An Opinion of the Women's Health Practice and Research Network of the American College of Clinical Pharmacy," *Pharmacotherapy: The Journal of Human Pharmacology and Drug Therapy* 34, no. 9 (September 1, 2014): 991–99, https://doi.org/10.1002/phar.1457.

33. Alicia T. Luchowski et al., "Obstetrician–Gynecologists and Contraception: Long-Acting Reversible Contraception Practices and Education," *Contraception* 89, no. 6 (June 1, 2014): 578–83, https://doi.org/10.1016/j.contraception.2014.02.004.

34. "Popularity Disparity: Attitudes About the IUD in Europe and the United States," Guttmacher Institute, November 12, 2007, https://www.guttmacher.org/gpr/2007/11/popularity-disparity-attitudes-about-iud-europe-and-united-states.

35. Ott, Sucato, and Adolescence, "Contraception for Adolescents."

36. "Practice Bulletin No. 168: Cervical Cancer Screening and Prevention," *Obstetrics & Gynecology* 128, no. 4 (October 2016): e111, https://doi.org/10.1097/AOG.0000000000001708.

37. Gauss, Julie W., Athur Mabiso, and Karen Patricia Williams. "Pap Screening Goals and Perceptions of Pain among Black, Latina, and Arab Women: Steps toward Breaking down Psychological Barriers." Journal of Cancer Education: The Official Journal of the American Association for Cancer Education 28, no. 2 (June 2013): 367–74. https://doi.org/10.1007/s13187-012-0441-1; Bergman, Sirena. "How Enduring Use of 150-Year-Old Speculum Puts Women off Smear Tests." The Independent, June 10, 2019. https://www.independent.co.uk/life-style/women/speculum-use-smear-tests-pain-women-cervical-screening-sexism-men-a8834771.html.

38. Diane E. Hoffmann and Anita J. Tarzian, "The Girl Who Cried Pain: A Bias Against Women in the Treatment of Pain," SSRN Scholarly Paper (Rochester, NY: Social Science Research Network, 2001), https://papers.ssrn.com/abstract=383803; Leslie Jamison, "Grand Unified Theory of Female Pain," *VQR Online*, Spring 2014, http://www.vqronline.org/essays-articles/2014/04/grand-unified-theory-female-pain; Joe Fassler, "How Doctors Take Women's Pain Less Seriously," *The Atlantic*, October 15, 2015, https://www.theatlantic.com/health/archive/2015/10/emergency-room-wait-times-sexism/410515/.

39. U.S. Department of Veterans Affairs Veterans Health Administration, "Provider Fact Sheet: Cervical Cancer Screening," June 2013, https://www.prevention.va.gov/docs/CervicalCProvider.pdf; "Practice Advisory; Screening Pelvic Examination," https://www.acog.org/Clinical-Guidance-and-Publications/Practice-Advisories/Practice-Advisory-Screening-Pelvic-Examination; Chris Crawford, "AAFP Recommends Against Pelvic Exams in Asymptomatic Women," April 25, 2017, https://www.aafp.org/news/health-of-the-public/20170425aafppelvicexam.html; Qaseem et al., "Screening Pelvic Examination in Adult Women."

40. Robert J. Carney and Donald W. Hardigree, "The Economic Impact of Gender-Neutral Insurance Rating on Women," *The Journal of Insurance Issues and Practices* 13, no. 2 (1990): 1–23; Robert Pear, "Women Still Pay More for Health Insurance, Data Shows," *The New York Times*, March 19, 2012, sec. Money & Policy, https://www.nytimes.com/2012/03/19/health/policy/women-still-pay-more-for-health-insurance-data-shows.html; "New NWLC Report: Discriminatory Health Insurance Practices Cost Women $1 Billion a Year,"

NWLC (blog), March 19, 2012, https://nwlc.org/press-releases/new-nwlc-report-discriminatory-health-insurance-practices-cost-women-1-billion-year/; Michelle Andrews, "Health Insurance Prices For Women Set To Drop," NPR.org, July 17, 2012, https://www.npr.org/sections/health-shots/2012/07/17/156895577/leveling-the-playing-field-for-women-s-premiums.

41. K. Aleisha Fetters, "Pap Smear FAQs," *Women's Health*, January 11, 2012, http://www.womenshealthmag.com/health/pap-smear-faqs.

42. I thank Nancy Delston for this point.

43. Jane Harrison-Hohner, "How Accurate Is My Pap Smear Result?" *WebMD* (blog), June 6, 2011, http://blogs.webmd.com/womens-health/2011/06/how-accurate-is-my-pap-smear-result.html.

44. Harrison-Hohner.

45. Surgery and chemotherapy are painful, distressing, and costly. While some surgeries, like cryosurgery, which freezes off cancerous cells, are minimally invasive and can be done in a doctor's office, other surgical treatments for cervical cancer are more severe. Chemotherapy is particularly burdensome because of the painful and long-lasting side effects. Total or radical hysterectomies are also a standard treatment for cervical cancer, involve a hospital stay and, of course, cause infertility due to the removal of the uterus. However, doctors should know that the increased use of Pap tests can lead to unnecessary diagnoses that can change the trajectory of a patient's life significantly and without reason. When the tests are not medically indicated and are themselves unnecessary, these risks are also unnecessary.

46. C. Hellsten, P.G. Lindqvist, and K. Sjöström, "A Longitudinal Study of Sexual Functioning in Women Referred for Colposcopy: A 2-Year Follow Up," *BJOG: An International Journal of Obstetrics & Gynaecology* 115, no. 2 (September 28, 2007): 210, https://doi.org/10.1111/j.1471-0528.2007.01503.x; Blanca R. Cendejas, Karen K. Smith-Mccune, and Michelle J. Khan, "Does Treatment for Cervical and Vulvar Dysplasia Impact Women's Sexual Health?," *American Journal of Obstetrics and Gynecology* 212, no. 3 (March 2015): 291–97, https://doi.org/10.1016/j.ajog.2014.05.039; Susanna Kola and Jane C. Walsh, "Patients' Psychological Reactions to Colposcopy and LLETZ Treatment for Cervical Intraepithelial Neoplasia," *European Journal of Obstetrics, Gynecology, and Reproductive Biology* 146, no. 1 (September 2009): 96–99, https://doi.org/10.1016/j.ejogrb.2009.05.005; Linda Sharp et al., "Factors Associated with Psychological Distress Following Colposcopy among Women with Low-Grade Abnormal Cervical Cytology: A Prospective Study within the Trial Of Management of Borderline and Other Low-Grade Abnormal Smears (TOMBOLA)," *Psycho-Oncology* 22, no. 2 (February 2013): 368–80, https://doi.org/10.1002/pon.2097; Annu Heinonen et al., "Health-Related Quality of Life and Perception of Anxiety in Women with Abnormal Cervical Cytology

Referred for Colposcopy: An Observational Study," *European Journal of Obstetrics, Gynecology, and Reproductive Biology* 169, no. 2 (July 2013): 387–91, https://doi.org/10.1016/j.ejogrb.2013.03.033; Gitte Lee Mortensen and Anny Lisbeth Adeler, "Qualitative Study of Women's Anxiety and Information Needs after a Diagnosis of Cervical Dysplasia," *Journal of Public Health* 18, no. 5 (October 1, 2010): 473–82, https://doi.org/10.1007/s10389-010-0330-1; Mélanie Drolet et al., "The Psychosocial Impact of an Abnormal Cervical Smear Result," *Psycho-Oncology* 21, no. 10 (October 2012): 1071–81, https://doi.org/10.1002/pon.2003; B. Bonevski et al., "Women's Experiences of Having a Colposcopic Examination: Self-Reported Satisfaction with Care, Perceived Needs and Consequences," *Journal of Obstetrics and Gynaecology: The Journal of the Institute of Obstetrics and Gynaecology* 18, no. 5 (September 1998): 462–70, https://doi.org/10.1080/01443619866804.

47. The American College of Obstetricians and Gynecologists, "Abnormal Cervical Cancer Screening Test Results" (January 2016).

48. Ibid.

49. Scott S. DeRossi and Elliot V. Hersh, "Antibiotics and Oral Contraceptives," *Dental Clinics of North America* 46, no. 4 (October 2002): 653–64.

50. Institute for Health Metrics and Evaluation. "Health-Related SDGs | IHME Viz Hub," 2017. http://vizhub.healthdata.org/sdg.; Tavernise, Sabrina. "Maternal Mortality Rate in U.S. Rises, Defying Global Trend, Study Finds." The New York Times, September 21, 2016. http://www.nytimes.com/2016/09/22/health/maternal-mortality.html.

51. US Hastings College of the Law, "Pregnancy-Related Conditions as Disabilities under the ADA," accessed March 15, 2017, http://worklifelaw.org/pubs/Preg-Accomm-Disabilities.pdf.

52. Janet Burlingame et al., "166: Episiotomies: Who Does Them and Do They Help?," *American Journal of Obstetrics & Gynecology* 212, no. 1 (January 1, 2015): S98, https://doi.org/10.1016/j.ajog.2014.10.212.

53. Lesley A Smith et al., "Incidence of and Risk Factors for Perineal Trauma: A Prospective Observational Study," *BMC Pregnancy and Childbirth* 13 (March 7, 2013): 59, https://doi.org/10.1186/1471-2393-13-59.

54. Kenneth J. Rothman, "Fetal Loss, Twinning and Birth Weight after Oral-Conctraceptive Use," *New England Journal of Medicine* 297, no. 9 (September 1, 1997): 468–71, https://doi.org/10.1056/NEJM197709012970903.

55. "Beyond Birth Control: The Overlooked Benefits Of Oral Contraceptive Pills," Guttmacher Institute, February 25, 2016, https://www.guttmacher.org/report/beyond-birth-control-overlooked-benefits-oral-contraceptive-pills.

56. "Birth Control: Benefits Beyond Pregnancy Prevention." WebMD, 2018. https://www.webmd.com/sex/birth-control/other-benefits-birth-control.

57. Michels, Kara A., Ruth M. Pfeiffer, Louise A. Brinton, and Britton Trabert. "Modification of the Associations Between Duration of Oral Contraceptive Use and Ovarian, Endometrial, Breast, and Colorectal Cancers." *JAMA Oncology* 4, no. 4 (April 1, 2018): 516–21. https://doi.org/10.1001/jamaoncol.2017.4942; Wright, Kristen Page, and Julia V Johnson. "Evaluation of Extended and Continuous Use Oral Contraceptives." *Therapeutics and Clinical Risk Management* 4, no. 5 (October 2008): 905–11.

58. Kara A. Michels et al., "Modification of the Associations Between Duration of Oral Contraceptive Use and Ovarian, Endometrial, Breast, and Colorectal Cancers," *JAMA Oncology* 4, no. 4 (April 1, 2018): 516–21, https://doi.org/10.1001/jamaoncol.2017.4942; Lisa Iversen et al., "Lifetime Cancer Risk and Combined Oral Contraceptives: The Royal College of General Practitioners' Oral Contraception Study," *American Journal of Obstetrics & Gynecology* 216, no. 6 (2017): 580.e1-580.e9, https://doi.org/10.1016/j.ajog.2017.02.002; Jennifer M. Gierisch et al., "Oral Contraceptive Use and Risk of Breast, Cervical, Colorectal, and Endometrial Cancers: A Systematic Review," *Cancer Epidemiology, Biomarkers & Prevention: A Publication of the American Association for Cancer Research, Cosponsored by the American Society of Preventive Oncology* 22, no. 11 (November 2013): 1931–43, https://doi.org/10.1158/1055-9965.EPI-13-0298; Collaborative Group on Epidemiological Studies on Endometrial Cancer, "Endometrial Cancer and Oral Contraceptives: An Individual Participant Meta-Analysis of 27 276 Women with Endometrial Cancer from 36 Epidemiological Studies," *The Lancet. Oncology* 16, no. 9 (September 2015): 1061–70, https://doi.org/10.1016/S1470-2045(15)00212-0; Laura J. Havrilesky et al., "Oral Contraceptive Pills as Primary Prevention for Ovarian Cancer: A Systematic Review and Meta-Analysis," *Obstetrics and Gynecology* 122, no. 1 (July 2013): 139–47, https://doi.org/10.1097/AOG.0b013e318291c235; S. Iodice et al., "Oral Contraceptive Use and Breast or Ovarian Cancer Risk in BRCA1/2 Carriers: A Meta-Analysis," *European Journal of Cancer (Oxford, England: 1990)* 46, no. 12 (August 2010): 2275–84, https://doi.org/10.1016/j.ejca.2010.04.018; Joan L. Walker et al., "Society of Gynecologic Oncology Recommendations for the Prevention of Ovarian Cancer," *Cancer* 121, no. 13 (July 1, 2015): 2108–20, https://doi.org/10.1002/cncr.29321.

59. Esther Roura et al., "The Influence of Hormonal Factors on the Risk of Developing Cervical Cancer and Pre-Cancer: Results from the EPIC Cohort," *PLOS ONE* 11, no. 1 (2016): e0147029, https://doi.org/10.1371/journal.pone.0147029; International Collaboration of Epidemiological Studies of Cervical Cancer et al., "Cervical Cancer and Hormonal Contraceptives: Collaborative Reanalysis of Individual Data for 16,573 Women with Cervical Cancer and 35,509 Women without Cervical Cancer from 24 Epidemiological

Studies," *The Lancet* (London, England) 370, no. 9599 (November 10, 2007): 1609–21, https://doi.org/10.1016/S0140-6736(07)61684-5; Victor Moreno et al., "Effect of Oral Contraceptives on Risk of Cervical Cancer in Women with Human Papillomavirus Infection: The IARC Multicentric Case-Control Study," *The Lancet* 359, no. 9312 (March 2002): 1085–92, https://doi.org/10.1016/S0140-6736(02)08150-3.

60. Iversen et al., "Lifetime Cancer Risk and Combined Oral Contraceptives"; Jennifer S. Smith et al., "Cervical Cancer and Use of Hormonal Contraceptives: A Systematic Review," *The Lancet* (London, England) 361, no. 9364 (April 5, 2003): 1159–67; Natthakan Vanakankovit and Surasak Taneepanichskul, "Effect of Oral Contraceptives on Risk of Cervical Cancer," *Journal of the Medical Association of Thailand = Chotmaihet Thangphaet* 91, no. 1 (January 2008): 7–12; Brittany M. Charlton et al., "Oral Contraceptive Use and Mortality after 36 Years of Follow-up in the Nurses' Health Study: Prospective Cohort Study," *BMJ (Clinical Research Ed.)* 349 (October 31, 2014): g6356; Gierisch et al., "Oral Contraceptive Use and Risk of Breast, Cervical, Colorectal, and Endometrial Cancers."

61. Rachel K. Jones, "Beyond Birth Control: The Overlooked Benefits Of Oral Contraceptive Pills."

62. Rachel K. Jones, "Beyond Birth Control."

63. Rachel K. Jones, "Beyond Birth Control."

64. John Stuart Mill, *Utilitarianism*, ed. George Sher, 2nd ed. (Hackett Publishing Company, 2002), 1; Wendy Donner, "Mill's Theory of Value," in *The Blackwell Guide to Mill's Utilitarianism*, ed. Henry West, 1st ed. (Wiley-Blackwell, 2006), 118.

65. Though Julia Driver argues consequentialists can accommodate partiality, too. Julia Driver, "Consequentialism and Feminist Ethics," *Hypatia* 20, no. 4 (Fall 2005): 197. Even if the practice was not harmful from a medical perspective, consequentialist or utilitarian reasoning might still rule it out. There might be utilitarian reasons for respecting bodily autonomy, individual choice, and informed consent. Additionally, the public policy implications of treating the dispensing of medical care in a punitive way would no doubt impact the cost-benefit analysis. I discuss these issues in chapter 4.

66. Philippa Foot, "The Problem of Abortion and the Doctrine of Double Effect," *Oxford Review* 5 (1967): 5–15.

67. Foot, 1.

68. Joseph T. Mangan, "An Historical Analysis of the Principle of Double Effect," *Theological Studies* 10, no. 1 (1949): 43.

69. Foot, "The Problem of Abortion and the Doctrine of Double Effect," 2.

70. DeMay, Richard M. "Should We Abandon Pap Smear Testing?" *Pathology Patterns Reviews* 114 (2000). http://ajcp.ascpjournals.org/content/supple-

ments/114/Suppl_1/S48.full.pdf; Melnick, Meredith. "Are Doctors' Exams a Barrier to Birth Control?" *Time*. Accessed May 28, 2015. http://healthland.time.com/2010/12/06/why-annual-exams-shouldnt-be-required-to-get-birth-control-pills/; Mencimer, Stephanie. "Holding Birth Control Hostage." *Mother Jones*, April 30, 2012. http://www.motherjones.com/politics/2012/04/doctors-holding-birth-control-hostage; Osterweil, Neil. "Experts Continue to Scale Back Annual Pap Smear." WebMD, 2015. https://www.webmd.com/cancer/cervical-cancer/news/20150501/pap-smear-cervical-cancer.

71. Mayo Clinic, "Pap Smear," July 25, 2019, http://www.mayoclinic.org/tests-procedures/pap-smear/basics/why-its-done/prc-20013038. Sirovich and Welch, "The Frequency of Pap Smear Screening in the United States."

3

IN CONCEIVABLE CARE

A Case of Medical Malpractice

Having established the real physical harms that attend denying patients access to contraception ostensibly for health reasons in chapter 2, I am in a better position to explore the legal ramifications here. Many patients experience the denial of contraception in service of other aims like pelvic exams and Pap tests as an inconvenience or annoyance. Given that 99% of women rely on hormonal birth control at some point in their lives and that a significant portion of doctors tie birth control renewals to other tests, it is possible to conclude that a very high number of women experience these obstacles. Is their experience a necessary side effect of a largely acceptable or even necessary practice? Are a few unintended harms necessary to achieve a larger public health purpose? Or is the practice of tying birth control prescriptions to other office visits like Pap tests a more pernicious activity? In this chapter, I argue that the practice actually meets much higher standards of harm. The decision in *Planned Parenthood v. Casey* states that, "The ability of women to participate equally in the economic and social life of the Nation has been facilitated by their ability to control their reproductive lives."[1] If I am right that this practice is harmful, it is a harm that has a large impact.

In this chapter, I argue that limiting access to oral contraceptives constitutes medical malpractice even if it is in service to larger health goals that physicians have for their patients.[2] To establish this point, I first explore the standard definition of medical malpractice. Although this definition is subject to change and varies by state, it has common underlying features that allow us to explore its application to this case generally. If the practice of withholding birth control access to gain compliance with Pap tests and other office visits does not meet each component of the definition, then it does not constitute medical malpractice generally. I then show how the practice meets each component of the definition. Next, I compare the case of doctors denying patients prescription birth control renewals until they come in for appointments to other similar medical contexts and explain why this case is unique. Lastly, I consider the practice of withholding other forms of contraception like LARC methods through a legal lens and conclude that it has relevant differences from the cases of monthly hormonal contraception but that denial of a LARC within an existing doctor-patient relationship could also count as negligence in some circumstances.

NEGLIGENCE AND MALPRACTICE

A general definition of medical malpractice is as follows: "The injured patient must show that the physician acted negligently in rendering care, and that such negligence resulted in injury. To do so, four legal elements must be proved: (1) a professional duty owed to the patient; (2) breach of such duty; (3) injury caused by the breach; and (4) resulting damages."[3] In this chapter, I argue that all four conditions are easily met in the case of birth control prescription renewal denials. But, before I apply the current legal context to the issue of birth control prescriptions, I first need to explain what each component means.

Negligence generally refers to a situation in which parties act or fail to act in a way that they ought to know would cause harm, though they do not. For example, if you should know better by a reasonable person standard, but you actually do not, you may be acting negligently due to your ignorance of the risks involved in your action. Negligence applies to the medical profession because doctors are held to a high standard with respect to knowing the risks of medical decisions and therefore can fall short of the standard even when they are ignorant of the risks they impose on their patients.

Establishing that the medical professional owes a duty to the patient in question is relevant because having medical expertise cannot make a doctor liable for any unrelated individual's poor treatment. If it did, then the mere existence of a patient in need could make every doctor equally liable for that patient's treatment, which is both an unreasonable standard for doctors to meet and an unnecessary protection for patients. And in fact, doctors may refuse to treat patients in a variety of legally protected scenarios. As long as doctors do not discriminate against protected classes in the accepting of patients, such as patients of a particular race or religion, they can generally choose which patients to accept into a practice. For example, I cannot sue a doctor for malpractice because she fails to treat me after she tells me her practice is already full and she is not taking on new patients. Instead, the duty of care is generally established by the doctor-patient relationship. Only after a doctor takes an individual on as a patient does the duty of care arise. Once the relationship commences, doctors are required to fulfill a medical professional role.[4]

Once it is established that the doctor owes a patient a duty of care because the doctor has agreed to treat that patient or has commenced treatment, the charge of medical malpractice next includes a breach of that duty. The breach of duty is a much more difficult component to prove than the existence of the duty and often relies on testimony of other medical professionals in the field. Generally, to prove that doctors breach a duty, one must first show what the standard of care is in the field. What do experts recommend in cases like the patient's? What is the established position of the medical community on similar cases? What would a reasonable doctor with comparable medical expertise do in the same case? When these questions have clear answers and the doctor acts against them, the doctor is subject to questions of negligence. Only if the doctor does not comply with the standard of care can one show that a breach of duty has occurred.

English tort law, on which American law is based, unsurprisingly uses a similar method to determine standard of care in what is now called the "Bolam test." The Bolam test gets its name from a 1957 case, *Bolam v. Friern Hospital Management Committee*. In that case, the judge, McNair J, states that,

> A doctor is not guilty of negligence if he has acted in accordance with a practice accepted as proper by a responsible body of medical men skilled in that particular art. Putting it another way round, a doctor is not negligent if he is acting in accordance with such a practice, merely because there is a body of opinion that takes a contrary view.[5]

According to that high court judge in the same case, doctors violate their duty when they, "obstinately and pig-headedly carry on with some old technique if it has been proved to be contrary to what is really substantially the whole of informed medical opinion."[6] When doctors use old techniques in the face of new evidence, or fail to stay abreast of established research, they mistreat their patients and act contrary to what a reasonable doctor would do in similar circumstances. That is why the high court judge explicitly discussed that possible scenario in the case and prohibited doctors from following outdated and disproved methods. English and American tort law, then, both have similar explanations of negligence in which doctors may not act against established medical opinion and must instead base their medical decisions on what a reasonable specialist would do given the current evidence.

It is possible for a doctor to have a duty of care to a patient, breach that duty, but through a stroke of luck, not injure the patient as a result of that mistreatment. In such cases, a patient would have no case to sue a doctor and no malpractice would occur. The third requirement for a malpractice suit is that an injury ensues as a direct result of the doctor's mistake. The type of injury most relevant to our case is physical harm. However, denial of a legal right also counts as an injury for these purposes. Although the denial of a legal right does not come up in this chapter, I will touch on it in later chapters, including chapter 4. Thus, even if one disagrees with my argument here that physical injury does arise, the case for medical malpractice may still exist.

Generally, exposure to unnecessary risk, though undoubtedly a harm in the ethical sense, does not count as harm in the legal sense. If it did, then by definition, any breach of duty would also count as injurious because failing to follow what a reasonable doctor would do in given circumstances would count as exposing a patient to unnecessary risk. If that were the case, then no further questions would be necessary to determine medical malpractice.

Instead, one must show that the breach of duty on the doctor's part resulted in some demonstrable harm to the patient, such as exacerbating an existing condition or causing a new one. This component therefore has two parts: first, that the patient did suffer an injury, and second, that the injury was caused by an act or omission on the part of the doctor. By comparison, not all injuries a doctor causes to a patient count as medical malpractice. If the injury is the result of a risky procedure and the patient willingly took on that risk before undergoing the intervention, then no malpractice would have occurred.

The last component of a medical malpractice case sets up its resolution. Determining damages in the way of pain and suffering helps show what is owed to the patient as a result of the doctor's negligence. Putting a dollar amount on the suffering caused by the injury allows for compensation. And if the patient's work were affected, such as through a pregnancy that required an unpaid leave, or from flare-ups from a disorder that affects work, then economic loss would also be included in this calculation. Damages are awarded to the patient if the case is successful in a court of law.

RECKLESSNESS

Doctors might be negligent when they cause harm unwittingly or without awareness of risks. Negligence, in which individuals ought to know about the risks in their behavior but do not, thus violating their duty to others, is not the only relevant problem in a medical context. A higher standard for liability would be recklessness, in which an individual is aware of the risks imposed on others but does not sufficiently attend to the risks, and hopes that the unintended consequence does not occur.[7] Recklessness involves foreseeing the negative consequences of one's actions but not intending that they come about. It is one step removed from malicious intent, in which one foresees the harm that comes about from one's actions and intends that the harm occur.

THE RIGHT TO REFUSE TREATMENT

In the next chapter, I look closely at informed consent and what it entails. Informed consent is both a legal and a moral doctrine, of which the right to refuse treatment is just one part. But the right to refuse treatment has clear lines of delineation and a case history of its own to protect a patient's decision not to have a medical intervention and thus can be considered separately. Several relevant laws and regulations protect the right to refuse treatment.[8] For example, the U.S. Code, as well as a number of states have specific laws on the books to protect the right to refuse treatment.[9] Several court decisions also protect this right.[10] These laws and cases generally center on the limits of the right to refuse treatment: what counts as being mentally competent; when may someone make a decision on behalf of another; what to do about children; what limits must be placed for dangerous individuals; how to treat end-of-life decisions; and similar difficult cases. The assumption is that the individual has a right to refuse treatment, but the landmark cases that reaffirm this right only come about when problems arise that would threaten that right. The question of when a limit must be placed on an individual's right to refuse treatment is philosophically and legally complex, but it does not relate to the average patient. That is because the average patient unequivocally retains the right to refuse treatment, especially when no questions arise as to competence, the gravity of the decision is not one of life or death, and no doubt surrounds the patient's explicit requests. In such cases, the right to refuse treatment is supposed to be protected for all individuals. If, however, doctors routinely and systematically infringe upon these rights when it comes to certain subsets of patients, questions remain about how and why the systematic abuse occurs.

APPLYING THE LEGAL CONTEXT TO THE CASE OF BIRTH CONTROL

In this section, I take the above analysis of medical malpractice and recklessness and apply them to the case of doctors denying birth control prescription renewals in service to other medical aims. Although I am not a lawyer and cannot dispense legal advice, I can analyze a very common trend in the medical field by reference to established law to determine its propriety and legal protection. And although an actual malpractice case would vary by state, would need a specific plaintiff who could testify to the harms resulting from the breach of duty, would need expert witnesses to testify on the plaintiff's behalf, and would need to convince a jury, my aim is not to win a particular sum of money for a patient but to explore some of the legal issues at stake in this very common practice.

A legal standard can also be a helpful motivator when recognizing and contextualizing the kind of harm done to patients as a result of the practice. Doctors should always take patient preferences, values, and complaints seriously. Yet they often do not and face no consequences. If the practice in question could meet the generalized definition of medical malpractice, then doctors might be more likely to take patient complaints seriously, avoid falling prey to this very common and very normalized practice in their field, and publicly decry other doctors who still engage in it. For example, a doctor who does not engage in the practice, but who is partnered with another doctor who does, should not allow the practice to continue under the assumption that it is simply a matter of individual variation and reasonable disagreement. Such a doctor could be liable for serious financial damages and would be more strongly motivated to hold partnered physicians to the legal standard. That is because a victim of medical malpractice may sue each individual physician in a partnership. Ignoring a partner's reliance on this sort of practice, then, would be a serious financial and professional risk.

Another reason that this sort of legal analysis can be helpful even if it does not succeed in getting damages is that it empowers patients to understand their legal rights. Patients with no other risk factors whose doctors require them to undergo yearly Pap tests just to continue treatment for an unrelated medical issue may find themselves distressed, physically harmed, or facing more serious repercussions, but may not know that they have any recourse. Explaining to uninformed doctors the ways in which the denial constitutes medical malpractice may not succeed in getting the patients' rights respected, but it may start the doctor along a process resulting in better treatment.

A third reason that this analysis is a valuable exercise is that on a certain level, it would be unfair not to treat this issue as medical malpractice. Ignoring a serious issue just because it happens very often is damaging to patients everywhere. And, if some are inclined to ignore medical malpractice and other forms of negligence in certain areas of the medical field just because they affect reproductive health or because the actions are taken against swaths of society very commonly facing discrimination, a larger issue of fairness is at issue. Treating citizens equally under the law regardless of reproductive status, gender, or sex is a central tenet of a fair system.

The relevance of this discussion then established, do the features of the practice meet the generalized definition of malpractice as given in the last section? Are doctors engaging in actions which amount to negligence when they deny patients access to birth control to serve other goals, even if they are never sued for this breach and even if no suit ever wins? As discussed above, a medical malpractice case must first establish a professional duty. Different legal and ethical issues arise when a doctor refuses to take a patient who needs birth control or when a pharmacist refuses to fill a birth control prescription. In the phenomenon I consider, in which the doctor withholds a birth control prescription refill until such time as the patient undergoes a pelvic exam or Pap test, the professional duty is established by the ongoing doctor-patient relationship. The doctor has accepted the individual as a patient. The patient has an ongoing relationship with the doctor. Typically, the issue would not even arise until the patient has been with the doctor for at least a year. When the situation does arise, the doctor has already prescribed the medication in question at least once previously. In such cases, the patient and the doctor have jointly concluded that the medication is working effectively and thus a refill rather than a first trial of the medication is in question. If patients find that the current prescription is not working or has worrisome side effects, they typically will seek out another consultation and no refill will be at stake. Such office visits will be unavoidable to discuss future directions of treatment. Though, if the doctor requires a Pap test or pelvic exam at this point even when the birth control prescription is not a renewal and is a first time dosage, the legal standards discussed here still apply. The question is not whether to start treatment, but whether to continue it. Furthermore, in such cases, the doctor has already agreed that the refill is in order and is recommending the patient continue treatment. Thus, a standard of care is clearly established.

In addition, that the doctor has a duty of care is not controversial. A doctor in these circumstances, who chooses to deny patients birth control until they receive a Pap test, would not likely question this component of the malpractice charge because the doctor's exhortation to undergo an added medical test implies the very duty of care at stake. It is only because the doctor is trying to fulfill a duty of care—and failing—that this issue arises. That is, it is only because the doctor wishes the patient to be properly screened for cervical cancer that the denial of other needed medical care comes into play.

In this context, physicians and patients have already worked together to find a birth control method that works. Physicians have already recommended the use of this birth control for the treatment of a variety of issues or birth control generally as the preferred treatment. Patients have already commenced treatment in some form. Any later changes mean the interruption or halting of a needed medical intervention already in progress. In such cases, a doctor making a decision to stop medical treatment on behalf of patients, without patients' consent or against their expressed wishes, for reasons entirely external to the issue at hand, would constitute the first component of negligence or medical malpractice.

Second, a medical malpractice case must establish that the professional duty was violated. The second condition, the breaching of the duty, is met when the doctor fails to prescribe the birth control. The professional duty owed to the patient is established by the standard of care. As noted above, standard of care in this case is first, not to require yearly Pap tests and second, not to tie birth control to such screenings.[11] Chapters 1 and 2 discuss how the practice violates the standard of care, and I appeal to those arguments here to define the professional duty. I argue that because every major medical organization recommends against both tying birth control to Pap tests and requiring yearly Pap tests in general, and because a preponderance of experts find problems with it, the standard of care is not to require such testing.

So, does the practice of withholding birth control "deviate from accepted norms of practice in the medical community"?[12] In some ways this question has an easy answer: Yes. Scientific evidence does not support the practice. That evidence is why established and reputable medical associations reject it. But the answer to this question is also controversial because so many doctors engage in this practice. As discussed in chapter 1, despite every major medical organization and association recommending against the practice, significant numbers of medical practitioners engage in it. Birth control prescriptions and Pap tests fall under an unlikely category of activities in which every doctor seems to recommend one thing and do another. This phenomenon is not entirely unprecedented. Some evidence suggests that the treatments doctors choose for themselves diverge from those they recommend to patients.[13] Other evidence suggests that doctors sometimes express commitment to including patients in decision-making but fail to do so in practice.[14]

Would calling an expert witness into court to determine what should be done in this case lead to the expert endorsing the doctor's decision instead of the medical evidence and the plaintiff's claims? If standards of care and norms of practice are determined by what most doctors do, and most doctors act wrongly, problems might ensue in making this case. It might be difficult to show that doctors are mistreating patients because the standard of care might be more difficult to establish in a court.

Two main reasons mean this concern is not damaging, however. First, while doctors likely do tend to require appointments for birth control prescription renewals, they may not testify as such in a court of law. That is because many doctors know the correct standard of care in this case, though they may not follow it for personal reasons. The framing of the question might matter here: "Should doctors tie birth control prescriptions to pelvic exams?" vs. "Do you tie birth control prescriptions to pelvic exams?" for example, might make a difference in how a doctor responds to a question.

Second, and more relevant for my purposes, proving in court that doctors act negligently is not my aim in this discussion. Since I am not suing for damages nor necessarily recommending any individual patient sue for damages, my argument merely relies on the fact that doctors do violate standard of care, not whether I can show that they do. To determine standard of care, it should be sufficient to stipulate that the overwhelming evidence and the support of major medical organizations show that the practice in question is unjustified. In fact, this case is precisely the sort of scenario the high court judge predicted might come about in *Bolam*, in which doctors may act "obstinately and pig-headedly" by defying scientific evidence even when doing so is commonplace. Similarly, in *Natanson v. Kline*, the courts rely on a "reasonable practitioner" standard in which disclosing risk to a patient is required, especially when the treatment in question is not established practice in the medical field.[15] The failure to prescribe a previously agreed upon treatment and the violation of the standard of care, then, comprise the breach of duty.

The third component of a medical malpractice case is that injury and damages must ensue. Clearly, injury does not occur in every case. Some instances will come about in which a doctor requires pelvic exams or Pap tests for birth control prescriptions, perhaps for a decade or more on end, and no direct injury comes about as a result to the patient. Perhaps the patient finds no burden in attending appointments, and always makes appointments well in advance of running out of the prescription. Or, perhaps the patient does run out of pills and temporarily has to go off birth control while waiting for an appointment, but has no underlying medical issue that birth control addresses, is not sexually active, and experiences no side effects resuming treatment. To prove that the phenomenon can and does fall under the heading of medical malpractice, and to prove that it is likely to lead to medical malpractice, it is not necessary to prove that it always does.

While they do not necessarily ensue in every case, chapter 2 explains the wide array of common harms, both large and small, that attend yearly Pap tests. These harms include, but are not limited to: stress, pain, time, cost, overdiagnosis, overtesting, and overtreatment. These side effects fall under the legal definition of "injury" discussed above and therefore meet the requirements for medical malpractice. And these sorts of injuries, or some combination or subset of them, are very likely to ensue, even if they do not necessarily ensue. As a result, and by relying on the arguments in chapters 1 and 2, I argue that withholding birth control is legally negligent.

Showing that these injuries are the direct result of the breach of duty is a complicated issue and depends on the injury to the patient. For example, although hormonal birth control may decrease the likelihood of endometrial and ovarian cancer, it is less clear that any individual case of needlessly denying a patient hormonal birth control is a contributing factor, let alone a cause, of a resulting cancer. That is because it is possible to have this kind of cancer even with perfect environmental conditions. By contrast, headaches and nausea, while uncomfortable and often very clearly the direct result of going on and off hormonal birth control, may be hard to diagnose or verify from an outside standpoint. These symptoms rely on patient reports. Furthermore, these issues are minor enough that a patient would be very unlikely to sue in response to them because the amount in damages would not be high enough to justify the inconvenience and expense of a court case.

Pregnancy is also a possible side effect, but it would be difficult to show that pregnancy is the direct result of a doctor's negligence. First, other activities are obviously required, such as sexual intercourse, for a patient to become pregnant, meaning that while the doctor may play a contributing role to the ensuing pregnancy by withholding birth control prescription refills, it may not be sufficient to establish the direct causal role needed for a malpractice case. Second, and relatedly, it would be difficult to prove that the pregnancy would not have happened otherwise, since birth control methods do sometimes fail. Third, patients know they are not covered by birth control when this sort of denial happens, unlike cases like birth control method malfunctions occurring unbeknownst to the patient.

While it is easy to see that these harms are the direct result of physician action by looking at overall population trends or upticks in incidences of side effects after doctors deny birth control to patients, they are much harder to prove in an individual context. Even the harms of overtreatment might be difficult to prove in a court of law because, while additional and unnecessary tests increase the likelihood of a false positive, it might be hard to show that any one particular extra test caused the false positive. Patients can get false positives testing at scientifically supported intervals, after all. Thus, the sorts of injuries that come about from follow-up tests after a false positive might be the cause of doctor negligence without that cause being verifiable.

But again, the point is not that I have the ability to prove this case in a court of law or that every instance of a doctor denying drug prescription renewal is an instance of medical malpractice. Instead, the larger point is that these types of actions on the part of doctors count as medical malpractice in a variety of cases and could reliably lead to instances of medical malpractice. And, this information lends credence to the argument that medical providers should avoid the practice.

I conclude, therefore, that the practice of denying patients birth control in service of Pap tests or pelvic exams meets the conditions of medical malpractice in at least some cases. If it is likely or even possible that the policy leads to this result, I argue it should be stopped entirely. That is, if doctors engage in a practice that breaches their professional duty and is likely to cause injury, then they should stop it, even if it does not always lead to injury and even if it is not possible to prove it leads to injury in a court of law.[16]

Recklessness is also relevant in this context. Given the strength of evidence against tying birth control to Pap tests and the longstanding recommendations not to do it, doctors arguably ought to know about the standard of care here, even if they actually do not. As argued in chapters 1 and 2, a notable percentage of doctors engage in a practice explicitly prohibited by major medical institutions. Mass ignorance on this particular recommendation seems unlikely. In at least some cases, doctors likely know about the standards of care, are aware of the risks involved in denying their patients needed medicine, and do it anyway. In such cases, they may hope the harm does not occur, wrongly believe the negative consequence to be unlikely, hope against evidence that the harm is unlikely, fail to stop and think about the harm, mistakenly view the conduct as justifiable in the face of the harm, make an error in calculating probability, or fail to understand the gravity of the harm.[17]

In fact, based on the arguments I present in chapters 4 and 5, recklessness is actually more likely than negligence in the case of doctors denying their patients birth control. If the purpose of withholding birth control is to achieve compliance with a medical test that a doctor deems necessary, then the negative consequence of actually forgoing that prescription is not intended. Doctors may know that at least some of their patients will fail to meet their requirements and thus suffer as a result; however, they intend for their patients to comply and therefore avoid those harms. Thus, they are likely aware of the risk but fail to understand the gravity of being denied birth control or making an error in the assessment of false positives that come about from yearly testing.

Alternatively, malicious intent seems very unlikely in these contexts. Doctors have incredible power over their patients. If they wanted to cause unintended pregnancy, cancer, or other negative consequences associated with the practice in question, they could easily do so without resorting to indirect means.[18] Furthermore, purposefully causing unwanted pregnancy or disease constitute actions that go beyond the scope of this book, which is directed at routine, systematic, and unrecognized injustice that attends actions even without malicious intent.

Finally, the right to refuse treatment is relevant here. Competent, rational adults of sound mind who put nobody else in danger, violate no state interest, and who are not making end-of-life decisions, have strong rights to refuse treatment. Yet in the case of Pap testing, this right is not respected because patients are coerced into accepting medical interventions. Doctors do not give patients a proper choice about whether they accept the Pap test because they are made to choose between getting the test or losing medical care that is incredibly valuable to them. The fact that these interventions violate standards of care in ways that ignore the countervailing evidence makes those interventions all the more suspect.

RELATED CASES

Another way of understanding this conclusion is to compare it to other related phenomena. For example, suppose a man is at high risk for prostate cancer, has a long family history of the disease, and is currently presenting symptoms.[19] It is in his own interest to receive a screening immediately, and his doctor tells him so. Suppose also that the man is on dialysis for kidney failure, a condition unrelated to prostate cancer. May the doctor discontinue the patient's dialysis to ensure compliance with the prostate exam? May the doctor even threaten to discontinue the needed dialysis in the hopes of incentivizing the patient to undergo the exam? The discontinuation of dialysis would likely be called negligence and the threat of it incredibly damaging. As necessary as the prostate exam may be, it has no bearing on the patient's kidney failure. Both medical interventions are necessary and one should not be used as a carrot or a stick. Moreover, as I discuss in the next chapter, the necessity of a medical intervention should not be used as a justification for withholding other, needed care because doing so is exploitive.

In this hypothetical scenario, the doctor has a duty of care to the patient because the doctor is currently treating him. The doctor also breaches duty when following the policy of withholding dialysis for prostate exams, a practice neither recommended by any major medical organization nor supported by any scientific evidence. In fact, since prostate cancer does not have much to do with kidney failure, no medical organization is likely to endorse the practice in the near future. The injury or damages occur if the patient fails to comply and loses access to dialysis, causing problems in quality of life. The causal connection between the deprivation of dialysis and the ensuing problems that occur is clear.

Another related case is also instructive. In the face of "anti-vaxxers," or parents who either oppose vaccines for their children or oppose them in the recommended time frame, some pediatricians refuse to accept as patients families who refuse vaccines. The doctors' justification is that since they cannot properly treat or protect a child when that child is unvaccinated, they also will not treat the child for ear infections or give well-child visits either. One might think that such cases are related because they also involve doctors incentivizing patients to undergo needed preventative care and deny treatment to unrelated conditions for this purpose.

However, the case does not constitute medical malpractice and is not analogous to the birth control case for a number of reasons. First, no duty of care exists between a prospective doctor and a patient who has not undergone any treatment yet. Doctors have wide latitude in picking and choosing patients. The first condition of a medical malpractice suit is not met, then.

Second, no breach of duty exists. Vaccinating all patients is the only recommended practice for pediatricians and all available evidence far and away supports this approach to treating children. Comparing the risk of vaccination in this case to the risk of yearly Pap tests in the other case highlights the differences. The risks of vaccination are tiny and minor, while the risks of false positives for overtesting and the risks of pregnancy for denying birth control are not.[20] Furthermore, the prevention vaccines provide is lifesaving, while the benefit of overtesting is not and the early testing is not valuable for its own sake, but rather requires further treatment to save lives.

Third, no reasonable injuries could be argued to come about as a result of these policies. If a child who cannot find a pediatrician falls ill with an ear infection, for example, it would be difficult to make the case that any one particular doctor is at fault for the delayed treatment. That result is partly due to the failure to meet the first requirement—without a doctor-patient relationship, no individual doctor can be blamed for the ensuing illness. And, of course, the ear infection itself would not be the direct result of any negligence on the part of the doctor. I am not evaluating the position from a public policy standard, considering whether pediatricians ought to engage in this behavior. For my purposes, it suffices to point out that unlike the birth control case, this similarly common case does not meet the conditions of medical malpractice.

Lastly, the case is different because it involves minors—individuals for whom others must make medical decisions on their behalf because they have not reached the age of legal consent yet. Suffice it to say, a legal adult is not the same as a child. Doctors and other caregivers acting paternalistically toward legal minors is often permitted or even required while the same paternalistic action directed at adults is not. The difference between treating minors paternalistically and treating adults paternalistically is significant for reasons I discuss in the next two chapters because it raises the specter of sexism.

LARC METHODS

In this chapter, I focus primarily on doctors and other medical professionals denying birth control drugs to patients: hormonal birth control administered in daily or monthly doses that the patient must administer to achieve continued protection, such as pills, patches, shots, and rings. However, LARC methods like implants and intrauterine devices (IUDs) also play a role in this discussion, and when it comes to medical malpractice, may have different results. That is because while pill, patch, shot, and ring prescription refills have the feature of continuing treatment of a condition through an already agreed-upon means, IUDs and other LARC methods are different.

LARC methods are different than daily or monthly hormonal contraception because they involve a new procedure that must be completed at each 5- to 10-year interval. Getting an IUD or implant renewal involves a procedure that only a medical professional can perform. Thus, while refusing a prescription renewal takes on the features of discontinuing medical care already in progress, refusing an IUD placement takes on the features of a doctor refusing to perform a particular procedure, a proposition that gives doctors more leeway generally.

However, just because state and federal limits protect doctors from performing procedures in some cases does not mean that those protections necessarily apply here. One major reason doctors can refuse to treat is that they do not have a standing relationship with the patient in question. Patients requesting an IUD placement from doctors they haven't seen in 10 years could justifiably be told that the doctor has no duty of care to them after such a long hiatus. However, I can stipulate that the patient seeking an IUD replacement does have a doctor-patient relationship with the doctor in question, since this occurs in at least some cases.

Another possible reason for refusal is triage. Doctors cannot always treat every patient due to constraints in time and resources. A doctor may justifiably refuse to treat, even if they have a relationship with the patient, if other patients have more urgent and more significant needs. However, again, that does not apply in at least some cases of placing an IUD. In at least some cases, doctors have enough time to perform the necessary treatment for all their patients. Furthermore, lack of time or triage considerations are not usually the reasons doctors give when they wish to avoid such procedures.

Doctors may also evaluate patients based on the likelihood that the patient's request is rooted in self-harm. Patients seeking access to LARC methods aim to protect themselves in most cases, either from pregnancy or the related conditions some hormonal LARC methods treat, not trying to fool a doctor into supplying drugs for an addiction or other problematic use of the doctor's time. This exception, then, does not apply to most cases either.

Thus, it is unlikely that a doctor would have a good reason to deny patients repeat LARC procedures. The procedure is a new consideration, but the reliance on the LARC method to treat the underlying cause is not. The problem with this discussion is that it overlooks the fact that doctors do not treat IUD and other LARC replacements similarly to hormonal birth control pill prescriptions. First, LARC renewals happen at much greater intervals than prescriptions, making it impossible to tie them to yearly Pap tests. The same issues of withholding care to ensure patients undergo unrelated and too-frequent tests do not then apply.

Second, LARC renewals are more likely to coincide with Pap test intervals that are medically justified, such as every three to five years. While that does not mean that doctors should withhold LARC procedures in service to Pap tests, it does mean that the risks of overtesting and false positives are reduced. This difference is relevant to the claims of medical harm that arise in the discussion from chapter 2. If the harms do not arise because no overtesting occurs, then the case for malpractice cannot be made.

Third, patients already have to come into a doctor's office to undergo a LARC procedure, making a required Pap test a less significant extra burden. Although extra appointments and invasive testing were deemed harms in chapter 2, those harms do not apply in the request for a LARC replacement. LARC methods essentially free patients from the excessive control some doctors wield over their patients with other forms of birth control. Thus, it is also unlikely that doctors would seek to deny patients repeat LARC procedures. Even if doctors have a policy of requiring Pap testing for birth control prescriptions, it is unlikely they would refuse to repeat a procedure previously done in this case.

Much more likely in cases of LARC methods is that a doctor would refuse to do a procedure for a LARC when a patient seeks it for the first time. Such cases are much more difficult to assess from a legal standpoint. Unlike a renewal, a first-time LARC request may not occur in an established doctor-patient relationship, suspending the duty of care. Also unlike a renewal, a first-time procedure request may be viewed as having more risks. That is because a larger subset of patients may request LARC methods than doctors think are well suited for them. A patient who has already had a LARC once is more likely to meet doctor-set criteria for eligibility. For example, a patient seeking a LARC for the first time may be younger; may not be in a stable, monogamous relationship; may be at higher risk for STDs; and may be switching from a monthly hormonal contraception that required yearly Pap tests and thus may have already received a false positive. On their face, these differences do not seem to be relevant to the question of administering LARC methods. None of them are connected to the physical features or risks of a LARC method, such as liver disease or risk of blood clots. However, doctors may still view such requests with added skepticism.

In chapter 2, I discussed the phenomenon of doctors denying LARC methods to patients. I then discussed reasons that doctors are more likely to deny young patients, non-monogamous patients, and patients at higher risk of STDs access to LARC methods. I also discussed reasons why these obstacles are not supported by major medical organizations or scientific evidence. Often, they involve doctors overinflating risks of LARC methods to some groups. LARC methods comprise the best methods for preventing pregnancy across the board despite being subject to unwarranted fears and misinformation among both doctors and patients. They also effectively and reliably treat a host of other conditions when they use hormone release as part of their treatment (a feature copper IUDs would not have, for example).

Denial of repeat LARC procedures, then, may meet the conditions of medical malpractice, but are unlikely to occur. First-time LARC procedure denials occurring within established doctor-patient relationships also meet these requirements and are also much more likely to occur. If a doctor with an established relationship with a patient receives a request for an IUD and denies it due to a misguided notion about the necessity or likelihood of monogamy, violating standards of care in the field, a patient would have much more standing.

However, proving damages in such cases also would be extremely difficult. While LARC methods of contraception can be orders of magnitude more effective than the alternative, it is difficult to prove a pregnancy after a LARC denial is caused by the breach of duty. Since abstinence is technically an option after a denial (though not an effective one), and since other pregnancy prevention alternatives are also possibilities, showing a causal connection between a LARC denial and a subsequent pregnancy is difficult, if not impossible. Too many other factors come into play.

In addition, even if it were possible to do so, pregnancy itself is treated variously by courts and some refuse to consider a pregnancy as a damage at all. A patient who sued for denial of a LARC and won might be able to win the cost of the medical expenses for wrongful pregnancy, but not for the raising of the child, which some courts refuse to consider as a damage due to the attending "joys of parenting." One might reasonably argue that this position on the part of a court is problematic because it does not take into account the agency of the patient, a topic I discuss in chapter 4. However, looking at the legal case specifically, it would be hard to show damages even if it were possible to show breach of duty in LARC denials.[21]

Pregnancy is, of course, not the only harm that could arise from a LARC method denial. Hormonal LARC methods treat a variety of other conditions already discussed. However, the same problems arise in finding damages for these harms, since other hormonal birth control methods could fulfill the same purpose. A patient denied a hormonal IUD could seek the pill to treat the same condition instead. Thus, proving damages as the direct cause of the breach of duty would be extremely difficult. The irony, of course, is that gaining access to these alternative hormonal treatments is also extremely difficult, as discussed already. However, since they merely require overcoming significant obstacles and are not entirely impossible, a legal case is harder to make.

CONCLUSION

In this chapter, I made the case that a large share of doctors engage in medical malpractice when they deny patients access to birth control after a previously established physician-patient relationship. This charge takes on more force when one accounts for the fact that most American women—99%—will at some point in their lives seek birth control. The decision to withhold birth control cannot be merely an issue of office policy or personal philosophy, then; a significant share of doctors in the obstetrics/gynecology field may meet the definition of medical malpractice.[22] That suggests a systemic issue in the medical field, and one that merits a deeper inquiry.

Although I argue that the phenomenon amounts to negligence, I do not maintain that a lawyer could necessarily prove malpractice in a court of law. A lot is at stake in a decision like this one, both because birth control is a partisan and politically charged issue and because it opens up the possibility of the courts being flooded with millions of lawsuits. Class action lawsuits might also be ineffective at stopping the practice. Although patients who have been harmed by the practice can join together to sue a single provider, many such class action lawsuits would have to be brought, since providers who engage in the practice are so numerous, often unrelated, and geographically dispersed. And, the issue is more complex than I have presented it here, since laws vary by state and judges and juries vary as well. But ultimately, the question is not whether the case can be proven in a court of law. Instead, I aim to start a conversation on how a practice that meets the definition of medical malpractice could become so widespread, why it was accepted for so long, why it continues, and instigate looking inward for the medical profession. Why is medical malpractice illegal in some cases and de facto legal in others? Why is negligence allowed, encouraged even, when reproductive health is concerned? In the next two chapters, I argue that this phenomenon is no accident. Significant reasons explain both why reproductive health is considered a class by itself when it comes to malpractice, and why this phenomenon must change. The application of law helps motivate and set the stage for this discussion, even if no legal case ever sees its day in court.

NOTES

1. O'Connor, Planned Parenthood of Southeastern Pennsylvania, Et Al., Petitioners 91–744 v. Robert P. Casey, Et Al., Etc. Robert P. Casey, Et Al., Etc., Petitioners 91-902, U.S. (U.S. Supreme Court 1992).

2. J. B. Delston, "When Doctors Deny Drugs: Sexism and Contraception Access in the Medical Field," *Bioethics* 31, no. 9 (November 2017): 703–10, https://doi.org/10.1111/bioe.12373.

3. B. Sonny Bal, "An Introduction to Medical Malpractice in the United States," *Clinical Orthopaedics and Related Research* 467, no. 2 (February 2009): 339–47, https://doi.org/10.1007/s11999-008-0636-2; Tom L. Beauchamp and James F. Childress, *Principles of Biomedical Ethics* (Oxford University Press, 2001), 118–19.

4. Julian Savulescu and Udo Schuklenk, "Doctors Have No Right to Refuse Medical Assistance in Dying, Abortion or Contraception," *Bioethics* 31, no. 3 (2017): 169, https://doi.org/10.1111/bioe.12288.

5. Bolam v. Friern Hospital Management Committee, No. 1 WLR 582 (1957).

6. Bolam v. Friern Hospital Management Committee.

7. James B. Brady, "Recklessness, Negligence, Indifference, and Awareness," *The Modern Law Review* 43, no. 4 (July 1, 1980): 381–99, https://doi.org/10.1111/j.1468-2230.1980.tb01599.x; G. R. Sullivan, "Intent, Subjective Recklessness and Culpability," *Oxford Journal of Legal Studies* 12, no. 3 (1992): 380–91.

8. Code of Federal Regulations, Title 42, Section 483.10(b) states in part, "The resident has the right to refuse treatment, to refuse to participate in experimental research, and to formulate an advance directive as specified in paragraph (8) of this section." "42 CFR 483.10 - Resident Rights," LII / Legal Information Institute, https://www.law.cornell.edu/cfr/text/42/483.10.

9. "42 U.S. Code § 9501 - Bill of Rights," LII / Legal Information Institute, https://www.law.cornell.edu/uscode/text/42/9501; "California Health and Safety Code - HSC," 1262.6(a)(3) § (2001), https://leginfo.legislature.ca.gov/faces/codes_displaySection.xhtml?lawCode=HSC&sectionNum=1262.6;

"215 ILCS 134/ Managed Care Reform and Patient Rights Act." (2000), http://www.ilga.gov/legislation/ilcs/ilcs3.asp?ActID=1265&ChapterID=22.

10. Union Pacific R. Co. v. Botsford, 141 United States (Supreme Court 1891); Schloendorff v. Society of New York Hosp., No. 105 N.E. 92, 93 (1914); C.J. Rehnquist, Cruzan by Cruzan v. Director, Missouri Department of Health, No. 497 U.S. 261 (June 25, 1990); In Re Brown, No. 478 So. 2d 1033 (1985).

11. Recent changes in guidelines mean that the standard of care for how frequently Pap tests should be offered have changed, not that there have been changes on recommendations to withhold other care in service of those screenings. The latter is always inappropriate.

12. Bal, "An Introduction to Medical Malpractice in the United States."

13. Frederik Joelving and Elaine Lies, "Doctors Don't Always Take Their Own Advice: Survey," *Reuters*, April 12, 2011, http://www.reuters.com/article/us-doctors-advice-life-idUSTRE73B0IZ20110412.

14. Rachel Zeuner et al., "Physicians' Perceptions of Shared Decision-making Behaviours: A Qualitative Study Demonstrating the Continued Chasm between Aspirations and Clinical Practice," *Health Expectations: An International Journal of Public Participation in Health Care and Health Policy* 18, no. 6 (December 2015): 2465–76, https://doi.org/10.1111/hex.12216.

15. J. Schroeder, Natanson v. Kline (Supreme Court of Kansas 1960).

16. Perhaps the risk of injury is very small. However, in this particular case, no benefit outweighs the injury, making even a small risk impermissible. No need for taking on risk would then justify the practice. The tradeoff between risk and reward is also not the doctor's to make in this instance, for reasons I discuss in the next chapter. I thank Larry May for this objection.

17. Brady, "Recklessness, Negligence, Indifference, and Awareness," 390.

18. Vanessa Romo, "DNA Test Reveals Fertility Doctor Used His Own Sperm To Impregnate Patient," NPR.org, April 4, 2018, https://www.npr.org/sections/thetwo-way/2018/04/04/599531061/dna-test-reveals-fertility-doctor-used-his-own-sperm-to-impregnate-patient.

19. Prostate cancer screenings are themselves similarly controversial due to high false positives.

20. Christine Overall, *Why Have Children?: The Ethical Debate*, Basic Bioethics (Cambridge, Mass: MIT Press, 2012), 115.

21. Paul, Regina Goulding. "Damages for Wrongful Birth and Wrongful Pregnancy in Illinois." Loyola University Chicago Law Journal 15, no. 4 (1984), p.811.

22. Similarly withholding care from patients in other domains is rare and illegal. For reasons I discuss below, such negligence is neither rare nor illegal in women's health.

4

PRE CONCEIVED NOTIONS

Some Ethical Considerations in Denying Patients Needed Care

The medical harms doctors do to patients when they deny needed drugs in service of unnecessary tests are both far-reaching and weighty. Chapters 1–3 focus on physical and medical harms and burdens placed on patients as the result of a medically questionable practice. Recognizing these physical harms is valuable both for settling the scientific debate and for identifying the legal protections available to patients. Though these harms do have implications for moral theories like consequentialism and utilitarianism, arguably too much emphasis is placed on medical harms to the exclusion of real and independent significant moral implications. Focusing only on the physical ramifications of these practices subtly implies that if they did patients good, they would therefore be permissible. But this attitude to the practice of withholding birth control for yearly Pap tests and pelvic exams is dangerous because it overlooks other impacts the practice has. It makes the practice subject to scientific, medical, and legal analysis, when in fact moral evaluation is also a requisite component of analysis.[1]

Even if yearly Pap tests were helpful, did not lead to any harm, and tying them to birth control prescriptions yielded better health overall for the patients in question, the practice would nevertheless be unjustified. An understanding of moral concepts shows that the practice cannot be justified even if the scientific and medical literature supported it.

Since these moral implications are significant and relevant whether or not the actions cause harm, the scientific and medical literature at best has limited importance, and at worst distracts from the high stakes at hand.

Specifically, I argue that limiting access to oral contraceptives with the aim of incentivizing cancer screenings and pelvic exams is morally problematic medicine because it violates patient autonomy, treats the patient paternalistically, fails requirements of informed consent, and upends the doctor-patient relationship. These reasons connect and overlap, but are not identical. Endorsing the existence of a self-legislating, independent being subscribing to a universal moral law is not necessary to demonstrate the wrong of the practice in question. I thus treat each reason separately for the purposes of those who reject such a conception of autonomy as well as connect the reasons conceptually for the purposes of those who endorse it. In the last section, I argue that the moral wrong rises to the level of a human rights violation.

First, the practice violates autonomy. Autonomy protects patients' pursuit of personal values but doctors violate it when they override patient decisions to accommodate their own values. Second, the practice is paternalistic. Paternalism plays a large role in doctors' rationalization for this practice. Withholding ongoing needed medical care is not morally permitted even if doctors desire patients undergo tests. The role of paternalism explains the necessity for scientific and medical evidence to show the practice is harmful and not for the patient's own good. Third, the practice violates the dictates of informed consent. Because it is exploitive and constitutes duress, the consent patients give to the tests is not morally legitimate. Fourth, the practice is not compatible with contemporary notions of the doctor-patient relationship. In fact, the practice arguably falls short of even outmoded views of doctor-patient relationships, meaning it would not be permissible even when it was started. Fifth, withholding birth control for Pap or pelvic testing is in violation of rights. In the last section, I consider rights to health care and reproductive rights and conclude that the practice is in violation of both.

AUTONOMY

When individuals act out of free will to pursue choices that reflect their considered opinions, they act autonomously. Carolyn McLeod distinguishes autonomy by stating that, "When *we* govern our own actions and choices, we are autonomous; when someone else does so, we are not."[2] Respecting autonomy acknowledges the full agency of actors as capable of setting their own goals and acting on them.[3] For example, a Kantian notion of autonomy is relevant in many such contexts because it prohibits treating rational nature as a mere means to someone else's end.[4] Immanuel Kant traces human dignity and worth to the idea that rational beings can give themselves universal law, saying,

> For, nothing can have a worth other than that which the law determines for it. But the lawgiving itself, which determines all worth, must for that very reason have a dignity, that is, an unconditional, incomparable worth; and the word *respect* alone provides a becoming expression for the estimate of it that a rational being must give. *Autonomy* is therefore the ground of the dignity of human nature and of every rational nature.[5]

For Kant, obeying the moral law we give ourselves is constitutive of autonomy.[6] Thus, treating patients as autonomous protects their right to govern themselves and allows them the authority to determine their own lives.[7]

Terrence Ackerman delineates two components of autonomous functioning: first, that it is "governed by plans of action that have been formulated through deliberation," and second, that it "issues, intentionally and voluntarily, from choices people make based upon their own life plans."[8] Taken together, Ackerman shows how central autonomy is in patient decisions on health care.

Autonomy is valued in biomedical ethics for many reasons, but at least in part because medical decisions are such an intimate feature of human life and often represent the deepest reflections of our values and character. Our bodies are an ineliminable part of the human experience, and the decisions that govern them are often an acknowledgement of this fact.

Autonomy is also relevant in biomedical cases because the decisions we make on our health, health care, and recovery are often made at our weakest and most vulnerable. Pain, suffering, sickness, disease, injury, and disability can impact the autonomous decision-making necessary to handle these issues. And yet, choices are unavoidable in these cases. If our autonomy is limited, then protecting or promoting our decision-making wherever possible becomes both a challenge and a necessity.

Competent individuals do not always make the best decisions for themselves.[9] Sometimes, even educated and intelligent competent individuals fall prey to failures in rationality, value short-term over long-term self-interest, lack self-awareness necessary to follow their own values, or even engage in self-deception that leads to choices they may not reflectively endorse. Adding in the complexity of knowledge required to make informed choices on medical decisions, makes good, let alone ideal decisions very difficult for any individual.

However, making the right decision should not be a requirement for having the power and responsibility to make a decision at all. The noted lawyer and burn victim survivor, Dax Cowart, argues that patients should be allowed to choose, even if they do not make correct decisions.[10] Dax Cowart fought hard during his hospitalization to be allowed to die rather than undergo excruciatingly painful experimental treatments. Later, he acknowledged his gratefulness to be alive and commented on his enjoyment of life. Crucially, this knowledge did not lead him to give up on the notion that patients ought to be able to choose and that he ought to have been able to choose. He does not argue he should have had to undergo medical procedures he did not want or unimaginable pain, even though the end result was a good one. He did not change his mind about what the right decision was at the time, but he has argued that even if he would have made the wrong choice about his treatment, he should have been free to make that wrong choice. After the accident, Dax studied to be a lawyer to protect others from the fate he suffered, in which he was subject to decision-making by his friends, family, doctors, and associates who had different religious values, personal values, and interests to serve than he did, despite full mental capacity.[11] Autonomy means the freedom to make mistakes.

One argument in favor of this position is the fact that despite weaknesses either in information or in reasoning abilities, individuals are best positioned to make choices for themselves given their information set. Even if I do not have a medical degree required to fully understand my own treatment options, I am still in a better position than my doctor to have the final say in the decision because I have access to a multitude of other relevant facts and information that allow me to incorporate opposing choices, because the doctor can provide me with the relevant medical information, and because the decision will have a bigger impact on me than anyone else. I have a better idea than most how well I can handle pain, how risk-averse I am, how much of a burden the worst-case scenarios will be, what kind of life I aim to lead, and how much I trust the doctors in charge of my care. In short, so long as my decisions do not endanger others, I can weigh my values and goals where outsiders cannot.

According to John Stuart Mill, "If a person possesses any tolerable amount of common sense and experience, his own mode of laying out his existence is the best, not because it is the best in itself, but because it is his own mode."[12] In other words, Mill acknowledges that people do not always make the best decisions, but still defends the idea that they ought to make decisions for themselves and ought to be protected in doing so. Partly, this fact is due to a wide variety in human experience, preference, and nature. And partly, this fact is due to the ultimate responsibility we desire for the directions of our own lives.

Mill defends autonomy, arguing that it is particularly valuable. He says that "individuality is one of the leading essentials of well-being."[13] For Mill, a quality like autonomy is actually constitutive of the good life. In part, that is because in deciding our future, we are fulfilling our highest human faculties:

> He who lets the world, or his own portion of it, choose his plan of life for him, has no need of any other faculty than the ape-like one of imitation. He who chooses his plan for himself, employs all his faculties. He must use observation to see, reasoning and judgment to foresee, activity to gather materials for decision, discrimination to decide, and when he has decided, firmness and self-control to hold to his deliberate decision.[14]

It is significant that Mill, a utilitarian, could defend individuality, choice, and autonomy as so prized.[15] Of course, this argument is not paradoxical because he argues that valuing autonomy will lead to good consequences.[16] That is why Mill famously argued that people should be free to make decisions for themselves whenever possible, even if some may think they are in a better position to decide for others.[17]

Respect for autonomy as protective of good outcomes is helpful for our purposes in a medical context.

This argument of Mill's might be among the hardest to understand from a medical perspective. Doctors devote their lives to saving patients and preserving health—any decision on the part of the patient that looks to be at odds with this mission is a difficult pill to swallow.[18] However, Mill makes the case that doing so can preserve good outcomes, achieve well-being, and protect patients from harm better than paternalism.[19]

But further, autonomy is also valuable in its own right. Even when people make decisions that differ from each other, even if people make wrong choices, and even as life and death matters, autonomy merits protection as an intrinsic value.[20] That is why the value of autonomy is viewed as distinct from medical benefit, most clearly seen in cases of lifesaving measures. For example, when discussing end of life decisions, Bonnie Steinbock argues that, "In general, a competent adult has the right to refuse treatment, even where such treatment is necessary to prolong life. Indeed, the right to refuse treatment has been upheld even when the patient's reason for refusing treatment is generally agreed to be inadequate."[21] In addition to being intrinsically valuable, autonomy is also very valuable. The freedom it protects for the direction of one's life is central to most conceptions of the good.

A feminist approach might require going even further. These facts about autonomy lead Susan Sherwin to argue that the scientific model of medicine itself is authoritarian and needs to be replaced with a new, feminist model of patient care that eliminates the hierarchy of the doctor over the patient.[22] Sherwin argues that "medicine cannot claim a uniquely privileged position for decision-making to appeal to the superior scientific training of its students."[23] Instead, a feminist model of health care would require the democratization of bioethics and egalitarianism in health care.[24]

Nevertheless, serious features in the medical context can limit autonomy and have outsized relevance in our discussion, as Sherwin herself notes.[25] Ackerman highlights four interacting potential constraints on autonomy: physical constraint, in which individuals face material restraints on autonomous decision-making or acting on those choices; cognitive constraint, in which individuals lack medical information or full mental capacities for autonomous functioning; psychological constraint, in which emotional features of patient circumstances limit autonomous functioning; and social constraint, in which "institutionalized roles and expectations that block considered choices" undermine autonomy.[26] Each type of constraint is sufficient to block autonomous decision-making or autonomous action on a considered life plan, but the obstacles can also intersect with one another, causing further problems for patients. For example, a patient might suffer from anxiety connected to a medical decision, upsetting a life plan or leading to unreflective choices and choices that violate longstanding values. But the same patient might also experience limited medical information necessary to make a successful choice. In fact, the lack of full medical information or feeling overwhelmed by medical information can actually lead to the sort of anxiety that would count as a psychological restraint on authentic decision-making.

Threats to autonomy from limited choices, oppression, and discrimination play a large role in feminist literature.[27] For example, if one's preferences and choices are shaped by discrimination and oppression, then they may not be reliable expressions of a considered worldview and may not be the best reflection of one's true autonomous desires. As Martha Nussbaum explains,

> If one does not know what it is like to feel well nourished, it is especially easy to be content with the undernourished state in which one lives; if one has never learned to read and is told that education is not for women, it is very easy to internalize one's own second-class status and learn not to strive for, or even desire, what tradition has put out of reach.[28]

For this reason, preferences that arise in oppressive scenarios in which people internalize their own limited options come to be known as "diseased," "adaptive," or "preference-deformation."

In the case of birth control prescriptions traded for Pap tests and other screenings, it is possible to identify the role of all of these constraints on autonomy. Bodily restrictions come about when doctors physically deny patients access to ongoing medical care or when they levy this care to achieve invasive and unnecessary medical testing. Cognitive constraint comes about when patients agree to such testing in the absence of knowledge that it is no longer recommended or necessary for health, and has not been recommended in the medical establishment for many years. Psychological constraint can come about in the fear and stress patients feel when they worry about losing access to birth control, in the avoidance behavior they engage in when dealing with doctor's appointments, in the anxiety they may feel about STD testing or cancer screening, and even in the emotional manipulation some doctors engage in when they attempt to instill fears in patients over the dangers of cervical cancer. For example, a doctor telling a story about a young patient who skipped her Pap test and ended up dying before the age of 30 from a preventable but aggressive form of cervical cancer can act as a psychological constraint on a patient who has full and accurate information about the benefits and risks of yearly Pap testing, but does not act on it due to irrational fears. Ackerman's social constraint can also play a part in this instance. Doctors taking on more paternalistic or robust advising in this instance can lead patients to second-guess their own free thinking and follow what they take to be a strong, institutionally supported physician role. Adaptive preferences can arise when patients come to expect limitations on their birth control access without recognizing these limitations as threats to their rights.

In such instances, one should not dismiss patients deviating from their ideal decision-making as trivial or small in the grander scheme of things. Such obstacles pose real risks to their autonomy and should be recognized as such. When patients lose control in these ways, they fail to act on their considered judgments, lack the ability to reflect on the problems they face accurately, or otherwise fall short of their aims in seeking medical care. They may make decisions that they do not endorse and that may damage their health or well-being in the long run.

According to Ackerman, however, the response to these limitations should not be to cede control in vulnerable situations but rather to do everything possible to promote autonomous decision-making, even if that means more robust acts on the part of doctors in intervening on patient choice.

Furthermore, as much as doctors think they know what is best for the patients, and as much as doctors tend to treat their patients paternalistically, many do not want these choices to begin with. Doctors may lament the life and death decisions they have to make for their patients and view these decisions as burdensome. They may feel troubled by the weight of these choices that they make for their patients, especially when the choice is between two awful options. Doctors may view these occasions as tragic yet connected to the life of a doctor without realizing that those decisions are not theirs to make. While they are right that certain life-and-death decisions are unique to doctors, such as triage decisions and decisions in emergencies when there is no time to consult with the relevant parties, other decisions that doctors may perceive as their unique burden are not actually theirs to make at all. For example, according to interviews in Dax's case, many of the people around Dax, including his doctors, felt torn and aggrieved over the unfortunate features of the case, including the fact that Dax did not want treatment for his injuries.[29] Nevertheless, they thought that the tough decision lay with them. Doctors may feel as though they are placed in a difficult position when a patient makes a choice to refuse lifesaving treatment. However, doctors need not bemoan the responsibility of a life-or-death decision when the patient refuses treatment because the decision ultimately lies with the patient, not the doctor.

In fact, feminists discuss the danger of minimizing the autonomy of patients for these reasons in just the context of Pap tests.[30] For example, historically, doctors have used finding precancerous cells in Pap smears as justification to coerce patients into hysterectomies that the patients were led to believe were required.[31] When doctors withhold medical information as impossibly complex or completely settled, they engage in fearmongering instead of protecting health.[32]

So far, my discussion has focused primarily on the fact that autonomy is valuable and as a result doctors ought to respect it. But a clear view of the role autonomy plays in the discussion goes much further. Not only are adult patients with rational capacity uniquely qualified to determine what best serves their interests in part due to privileged information they have about their own values, goals, and preferences, but also to go against these decisions treats them as less than persons. The argument is not just that respecting autonomy is good, but also that denying it is unacceptable.

Autonomy is an extremely weighty moral value; overriding it requires an equally weighty or weightier reason. In biomedical contexts, variation in individuals' goals and values means they should have as much choice as possible in pursuit of those goals. A longer life is not always valuable to patients who endure extreme and untreatable suffering; a better quality of life is not always valuable to patients who think any medical intervention disrupts God's plan. Adhering to patient values protects their autonomy.[33]

Overriding or ignoring patient choice is disrespectful of their autonomy, even when it falls short of medical negligence or malpractice, because it upsets their decision-making and values. For example, doctors should respect the decision of a patient who does not want a screening for Huntington's disease, despite having a 50% chance of having it, without threatening other sorts of care.

Some do not value autonomy, or value it only instrumentally, and my argument does not require commitment to this concept.[34] Before I move to related arguments, however, I first consider and reject several objections to reliance on autonomy in these contexts.

First, one could value autonomy, but think it is defeasible. Even if this value can be overridden in the medical context in certain limited scenarios, it would be odd to say doctors do not need to respect autonomy or gain consent for medical procedures, so long as doctors find those procedures valuable. To make autonomy so defeasible would be to make it utterly irrelevant in the medical context, only required in the most circumspect or worthless medical interventions.

Some might argue that while in general it is possible respect autonomy in biomedical cases, overriding those decisions is permissible when patient choices have impacts on the broader population. For example, requiring vaccination against preventable diseases,[35] or screening and quarantining individuals during an outbreak might be instances in which respect for autonomy does not protect the patient against all medical intervention.[36] While these cases are complex and theoretically interesting, I argue they do not apply to the argument at hand because no immediate threat to others attends failures to get Pap testing. And, while STD testing has a public health benefit, stigmatizing STDs is likely to have the opposite effect.[37] In fact, since I already argued that Pap testing at the frequency it is currently required by most clinicians is not even beneficial for the individual in question, let alone for the community at large, these potential limits on autonomy are inapplicable.

Sarah Conly gives several main objections to the value of autonomy, arguing that a paternalistic government set up to defend citizens from bad choices is justified.[38] She argues that autonomy has two main weak points: first, that individuals often lack the full information necessary to make successful choices for themselves; and second, that individuals often lack the full rationality necessary to use full information well. In the face of these two weaknesses, Conly argues that paternalism, which I discuss below, is sometimes justified.

The major proponents of autonomy tend to incorporate these objections into their arguments for autonomy.[39] Nobody argues that respect for autonomy means people will always act in their own self-interest, or that people will always make the best choices. Instead, defenders of autonomy tend to argue that making mistakes is required for full acceptance of autonomy. They also argue that the risk of making mistakes is not as great as the risk of paternalistic forces getting it wrong. The ability to make mistakes is often a downside people are willing to accept to control their own destinies. Autonomy, despite its detractors, is a salvageable value.[40]

In addition, Conly's reasons to accept paternalism do not apply in this particular instance. First, Conly and other critics of autonomy do not argue that paternalism is justified in all cases. That leaves the door open for individual decision-making. Second, the reasons Conly gives for thinking autonomy is flawed do not apply in these cases. If full information is lacking, and I have argued that it is, then an exhortation to accurate information pulls in favor of rejecting the paternalistic practice, not accepting it. When patients accept the burden of yearly Pap tests so as to ensure uninterrupted access to hormonal birth control pills, they generally do so in the absence of full information that annual tests are not justified by evidence-based practice. Accurate information would not lead them to accept the paternalistic practices; it would lead them to reject those practices. Similarly, patients' rationality is not in question when they express preferences not to undergo yearly testing. A complex constellation of values is compatible even with missing a necessary Pap test and retaining access to birth control. This calculus is completely rational. After all, two harms—no needed testing and no birth control—do not make a benefit.

Furthermore, if relevant information on the part of patients would support this practice, which I argue that it does not, it does not follow that the practice is therefore justified. Perhaps a robust marketing campaign touting the benefits of regular Pap testing would be a better and more respectful way of ensuring full information on the part of patients without jeopardizing their health in other ways. For example, as controversial as the American campaign for mammograms is, it is still a better option than withholding other care until they undergo a needed mammogram. Similarly, a popular campaign recommending regular Pap testing might be more effective and lead to better outcomes than withholding birth control to achieve these goals. It might be more effective because it will give patients more accurate information about testing—yearly testing is not actually recommended—and it might lead to better outcomes because it would not put patients at risk for pregnancy and other related conditions.

And in fact, the controversy surrounding mammogram advertising is relevant to the concerns about using paternalism to ensure patients act in their own best interest. New data suggest that mammograms are neither needed nor helpful at the interval they have popularly been recommended.[41] Instead, too much testing has led to overtreatment, just as has happened in the case of Pap testing.[42] As much as experts might like to think that they have full information and that patients making different choices are failing in some way, the fact is that scientific evidence is not settled on every such issue. Furthermore, mammograms have perhaps been emphasized too much at a time when women face bigger health threats from other diseases than breast cancer, such as heart disease.[43] An advertising push for mammograms belies the point that testing for other diseases is also essential and may even be more essential for good health outcomes. Similarly, as I argued in chapter 2, too much emphasis on Pap tests suggests that they have an outsized importance compared to other forms of health care, like birth control. In fact, pregnancy is more likely to occur than cervical cancer and can also be fatal in some circumstances.[44] Ensuring access to birth control, even where patients fail to undergo Pap testing, is essential for public health.

Other objectors see value in autonomy but argue that it ought not play a big role in biomedical ethics specifically. Onora O'Neill is one such scholar arguing that autonomy is compromised in biomedical ethics particularly. Says O'Neill, "the notion that we could be 'ideal rational patients' cannot stand up to a moment's scrutiny."[45] O'Neill goes on to argue that because reductions in autonomy are endemic in patients, paternalism must pick up the slack and fill the need left by compromised choice. Although O'Neill is undoubtedly correct that patients—even healthy ones—face reductions in autonomy and increased vulnerability due to their status as patients, not all patients are sick, infirm, or have disabilities. A perspective on health care that only allows for interaction with sick patients would be itself diseased; all individuals require preventative care. Clichés aside ("An ounce of prevention is worth a pound of cure"), preventative care is actually a necessary component of a complete health care regimen. If patients are denied access to vaccines, checkups, and other prophylactic medicine, they most likely do not have access to good health care.

Furthermore, such preventative care itself exists on a continuum. An immunocompromised individual living in a nation without herd immunity against a deadly disease and living near contagions for that disease lives with much more risk and is much more in need of care than someone living absent these conditions. Though neither individual is sick, perhaps this view suggests the former patient has more limited autonomy than the latter due to this vulnerability. Similarly, patients with illnesses who are living in remission due to successful treatment are not the same as patients suffering from grave symptoms, and may not even view themselves as sick.

In the present example, there is no reason to view a normal, healthy adult with functioning ovaries and fallopian tubes as sick qua gynecology patient, despite needing access to drugs to prevent pregnancy.[46] Similarly, the fact that an individual is in possession of a cervix does not imply that person is sick or has reduced autonomy. Are all such people necessarily vulnerable or have had their autonomy compromised simply because they are susceptible to pregnancy and cancer? Such a notion does not stand up to a moment's scrutiny. Agreeing with O'Neill's thesis, then, does not require permitting paternalism in the particular case in question.

In response to the argument O'Neill considers, it is possible to acknowledge an array of ways that health can compromise autonomy, including the very nature of the doctor-patient relationship; further steps may be taken to protect individuals whose autonomy is reduced, no matter how small, without accepting the notion that paternalism permissibly can always expand to address these reductions or that paternalism is morally called for in any such situation. This leaves autonomy conceptually in the clear. This point also explains why O'Neill argues that, "Respect for autonomy requires that consent be possible to fundamental aspects of actions and proposals, but allows that consent to trivial and ancillary aspects of action and proposals may be absent or impossible."[47]

Among those who deny the existence of autonomy altogether, some hold the view that it is a culturally specific notion that is not found at all in geographically distinct areas and thus is not universal or is problematic. For example, Willy De Craemer makes such a case in his article, "A Cross-Cultural Perspective on Personhood."[48] De Craemer argues the Buntu languages found in parts of Africa do not have a close approximation of the English word "person." While people have individuated names, suggesting separateness to some extent, these names are a reflection of their familial ties, social status, and other relative positions in a community rather than their separateness or uniqueness.[49] Interconnectedness, roles and positions, relationships, and family play a larger role in the culture, and people's natures are seen as in flux as well as composite, sometimes being represented as having multiple souls.[50]

Do these attitudes toward individuality and autonomy translate to differing attitudes toward family planning and reproductive health? Fertility and population growth are higher in the countries De Craemer considers, social status sometimes depends on large families, and desire for birth control methods is relatively lower.[51] For example, women who cannot bear children may sometimes be regarded as less than persons and this feature of society can lead to less interest in birth control.[52] Yet, this interest in birth control that is supposedly low actually exceeds half the population.[53] In addition, respect for "other cultures" can sometimes mask a tolerance of sexism or oppression of women.[54] Indeed, surveys of populations in question suggest that the differential between women who desire birth control and their male partners who reject it approaches 30%.[55] A large proportion of women in these countries who want contraception lack access.[56]

Furthermore, linking birth control to Pap tests and pelvic exams is an anachronism unique to the United States, making the culture of autonomy relevant even if it is not universal. Lack of access in other countries include a host of significant barriers, many of them gender-based, but the phenomenon of a doctor cutting off a previous supply for the purposes of imposing other health considerations on the patient is not one of them.[57] In fact, with just a handful of exceptions, oral contraception is available in most African countries without a prescription.[58] These sorts of objections, then, even if theoretically powerful against autonomy in some cases, do not hold significant sway in this context and fail to provide conceptual guidance for the issue at hand. Particular objections to autonomy do not hold purchase for a doctor's defense of this phenomenon.

PATERNALISM

Definitions of paternalism vary, but generally accounts include two components: 1) aiming at the patient's best interests; and 2) overriding the patient's consent, will, or rights. Alan Goldman, for example, gives this account: "We may define paternalism as the overriding or restricting of rights or freedoms of individuals for their own good."[59]

The argument in chapter 2 should be sufficient to rule out the possibility that the practice is justified by paternalism. Tying birth control to Pap tests causes so many physical and mental harms that it likely does not support the patient's best interest. Even those who object to or dismiss autonomy can work within the framework of an incredibly reductionist definition of paternalism, which only requires that patients have interests that are being pursued or preferences that are being denied. However, such a definition of paternalism could not plausibly support the phenomenon of denying patients needed medical care because it violates the patient's best interests.

Nevertheless, suppose no risks attended Pap tests. Suppose they never caused pain or worry. Suppose no false positives ever arose, and thus no harms were ever done by overtesting, overtreatment, or unnecessary surgeries. Suppose they cost patients no money and suppose the opportunity costs of the time spent in appointments evaporated.[60] But suppose the benefits of Pap tests and pelvic exams remained: these screenings saved many lives. Would doctors thereby be justified in withholding oral contraceptives until patients undergo beneficial tests? I argue they would not. Even if no medical harms arose from limiting access to birth control, threats to the well-being of patients would still persist through violations like paternalistic attitudes.

Requiring medical interventions, even if they are for the patient's own good, is not within the realm of doctor choice.[61] Doctors can make recommendations, but they cannot permissibly use coercive tactics to gain compliance. Paternalism in the medical realm is a danger to patients and doctors should be careful about imposing their own conceptions of the good on their patients. When a patient engages in informed refusal, appropriate responses include clearly documenting the refusal and raising the issue again, but not withholding care. Paternalism was once standard in the medical profession because doctors saw themselves as being in a better position to decide what is best for the patient than those patients themselves. Now, it is a holdover from a different era.[62]

As discussed above, O'Neill proposes the idea that insofar as autonomy is limited, paternalism must fill in the gaps. Outlining this view, she says, "Where autonomy is standardly reduced, paternalism must it seems be permissible; opposition to medical paternalism appears to reflect an abstract and inaccurate view of human consent which is irrelevant in medical contexts."[63] This view makes sense in view of the various ways patients are unable to exercise full decision-making power. One reason this view is powerful is that nobody—patient or not—has full autonomous decision-making power. We all experience reductions and limitations to various degrees and for various reasons. A failure to engage in complete and thorough self-reflection, a distracting pain, or a desire to please, in conflict with other values, can all reduce our autonomy. But if everyone experiences a reduction of autonomy to some extent—or put another way, if not everyone is a perfect self-legislating ideal—then by the lights of this view, paternalism is always justified. If falling short of an ideal of autonomy justifies paternalism, then doctors are morally justified in exercising an incredible amount of control over patient health care. This idea then puts patients in a dangerous position because it leaves them no moral recourse when a doctor violates their expressed wishes.

I can also challenge this conclusion by arguing that paternalism need not fill the gaps in autonomy in every case. If paternalism inherently requires acting against the patient's will, and if paternalism is inherently coercive, then there may be other ways to make up for limitations in autonomy that avoid this pitfall. For example, a living will or advance directive can give medical practitioners avenues to a patient's autonomous decisions without resorting to paternalism. Similarly, designating a power of attorney could help a patient fill in the gaps in autonomy without being subject to paternalism.[64] Discussions with the patient also can help in this regard. Ensuring patients understand the background at stake and alleviating their fears can go a long way toward supporting their choices. Even patients who willingly cede to their doctor the relevant choice cannot be said to be subject to paternalism, since paternalism by its very nature must be done against consent. Thus, it is possible to resist the notion that the inevitable gaps in autonomy must be filled by something as powerful and dangerous as paternalism.

O'Neill acknowledges as much, saying, "To respect others' autonomy requires that we make consent *possible* for them, taking account of whatever partial autonomy they may have."[65] She reckons with the fact that doctors may have to do more to enhance the autonomy of limited patients rather than necessarily step in with coercive and paternalistic measures. O'Neill takes account of partial autonomy in a way that does not necessarily lead to paternalism but leaves the door open for paternalism where autonomy is absent. O'Neill states, "When patients' partial autonomy constrains medical practice, respect for patients may demand action which avoids not only deceit and coercion but also manipulation and paternalism; but where autonomy is absent there is no requirement that it be respected."[66] Thus, drawing the line between partial autonomy and no autonomy takes on heightened importance. I have already catalogued ways in which a patient's autonomy may seem to be absent but must still be respected. For example, a patient in a coma may be literally lacking in autonomous capacity, but with a living will, still in some sense has autonomy that must be respected. Staving off paternalism would be possible where partial autonomy persists.

INFORMED CONSENT

Informed consent is a crucial tenet of medical ethics. Consent has several features: patients must be informed, must understand the risks and benefits of a treatment, must be competent to make the decision, and must make the choice voluntarily.[67] These four attributes of consent must all be met for consent to be considered morally valid in human experiments according to the Nuremberg Code.[68] A variety of overlapping branches of philosophy incorporate notions of informed consent, including normative ethics, political philosophy, philosophy of law, social philosophy, and applied ethics such as sexual ethics. For example, versions of informed consent play a central role in contractualism,[69] social contract theory,[70] theories of democracy,[71] legal contracts,[72] notions of promising,[73] marriage,[74] and sexual conduct.[75]

No one can truly have full information because an infinite amount of information might be relevant to each component of a medical decision. Instead, being fully informed is sometimes broken out into two conditions: a doctor disclosing the relevant information and the patient actually understanding it. This distinction helps highlight the fact that patients may not understand the information given to them, and if they do not, the condition has not been met. While the former is certainly essential for a legal definition of consent, the latter only works for consent in a moral sense. After all, epistemological difficulties attend knowing whether a patient truly has understood the practice in question. However, it would be helpful for doctors to consider this requirement a gold standard in the practice, because it may incentivize them to discuss the procedure in such a way as to ensure the patient exhibits understanding. Furthermore, what counts as relevant or sufficient information may depend on the gravity of the choice, where a more difficult choice would require more information and a less difficult one requires less.[76]

In the practice relevant to our discussion, it is not clear either that the doctor has disclosed enough information to obtain informed consent or that the patient has understood the information enough. For one thing, requiring a Pap test for a birth control prescription spreads misinformation about birth control. For example, it suggests that it is unsafe to take birth control without such tests. The practice may also lead patients to believe that they need yearly Pap tests. When patients believe these measures are necessary, they may make trade-offs in their overall health considerations that are a net loss to them. They may choose a yearly Pap test that is medically unnecessary over a biopsy of a suspicious mole that is medically indicated due to constraints in time and money that do not allow for both. When doctors deceive patients, they prevent patients from making choices that reflect their best interests. An OB/GYN may not even be aware of other needed medical care the patient is forgoing to comply with Pap testing. As a result, the condition of informed consent has not been met.

In addition, the practice spreads the misinformation that knowing whether one has cervical cancer is more significant than the conditions that hormonal birth control treats. When patients believe this fiction, they operate on the assumption that birth control is much less essential to their health than it actually is, and that annual cancer screenings are much more essential to their health than they actually are. These skewed priorities that doctors endorse can lead to poor decision-making in the future and undermine informed consent.

It is no surprise, then, that anecdotally patients tend to hold beliefs inconsistent with a full understanding of the practice. For example, they may believe that there is some medical necessity for birth control to be linked to cancer screenings, that yearly cancer screenings are recommended, and that they would be worse off if their doctor did not link these procedures. In fact, for doctors to be sure that the patient did not hold some combination of these beliefs while still continuing with the practice, they would have to ask their patients leading questions that would be antithetical to their purposes. Asking a patient, "Are you aware that my personal requirement that you get a yearly Pap test is neither medically necessary nor supported by scientific evidence?" while theoretically possible within a given doctor's protocols, is very unlikely to occur. If it did, the understanding the patient receives may precipitate that patient leaving the doctor or getting a prescription elsewhere. It is safe to say, then, that the practice is very unlikely to meet the first condition of informed consent, as defined by the Nuremberg Code.

The second condition, that patients understand the benefits and risks, is related to this discussion and also not traditionally met. A full understanding of the risks would mean that the patient is aware of the kind of medical background provided in chapter 2, which is highly unlikely in this case. Doctors are not likely to spell out the risks of Pap tests when they are so adamant that their patients get them. They are even less likely to inform their patients of the added risks of getting Pap tests more often than evidence suggests is effective, such as the higher likelihood of false positives and the ensuing harms of overtreatment. Would doctors requiring yearly Pap tests be inclined to tell their patients that Pap tests are sometimes only recommended every three to five years and that getting the test more causes increased risk of harm? Having truly informed patients would undermine their personal goals, while keeping patients in the dark would better suit their values. Nothing about the practice of tying birth control to Pap tests rules out this forthrightness on the part of doctors, meaning the consent is not necessarily uninformed. But it is more likely to be uninformed.

In fact, even requiring that the patient be aware of benefits highlights the deficient nature of the practice, since it would be extremely difficult to identify any. While there may be some subgroup of patient that could benefit from yearly testing but who is not currently included in standard recommendations, no category of patient benefits from the removal of birth control access, keeping in mind that not everyone who has access to birth control necessarily uses it. If we imagine some future, technologically advanced Pap test that has a far lower rate of false positives—perhaps we could imagine one with no false positives at all—eliminating the risk of overtreatment altogether would be insufficient to create a recommendation for yearly testing. For example, false positive tests are relatively rare in pregnancy testing, but that does not mean that patients should increase the incidence of testing for this condition.

The third condition for informed consent is that the patients be competent to make medical decisions for themselves. A patient may be incompetent to make medical decisions if deficient in rational capacity, too sick to understand what is going on with her body, drunk or high on drugs that impair reasoning ability, or subject to some other condition that would likely also interfere with routine checkups. Whether or not a doctor would impose the restrictions discussed in this chapter on such a patient is unclear. However, such patients would need other competent individuals to make decisions on their behalf, and in that case, the condition would apply again. The circumstances under which a doctor would permissibly make decisions on the patient's behalf without a power of attorney are so rare as to not apply for routine cancer screenings and only are relevant in extreme life-and-death emergencies.

The last condition requires that the consent not be under duress. Duress can take many forms, including the limiting of options. For example, a criminal who threatens your money or your life is technically giving you a choice, but your decision to hand over your money could not be construed as consensual because such a decision was made under duress and with limited options. Withholding contraceptives to force a specific test violates consent because it takes away a treatment the doctor and patient have jointly decided is necessary and limits options to achieve compliance.[77]

Despite failing a general notion of informed consent, perhaps informed consent is itself of limited moral concern. As Jay Katz points out, informed consent was originally developed as a legal, not a moral model. As such, it has two main limitations for guiding our moral evaluations: first, the standard comes from outside the field, especially as it is conceived in contemporary American society. Second, due to its legal framework, it is viewed as a minimum and not an ideal. That is, when aiming to achieve the standard of informed consent, doctors may aim at divulging the minimum amount of information necessary to avoid legal liability.[78] Of course, in this case, they do not even do that, as argued in chapter 2. Perhaps doing so would not be enough to put them in the clear morally with respect to this practice. It is difficult to imagine under what circumstances fully informed patients would agree to be subject to these restrictions, but if they did, the doctors' actions would support, and not restrict, their patients' choices.

The value of informed consent and respect for truth can also flow from the concept of autonomy. Susan Cullen and Margaret Klein state,

> Respect for persons bars the deception of patients. When the deception is for the physician's benefit, the wrong is obvious. Yet even when the deception is intended to benefit the patient, the physician's good intention doesn't alter the fact that the deception violates the patient's autonomy.[79]

In the case of birth control discussed here, perhaps the deception benefits the physician, since the physician sees patients more often and gets more money. But speaking charitably, the physician will most likely attribute the practice to a need to pursue the patient's own good. As Susan Cullen and Margaret Klein make clear, making patients believe they need a Pap test for pregnancy protection when they do not is deceptive and the need for a Pap test is not a sufficient reason to deceive. What is needed is respect for patients to make their own choices about the direction of their lives. Patient knowledge is needed to do that. Thus, Cullen and Klein argue that "When knowledge is power, ignorance is slavery."[80]

This discussion has served to show that the practice fails standard definitions of informed consent and falls short of both a legal and moral standard protecting patients. But it perhaps has not conveyed the severity of the issues at stake in this question. A central tenet and arguably the foundational standard holding up all of bioethics is the idea that a patient has irrevocable power to refuse treatment. When doctors violate this pillar of ethical theory, they arguably cross the most dangerous threshold possible in this context.

Of course, doctors do sometimes perform medical procedures without the patient's consent, such as in emergency scenarios in which the patient is not conscious and there is no time to contact family members. However, when doctors and medical professionals act in these cases, they do so as a means of fulfilling what the patient would want in the circumstances, not violating consent or overriding patient desires. As Douglas S. Diekema writes, "The failure to obtain informed consent constitutes a battery under the law, for which a physician might be either criminally or civilly liable. This right to refuse treatment and grant informed consent does not disappear for individuals who are incompetent. Rather the right is one that must be exercised for them."[81] For example, Do Not Resuscitate (DNR) orders are used in just such scenarios to protect patients from medical interventions that they would not want in emergency situations but that doctors may otherwise assume that they would want to save their lives. Doctors withholding intubation or CPR in a DNR case show that respecting the patient's wishes to avoid medical care is valued over and above saving lives.

DOCTOR-PATIENT RELATIONSHIP

In describing Dr. Mary Halton, Margaret Sanger states that, "She has what to my mind is the attitude of the real physician; that it is not enough merely to cure ailments—surroundings, heartaches, privations must also be given attention."[82] The doctor-patient relationship plays a large role in the scholarship on the ethics of medical decision-making in part because biomedical ethics is a form of professional ethics in which the role of the professional—in this case the medical provider—helps determine behavioral standards.

In some senses, the idea of a doctor-patient relationship fails to take into account contemporary experiences in America. Discussing the correct or ideal model of a doctor-patient relationship presupposes that everyone has access to a doctor and that any relationship at all is possible, let alone a morally justified one. Today, individuals may not have full health care coverage, may not have a longstanding relationship with a doctor, may only see a doctor in emergency scenarios in which a discussion is difficult or impossible, or may only see a doctor for a few short minutes at a time. Still, applying the various models of doctor-patient relationships to the case of birth control access is informative because first, establishing an ideal helps delineate what to work toward; second, establishing bad models helps us understand what to rule out; and third, if all relevant models rule out the practice under discussion, then we have a better understanding of the theoretical basis—or lack thereof—for the current treatment of patients regarding reproductive health.

In the *Laws*, Plato gives a comparative analysis of free doctors and slave doctors. Although he is primarily interested in politics and legislation, his analogy here is instructive.[83] The Athenian in the dialogue states of slave doctors that,

> This kind of doctor never gives any account of the particular illness of the individual slave, or is prepared to listen to one; he simply prescribes what he thinks best in light of experience, as if he had precise knowledge, and with the self-confidence of a dictator. Then he dashes off on his way to the next slave-patient, and so takes off his master's shoulders some of the work of attending the sick. (*Laws* 720c3-d1)[84]

Here, the subject in question not only treats slaves, but also may be a slave himself. The result in such cases is that a full investigation into the symptoms, a clear diagnosis, and a proper explanation of treatments are not an option. The limited approach to treatment is thus twofold: that the clinicians themselves may not be fully trained and that the slaves are not educated enough or wealthy enough to understand or pay for better treatment. A free doctor acts differently:

> The visits of a free doctor, by contrast, are mostly concerned with treating the illnesses of freemen; *his* method is to construct an empirical case-history by consulting the invalid and his friends; in this way he himself learns something from the sick and at the same time he gives the individual patient all the instruction he can. He gives no prescription until he has somehow gained the invalid's consent; then, coaxing him into continued cooperation, he tries to complete his restoration to health. (*Laws*, 720d1-e1)

In his account of the free doctor, Plato, through the Athenian, demonstrates how consent is an integral part of the doctor-patient relationship. Plato's *Laws*, dated 348 BCE, recognizes the value of informed consent for proper treatment. Even 2,300 years ago, in a different continent, culture, and political regime, similar values for doctors' responsibilities applied.

Plato's analysis provides two other helpful threads for my purposes. One is that the doctor-patient relationship in question, which relies on dictatorial approaches to treatment and can be viewed as paternalistic only if viewed charitably, is a relationship that demonstrates a lack of standing for the patient. We do not treat free people in this way. Only those who are already oppressed would be subject to this sort of care. And that is true presumably because one does not explain the diagnosis or treatment to someone in such a position. Viewing one's patient as slave-like can potentially lead a doctor to engage in differential treatment.

The other point that is instructive from Plato is that the failure to obtain informed consent may not just be due to (perceived) deficiencies on the part of the patient; failure to obtain informed consent is actually evidence of deficiencies on the part of the doctor. Clinicians engage in this truncated practice when they are not competent to give a full diagnosis or do not have the education or freedom to invest in each patient. Care without informed consent is not merely a different style, such as "paternalistic" care; it is demonstrably worse care. Bad ethics makes for bad medicine.

Thus, Plato, writing in a different time and culture—and about a different subject!—can still give us valuable insights into contemporary American health care. But this discussion only scratches the surface of what a better doctor-patient relationship would look like.

Ezekiel J. Emanuel and Linda L. Emanuel in their article, "Four Models of the Physician-Patient Relationship," discuss the paternalistic, informative, interpretive, and deliberative relationships doctors can have with their patients.[85] The paternalistic model most closely approximates the relationship doctors aim at when they decide to withhold medication until such time as their patients undergo added testing. However, it is striking that by Emanuel and Emanuel's landmark definition, this practice fails even to meet the standard of the paternalistic model. According to Emanuel and Emanuel, in a paternalistic model, doctors act as authoritative guardians, either selectively choosing which information would convince their patients to make the desired choice, or simply telling the patients which action will be taken for their treatment.[86] In this model, it is assumed that patients and doctors share the ultimate goal of health and choose treatments accordingly. Does withholding birth control until patients undergo Pap or pelvic testing fit the paternalistic model of the doctor-patient relationship? In short, no: in chapter 2 and above, I reviewed evidence that a yearly Pap test or pelvic exam does not best achieve health for the patient.

How can we know that a practice fails to meet a given model of a physician-patient relationship unless we know exactly how that practice is implemented? Perhaps it is done in an open, caring, and deliberative way. Perhaps the doctor is transparent and gives full information. First, these features are not required of the paternalistic model. Paternalistic doctors do not give full information; they select the information they provide to achieve the outcome they wish. They do not deliberate with their patients; that interaction best fits a different model.

But second, the strict and controlling nature of the practice provides a clue as to how the practice would have to be implemented. Doctors cannot be viewed as successfully persuading their patients to undergo a test if they have to withhold medical care to achieve compliance with that test, because if the patients were persuaded, doctors would not need to implement a threat. When a mob boss is "very persuasive" in eliciting preferred behavior through threat of physical violence, that description is facetious. The mob boss does not actually convince anyone of a position or use arguments to move anyone intellectually. Mob bosses do not need threats if they actually persuade.

Perhaps doctors using this practice fall closer to the extreme of paternalism, of which Emanuel and Emanuel say, "At the extreme, the physician authoritatively informs the patient when the intervention will be initiated."[87] Presumably, this description most accurately fits what a doctor would have to do to successfully implement the practice in question. However, even this description fails to approximate the pressure exerted by the doctor on the patient in this case. A doctor does not merely say, "It is time for your routine Pap test, which will take place in the next month," which would exemplify the type of pressure described by the authors' account. Instead, a doctor imposes another layer of control: "It is time for your routine Pap test. I will take away the treatment options for your other conditions and your preferred method of pregnancy prevention if you do not comply."

Doctors do sometimes engage in such activity, and are very likely to have done so decades ago. For example, in Dax Cowart's case, discussed above, the patient's decision was overridden and he was forced to undergo treatment he did not want. However, even in this case, attempts were made to determine whether he was fit to make decisions for himself. In an effort to prove himself able to govern his own care, he underwent psychological evaluation. Even when doctors were treating a patient against his will, they paid lip service to the idea that he was potentially competent on his own to make decisions for himself. Ultimately, when his choices were overridden, they were not done to give the doctors sole control over the patient's care: Dax's mother, who consented to each treatment, was given the power to do so. Thus, even this paradigmatic example of physician paternalism, which took place under completely different medical norms in 1973, still gives less power to doctors and more power to patients than routine checkups for many women today.

Third, the nature of the offer again precludes the sort of back and forth that would be evident in a more deliberative model. Consider a revised offer: "You and I agree that Pap tests are necessary for your health, but you and I also agree that you may fail to come in at regular intervals for proper testing. To ensure you live up to the choices you make for yourself now, with considered objectivity, may I withhold other care from you until you undergo this testing which you yourself agree is valuable?" Such an offer would perhaps allow us to reframe the phenomenon under consideration in a more open model. But it is very unlikely that doctors and patients have such exchanges. It is unlikely because the kind of discussion necessary to come to such a conclusion could not possibly lead to such a high percentage of doctors making the same exact trade with every single patient. Surely some patient would say, "Yes, I agree that you should withhold something from me to ensure Pap testing, but I think it should be mammograms, not birth control." It is also unlikely because the kind of discussion necessary to come to such a conclusion would involve informing the patient of the pros and cons of Pap testing to a degree that would allow patients to realize annual Pap testing is not inherently more consequential for their health than birth control. And, of course, a doctor engaging in such a negotiation is not appropriate. While it is helpful for doctors to have discussions with their patients, establish patient values and goals, and determine the patient's preferences expressly, it is not the job of the doctor to act as an enforcer.

Additionally, Emanuel and Emanuel offer compelling arguments against this model for a physician-patient relationship.[88] First, the model fails to incorporate other potential patient values that individuals may seek when using medical care. For example, patients may seek quality of life over health, religious goals, work or family commitments over their health, and may have different cost-benefit analyses and risk aversion than their doctors. In fact, patients may even have different ideas of health than their doctors. For example, a recovering stroke patient may have the goal of returning to their pre-stroke abilities (e.g., walk as I used to walk), while a caregiver may have functional goals (e.g., get around, however best that can be accomplished). Thus, for the patients, "health" might mean their previous state, and for the doctors, "health" might mean a new normal.

Second, paternalism does not allow for a robust conception of autonomy. Emanuel and Emanuel define the notion of autonomy used in the paternalistic model of autonomy as "patient assent."[89] In some sense, patients do agree to undergo testing in compliance with this model, albeit without full information and without full freedom of choice. But it is hard to imagine patients "assenting" to this model of assent under normal circumstances. And such a notion of assent relies on an understanding of patient autonomy in which patients are not interested in or do not care about the relevant information necessary to make their health-care choices. But such assent is problematic both because it lacks a fuller understanding of assent and because it relies on a problematically thin notion of autonomy.

If patients indicate to their doctors that they are overwhelmed by the choices necessary, or have no wish to understand the medical concepts the doctor explains either because they are uninterested or because they lack an educational background they deem necessary to understand, then perhaps doctors would be justified in stepping in and filling in the gaps in patient autonomy. However, no evidence suggests that this concession regularly occurs when patients are denied full information and full choice. And a concern arises about such patients: do they belong to particularly vulnerable groups in society? Are they at vulnerable points in their lives? If so, taking away their decision-making power can be damaging to them overall. A real danger lurks where patients do not have the ability to determine their own health choices.

Yet, the routine checkups under consideration are yearly events. They generally cover average, healthy adults. The difficulties of empowering people too sick to speak, suffering from unendurable pain, or undergoing powerful treatments like chemotherapy or major surgeries are significant but distinct. As such, there is no reason to think that their autonomy is undermined in ways that would justify these extreme measures.

If paternalism does not justify the practice, and itself is problematic, what about other possible models of the doctor-patient relationship? Emanuel and Emanuel consider the informative model of the relationship, in which the main purpose is to provide the patient with whatever relevant facts they are missing to execute their will.[90] In this model, patients already know and are familiar with their personal values and how to achieve them; they merely lack the medical knowledge necessary to follow their established plans. The doctor steps in and informs the patient and the patient makes the ultimate choice. Of course, some problems attend this model from both sides. From the physician side, the model reduces a doctor from an empowering caretaker to a medical textbook. From the patient side, the model assumes a view of autonomy in which the patient has fixed and defined values and merely lacks information to implement them. In both cases, this view is lacking, and Emanuel and Emanuel make these objections known. Nevertheless, it is helpful to point out that the practice in question cannot possibly fit this model of the physician-patient relationship. Key information is deprived from the patient when a doctor ties birth control to other features of health care. The informative model cannot support a practice that has demonstrable negative effects on patients and that deprives them of rights and goods.

A third model Emanuel and Emanuel discuss is the interpretive model of the physician-patient relationship, in which the physician plays an active role in eliciting the patient's values and preferences and helps formulate a plan that achieves them.[91] The authors discuss problems with this model, too, such as doctors lacking expertise to tease out these difficult issues or the necessity of the doctor presenting new values to the patient. For example, doctors with patients who smoke and who also fully resign themselves to early deaths may wish to make a plea for their patients valuing health higher in their set of priorities. Doing so would go against the interpretive model. But again, the practice in question fails this model, too, because doctors do not attempt to uncover patient values and in fact may overrule them when presenting the stark choice of invasive testing or losing other health-care access. And, since I argued above that the doctor knows and relies on the patient highly valuing birth control access to achieve compliance with Pap testing, the practice fails the interpretive model not because the doctor is unaware of the patient's values but because the doctor overrides them.

The last model that Emanuel and Emanuel consider and that plays a big role in the literature on these issues is the deliberative model.[92] This model allows an interchange between the doctor and patient on the values relevant to health-care decision-making and on the options themselves and how they would embody those values. Like the interpretive model, the doctor may help the patient draw out what values are relevant. Like the informative model, the doctor also helps provide information about all the options available. According to the authors, autonomy in the deliberative model looks like "moral self-development; the patient is empowered not simply to follow unexamined preferences or examined values, but to consider, through dialogue, alternative health-related values, their worthiness, and their implications for treatment."[93] This fuller conception of autonomy in use in the deliberative model is the only version of autonomy among the four options the authors consider that looks like a robust conception fit for self-determination. According to the authors, this fuller notion of autonomy is necessary for an accurate picture of the ideal worth striving for. They say,

> Autonomy requires that individuals critically assess their own values and preferences; determine whether they are desirable; affirm, upon reflection, these values as ones that should justify their actions; and then be free to initiate action to realize the values. The process of deliberation integral to the deliberative model is essential for realizing patient autonomy understood in this way.[94]

Doctors are uniquely positioned to have this exchange with the patient. As was clear from the other competing models, the deliberative model is not compatible with the practice I consider here. The give-and-take necessary to exemplify this model would not allow for the coercive measures doctors use in gaining compliance from their patients. In addition, the practice is not compatible with varying patient values and priorities. Some patients may rely less heavily on hormonal contraception because they do not use it to treat other conditions or because they also rely on male or female condoms as birth control or both. Some patients may prioritize cancer screenings more highly for any number of reasons. But some patients will not share these values or commitments and for them, the deliberative model would reveal the oppressive nature of the practice in question. In fact, it is hard to imagine a doctor using the practice even among the population prioritizing screenings highly, since patients who care a great deal about cancer screenings would not need threats to incentivize their behavior. And, patients who do not rely heavily on hormonal birth control prescriptions may have strong negative reactions to doctors taking them away.

Emanuel and Emanuel's deliberative model bears some resemblance to Ackerman's notion of what the purpose of a doctor-patient relationship should be. Says Ackerman, "The physician is attempting to alter the fundamental ability of patients to carry through their life plans. To accomplish this delicate task requires a personal knowledge about and interest in the patient."[95] The kind of caretaking interest the doctor has in the patient is not compatible with the informative model and the cooperative nature of the relationship is not compatible with the paternalistic or interpretive model. Ackerman emphasizes the development of the patient, much like the Emanuels do in discussing the deliberative approach. Although I do not aim to minimize any vital differences between Ackerman and the Emanuels' model, it is relevant to see that Ackerman, too, rules out the kind of coercive threatening required for the implementation of the practice in question.

Although Emanuel and Emanuel's four models of physician-patient relationships are not exhaustive, they help paint a picture of what possibilities and ideals are available for the discussion. Since none are compatible with threats, bribes, coercive behavior, withholding information necessary to decision-making, or overriding expressed patient values, none are compatible with the practice as used in the medical field. A successful doctor-patient relationship would not rely on withholding birth control prescriptions in service of Pap testing or pelvic exams.

HEALTH-CARE RIGHTS, DISTRIBUTIVE JUSTICE, REPRODUCTIVE RIGHTS, AND OTHER MORAL CLAIMS TO HEALTH CARE

The principles of bioethics and of moral theory more generally cannot support the practice in question and in fact give us strong reason for rejecting it. Autonomy, paternalism, informed consent, and the doctor-patient relationship give us reasons to think the practice is immoral and unacceptable. And yet, more fundamental rights may be at stake in this issue. If health care itself is a right, meaning that all patients should have access to it, then the denial of health care in this instance constitutes a right violation.[96]

Why think that rights to health care are universal human rights? Although current legal and contractual global documents cannot answer this question, it is significant that they place a high emphasis on the right and earn broad support. The United Nations Universal Declaration of Human Rights (UDHR) written under the leadership of Eleanor Roosevelt after World War II and signed unanimously by the United Nations in 1948, which now boasts close to 200 signatories, is one indication of the value of health care.[97]

Article 25 lists health care as a universal right, the denial of which would constitute harm to any human being. In fact, this statement of the right to health care is much stronger than one might otherwise assume, since the right to health care, which it is generally possible to guarantee, does not necessarily mean the right to health, which it is generally presumed impossible to guarantee, barring future technological and medical advances. But health care for the purpose of guaranteeing a certain standard of living is exactly what is listed as a universal right in this document.

Article 25 also underlines the importance of motherhood and childhood to protect human well-being. Although the health care in question is often aimed at preventing motherhood, the special emphasis placed on that position shows just how dangerous and significant it is in a human life. And, since many people seeking access to birth control are already mothers, ensuring their protection should allow for the timing and spacing of any future children as well as protecting their health more generally.

Other major global institutions back the UDHR emphasis on the provision of medical care, such as the United Nations International Covenant on Economic, Social, and Cultural Rights.[98] As opposed to the UDHR, this document has an even higher bar, seeking "the highest attainable standard" of health. That language is echoed in the United Nations Convention on the Rights of Persons with Disabilities (CRPD), which mentions health 20 times.[99] There, the "highest attainable standard of health" is also guaranteed as a right, with special emphasis on the guaranteeing of this right for people with disabilities and gender-sensitive care.

The United Nations International Convention on the Elimination of All Forms of Racial Discrimination lists in Article 5, part d, section iv the civil right of "the right to public health, medical care, social security and social services."[100] Here, the language of civil rights applies to public health and medical care is specifically required to prevent racial discrimination. The Convention on the Elimination of All Forms of Discrimination Against Women (CEDAW) most specifically of all the Conventions describes the features of the case in question.[101] It highlights access to family planning and demonstrates the value of birth control access for elimination of sex-based discrimination.

The focus so far has been on United Nations conventions because they bear the most relevance on our contemporary application of human rights theory, enjoy the widest possible support, and come the closest to having "teeth" in terms of the enforcement and backing of a global institution of great influence and power. Nevertheless, moral, not legal rights are what matters here. Enforcement mechanisms are not central to the question of whether someone has a right; they are relevant only to the question of whether that right is respected. In this case, the relevant right clearly is not being respected, so the point is only to investigate whether it is in fact a right.

One reason to think that health care is a right is that it is "special" in the sense that it is required for opportunity and because equality of opportunity is so central to the fair distribution of social goods.[102] More specifically, health care pertains to basic, objective needs all people have and deviations from this standard count as diseases meriting treatment. Norman Daniels finds that,

> . . . impairments of normal species functioning reduce the range of opportunity we have within which to construct life-plans and conceptions of the good we have a reasonable expectation of finding satisfying or happiness-producing. Moreover, if persons have a high-order interest in preserving the opportunity to revise their conceptions of the good through time, then they will have a pressing interest in maintaining normal species functioning by establishing institutions—such as health-care systems—which do just that.[103]

In other words, first, we use a basic, biomedical understanding of health and disease, one that is based on human need. Then, we can characterize life plans of reasonable people as all in some sense dependent on the protection of health and the treatment of disease because functional impairments limit opportunity.[104] And, in fact, we should give special consideration to these needs. Daniels states,

> ...by keeping people close to normal functioning, healthcare preserves for people the ability to participate in the political, social, and economic life of their society. It sustains them as fully participating citizens—normal collaborators and competitors—in all spheres of social life.[105]

Participating in society at all, then, relies on notions of health and health care. Since, as Amartya Sen argues, democratic participation is plausibly conceived as a human right in part because it is constitutive of the good life and bare notions of well-being require it, a right that protects the ability of citizens to exercise that right would be of high value.[106]

According to Daniels, the distribution of health care is part of justice because health care is one way to meet to protect fair equality of opportunity. To the extent that theories of justice are required to protect fair equality of opportunity, health-care distribution must be part of them.[107] And health care likely involves insurance schemes which themselves need to be distributed fairly, since protection of the kind of health needed for social participation requires taking into account vast inequalities in distribution of health and the high expense of treating these inequalities.[108]

Some who deny rights to health care aim to distinguish "positive" from "negative" human rights, with the aim to place "negative" rights as higher priority, more basic, or even existing to the exclusion of "positive" rights.[109] According to this view, whereas negative rights require no action on the part of others and merely focus on the value of non-intervention, positive rights do require others to perform positive acts in defense of the rights in question, meaning that too much is required to protect them. The language of "civil and political" rights or freedom from interference rights can refer to negative rights and "social and economic rights" or "security rights" can refer to positive rights.

Two major problems attend such arguments. First, these arguments primarily tend to be found in American civil discourse, making them liable to objections that they are culturally specific and not of universal import. However, this book is primarily aimed at practices found in the United States. More to the point, the so-called negative rights often rely on positive rights. To ignore the connection between civil rights and economic rights means failing to notice that freedom of association requires the ability to leave the home and that freedom of speech requires some level of education.[110] In fact, a basic level of education may be more influential than any other sort of protection the government provides.[111]

Some theorists have argued that the theoretical distinction between these rights cannot be upheld in a consistent manner. For example, the distinction between acts and omissions might itself be flawed since intentions and consequences can remain constant across acts and omissions.[112] Henry Shue has convincingly argued that the distinction breaks down because "negative" rights often do require positive acts on the part of others and that "positive" rights often do require mere omissions on the part of others.[113] As a result, the traditional divide between the two types of rights cannot be upheld. That means either negative, security rights are less basic than generally viewed (a conclusion many are unwilling to accept) or that positive, subsistence rights are more basic than generally viewed (a conclusion Shue argues we should adopt).

Shue's argument about security points out that while personal decisions not to violate someone's physical security generally fall under the category of omissions, the concept of protecting the right itself is much broader. It encompasses a variety of different acts and institutions put in place to uphold the right, such as the military, police, courts, prisons, and other social institutions.[114] Thus, institutions to uphold negative rights might be large and expensive, while the institutions necessary to protect positive, subsistence rights might be much more sparse, inexpensive, and less complicated.[115] The moral and logical distinctions between these types of rights cannot be maintained. Thus, access to health care is not substantively different and in fact is an extension of physical security necessary to exercise our other rights.

Shue's argument takes on more force in the particular issue at stake in birth control prescription refills. Denial of birth control is literally a threat to physical security, and not just subsistence or socio-economic rights. Being prone to pregnancy, for example, especially in a country with a very high maternal mortality rate, is a threat to life itself. Furthermore, since the question of paying for the pills is not at stake, and since no procedure or medical intervention is required for protecting the patient's health (indeed, I am arguing for the elimination of a procedure), no onerous positive acts are required by others outside of the simple writing of a prescription. Thus, a negative security right is just as plausibly at stake here as a positive health-care right, showing how the distinction can break down.

Some feminists also suggest that the focus on negative rights and freedom from the state to the exclusion of positive rights is damaging to women, women's interests, and a variety of central requirements to thrive.[116] A feminist analysis would then require respect for positive rights such as health-care rights.

However, the protection of access to health care does not necessarily settle the questions raised in this chapter. Having a right to health care does not necessarily mean any particular provider has to fulfill it. I may have a right to abortion, but do I have a right for a particular doctor to perform it? This second right is more controversial. Legally, doctors may refuse treatment for patients if their offices are too busy, if they don't accept the patient's insurance, if the patient cannot pay for the costs, and a host of other reasons, none of which meet the criteria for medical malpractice, as discussed in chapter 2. Legally, it is just not true that someone may walk into any office and demand service from doctors.

To the extent these rights exist, they are *in rem* rights; not the *in personam* rights discussed in chapter 3. As such, it is more difficult to point out a specific person effectively denying the relevant rights such that they may be easier to ignore. Nevertheless, the ability to make a broad claim that applies to everyone, and therefore that everyone has a stake in, is a powerful moral tool in convincing others to respect rights. And, for reasons discussed in chapter 3, the doctors denying patients birth control are guilty of more than just committing legal negligence if they are also additionally denying a human right.

Judith Jarvis Thomson describes this concern when she argues that I may have a right to life, but no claim on Henry Fonda to lay his cool hand on my fevered brow, even if that is all that is required to save my life.[117] I may be able to demand such service from an emergency room or other service providers that are not permitted to turn patients away. But emergency rooms are prohibitively expensive, even for OTC medications like Tylenol. By contrast, I do have moral claims to demand service from a provider who has already commenced my treatment. That possibility is discussed in chapter 2. While that certainly limits the claims for a broader argument on contraception access, it is sufficient to cover the cases discussed here, in which treatment has started and at some later date, a doctor withholds access.

What about rights to contraception specifically? Since reproductive rights are a central feature of health care, it stands to reason that rights to health care include reproductive rights.[118] Reproductive rights themselves include a range of rights of varying importance, of which rights to contraception play a prominent role.[119] Contraception protects against a condition, pregnancy, that can lead to greater risk of death in addition to risks of lifelong disabilities and other irreversible conditions, grave and minor; treats a variety of diseases and syndromes, including endometriosis and polycystic ovary syndrome; and also protects against other diseases, including ovarian cysts and a variety of different cancers.

But the right to contraception goes further than just protection against and treatment of major physical medical issues. Contraception is also a core component of a broader right to privacy. A long history of United States Supreme Court cases protect a legal right to privacy based in the Fourteenth Amendment.[120] For example, *Union Pacific Railway Co. v. Botsford* 141 U.S. 250 (1891) protects against a court forcing a plaintiff to undergo a medical procedure.[121] This case is one of many used as precedent for a right to personal privacy under the Constitution covering at least access to contraception.[122] The court later extended that right to include abortion access, too, saying "This right of privacy, whether it be founded in the Fourteenth Amendment's concept of personal liberty and restrictions upon state action, as we feel it is, or, as the District Court determined, in the Ninth Amendment's reservation of rights to the people, is broad enough to encompass a woman's decision whether or not to terminate her pregnancy."[123] The reasons the court goes on to give include the decision to have a pregnancy, reasons which also easily apply to contraception. In his court opinion, Justice Blackmun continues,

> Specific and direct harm medically diagnosable even in early pregnancy may be involved. Maternity, or additional offspring, may force upon the woman a distressful life and future. Psychological harm may be imminent. Mental and physical health may be taxed by child care. There is also the distress, for all concerned, associated with the unwanted child, and there is the problem of bringing a child into a family already unable, psychologically and otherwise, to care for it. In other cases, as in this one, the additional difficulties and continuing stigma of unwed motherhood may be involved. All these are factors the woman and her responsible physician necessarily will consider in consultation.[124]

That is, a Fourteenth Amendment right to liberty, which encompasses privacy, extends to decisions of reproductive choice. Medical harm, as well as the right to make intimate choices about the direction of one's own life protect these features. Denial of a right to contraception, then, is a much graver issue than previously determined. Even if one rejects the international courts and United Nations stipulations of rights to health care, an American right to liberty and privacy still protect contraception in this case.

A range of different philosophers discussing the issues concur that reproductive rights are central to the direction of our lives and of intimate importance in our personal lives. For example, Ronald Dworkin argues in *Life's Dominion,* that, "The principle of procreative autonomy, in a broad sense, is embedded in any genuinely democratic culture."[125] Similarly, O'Neill argues that,

> In this way of thinking, reproductive or procreative autonomy is on a par with freedom of thought and conscience, and of equally profound importance. If our reproductive decisions express our deepest sense of who and what we are, then the way is seemingly open for arguing that reproductive autonomy must be more than a right to accept or refuse reproductive treatments and technologies others

> offer, and that it must include a wide right to self-determination and self-expression in reproductive matters.[126]

In other words, O'Neill argues that the right to reproductive choice is embedded in a broader right for freedom of thought and that self-determination in these matters must therefore be respected.

So far, I have considered whether health-care access is a right and argued that under any major conception of rights, it is. But being a rights theorist is not required to understand and defend this point. Even those who reject rights theory can plausibly still accept the conclusions of this section. If, instead of defending a right to health care, we interpret this claim as merely the overarching and strong fundamental obligations to provide health care from a moral perspective absent any subscription to rights, we can still gain the support of other views.

For example, a capabilities approach is opposed to rights approaches in major part because traditional conceptions of rights have made just this distinction between positive and negative rights, a distinction that focuses on negative liberty to the detriment of women.[127] Rights approaches also tend to ignore the home, and are sometimes specifically designed to ignore "private realms" where men are the master of their domain, causing the proliferation of domestic violence and the lack of bodily integrity for women.[128] If we reject rights in favor of capabilities, however, in part because rights fail to adequately protect women's interests, we are not thereby rejecting the great moral import of health care. In fact, Nussbaum specifically highlights the value of reproductive health in her list of capabilities.[129] Other capabilities theorists like Sen also highlight the value of health, especially within the family.[130] Thus, a rejection of rights theory in favor of the capabilities approach does not remove or lessen the value of health-care access.

Similarly, utilitarian theories that reject rights still place a great emphasis on health, as discussed in chapter 2. For example, Peter Singer argues as much, making universal access to health care a major tenet of his views.[131] And, since population control is arguably connected to hunger and poverty relief, Singer would also be committed to birth control access, as he makes clear in his writings.[132]

While not exhaustive, the point of this section is to demonstrate that rights theories commit us to protection of birth control access. But further, no prior theoretical commitments are required to understand a basic and foundational interest of overarching value in access to contraception. Rights theorists, those who oppose rights, utilitarians, and capabilities approaches alike can understand and support those claims.

CONCLUSION

Just as good moral philosophy needs science, medicine, and clear empirical evidence to identify and articulate major social problems, good science and medicine need moral philosophy. The argument of this chapter is that becoming a good doctor and a good scientist requires an understanding of the moral features of the case. Doctors cannot meet the needs of a patient without understanding their values and interests. In fact, they can do grave harm to their patients without this knowledge, violating their very role as physicians. Science can uncover valuable connections between contraception and other conditions, but it can neither pursue answers to questions that will help people nor apply the results of its advances without the use of moral philosophy. Tying birth control to Pap tests fails compliance with influential concepts of medical ethics; it also violates human rights. In this chapter, I fill the gap in the literature surrounding doctor-reliant access to contraception by offering the moral treatment required to settle significant and influential patient interests and needs.

NOTES

1. It is beyond the scope of this chapter to give an exhaustive account of what every moral theory has to say about the practice. In fact, my aim is not even to give an account of the representative theories in bioethics, nor every issue that arises in medical professionalism. For example, I do not consider how the practice may be in violation of virtue ethics or care ethics, though I also do not think that these moral theories would permit the practice. Edmund D. Pellegrino, "Professing Medicine, Virtue Based Ethics, and the Retrieval of Professionalism," in *Working Virtue: Virtue Ethics and Contemporary Moral Problems*, ed. Rebecca L. Walker and Philip J. Ivanhoe (Clarendon Press, 2007), 70. Dorene F. Balmer et al., "Caring to Care: Applying Noddings' Philosophy to Medical Education," *Academic Medicine* 91, no. 12 (December 2016): 1621, https://doi.org/10.1097/ACM.0000000000001207; Margaret A.

McLaren, "Feminist Ethics: Care as a Virtue," in *Feminists Doing Ethics*, ed. Peggy DesAutels and JoAnne Waugh (Rowman & Littlefield, 2001), 112.

2. Carolyn McLeod, "How to Distinguish Autonomy from Integrity," *Canadian Journal of Philosophy* 35, no. 1 (March 2005): 108.

3. Susan Sherwin, "A Relational Approach to Autonomy in Health Care," in *Politics Of Women's Health: Exploring Agency and Autonomy* (Philadelphia: Temple University Press, 1998), 33; Krista K. Thomason, "Shame and Contempt in Kant's Moral Theory," *Kantian Review* 18, no. 2 (July 2013): 223, https://doi.org/10.1017/S136941541300006X.

4. Berit Brogaard, "Sex By Deception," in *Oxford Handbook of Moral Psychology*, ed. John Doris and Manuel Vargas (Oxford University Press, Forthcoming).

5. Immanuel Kant, *Kant: Groundwork of the Metaphysics of Morals*, ed. Mary Gregor (Cambridge University Press, 1998), 43.

6. Harry G. Frankfurt, *Necessity, Volition, and Love* (Cambridge, U.K.; New York: Cambridge University Press, 1998), 130. I thank Krista Thomason for input on this section.

7. Amy Gutmann, *Liberal Equality* (CUP Archive, 1980), 33.

8. T. F. Ackerman, "Why Doctors Should Intervene," *Hastings Center Report* 12, no. 4 (August 1982): 14–17.

9. Tracy Isaacs, "Feminism and Agency," *Canadian Journal of Philosophy* 32, no. sup1 (January 2002): 129–54, https://doi.org/10.1080/00455091.2002.10717585.

10. Robert A. Burt and Dax Cowart, "Confronting Death: Who Chooses? Who Controls? A Dialogue between Dax Cowart and Robert Burt," *Yale Law School Faculty Scholarship Series* 706 (January 1, 1998): 17, https://pdfs.semanticscholar.org/d478/88dce40390296abca7c13d6f9e0aec304264.pdf.

11. Burt and Cowart, 17.

12. John Stuart Mill, *On Liberty*, ed. Elizabeth Rapaport (Hackett Pub Co, 1978), 64.

13. John Stuart Mill, *On Liberty*, 54.

14. John Stuart Mill, *On Liberty*, 56.

15. Onora O'Neill, "Paternalism and Partial Autonomy," *Journal of Medical Ethics* 10 (1984): 173.

16. Mill may have a more robust conception of autonomy here than I allow. I thank Eric Brown for this point. In that case, his argument would be more relevant as an ideal than a standard.

17. Note also J. David Velleman, "A Right of Self-Termination?," *Ethics* 109, no. 3 (1999): 608, https://doi.org/10.1086/233924.

18. This point may be difficult for doctors to accept even if the realm of patient autonomy is relatively narrow, such as refusing medical intervention.

For example, patients may not permissibly demand doctors fulfill their every wish, and we need not argue that a robust conception of autonomy require deference in all cases. For example, the competency at issue in many notions of autonomy may include a reasonable person standard which attends to medical knowledge and expertise. One way I can sidestep the conflict between medical expertise and patient autonomy is by relying on instances of doctors violating the scientific evidence and the standard of care, which is the focus of most of the case studies in this book.

19. Of course, Mill's analysis of autonomy in a consequentialist theory is not without its detractors. According to O'Neill, the evidence for Mill's position is lacking, not in the least because some patients do not want full control over their choices. O'Neill, "Paternalism and Partial Autonomy." For ways that doctors can support the autonomy of patients even where they meet with resistance to full decision-making control, see the discussion of Emanuel and Emanuel below. Furthermore, a utilitarian framework like Mill's cannot universally defend autonomy in all cases, since, if a situation arises in which it maximizes utility in the aggregate to violate autonomy a utilitarian will defend the violation. David Lyons, *Forms and Limits of Utilitarianism* (Clarendon Press, 1965).

20. Ronald Dworkin et al., "Assisted Suicide: The Philosophers' Brief," *The New York Review of Books*, March 27, 1997, 41–47.

21. Bonnie Steinbock, "The Intentional Termination of Life," *Ethics in Science & Medicine* 6, no. 1 (1979): 59–64.

22. Susan Sherwin, *No Longer Patient: Feminist Ethics and Health Care* (Temple University Press, 1992).

23. Sherwin, 148.

24. Sherwin, 240.

25. Sherwin, 140.

26. Ackerman, "Why Doctors Should Intervene."

27. Martha C. Nussbaum, *Sex and Social Justice* (Oxford New York Athens: Oxford University Press, 2000), 152; Isaacs, "Feminism and Agency," 132; Shay Welch, *Existential Eroticism: A Feminist Approach to Understanding Women's Oppression-Perpetuating Choices* (Lexington Books, 2017), 42; Ann E. Cudd, "The Paradox of Liberal Feminism: Preference, Rationality, and Oppression," in *Varieties of Feminist Liberalism*, ed. Amy R. Baehr and Anita Allen (Rowman & Littlefield Publishers, 2004), 37–61.

28. Nussbaum, *Sex and Social Justice*, 151.

29. Donald Cowart et al., *Dax's Case* (New York: Filmakers Library, 1984).

30. Sherwin, *No Longer Patient*, 143.

31. Sue Fisher, *In the Patient's Best Interest: Women and the Politics of Medical Decisions* (Rutgers University Press, 1986), 3.

32. Sherwin, *No Longer Patient*, 143.

33. In his refutation of paternalism, Alan Goldman makes a case for this difference in values between doctors and patients, pointing out that while to doctors, health and life have utmost value, most individuals place value on other considerations, as evidenced by risky behavior and even on federal budget spending, which allocate funds to pursuits beyond health. Alan H. Goldman, *The Moral Foundations of Professional Ethics* (Rowman & Littlefield Pub Incorporated, 1980), 180.

34. Julius M. Moravcsik, "The Role of Virtue in Alternatives to Kantian and Utilitarian Ethics," *Philosophia* 20, no. 1–2 (July 1990): 33–48, https://doi.org/10.1007/BF02382583; Jeremy Bentham, *The Collected Works of Jeremy Bentham: An Introduction to the Principles of Morals and Legislation* (Clarendon Press, 1996).

35. I take up opposition to vaccines in chapter 8.

36. Though it is questionable whether quarantining an individual counts as a medical intervention, since it is not technically a treatment.

37. Shayna D. Cunningham et al., "Relationships Between Perceived STD-Related Stigma, STD-Related Shame and STD Screening Among a Household Sample of Adolescents," *Perspectives on Sexual and Reproductive Health* 41, no. 4 (December 2009): 225–30, https://doi.org/10.1363/4122509; Jessica L. Morris et al., "Sexually Transmitted Infection Related Stigma and Shame Among African American Male Youth: Implications for Testing Practices, Partner Notification, and Treatment," *AIDS Patient Care and STDs* 28, no. 9 (September 1, 2014): 499–506, https://doi.org/10.1089/apc.2013.0316.

38. Sarah Conly, *Against Autonomy: Justifying Coercive Paternalism* (Cambridge University Press, 2013).

39. Sherwin, for one, denies the either/or fallacy of paternalism versus autonomy. Sherwin, *No Longer Patient*, 140.

40. Isaacs, "Feminism and Agency," 139.

41. Corliss, "New Mammography Guidelines Call for Starting Later and Screening Less Often - Harvard Health Blog," Harvard Health Publishing, October 21, 2015. https://www.health.harvard.edu/blog/new-mammography-guidelines-call-for-starting-later-and-screening-less-often-201510218466. I discuss this further in chapter 8.

42. Neighmond, "The Hidden Cost Of Mammograms: More Testing And Overtreatment," NPR.org, April 13, 2015, sec. Morning Edition. http://www.npr.org/sections/health-shots/2015/04/13/398818949/the-hidden-cost-of-mammograms-more-testing-and-overtreatment.

43. Centers for Disease Control and Prevention, "Heart Disease Facts & Statistics" August 24, 2017, https://www.cdc.gov/heartdisease/facts.htm. I discuss this point further in chapter 8.

44. Sabrina Tavernise, "Maternal Mortality Rate in U.S. Rises, Defying Global Trend, Study Finds," *The New York Times*, September 21, 2016, http://www.nytimes.com/2016/09/22/health/maternal-mortality.html; Nina Martin and Renee Montagne, "U.S. Has The Worst Rate Of Maternal Deaths In The Developed World," NPR.org, May 12, 2017, http://www.npr.org/2017/05/12/528098789/u-s-has-the-worst-rate-of-maternal-deaths-in-the-developed-world. I discuss this point further in chapter 7.

45. O'Neill, "Paternalism and Partial Autonomy," 174.

46. Though note Devora Shapiro, "Should Pregnancy Be Considered a (Temporary) Disability?," *IJFAB: International Journal of Feminist Approaches to Bioethics* 11, no. 1 (February 2018): 91–105, https://doi.org/10.3138/ijfab.11.1.91.

47. O'Neill, "Paternalism and Partial Autonomy," 176.

48. Willy De Craemer, "A Cross-Cultural Perspective on Personhood," *The Milbank Memorial Fund Quarterly. Health and Society* 61, no. 1 (1983): 19–34, https://doi.org/10.2307/3349814.

49. De Craemer, 22.

50. De Craemer, 23.

51. Cleland, Ndugwa, and Zulu, "Family Planning in Sub-Saharan Africa: Progress or Stagnation?," World Health Organization, November 4, 2010, http://www.who.int/bulletin/volumes/89/2/10-077925/en/.

52. De Craemer, "A Cross-Cultural Perspective on Personhood," 24.

53. Cleland, Ndugwa, and Zulu, "Family Planning in Sub-Saharan Africa."

54. Martha C. Nussbaum, "Judging Other Cultures: The Case of Genital Mutilation," in *Sex & Social Justice* (New York: Oxford University Press, 1999), 118–29.

55. Cleland, Ndugwa, and Zulu, "Family Planning in Sub-Saharan Africa."

56. "Family Planning/Contraception," http://www.who.int/mediacentre/factsheets/fs351/en/.

57. "Family Planning/Contraception."

58. "Global Oral Contraception Availability," OCs OTC Working Group, August 1, 2019, http://ocsotc.org/wp-content/uploads/worldmap/world-map.html.

59. Goldman, *The Moral Foundations of Professional Ethics*, 161.

60. It is harder to suppose no harms attend birth control cessation, since by definition, it would increase the risk of pregnancy, which is harmful to those who do not want to get pregnant.

61. Julian Savulescu and Udo Schuklenk, "Doctors Have No Right to Refuse Medical Assistance in Dying, Abortion or Contraception," *Bioethics* 31, no. 3 (2017): 170, https://doi.org/10.1111/bioe.12288.

62. The reason why paternalism persists in some fields even where it is vilified in others is a topic I take on later in the book.

63. O'Neill, "Paternalism and Partial Autonomy," 174.

64. Dana Howard, "The Medical Surrogate as Fiduciary Agent," *The Journal of Law, Medicine & Ethics* 45, no. 3 (September 1, 2017): 402–20, https://doi.org/10.1177/1073110517737541.

65. O'Neill, "Paternalism and Partial Autonomy," 175.

66. O'Neill, 177. Elsewhere, O'Neill also allows for the limited role of paternalism. She states, "we can accept that medical paternalism has a limited, but indispensable, role in the treatment of those who are temporarily or permanently unable to consent or refuse, but not beyond." Onora O'Neill, *Autonomy and Trust in Bioethics* (Cambridge University Press, 2002), 152. But she also provides strong opposition to paternalism in broad strokes: "However, even if medical paternalism can benefit some patients, it is ethically unacceptable for two reasons. First, it unnecessarily gives professionals powers that can also be used to harm patients. Second, even the proper use of those powers—paternalists assume that they will only be properly used—requires and condones an unnecessary degree of coercion or deception." O'Neill, 151.

67. Ruth R. Faden, Tom L. Beauchamp, and Nancy M. P. King, *A History and Theory of Informed Consent*, 1 edition (New York: Oxford University Press, 1986).

68. "Permissible Medical Experiments," Trials of War Criminals before the Nuremberg Military Tribunals under Control Council Law (Washington, D.C.: U.S. Government Printing Office, 1949), https://history.nih.gov/research/downloads/nuremberg.pdf.

69. David P Gauthier, *Morals by Agreement* (Oxford: Clarendon Press, 1986), 26; Thomas Scanlon and Alford Professor of Natural Religion Moral Philosophy and Civil Polity T. M. Scanlon, *What We Owe to Each Other* (Harvard University Press, 1998), 153; Onora O'Neill, "Constructivism VS. Contractualism," *Ratio* 16, no. 4 (December 2003): 319–31, https://doi.org/10.1046/j.1467-9329.2003.00226.x.

70. Plato, *Plato: Five Dialogues* (Hackett Pub Co Inc, 1981), 51e; John Locke, *Second Treatise of Government*, ed. C. B. Macpherson (Indianapolis, Ind: Hackett Publishing Company, Inc., 1980), 13; Hanna Pitkin, "Obligation and Consent—I," *The American Political Science Review* 59, no. 4 (December 1, 1965): 990, https://doi.org/10.2307/1953218; John Rawls, *A Theory of Justice*, Rev. ed (Cambridge, Mass: Belknap Press of Harvard University Press, 1999), 302; Jean Hampton, *Hobbes and the Social Contract Tradition* (Cambridge University Press, 1988), 267; Larry May, *Crimes Against Humanity: A Normative Account* (Cambridge University Press, 2005), 44.

71. Amartya Kumar Sen, "Democracy as a Universal Value," *Journal of Democracy* 10, no. 3 (1999): 10, https://doi.org/10.1353/jod.1999.0055; David M. Estlund, *Democratic Authority: A Philosophical Framework* (Princeton, NJ: Princeton University Press, 2009), 117; Carole Pateman, *The Disorder of Women: Democracy, Feminism, and Political Theory* (Stanford University Press, 1989), 72.

72. "Contract," LII / Legal Information Institute, August 6, 2007, https://www.law.cornell.edu/wex/contract; Larry Alexander, "The Ontology of Consent," *Analytic Philosophy* 55, no. 1 (2014): 102–13, https://doi.org/10.1111/phib.12035.

73. Aristotle, *Nicomachean Ethics*, trans. Terence Irwin, 2nd ed. (Hackett Publishing Company Inc., 1999), 1127a–1127b; Heidi M. Hurd, "The Moral Magic of Consent," *Legal Theory* 2, no. 2 (June 1996): 121–46, https://doi.org/10.1017/S1352325200000434.

74. Brake defends the view that wedding vows rely on love and spousal roles but describes marriage and promising in Elizabeth Brake, *The Marriage Promise: Is Divorce Promise-Breaking?* (Oxford University Press, 2012), 24, https://www.oxfordscholarship.com/view/10.1093/acprof:oso/9780199774142.001.0001/acprof-9780199774142-chapter-2.

75. "Sexual Offense Prevention Policy (SOPP) & Title IX," *Antioch College* (blog), 1991, https://antiochcollege.edu/campus-life/sexual-offense-prevention-policy-title-ix.

76. Alec Buchanan, "Mental Capacity, Legal Competence and Consent to Treatment," *Journal of the Royal Society of Medicine* 97, no. 9 (September 2004): 415–20.

77. The practice also upsets the doctor-patient relationship, leading to abuse or neglect and undermining trust, discussed below.

78. Jay Katz, "Informed Consent—Must It Remain a Fairy Tale?" *Journal of Contemporary Health Law and Policy* 10 (1994): 69.

79. Susan Cullen and Margaret Klein, "Respect for Patients, Physicians, and the Truth," in *Intervention and Reflection: Basic Issues in Medical Ethics*, ed. Ronald Munson, 8 edition (Belmont, CA: Cengage Learning, 2007), 157.

80. Cullen and Klein, 155.

81. Douglas S. Diekema, "Parental Refusals of Medical Treatment: The Harm Principle as Threshold for State Intervention," *Theoretical Medicine and Bioethics* 25, no. 4 (2004): 243–64.

82. Margaret Sanger, *The Autobiography of Margaret Sanger*, Dover Ed edition (Mineola, New York: Dover Publications, 2004), 212.

83. For a discussion of Plato in this context, see Emanuel and Emanuel, "Four Models of the Physician-Patient Relationship."

84. Plato and John M. Cooper, *Complete Works*, ed. D. S. Hutchinson (Hackett Publishing Company Inc., 1997).

85. Ezekiel J. Emanuel and Linda L. Emanuel, "Four Models of the Physician-Patient Relationship," *The Journal of the American Medical Association* 267, no. 16 (April 22, 1992), http://www.antoniocasella.eu/salute/Emanuel_1992.pdf.

86. Emanuel and Emanuel, 2221.

87. Emanuel and Emanuel, 2221.

88. Emanuel and Emanuel, 2224.

89. Emanuel and Emanuel, 2221.

90. Emanuel and Emanuel, 2221.

91. Emanuel and Emanuel, 2221.

92. Emanuel and Emanuel, 2222.

93. Emanuel and Emanuel, 2222.

94. Emanuel and Emanuel, 2225.

95. Ackerman, "Why Doctors Should Intervene."

96. Loretta Ross and Rickie Solinger, *Reproductive Justice: An Introduction*, First edition (Oakland, California: University of California Press, 2017), 117.

97. General Assembly U.N., "Universal Declaration of Human Rights," December 10, 1948, http://www.unhcr.org/refworld/docid/3ae6b3712c.html. Article 25 reads in full: "(1) Everyone has the right to a standard of living adequate for the health and well-being of himself and of his family, including food, clothing, housing and medical care and necessary social services, and the right to security in the event of unemployment, sickness, disability, widowhood, old age or other lack of livelihood in circumstances beyond his control.(2) Motherhood and childhood are entitled to special care and assistance. All children, whether born in or out of wedlock, shall enjoy the same social protection."

98. Article 12, Section 1 of the United Nations International Covenant on Economic, Social, and Cultural Rights states: "The States Parties to the present Covenant recognize the right of everyone to the enjoyment of the highest attainable standard of physical and mental health." "International Covenant on Economic, Social and Cultural Rights," January 3, 1976, http://www.ohchr.org/EN/ProfessionalInterest/Pages/CESCR.aspx.

99. Article 25 states in part, that

> States Parties recognize that persons with disabilities have the right to the enjoyment of the highest attainable standard of health without discrimination on the basis of disability. States Parties shall take all appropriate measures to ensure access for persons with disabilities to

> health services that are gender-sensitive, including health-related rehabilitation. In particular, States Parties shall:
>
> 1. Provide persons with disabilities with the same range, quality and standard of free or affordable health care and programmes as provided to other persons, including in the area of sexual and reproductive health and population-based public health programmes. . .

Aart Hendricks, "UN Convention on the Rights of Persons with Disabilities," *Eur. J. Health L.* 14 (2007): 273.

100. "International Convention on the Elimination of All Forms of Racial Discrimination," January 4, 1969, http://www.ohchr.org/EN/ProfessionalInterest/Pages/CERD.aspx.

101. Article 12 states that:

> 1. States Parties shall take all appropriate measures to eliminate discrimination against women in the field of health care in order to ensure, on a basis of equality of men and women, access to health care services, including those related to family planning.
> 2. Notwithstanding the provisions of paragraph I of this article, States Parties shall ensure to women appropriate services in connection with pregnancy, confinement and the post-natal period, granting free services where necessary, as well as adequate nutrition during pregnancy and lactation.

Convention on the Elimination of All Forms of Discrimination against Women. December 18, 1979. https://www.ohchr.org/en/professionalinterest/pages/cedaw.aspx

102. Norman Daniels, "Health-Care Needs and Distributive Justice," *Philosophy & Public Affairs* 10, no. 2 (1981): 146–79. Maslow's hierarchy of needs also reflects this point, since physiological needs are at the bottom of the pyramid and must be met first before self-actualization can be achieved. A. H. Maslow, "A Theory of Human Motivation," *Psychological Review* 50, no. 4 (1948): 370–96.

103. Daniels, "Health-Care Needs and Distributive Justice," 154.

104. Daniels, 159.

105. Norman Daniels, "Justice, Health, and Healthcare," *American Journal of Bioethics* 1, no. 2 (2001): 3.

106. Sen, "Democracy as a Universal Value."

107. Daniels, "Health-Care Needs and Distributive Justice," 161.

108. Daniels, "Justice, Health, and Healthcare," 4.

109. H. Tristram Engelhardt, Jr., "Rights to Health Care, Social Justice, and Fairness in Health Care Allocations: Frustrations in the Face of Finitude," in *The Foundations of Bioethics* (Oxford University Press, USA, 1996), 375–410.

110. Martha C. Nussbaum, "Capabilities and Social Justice," *International Studies Review* 4, no. 2 (2002): 128.

111. For example, Thomas Jefferson argues that, "The basis of our governments being the opinion of the people, the very first object should be to keep that right; and were it left to me to decide whether we should have a government without newspapers or newspapers without a government, I should not hesitate a moment to prefer the latter. But I should mean that every man should receive those papers & be capable of reading them." Thomas Jefferson, "Thomas Jefferson to Edward Carrington," January 16, 1787.

112. In fact, the distinction between acts and omissions is itself plausibly questioned as lacking moral merit. James Rachels, "Active and Passive Euthanasia," *Bioethics: An Introduction to the History, Methods, and Practice*, 1975, 77–82.

113. Henry Shue, *Basic Rights: Subsistence, Affluence, and U.S. Foreign Policy* (Princeton University Press, 1996), 37.

114. Shue, 37.

115. Shue, 39.

116. Nussbaum, "Capabilities and Social Justice," 128.

117. Judith Jarvis Thomson, "A Defense of Abortion," *Philosophy & Public Affairs* 1, no. 1 (Fall 1997): 47–66.

118. Christine Overall, *Why Have Children?: The Ethical Debate*, Basic Bioethics (Cambridge, Mass: MIT Press, 2012), 19–20.

119. Allen Buchanan et al., *From Chance to Choice: Genetics and Justice* (Cambridge: Cambridge University Press, 2001), 213.

120. Griswold v. Connecticut, United States (Supreme Court 1965); Eisenstadt v. Baird, United States (Supreme Court 1972); Roe v. Wade, 410 United States 113 (Supreme Court 1973).

121. Union Pacific R. Co. v. Botsford, 141 United States (Supreme Court 1891).

122. Griswold v. Connecticut, United States; Eisenstadt v. Baird, United States.

123. Roe v. Wade, 410 United States.

124. Roe v. Wade, 410 United States.

125. Ronald Dworkin, *Life's Dominion: An Argument About Abortion, Euthanasia, and Individual Freedom* (Knopf Doubleday Publishing Group, 2011), 167.

126. O'Neill, *Autonomy and Trust in Bioethics*, 56.

127. Nussbaum, "Capabilities and Social Justice," 128.

128. Nussbaum, "Capabilities and Social Justice"; Charlotte Bunch, "Women's Rights as Human Rights: Toward a Re-Vision of Human Rights," *Human Rights Quarterly* 12, no. 4 (November 1, 1990): 486–98, https://doi.org/10.2307/762496.

129. Martha C. Nussbaum, "Capabilities and Human Rights," in *Global Justice and Transnational Politics: Essays on the Moral and Political Challenges of Globalization*, ed. Pablo De Greiff and Ciaran Cronin, Studies in Contemporary German Social Thought (Cambridge, Mass: MIT Press, 2002).

130. Amartya Kumar Sen, "Development as Capability Expansion," *The Community Development Reader, 2nd Ed.; DeFilippis, J., Saeger, S., Eds*, 1990, 319–327.

131. Peter Singer, *The Life You Can Save: Acting Now to End World Poverty* (Random House Publishing Group, 2009); Peter Singer, "Why We Must Ration Health Care," *The New York Times*, July 19, 2009, http://www.nytimes.com/2009/07/19/magazine/19healthcare-t.html?pagewanted=all; Peter Singer, *Animal Liberation* (Random House, 2015).

132. Peter Singer, "Famine, Affluence, and Morality," *Philosophy and Public Affairs* 1, no. 1 (Spring 1972): 229–43.

5

FERTILE GROUND FOR BIAS

Medical Sexism Explains the Practice

In this chapter, I argue that medical sexism explains, but does not justify the practice of withholding birth control to ensure patients undergo needed tests. If I am right in chapter 1 that the practice exists, in chapter 2 that it causes physical harm to patients, in chapter 3 that it violates contemporary American law, and in chapter 4 that it violates a wide range of moral precepts, the question remains as to why it persists. Why does it occur at such a high frequency, and why has it persisted for so long after it was generally known that the practice was harmful and violated basic principles in science and morality? We need to know the answer to these questions because understanding the causes of an unjust practice are the first step towards eliminating it. Angela Davis states that, "Birth control—individual choice, safe contraceptive methods, as well as abortion when necessary—is a fundamental prerequisite for the emancipation of women."[1] If birth control access is required for emancipating women, what of birth control denials?

Without understanding the causes of an unjust practice, responses would likely be inefficient, ineffective, and inadequate. They would be inefficient, since responses would likely spend time and effort on misguided activities; they would be ineffective, since the underlying cause could emerge again in a different area creating more injustice; and they would be inadequate, since responses would address the symptoms alone. Correctly identifying the aim of our efforts is crucial toward progress in part because convincing the perpetrators of these harms to change their ways requires identifying what compels them to do it.

Why, then, do doctors act paternalistically in this arena when their patients often explicitly and vocally protest their methods? Paternalism is on its way towards eradication from the field; even where it persists doctors generally do not openly subscribe to it. Doctors generally do not admit to, nor would they want to admit to forcing patients to undergo procedures they do not want.[2] However, for some reason, paternalism survives particularly in areas traditionally conceived of as "women's health."[3] I argue this fact is not an accident. Paternalism is the expected response to patients who are not thought to be fully autonomous, who need others to look out for their best interests, or who are infantilized in significant ways, as the patients of obstetrics and gynecology often are. As a result, it is no surprise that paternalism persists in this area while it is more often condemned elsewhere in the medical field.

In this chapter, I also consider alternative explanations for the practice. For example, perhaps the financial rewards of requiring extra appointments explain why doctors engage in this practice.[4] Maybe doctors are not sexist but rather just want more money.[5] However, I ultimately find these explanations lacking. If financial reasons were the explanation, these practices would arise equally in all areas of medicine. Instead, no significant reports exist of doctors withholding, for example, Viagra prescription refills until patients undergo colonoscopies.[6] Even if financial considerations did weigh into the practice, medical sexism could also figure in causally. In fact, medical sexism may be what permits doctors to use the avenue of financial exploitation, just as other marginalized communities could be more easily exploited financially.[7] Medical sexism can still be a cause even if such other factors also contribute.

WHAT IS MEDICAL SEXISM?

In this book, I apply the term "medical sexism" to the phenomena I describe. To properly argue that the practice falls under the category of medical sexism, I first need to identify what I mean by the term.[8] Since there are a variety of types of sexism, including oppositional sexism and cissexism, it is useful to focus on what is sometimes referred to as "traditional sexism." Marilyn Frye's claim of a "culture which exists[s] to support a morally and scientifically insupportable system of dominance and subordination" is compatible with my view.[9] Broadly speaking, traditional sexism consists in a hierarchy[10] of maleness or masculinity over femaleness or femininity.[11] Medical sexism, then, narrows the scope to focus on the medical context. Thus, medical sexism consists in the hierarchy of maleness or masculinity over femaleness or femininity in the medical context. For example, medical sexism uses medical means or medical ends to uphold, assert, or achieve that hierarchy.

In her book, *Whipping Girl: A Transsexual Woman on Sexism and the Scapegoating of Femininity*, Julia Serano defines traditional sexism as the *belief* in this hierarchy.[12] For the purposes of this chapter, I abstract away from this more narrow definition because I aim to include impacts, behavior, systems, and institutions, which are in line with this hierarchy but fall short of beliefs or the individuals who hold them. That inclusion of systems and institutions is especially relevant if, as Marilyn Frye argues, "the locus of sexism is primarily in the system or framework, not in the particular act."[13] For example, an organization that, as a whole, pays work associated with women and femininity less than comparable work associated with men and masculinity may employ a large proportion of people who do not literally believe that femaleness and femininity are inferior to maleness and masculinity. But they may nevertheless contribute to, support, or otherwise take part in work and decisions which negatively impact women for morally arbitrary reasons. That is, institutional sexism may pervade organizations even where no individuals are themselves sexist. Yet, to adequately respond to the injustices I tackle in this book, we need to include this institutional hierarchy and not just individual action.

In addition, implicit bias may lead to individuals making decisions or engaging in microagressions that are sexist without explicitly or self-consciously being committed to sexist beliefs.[14] This definition, then, allows for both institutional and implicit bias. The definition I rely on also makes space for other intersecting areas of oppression, such as classism and racism that women face, many of which they face qua women. After all, the hierarchy of maleness or masculinity over femaleness or femininity can overlap and intersect with other significant and influential hierarchies that play a large role in individuals' lives.[15]

This definition is also broader than an approach to medical sexism that focuses only on oppression or discrimination. Defining sexism as oppression directed toward people who are, appear to be, or have attributes associated with women includes a variety of unjust treatment and discrimination, but does not include other cases that fall under the umbrella of medical sexism on my definition, such as sexist attitudes, beliefs, tendencies, comments, and microaggressions that may fall short of behavior, discrimination, and control. Furthermore, the same action (denying a patient access to birth control without added tests) might be oppressive to some (for whom the added tests are outside of their reach) while relatively inconsequential for others (for whom the added tests are valuable and easily met).

This feature of the definition also opens the way for intersectionality, since at least in some cases, a person's sex or gender alone may be insufficient to explain unjust treatment, even though when combined with other hierarchies like racism, classism, ageism, ableism, or anti-Semitism, it together creates or highlights features of sexism.[16] In reality, for this reason, creating stark divisions between different hierarchies can leave some forms of injustice unaddressed or unnoticed.[17] The myth of "the Jewish mother" is an example of this phenomenon. In one description, "The Jewish mother stereotype isn't pretty. It depicts someone needy, neurotic, clingy—a guilt-shooting laser whose entire identity comes from her children . . . as suffocating, whining, melodramatic, demanding grief givers."[18] The image, used to belittle and ignore Jewish women, cannot exist without an understanding of intersecting identities because Jewish men are not subject to the same stereotype nor are all women. Similarly, women of different races are not subject to the same stereotypes, suggesting that race has a central role in hierarchies; men and women of the same race are not subject to the same stereotypes, suggesting that sex is also necessary for a complete understanding of hierarchies.[19] Furthermore, these groupings are not static or complete. Patricia Hill Collins points out that, "Depending on the context, individuals and groups may be alternately oppressors in some settings, oppressed in others, or simultaneously oppressing and oppressed in still others."[20] Because more than one hierarchy influences our lives, and these hierarchies are overlapping and mutually influential, these results would not be surprising. That our identities can be complex in this way also highlights the problems with being forced to place one identity over another.

Can the definition be criticized on these grounds, if I am wrong to separate femaleness and femininity from other forms of oppression at all?[21] Arguably there is some value in defining sexism alongside other sorts of hierarchies like classism and racism instead of grouping them together in a single unified whole. After all, a black woman may be subjected to forms of discrimination that follow her no matter what her class or level of wealth, making the distinction between class and race valuable, while a trans woman may be subject to certain forms of discrimination that a cis woman is not, making the distinction between cissexism and traditional sexism helpful. Thus, I aim for a definition of medical sexism that can be used to advance intersectional feminism without collapsing all forms of oppression.

However, the definition I use for this purpose also differs from some definitions. For example, Barbara Smith states that,

> The reason racism is a feminist issue is easily explained by the inherent definition of feminism. Feminism is the political theory and practice that struggles to free *all* women: women of color, working-class women, poor women, disabled women, Jewish women, lesbians, old women—as well as white, economically privileged, heterosexual women. Anything less than this vision of total freedom is not feminism, but merely female self-aggrandizement.[22]

While I agree with Smith that feminism must include the groups of women she discusses, for the purposes of this chapter, I use a broader definition. If sexism can have effects that reach people who are not women, feminism must also address these issues. For example, a boy who is bullied for perceived feminine traits may be the subject of sexism, since what he suffers from is the hierarchy of masculinity over femininity, despite being male.[23] My definition of sexism, then, is meant to include all the women Smith recognizes in an intersectional fashion while also acknowledging that men can be subject to constraints of sexism.

The purpose of defining medical sexism is to consider whether the practice in question of restrictive contraceptive care is medical sexism. Some doctors may not hold sexist attitudes and may even disagree with the practice, but feel forced into it due to broader expectations in their fields or offices. But beliefs are not required for the attribution of medical sexism. Other doctors may not be operating under institutional sexism, and may not hold sexist attitudes or beliefs, but may implicitly follow the practice or accept the practice due to implicit bias. Still other doctors may explicitly hold sexist attitudes or beliefs, but not recognize them and fail to identify as sexist themselves. They might tolerate the practice where they would not tolerate other similar denials of health care to patients because of this sexism, without recognizing it as such. That does not mean the implications of their actions and expectations are any less a case of medical sexism for the patients in question. The actions of doctors who harbor no sexism can have unequal and unfair implications for their patients.

In addition, the consequences of the behavior have differential impacts on differing populations, making it difficult to identify a single oppressive result. Furthermore, the mindset of the doctor is both impossible to discern and of dubious influence over the medical sexism of the actions, complicating matters. Another layer for this discussion is that, as a result of all these previous difficulties, telling an accurate causal story is problematic, meaning that medical sexism will not be the only plausible explanation of the phenomenon. So, even if we could agree on a definition of medical sexism, and understand the consequences and intentions of the act accurately and consistently, we may still have difficulty attributing any particular instance as medically sexist.

Evaluating the phenomenon in question to determine whether it is medical sexism is controversial. The definition of medical sexism itself is debatable, making the attribution of the charge subject to disagreement. Ultimately, it is incredibly difficult to prove the charge of medical sexism. However, given the definition I defend, the standard excuses do not lessen its application. Is medical sexism a plausible interpretation of the practice, given the definition above and with the understanding of the practice from chapters 1–4? In the next section, I argue that medical sexism does explain the practice.

MEDICAL SEXISM EXPLAINS THE PRACTICE

When doctors require patients to undergo pelvic exams or Pap tests before they will release a birth control prescription, I argue that medical sexism is a successful explanation their actions and the best explanation. First, as discussed in chapter 1, the practice is routine.[24] Furthermore, a disconnect between what the medical field endorses and what doctors actually do in practice shows that doctors are diverging from the scientific consensus, leaving value-laden reasons as a possible explanation. Doctor beliefs are known to influence treatment in a variety of care options for women.[25]

Second, as argued in chapters 1 and 2, the practice does patients identifiable and demonstrable harm. And, as discussed in those chapters, doctors may know that they are causing their patients harm, as that knowledge is central to the motivation for the practice. If and to the extent that doctors engage in a practice that predictably increases the risks of harms to patients and do so because it has this result, they are not acting paternalistically. Doctors may be making trade-offs with the patient's health, even though those tradeoffs are not theirs to make. That is, because they think that the risk of harm will achieve good results, their motivations also include elements of paternalism despite not acting in the patient's best interest.

So, doctors deny patients access to a central medical need, and may do so purposefully. That leads to the arguments in chapter 3: doctors violate the law when doing so because they engage in medical malpractice. This legal interpretation means they are putting their very practices, roles, and integrity on the line just so they can deny a few patients access to needed medical care. A lot is at stake here.

Chapter 4 amplifies these issues by bringing them beyond a legal context to a moral one. I argue there that the harms of engaging in the practice far exceed any specific physical result discussed in chapter 2 because doctors deny their patients autonomy when they engage in the practice, act paternalistically, fail to obtain informed consent, and commit a variety of rights violations. If you deny patients their autonomy and make a medical decision on their behalf against the patients' wills, and those decisions turn out well for the patients in terms of physical health, then you can plausibly make the claim that you have caused no physical harm while nevertheless causing real moral wrong worth considering.

Using the understanding of chapters 1–4, I argue that a hierarchy is occurring here, placing some patients in a lower status. This lower status makes them more vulnerable to harm, gives them less protection of the law, and allows them less ability to fulfill their preferences than other patients similarly situated. While patients are already in a vulnerable position, this practice lowers their overall power and puts more obstacles in their way. The group of patients affected is significant considering these points.

So far, in chapters 1–4, I have described the group of patients affected in gender-neutral ways, because the practice affects a variety of different people regardless of their gender. Not all women need birth control. Some are not sexually active, some are trying to get pregnant, some are already pregnant, some have no underlying medical issues to address, and some cannot get pregnant. Not all people who need birth control are women. Some are young girls. Some are adult men. For example, a trans man, especially one who is not seeking a medical transition, may be in need of birth control at various times throughout his life. Some are intersex. For example, someone with Swyer syndrome might need the hormones in birth control without needing its contraceptive properties.[26] Some people who need birth control might be without gender. For example, someone who has a uterus and is genderless might need birth control.[27] Some people needing birth control may have two or more genders. For example, someone bigender, trigender, or pangender and who has particular hormonal or contraceptive needs might require a doctor's prescription for birth control.

If not all women need birth control, and not all people needing birth control are women, meaning womanhood is neither necessary nor sufficient for this medical need, then why think it relates to sexism at all? As established above, an action can be sexist without being directed to a woman. What is required instead is a systemic, institutional hierarchy that lowers the relative status of femaleness or femininity. One feature of the definition of medical sexism above is that it does not define sexism as directed solely at women and does not use the term "woman."[28] Since anyone or anything can exhibit femaleness or femininity, this definition highlights implications such as that some men may be the targets of sexism, some women may be the recipients of privilege, some people who are nonbinary may be targeted for resisting classification in the hierarchy, and some people may experience prejudice and privilege to varying degrees in various medical contexts, among other features. Relatedly, this definition does not describe femininity and masculinity as exhaustive, resisting a binary or oppositional description of the terms.

But that raises a further question: If some people who have the medical need of birth control are not female or feminine, such as someone who is not female or feminine and has a uterus, then how could sexism arise?

This question cuts to the heart of so much sexism in the world. When people in caregiving professions are discriminated against, underpaid, and face higher incidences of sexual assault and violence, why do some cry sexism? Not all caregivers are women and not all women are caregivers; being a woman is neither necessary nor sufficient for being a caregiver. Furthermore, there is nothing essentially female or feminine about caregiving professions like nurses or childcare professionals.[29] Nevertheless, caregiving professions are predominantly made up of women, and women sometimes are encouraged or even pressured into entering caregiving professions.[30] That relationship, even if it is socially constructed, is all that is needed to understand the connection between undervaluing caregiving and sexism.

In fact, if one thinks sex, gender, and professions as a whole, like nursing, are social constructs, there may not be anything essential about them. That does not mean social constructionists deny the existence of sexism in general. It just means they acknowledge that some characteristics, body parts, actions, clothing, and professions are associated with femaleness or femininity, despite not needing to be a woman to have or do or wear these things.[31] In a society where theoretical mathematics is associated with women's work, that profession might be underpaid and undervalued due to this association.[32] In a society where theoretical mathematics is associated with men's work, that profession might be overpaid and overvalued, due to this association.[33] Nothing about theoretical mathematics is gendered. But sex discrimination can still occur in this context through cultural associations.[34]

In this instance, instead of theoretical mathematics being culturally associated with one gender over another, a certain set of sexual anatomy is culturally associated with one gender over another and may therefore be the subject of sexism. Vulvas, vaginas, clitorises, cervixes, uteruses, fallopian tubes, ovaries, and other body parts are associated with femaleness or femininity culturally, and the people who have these body parts are often associated with women. As a result, the set of people seeking treatment and medical care from obstetricians and gynecologists are people associated with women, whether or not any one individual patient actually is a woman. For the purposes of sexism on my definition, it ultimately may not matter if the patients themselves are women if they are associated with women culturally.

This group of patients, whatever their sex or gender, faces injustices; this group of patients is associated with femaleness or femininity; and this group is predominantly made up of women. It is no surprise, then, in a culture where femaleness and femininity are placed below maleness and masculinity in a hierarchy, that this set of patients would face differential treatment, unjust behavior, and that when these wrongs do occur, that medical sexism occurs. It is not an accident that this set of patients receives treatment that ordinarily would be described as medical malpractice in any other context. Given the existence of sexism, this result could be expected. And, when this group of people are treated differently than other groups of patients, there is good reason to think that medical sexism is afoot.

If the injustice occurs and if it occurs in a way that affects people associated with femaleness or femininity, whether or not they are female or feminine, does the particular type of injustice occurring make sense as a sexist set of behaviors? Just looking at the context of chapter 3, this result may not be obvious. Medical malpractice occurs in a range of different contexts and for a range of different reasons. When it comes to medical negligence, mistakes and ignorance of doctors also come into play.[35] However, the specific type of medical malpractice occurring in this instance is not a simple issue of making a misdiagnosis or a mistake like a surgical error. The type of malpractice occurring is systematic and involves a combination of overtreatment, denial of treatment, and physical harm. Central to the malpractice occurring is the paternalistic attitudes of the doctors, which lead to overriding autonomy and violating informed consent. Why would doctors systematically override a whole set of patients' autonomy and treat them paternalistically? Answering that question without understanding that group of patients is associated with femaleness or femininity would be incomplete.

Thus, I argue that doctors are mistreating groups of patients who are already marginalized in society. They are not denying the autonomy of patients belonging to a privileged or dominant group; they are denying the autonomy of a group who is undervalued. And, given the track record of malpractice suits against doctors engaging in the practice—nonexistent—they are getting away with it every time they do it. Why are doctors able to treat patients paternalistically at such a high rate with no consequences or accountability? Why are doctors looking at a historically marginalized group and assuming they cannot make decisions for themselves or assuming they are not fully autonomous human beings?

At best, the practice in question infantilizes women and other patients associated with women, purporting to know what is best for them and choosing that course of action without their input. When one individual infantilizes another individual, it is difficult to conclude structural or systematic discrimination or oppression has occurred. But when doctors infantilize a group of patients who are predominantly women or associated with women, with no ramifications, sexism starts to look like a central feature of the practice, because discrimination is occurring and that discrimination is sex-based.[36]

But at worst, the practice seeks obedience over health outcomes and objectification over recognition of personhood. Since the understanding that yearly testing does not produce good health outcomes and sometimes produces bad outcomes is longstanding, widely known, and generally accepted, as discussed in chapters 1 and 2, at least some doctors likely continue the practice in the knowledge that it is not doing their patients any good. This attitude fails to even comply with basic paternalistic standards because paternalism requires that actions overriding patient autonomy be done for patient good. So what, then, would be the aim in these cases?

Perhaps, more than anything else, doctors seek obedience from this class of patients, to no particular health aim. Patients who object to overtesting may be belittled, criticized, or subject to scare tactics despite doctors knowing that their patients are right. Obedience displaces health as the ultimate aim of testing. As discussed in chapter 4, when doctors withhold birth control prescriptions to ensure that patients come in for testing, and especially when they never have to actually make good on their threats because their patients do submit to testing, they have acted against the Hippocratic Oath, the principle of nonmaleficence, patient preference, positive health outcomes, informed consent, and medical malpractice, but they have successfully achieved a compliant patient.

Objectification of patients may also play a role. As the nonconsensual pelvic examinations of unconscious patients testifies,[37] patients may be seen as mere objects for use, such as for use in medical experimentation and training, rather than full persons with autonomy and personal goals. When full moral personhood is denied, doctors have greater perceived freedom to treat patients in a way that more closely approximates legal negligence than successful care. Patients are not seen as full persons and are not individualized, but rather stereotyped as a group that is unlikely to do what is necessary to achieve the best possible health outcomes. In fact, yearly Pap tests, which have never as such been recommended by the scientific evidence, can be seen in this context as a punishment for the perceived inability to follow prudential self-interest. That is, since women cannot be trusted to take care of their own health and get a test at the proper intervals, doctors subject them to testing at *higher* intervals. This practice may objectify women or may persist due to underlying objectification already present.

In fact, the very nature of most birth control pill prescriptions involves some of these same elements of infantilizing women or not trusting them, and as a result requiring them to undergo added hassle. While doctors and bioethicists debate the ethical permissibility of placebos,[38] most oral birth control prescriptions contain a week of placebo pills without a comparable ethical debate.[39] Other comparable treatment that requires patients to take added pills or placebo treatments as standard practice and not in the context of a clinical trial, experimental treatment, or incurable condition, is vanishingly rare. Other treatments exist for which pills are not taken every single day, yet patients are trusted to remember their treatment without the expectation of a placebo pill needed.[40] As a result of these placebo pills, risks may arise. For example, one pharmaceutical company recalled around 170,000 packs of oral contraceptives when the placebo pills were mislabeled.[41]

So far, I have focused primarily on what Serano calls "traditional sexism," in which a hierarchy of maleness or masculinity over other genders and gender expressions is maintained. But Serano also discusses another form of sexism, called "oppositional sexism," which is relevant in this context as well.[42] Oppositional sexism does not rely primarily on a hierarchy but instead exists to maintain an opposition of maleness and masculinity against femaleness and femininity. Since these two genders are considered opposites, it implicitly upholds a binary, in which these are the only two valid genders and gender expressions. However, the binary is not the only problem Serano identifies in oppositional sexism. When the two genders are viewed as opposites, then they are also viewed as mutually exclusive. If light and dark are opposites, something cannot be light and dark at the same time. If men and women are opposites, someone cannot have attributes associated with both at the same time. That most people fall into the categories of male and female is thus not the primary target of her analysis when the mutual exclusivity causes significant harm across the board.

Oppositional sexism may also play into the phenomenon of denying patients birth control refills until they undergo added tests. Even if doctors do not turn patients away at the outset of treatment, and offer needed prescriptions to treat manageable symptoms, they may still go on to deny those same patients continuity of treatment later on. When patriarchal attitudes lead people to associate men with positive stereotypes, like that they are authoritative, rational, in control, or self-determining, oppositional sexism implicitly leads to association of women with the opposite stereotypes, such as that they are unreliable, irrational, weak, or dependent. If women are implicitly or explicitly associated with these characteristics, then doctors may feel justified—even obligated—to override patient preference, which itself may be viewed as flighty, childish, or needy. Seeking to control such patients would be helpful and natural. Similarly, if doctors themselves are in a position of control, authority, and have relevant expertise, then their patients must be the opposite and so acting paternalistically would be necessary.

Sexism, both as a hierarchal understanding of the world and as a version of opposition (absent any hierarchy) can help explain a phenomenon that is otherwise without any parallel in the medical field. Why do some share of doctors engage in a practice so negligently harmful to their patients that it literally meets the definition of medical malpractice and do so in a way that impacts virtually every woman in society at some point in her life? The infantilization of women in a society characterized by patriarchal attitudes can explain it. Why do the majority of doctors engage in this systemic denial of patient rights toward most women—which is to say, most patients—without ever facing a lawsuit or medical malpractice case that would implement existing laws for the protection of patients? Perhaps they get away with it because women are not seen as meriting rights protections, as lower status members of society, or because the denial of rights is not seen as such when it is directed at women. Why do scientific advances in women's health, such as lifesaving cancer screenings and effective birth control options get turned into methods of behavior control on a massive scale spanning decades? Potentially helpful medical interventions can be weaponized to use against women if women are not seen as competent to direct their use. Why do physicians view choices traditionally falling within the realm of bodily autonomy as within their own dominion?[43] One explanation is that women are not seen as having bodily autonomy to begin with.[44]

In fact, in the context of historical battles of sexism, this result is predictable. Historically, these battles have often been waged on the territory of women's bodies. Reproductive autonomy, domestic abuse, sexual assault, female genital mutilation, and dowry killings are examples of sexist attitudes and beliefs—patriarchal power—wielded over and located on bodies themselves.[45] Human rights theorist Charlotte Bunch makes this point when she argues,

> Female subordination runs so deep that it is still viewed as inevitable or natural, rather than seen as a politically constructed reality maintained by patriarchal interests, ideology, and institutions. . . . The physical territory of this political struggle over what constitutes women's human rights is women's bodies. The importance of control over women can be seen in the intensity of resistance to laws and social changes that put control of women's bodies in women's hands: reproductive rights, freedom of sexuality whether heterosexual or lesbian, laws that criminalize rape in marriage, etc. Denial of reproductive rights and homophobia are also political means of maintaining control over women and perpetuating sex roles and thus have human rights implications.[46]

I have already argued that this practice constitutes a denial of rights in chapter 4. Here, Bunch gives us further arguments to think that reproductive rights are human rights. If the political fight over women's rights occurs on the domain of women's bodies, as Bunch gives us reason to believe, then the denial of reproductive autonomy and control is an integral part of the subordination of women more generally.

DOCTOR IGNORANCE

Birth control denials are not standard across the medical field. Older doctors are more likely to impose restrictions on patients, as discussed in chapter 1.[47] However, lack of awareness of the guidelines is unlikely to explain the phenomenon.[48] First, the trend is not moving in the right direction, as discussed in that chapter. That is, it is not true that significantly fewer doctors today require exams for birth control than they did several decades ago. As a result, outdated training alone or guideline fatigue, in which too many changes in guidelines make it harder for doctors to comply with them or to stay up to date, does not explain the practice.

Second, enough doctors are requiring the exams that the problem is clearly systemic and not a matter of individual preference. That is, age alone cannot explain the practice. The commonality in the reliance on the practice suggests that broader societal commitments and attitudes are at stake.

Third, the guidelines have been around for decades and span every major medical organization.[49] Thus, lack of information about standards of care is not a plausible explanation of the phenomenon. Even if older doctors were more likely to receive training sanctioning the practice, that does not explain how they have remained in the dark since their training. In addition, even if some doctors truly are unaware of the field standards, this would be negligent ignorance and not defensible.

Of course, it may be the case that the average time for a change in protocol to make its way through the medical field takes years. Some studies suggest that it takes a full 17 years for a protocol change to take hold.[50] In that case, we would expect full compliance with the 2009 directive to space the tests further than every year, be achieved in 2026.[51] But this point assumes that yearly testing was definitively recommended in earlier, 2003 guidelines. Not only do the 2003 guidelines fall short of recommending yearly testing, but they also make no mention of tying birth control prescriptions to cervical cancer screenings.[52]

In fact, the guidelines point to indirect evidence that screening every three years is the proper interval for best practices. The 2003 recommendation updates 1996 recommendations, but even the 1996 recommendations point to a three-year interval for most patients. In fact, despite acknowledging that nearly all doctors recommended yearly tests to patients in the mid-1980s, the primary purpose of the 1996 guidelines were to update the recommendation from testing every 10 years. The report states, "There is little evidence that women who receive annual screening are at significantly lower risk for invasive cervical cancer than are women who are tested every 3–5 years."[53] As a result, the report recommends against yearly testing, even as they acknowledge 97% of doctors do it. Thus, even a generous allotment of two decades to ensure doctors have full understanding of guidelines before relinquishing a practice suggests that this practice in particular should not have made it to the new millennium.

Fourth, medical guidelines should not be required since these guidelines focus almost exclusively on physical instead of moral harm to patients. As discussed in chapter 4, much deeper harms are imposed on patients, regardless of whether or not the practice leads to physical harms. That means doctors are flouting ethical standards and not just industry practice. The fact that older doctors are more likely to implement the practice than younger doctors could be due to higher incidence of sexism in this population rather than lack of awareness about standards. Medical guideline changes that have failed to be disseminated throughout the population fails as an explanation also because no good justification existed for linking the test to birth control in the first place. Requiring a high standard for evidence in delinking the practices without requiring a high standard of evidence in linking the practices is a double standard that has no basis.

A more likely explanation could be the availability heuristic. Doctors are likely to remember cases where aggressive forms of preventable cancers took the lives of their patients, and may therefore insist on extra testing to prevent repeat occurrences. However, the same objections apply to this potential justification as the last one. If the availability heuristic were the only such contributing factor to the practice, mandatory testing and the attendant withholding of other treatments would occur much more, in many more areas of medicine, and at much higher rates. Instead, the practice seems to be confined to a narrower subset of the population.

Another reason to understand the practice as having sexist origins and explanations is to compare it to treatment of patients in other contexts. In obsterircs and gynecology, patient preference for a medical intervention is denied so as to preserve a flawed notion of the patient's interests. In other areas of medicine, the opposite often happens: medical providers act questionably because they want to make their patients happy and satisfied.[54] For example, in the cases of prescribing antibiotics,[55] prescribing opioids,[56] coronary heart disease stent procedures,[57] placebos,[58] diagnoses of ADD and ADHD,[59] and other medical treatments, doctors often follow preferences without the necessary scientific data backing up the intervention's usefulness. In at least some of these cases, such as the prescribing of antibiotics, tests that are actually medically relevant and should be required before the dispensing of a medication are not used. For example, prescribing antibiotics for flu-like symptoms or symptoms of a viral infection is not justified because antibiotics cannot treat viruses; are very likely to do damage, such as to the patient's digestive tract or to the prevalence of antibiotic-resistant strains of infections; and are incredibly invasive. A preliminary test to ensure that the patient has a bacterial infection would at the very least be merited. However, many patients want and expect medication like antibiotics if they are sick and visit a doctor. Doctors are sometimes pressured into making sure their patients are happy, even to the detriment of their patient's long-term health. Such cases are extremely common. An estimated 30% of all antibiotic prescriptions are considered unnecessary.[60]

This practice is problematic, to be sure, but lots of examples exist in which doctors want so much to make their patients happy that they are willing to do scientifically dubious actions. Incentives for overtesting and overtreating are great, meaning that prescribing antibiotics for viruses is part of a large problem in the medical field. The phenomenon of withholding birth control for the scientifically dubious goal of getting patients to undergo more Pap tests is, of course, the opposite of the above practices wherein doctors overprescribe treatments to make patients happy, even if the doctors do not believe that the treatments will help. In the withholding birth control case, so far are doctors from trying to please their patients that they go directly against the expressed wishes of the patients and the recommendations of their own field to achieve a goal that at best does no harm to the patient.

SEXISM RESULTS EVEN WITHOUT SEXIST MOTIVES

In this particular case of withholding birth control, skeptics of the sexism charge could point out that the phenomenon may have other causal explanations. That the phenomenon has other explanations does not, of course, prove that sexism also does not contribute. A single event can have more than one explanation and the reasons may themselves be overdetermined, meaning that any one explanation would be sufficient to bring it about. Similarly, a single event can also have more than one necessary contributing factor, any one of which may be insufficient to bring it about. If it is necessary or sufficient, then it would be a contributing factor to the event. As we will see later, though, even that is not the end of the story, since a phenomenon without a sexist cause can still have a sexist result through disproportionate harm.

So, finding another competing cause for the result in question, such as the financial gain of the doctors in question, would not be enough to show that medical sexism does not also have a role to play in the practice. However, while other competing explanations do not show that the phenomenon is not sexist, it is instructive to see how they also fail to provide complete explanations of the practice. In the next section, I consider the possibility that financial exploitation explains why doctors force patients to undergo unneeded tests and argue that the sexism charge still stands. I show that sexism has more explanatory power than financial exploitation. Here, I apply the definition of medical sexism given above to explain how the practice may have sexist impacts even if no individual doctor holds sexist attitudes or beliefs.

Proving sexist intent is not the only way to show that a practice is sexist. Actions and statements that look sexist can have plausible, nonsexist explanations, and it is difficult to definitively prove that someone has sexist attitudes or beliefs. But for a practice to be sexist or discriminatory against women, it does not strictly have to depend on sexist intent. First, evidence on implicit bias shows that some sexist decisions or actions may be unconscious and not available to the agent.[61] Agents can be sexist without knowing it. But second, even implicit bias is not required for the purposes of this argument. Decisions and practices can have a disparate impact without a sexist intention necessarily behind the origins of the practice or rule. If the practice disproportionately harms women, as I have argued in chapters 2 and 3 that this practice does, and if the practice has an effect that means women cannot maintain a certain level of health, then the practice can be properly described as discriminatory without the necessity of showing intent.

Requiring tests for the prescription of a drug is generally appropriate. It would be irresponsible to prescribe treatment without first testing that the treatment is necessary. For example, doctors would not prescribe antibiotics to treat strep throat unless they first checked the patient for symptoms or did a formal throat culture. Similarly, not all tests need strictly to be directed at the condition itself. If a treatment has potentially dangerous side effects, further tests may be warranted. For example, if a drug treatment is dangerous to the liver, a doctor might do a liver function test first to ensure that the treatment does not present too great of a risk to the patient. A rule that requires a test before a prescription, then, is not wrong on the face of it. In fact, such a rule is relatively neutral.

However, requiring tests before giving out prescription renewals disproportionately harms women and other groups marginalized in society. In fact, as argued in chapter 3, it constitutes a denial of needed medical care that, as argued in chapter 2, can lead to irreversible harm.

De jure discrimination, therefore, is not at stake. But de facto discrimination, in which a policy causes disproportionate harm in reality even if not explicitly in law, is still relevant. De facto discrimination is difficult to determine. But, as argued in chapter 1, the practice is occurring. To the extent that it ever did occur and to the extent that it still does occur, de facto discrimination also occurs, with or without malice on the part of medical professionals, insurance companies, or any other contributing party.

FINANCIAL EXPLOITATION AND INSURANCE REQUIREMENTS

Financial exploitation is a simple explanation of current practices and a very likely contributing factor.[62] Yearly visits are lucrative and can sustain a practice. However, financial exploitation does not sufficiently explain this phenomenon, because this phenomenon of paternalistic behavior and conditional treatment is not equally spread out in different areas of the profession. While doctors may be guilty of disrespecting patients, the attitudes that may underlie some doctors' opinions do not obviously translate to paternalistic behavior. Doctors do not generally withhold one sort of care until their patients undergo another. For example, if a third of all money spent on health goes to unnecessary care, then a lot more people than just women are likely receiving unnecessary tests, not to mention surgeries, and other medical interventions.[63] But overtreatment by itself is not the subject of this discussion and constitutes a different, though significant issue affecting the average American.[64]

For example, dermatologists do not commonly withhold medications for cosmetic skin conditions until their patients get cancer screenings.[65] Such medications are arguably much less necessary for a patient's health than birth control, since cosmetic skin conditions are not the source of debilitating pain as endometriosis may be, are not a matter of life-and-death care as pregnancy may be, and are not central to the patient's self-conception as parenthood may be. Instances of doctors withholding treatment might be relatively common and discussed broadly, but as discussed in previous chapters, the unifying feature behind such cases is that doctors believe that the treatment being withheld is bad for the patient. In the birth control case, the doctor and the patient agree that the treatment being withheld is good for the patient. Precisely because the treatment in question is necessary for the patient's wellbeing does the doctor withhold it to get the patient to comply with other tests.

While women's choices are commonly disregarded in OB/GYN contexts, similar practices are uncommon in doctors' policies toward cisgender men. It not only illegal for doctors to withhold needed medical care to men, as discussed in chapter 3, but also exceedingly rare, even so as to act in their patients' best interests.[66]

In addition, no evidence suggests insurance companies make the same calculations to exploit female patients for financial gain. First, the Affordable Care Act mandates Pap tests, pelvic exams, and contraception itself be covered.[67] Second, the ACA mandates that women not be charged more than men for health care.[68] Prior to its implementation, women paid 50–80% more than men in health insurance premiums due to gender rating.[69] But if health insurance companies interpreted more reliance on health insurance to mean more expenses, then they would not have any incentive to force women to use health insurance more than needed. Third, pregnancy, birth, and child dependents all can cause great expenses for health insurance companies. Insurance companies have a vested interest in avoiding unwanted pregnancies for their customers, which means that obstacles to procuring contraception are not financially incentivized.

Of course, in other areas of medicine, the medical field also lags behind the scientific advancements that would show their practices were wrong.[70] And, in some cases, financial incentives are a plausible explanation of the behavior.[71] For example, doctors and for-profit medical care professionals may be guilty of exploiting diabetes patients in kidney failure by referring them to years-long and debilitating dialysis treatments rather than transplants, which offer better health outcomes.[72] When patients face kidney failure, either due to diabetes or some other kidney disease, patients may live 10 years longer after transplant than with dialysis.[73] Dialysis itself requires tens of billions of dollars' worth of care every year for thousands of treatment centers nationwide.[74] Medicare, which covers End-Stage Renal Disease (ESRD) for patients of any age,[75] plays a large role in this debate, as do private health insurance companies.[76] Does the proliferation of dialysis treatment over organ transplants demonstrate that doctors act paternalistically and in a financially exploitive way toward patients, making the case described thus far in this book no different?

Kidney disease is not analogous to birth control and Pap tests for a variety of reasons. First, while it is true that patients may rely on dialysis at a very high rate when kidney transplants would be a better treatment option for them overall, both groups of patients receive treatment for their conditions.[77] We cannot say the same of patients denied birth control in service of other lifesaving tests.

Additionally, the patients facing barriers to kidney transplants are not denied in service of some other interest they have. Transplantation is not withheld in service of cancer screenings, dietary change, or use of some other feature of the patient's health as a bargaining chip. Arguably, this feature of ESRD is worse than the situation of birth control, since the treatment barriers are not in service of the patient's well-being. However, we have already established that using birth control as a bargaining chip to gain compliance with yearly Pap tests fails to improve patient well-being. Additionally, if the average dialysis patient endures financial exploitation, combining it with the denial of other needed care does not compound it.

Next, it is possible that medical providers may fail to properly inform dialysis patients on transplants or give full information about transplants in a consult, just as they may fail to properly inform patients seeking birth control that LARC methods might be better suited to their needs.[78] But in the case of dialysis, doctors are not literally putting a direct obstacle in the path of a patient who explicitly asks for it.

Also, the financial differences are such that financial exploitation is not a simple explanation. Dialysis can cost about $88,000 each year per patient.[79] Alternatively, a kidney transplant can cost about $262,000 per patient.[80] Since a kidney transplant is likely to last longer than three years, it offers clear benefits over dialysis. But, the much higher upfront cost makes the comparison closer to that of IUDs versus birth control pills. Of course, Medicare covers both dialysis and transplants equally and the ACA mandates contraception coverage, so cost to the patient is not a simple explanation of the phenomena. Although a patient choosing dialysis is likely to require more costly treatment over time, the upfront costs of transplants are so much higher that a company making a purely financial decision would have to forgo an immediate payment in the hopes of accruing that same sum over the ensuing years, assuming no other health complication befalls the patient. Corporations are usually expected to take into account the time value of money such that it would take longer to recoup the cost of forgoing more money sooner.

Another difference between understanding the causes of overusing dialysis by comparison to the causes of overusing Pap testing is that no triage consideration attends birth control prescriptions, while a discussion of dialysis must take into account that simply not enough kidney transplant options are available for everyone.[81] The average time spent on a kidney transplant waiting list is four to five years.[82] If more people were organ donors, or more living donors were willing to give kidneys to people on dialysis, the financial exploitation would be the only possible explanation of dialysis.[83] However, since it is not possible, under current conditions, for everyone in need of a kidney to receive one, dialysis treatment centers are inevitable. This problem is compounded by the fact that patients actually get better outcomes if they get kidney transplants earlier: more people are in need of kidneys than even the hundreds of thousands currently in kidney failure.[84]

Although financial exploitation is certainly a contributing cause to consider, and very likely influential in Pap testing just as in other cases, we should not overlook systemic injustice either. If financial exploitation were the only relevant factor, then there might not be a difference in patients of differing groups, since all are equally covered by Medicare reimbursements. In reality, however, disadvantaged groups are more likely to be given the relatively less effective recommendation of long-term dialysis, whereas privileged groups are more likely to be referred for transplant, as discussed in chapter 8.[85] Those most affected by ongoing dialysis treatment in lieu of lifesaving transplants are those who already belong to a disadvantaged group, like those who are of lower socioeconomic status. Incidentally, women have been 30% less likely to receive kidney transplants historically.[86] It is virtually impossible to remove sexism or injustice from the discussion. This point also helps underline the fact that financial exploitation is not independent of systemic injustice but also arises where systemic injustice is already in place. That is, it is easier to financially exploit patients who are already disadvantaged in society. As a result, mistreatment compounds when disadvantaged groups overlap, which is why intersectional feminism highlights these features of injustice.[87]

The identification of the practice as financially motivated and as motivated by sexism are not mutually exclusive. Doctors can have both motives because their motives can be overdetermined. In addition, sexism can intersect with other forms of hierarchy and oppression. To be sure, the practice targets women and patients associated with femaleness. However, it hits poor patients the hardest. Sexism and classism can interact in ways that make intersectional feminism the correct response, whether or not the motive is primarily sex and gender-based or primarily class-based. Often, financial exploitation is only found among vulnerable groups, in which a marginalized group is being leveraged for its vulnerability. What is necessary for my argument is not to prove that no financial exploitation applies, but rather that financial exploitation is an injustice to patients, that it is more likely to fall on marginalized groups, that it can intersect with other forms of systemic injustice, and that it must be eradicated.

If financial exploitation were the reason for the practice, then it would be possible to identify better treatment and more respectful treatment of female patients when doing so is in the doctor's financial interest. In chapters 6, 7, and 8, I discuss relevant cases in more detail. Certainly in some instances, I argue that mistreatment of women does involve expensive procedures that they do not need and are ultimately harmful, like C-sections, episiotomies, and mammograms. But in other instances, the harmful and paternalistic behavior yields no financial gains, like bed rest, pelvic exam training, and breastfeeding policies. And in still other instances, the same sort of paternalistic denials of autonomy attend practices that are a net financial loss to a doctor, such as denials of abortion, organ transplantation, heart disease treatment, treatment of trans patients, autoimmune disorder diagnoses, and medical research. So, financial exploitation not only cannot explain why women bear the brunt of paternalistic policies, which disproportionately impact them, but also fails to explain why paternalistic policies are so commonplace when no financial gains, and in fact financial losses, accrue to doctors.

I have argued against the possibility that financial exploitation can alone explain the practice. But suppose I am incorrect. Suppose that doctors engage in this practice not due to any sexism whatsoever. Suppose that they do it merely out of greed. It is still necessary to highlight this behavior and attitude of greed and exploitation as wrong. Just because doctors may not be sexist when they require added appointments does not mean that their behavior is morally permissible.

CONCLUSION

Many causal factors may come into play when understanding the root cause of such a prevalent and predatory practice existing for decades. The reason why I highlight sexism in particular is that sexism has a unique explanatory value in understanding the practice and its historical context. Gender-based discrimination can explain what is going on where other considerations cannot. Financial discrimination may be at play, but it does not explain why this practice is directed primarily at women. Doctors wishing to act in their patients' best interest is possible, but does not explain why they do so when the testing yields a net harm. It also does not explain why doctors would require Pap testing in exchange for birth control, instead of vaccination against HPV, which would prevent against the disease that causes cervical cancer.[88] Demands from insurance companies may contribute, but do not explain why insurance companies would make these demands of doctors, especially when overtesting, overdiagnosis, and propensity to pregnancy are not in their financial interests. A lag in compliance with new standards could be a contributing factor, but does not explain why the standards would require the practice in the first place, since no medical reason ever justified the practice; how it became so widespread against standard updates; why it persists so many years after a guideline would normally be implemented among clinicians; why doctors would comply with a guideline that was in opposition to their very role; why doctors selectively ignore scientific evidence in this but not other cases; or why doctors continue to follow other problematic policies, like bed rest, discussed in chapter 7, which also never had any scientific basis. Patient preferences for extra testing might contribute to doctors offering tests more often then is recommended, but does not explain why violating patient preference for birth control occurs alongside yearly testing. The desire to resist liability for a patient's life-threatening disease might contribute to doctors requiring extra tests, but doctors' concerns about avoiding medical malpractice litigation do not explain why they engage in the definition of medical malpractice to avoid it. The argument highlighting sexism is in part an argument from explanation.

In this chapter, I also argued that doctors are in part responsible for this mistreatment of patients, since they impose the standard, they withhold prescriptions for unnecessary tests, and since they test at intervals that are harmful to patients. However, if I am incorrect about this, too, and doctors do not contribute to the practice, but the practice instead can be attributed to insurance company mandates, the injustice still stands. Recognizing discrimination where it exists, correctly identifying it as discrimination, and using that identification to eliminate the practice, is necessary whether or not there are multiple implicated parties.

NOTES

1. Davis, *Women, Race, & Class*, 202.

2. Though of course unconscious sexism is also possible as discussed later in the chapter. Cudd and Jones, "Sexism."

3. Although reproductive health and birth control are not actually "women's issues," since they affect trans men, nonbinary, and genderqueer people, that attribution often persists of obstetrics and gynecology and may be influencing the field as a whole.

4. Elliott, *White Coat, Black Hat*, xi; Oreskes and Conway, *Merchants of Doubt*, 11, 136 and elsewhere; Andersen and Kuhn, *What the Health*.

5. Elliott, *White Coat, Black Hat*, 16.

6. For example, expensive and unnecessary screening and diagnostic testing for prostate cancer is widely reported, but what is not reported is withholding certain types of care from patients until they undergo testing. Welch, Schwartz, and Woloshin, *Overdiagnosed*, 49.

7. Elliott, *White Coat, Black Hat*, 2.

8. Frye, *Politics of Reality*, 17; Welch, *Existential Eroticism*, 36.

9. Frye, *Politics of Reality*, 35. Frye's definition itself might be both too narrow and too broad for my purposes: "The term 'sexist' characterizes cultural and economic structures which create and enforce the elaborate and rigid patterns of sex-marking and sex-announcing which divide the species, along lines of sex, into dominators and subordinates. Individual acts and practices are sexist which reinforce and support those structures, either as culture or as shapes taken on by the enculturated animals." Frye, 38. Her definition may be too narrow for my purposes because she talks only of cultural and economic structures, though one could imagine other similar structures being at stake, such as in my case, legal and health-care structures. This definition may also be too narrow for my purposes because a single person can encapsulate both patterns, as she herself acknowledges, and be punished as a result of crossing those barriers. But the definition may also be too broad insofar as I aim to include acts and practices that fall short of creating and enforcing these hierarchies or that fall short of reinforcing and supporting those structures.

10. Cudd, "The Paradox of Liberal Feminism: Preference, Rationality, and Oppression," 38; Welch, *Existential Eroticism*, 36.

11. Serano, *Whipping Girl*, 14; Battersby, *The Phenomenal Woman*, 20; Young, *On Female Body Experience*, 5. Or note: "Though there are certainly patent cases of sexism, on many definitions sexism is often only identifiable by its symptoms or consequences. We can quite readily explain that, if some distribution of opportunities systematically deprives women of what is offered to men, and there is no apparent overriding reason which justifies such a

distribution, then we have a clear prima facie case of sexism. As a general claim this seems to us both undeniable and unassailable. The idea that sexism involves systematic inequality is, in short, a commonly recognized working definition." Cudd and Jones, "Sexism," 103.

12. Serano, *Whipping Girl*, 14.

13. Frye, *Politics of Reality*, 19.

14. Brogaard, "Bias-Driven Attention, Cognitive Penetration and Epistemic Downgrade"; Cassad et al., "How Sexism Undermines the Advancement of Women in Science, Technology, Engineering, and Mathematics," 132.

15. Harris-Perry, *Sister Citizen*.

16. Crenshaw, "Demarginalizing the Intersection of Race and Sex: A Black Feminist Critique of Antidiscrimination Doctrine, Feminist Theory and Antiracist Politics."

17. Crenshaw, "Mapping the Margins." Roberts, *Killing the Black Body*, 8.

18. Ingall, *Mamaleh Knows Best*, 10–11.

19. For example, Kathryn T. Gines's definition of proto-intersectionality is relevant here: "identifying and combating racism and sexism—through activist organizing and campaigning—not only as separate categories impacting identity and oppression, but also as systems of oppression that work together and mutually reinforce one another, presenting unique problems for black women who experience both, simultaneously and differently than white women and/or black men." Gines, "Race Women, Race Men, and Early Expressions of Proto-Intersectionality, 1830s–1930s," 14. Gines goes on to quote Anna Julia Cooper's words in 1892 in this context. Cooper writes, "The colored woman of to-day occupies, one might say, a unique position in this country. In a period of itself transitional and unsettled, her status seems one of the least ascertainable and definitive of all the forces which make for our civilization. She is confronted by both a woman question and a race problem, and is as yet an unknown or an unacknowledged factor in both." Cooper, *A Voice from the South*, 134.

20. Collins, *Black Feminist Thought*, 265.

21. Harris-Perry, *Sister Citizen*, 33; Kozma and Schroer, "Purposeful Nonsense, Intersectionality and the Mission to Save Black Babies," 112.

22. Smith, "Racism and Women's Studies," 96.

23. Serano, "Trans-Misogyny Primer"; Smith, "Racism and Women's Studies," 96. That does not mean that the problem rises to the level of oppression. Frye, *Politics of Reality*, 14.

24. Stewart et al., "Clinical Breast and Pelvic Examination Requirements for Hormonal Contraception"; Schwarz et al., "Cervical Cancer Screening Continues to Limit Provision of Contraception"; Qaseem et al., "Screening Pelvic Examination in Adult Women"; Melnick, "Are Doctors' Exams a Barrier

to Birth Control?"; Debbie Saslow, "American Cancer Society Expert Voices Blog: Is a Pap Test Necessary Every Year?," Cancer.org, March 14, 2012, http://www.cancer.org/Cancer/News/ExpertVoices/; Henderson et al., "Pelvic Examinations and Access to Oral Hormonal Contraception"; Yu et al., "Obstetrician-Gynecologists' Beliefs on the Importance of Pelvic Examinations in Assessing Hormonal Contraception Eligibility."

25. Erdely, "Doctors' Beliefs Can Hinder Patient Care."

26. Azidah, Nik Hazlina, and Aishah, "Swyer Syndrome in a Woman with Pure 46, XY Gonadal Dysgenesis and a Hypoplastic Uterus."

27. Similarly, those who are agender or nongender, genderfree, neutrois, or nonbinary and have a uterus may need contraceptives.

28. Freeman and López, "Sex Categorization in Medical Contexts," 244.

29. Young, *On Female Body Experience*, 5.

30. National Alliance for Caregiving, "Caregiving in the U.S. 2015," 6.

31. These notions can also pull apart. One can think gender is a social construct, but not sex, or vice versa. For example, Thomas W. Laqueur argues that in pre-Enlightenment views, "*sex,* or the body, must be understood as the epiphenomenon, while *gender*, what we would take to be a cultural category, was primary or 'real.'" Laqueur, *Making Sex*, 8.

32. Shetterly, *Hidden Figures*, 114.

33. Saini, *Inferior*, 5. and elsewhere.

34. Saini, 8; Miller, "As Women Take Over a Male-Dominated Field, the Pay Drops."

35. Of course, women also may be more likely to receive medically negligent care in the first place. Brown and Hughes, *The Medical Malpractice Crisis and Poor Women*.

36. Brennan, "Feminist Ethics."

37. Friesen, "Educational Pelvic Exams on Anesthetized Women." I discuss this point further in chapter 7.

38. Schattner, "The Placebo Debate."

39. "Do You Need to Take the Last Week of Birth Control Pills?" Medically reviewed by Alan Carter, PharmD on November 8, 2018—Written by James Roland. https://www.healthline.com/health/birth-control/last-week-of-birth-control-pills.

40. Jafari et al., "Efficacy of Alternate-Day Dosing versus Daily Dosing of Atorvastatin"; Reindl, Wright, and Wargo, "Alternate-Day Statin Therapy for the Treatment of Hyperlipidemia."

41. Chiu, "'Unintended Pregnancy.'"

42. Serano, *Whipping Girl*, 13.

43. Savulescu and Schuklenk, "Doctors Have No Right to Refuse Medical Assistance in Dying, Abortion or Contraception," 166.

44. Female doctors can perpetuate these myths and systemic justices just as male doctors can.

45. Schechter, *Women and Male Violence*, 6; Crenshaw, "Mapping the Margins," 1241; Friedman, *Autonomy, Gender, Politics*; Gray, "Original Habitation:"

46. Bunch, "Women's Rights as Human Rights," 491.

47. Henderson et al., "Pelvic Examinations and Access to Oral Hormonal Contraception."

48. Abadir et al., "Influence of Qualitative Research on Women's Health Screening Guidelines."

49. Center for Disease Control, "US Selected Practice Recommendations for Contraceptive Use, 2016 Appendix C: Examinations and Tests Needed Before Initiation of Contraceptive Methods." Amir Qaseem et al., "Screening Pelvic Examination in Adult Women: A Clinical Practice Guideline From the American College of Physicians Screening Pelvic Examination in Adult Women," *Annals of Internal Medicine* 161, no. 1 (July 1, 2014): 67–72, https://doi.org/10.7326/M14-0701. The American College of Obstetricians and Gynecologists, "Committee Opinion, Number 544 Over-the-Counter Access to Oral Contraceptives."

50. Morris, Zoë Slote, Steven Wooding, and Jonathan Grant. "The Answer Is 17 Years, What Is the Question: Understanding Time Lags in Translational Research." *Journal of the Royal Society of Medicine* 104, no. 12 (December 2011): 510–20. https://doi.org/10.1258/jrsm.2011.110180.

51. Moyer, Virginia A. "Screening for Cervical Cancer: U.S. Preventive Services Task Force Recommendation Statement." *Annals of Internal Medicine* 156, no. 12 (June 19, 2012): 880. https://doi.org/10.7326/0003-4819-156-12-201206190-00424.

52. "Screening for Cervical Cancer." *American Family Physician* 67, no. 8 (April 15, 2003): 1759.

53. U.S. Preventative Services Task Force, *Screening for Cervical Cancer*.

54. Robbins, "The Problem With Satisfied Patients."

55. Belluz, "Why Doctors Overprescribe Antibiotics — Even in Cases Where They're Useless"; Dempsey et al., "Primary Care Clinicians' Perceptions about Antibiotic Prescribing for Acute Bronchitis"; Linder and Singer, "Desire for Antibiotics and Antibiotic Prescribing for Adults with Upper Respiratory Tract Infections"; Linder et al., "Time of Day and the Decision to Prescribe Antibiotics."

56. Belluz, "Why Doctors Overprescribe Antibiotics — Even in Cases Where They're Useless."

57. Epstein, "When Evidence Says No, But Doctors Say Yes."

58. Carvalho et al., "Open-Label Placebo Treatment in Chronic Low Back Pain"; Resnick, "The Weird Power of the Placebo Effect, Explained"; Tuttle et al., "Increasing Placebo Responses over Time in U.S. Clinical Trials of Neuropathic Pain"; Kaptchuk et al., "Placebos without Deception."

59. Hawthorne, *Accidental Intolerance*, 88.

60. Center for Infectious Disease Research and Policy, "Overuse and Overprescribing of Antibiotics."

61. Brogaard, "12 Ways to Spot a Misogynist."

62. Elliott, *White Coat, Black Hat.*

63. Brownlee, *Overtreated*, 5.

64. Brownlee, 5.

65. Cancer screenings are not recommended for asymptomatic patients the same way Pap tests are, which is a significant difference between the two practices. Similarly, the percentage of patients seeking treatment from a dermatologist is much smaller than those seeking contraception. But if the purpose of the added screenings is merely financial and not for the patient's own good, then any practice that requires extra screenings would be financially incented, especially if it captures a large subsection of the population. Wernli et al., "Screening for Skin Cancer in Adults."

66. As discussed, no analogy exists in men's health, such as withholding needed medical care for the purpose of getting men to undergo prostate exams. When men are denied health care, it is primarily for reasons related to lack of insurance prior to the passage of the ACA. A.Wilper et al., "Health Insurance and Mortality in US Adults."

67. HealthCare.gov, "Preventive Care Benefits for Women."

68. Kahn, "The End of Gender Rating"; Andrews, "Health Insurance Prices For Women Set To Drop"; Obama, "Read Obama's Full Remarks on Supreme Court Ruling."

69. Brown, "Women Pay up to 50% More for Health Insurance Premiums"; Garrett, "Turning to Fairness."

70. Prasad et al., "A Decade of Reversal."

71. Raymond, "Opioid Manufacturer Insys Files for Bankruptcy after Kickback Probe."

72. Waterman et al., "Living Donor Kidney Transplantation."

73. Stokes, "Consequences of Frequent Hemodialysis"; Oniscu, Brown, and Forsythe, "How Great Is the Survival Advantage of Transplantation over Dialysis in Elderly Patients?"

74. Humer and Copley, "FOCUS-U.S. Seeks to Cut Dialysis Costs with More Home Care versus Clinics."

75. Department of Health & Human Services, "Medicare Coverage of Kidney Dialysis & Kidney Transplant Services."

76. Childers et al., "A Comparison of Payments to a For-Profit Dialysis Firm From Government and Commercial Insurers."

77. Kucirka, Purnell, and Segev, "Improving Access to Kidney Transplantation"; Kazley et al., "Barriers Facing Patients Referred for Kidney Transplant Cause Loss to Follow-Up"; Fowler, "Accountability of Dialysis Facilities in Transplant Referral"; Patzer et al., "Variation in Dialysis Facility Referral for Kidney Transplantation Among Patients With End-Stage Renal Disease in Georgia." In addition, as discussed in chapter 8, many of the barriers to transplant access are connected to sex and race.

78. Waterman et al., "Assessing Transplant Education Practices in Dialysis Centers"; Harper et al., "Counseling and Provision of Long-Acting Reversible Contraception in the US"; Tang, Maurer, and Bartz, "Intrauterine Device Knowledge and Practices."

79. Shinkman, "The Big Business of Dialysis Care."

80. Rancic et al., "Economic Evaluation of Pharmacogenetic Tests in Patients Subjected to Renal Transplantation."

81. Organ Procurement and Transplantation Network Minority Affairs Committee, "Educational Guidance on Patient Referral to Kidney Transplantation."

82. Organ Procurement and Transplantation Network Minority Affairs Committee, "Educational Guidance on Patient Referral to Kidney Transplantation."

83. I discuss organ donation in chapter 8.

84. Sakhuja et al., "Underutilization of Timely Kidney Transplants in Those With Living Donors."

85. Gillespie et al., "Sex Differences and Attitudes toward Living Donor Kidney Transplantation among Urban Black Patients on Hemodialysis"; "Older Women Less Likely than Men to Be Listed For Kidney Transplants; Patzer et al., "Variation in Dialysis Facility Referral for Kidney Transplantation Among Patients With End-Stage Renal Disease in Georgia."

86. McMurray et al., "Gender Disparities in Clinical Decision Making."

87. Crenshaw, "Beyond Racism and Misogyny: Black Feminism and 2 Live Crew," 112.

88. McClung et al., "Trends in Human Papillomavirus Vaccine Types 16 and 18 in Cervical Precancers, 2008–2014."

6

A TYPICAL TREATMENT

Abortion

In the last chapter, I argued that medical sexism helps explain the origination of a flawed practice of tethering necessary birth control prescriptions to unnecessary cancer screenings as well as the continuation of the practice well past the point at which any evidence could justify it. Although I argued that medical sexism is not the only possible explanation, I argued that it was a significant component of a complete explanation. For example, while financial incentives may be a contributing factor to the prevalence of the practice, they cannot explain it by themselves, since financially exploiting patients is more feasible when those patients are already disadvantaged in other ways. Using the argument that medical sexism is at play in the case of birth control prescriptions and Pap testing, I am on stronger ground to understand other major cases in reproductive care, like abortion. In this chapter, I argue that medical sexism is one explanation for current and proposed abortion practices in the United States, just as it is one explanation for birth control practices. This lack of adequate concern for women, more than any sort of moral commitment to fetuses, allows proposed or actual policies that harm women.[1] In fact, identifying medical sexism as having an explanatory role in contraception, where there is no fetus, helps make progress on cases like abortion, where there is a fetus.[2]

When pregnant people seek abortion and their preferences are overridden in denying them abortion access, they lack consent and their autonomy is denied, just as it is in birth control restrictions. If autonomy is systematically or commonly denied in both abortion and birth control cases, and not denied as systematically or as commonly in other cases, medical sexism may be at root. For example, male condoms are not generally prohibited or regulated; male condoms are classified as a Class II medical device while female condoms are classified as a Class III medical device requiring more regulatory oversight and a more difficult FDA approval.[3] However, abortion access differs from birth control access in significant ways. Most notably, in the case of abortion, a very obvious answer could explain why patient autonomy is overridden: the fetus.

Nevertheless, with the understanding I explore in chapter 5, I defend another explanation at play and another common thread between the cases. The case of contraception includes the same attitudes, behaviors, and practices, but no fetus exists. With denials of contraception, autonomy is overridden, but not to ensure the protection of a fetus's moral status or rights. Coming to a fuller understanding of birth control before progressing to an analysis of abortion allows more insight on an emotionally fraught and extremely controversial issue like abortion, and more clarity on the role of the fetus in denials of care.

In plenty of instances of abortion, the fetus does not "have" autonomy in any identifiable way; fetuses without brains are hardly an example of beings with the right to make conscious decisions for themselves such as would be required to respect their autonomy.[4] But, since some wish to count the fetus as a being worthy of full moral personhood, rights, and autonomy at the moment of conception as a single-celled zygote, I put aside such cases as under dispute. Instead, by incorporating the restriction of access to birth control into the list of medical situations in which patient choice is overridden, I identify medical sexism as an underlying reason for the widespread abuse of patient autonomy in abortion cases, regardless of the moral status of the fetus.

Medical sexism tends to come from doctors and other health-care providers, but this category can be expanded when politicians and other government officials use medical reasons as a pretext to control classes of patients without the support or input of the medical community. The legislators and courts making decisions about abortion can also engage in medical sexism insofar as their ostensible concerns are about public health, safety, and life. Insofar as policymakers can engage in medical sexism, their actions fall within the scope of this book.[5]

ABORTION RESTRICTIONS AND THE MEDICAL FIELD

Just as I criticized the medical field independent of the various judicial and legislative checks on women's access to birth control, often going above and beyond the law in restricting access to birth control, so is the medical field an independent check on access to abortion, often going above and beyond the various judicial decisions and legislative restrictions there, too. *Roe v. Wade* and the attendant Supreme Court decisions protecting the constitutional right to abortion ensure that abortion is legal in the United States. But even without any legislative restrictions, that does not mean that it is accessible. If abortion is de jure legal, but no doctor is willing to perform it, then it is de facto out of the reach of many women.[6]

For example, the distances women have to travel to gain access to abortion are great and holding steady.[7] Around a fifth of women have to travel more than 40 miles to reach an abortion provider, and for women who live in rural areas, that distance can exceed 180 miles on average.[8] Why are patients traveling so far to gain abortion access when most Americans, including people in rural areas, live no more than four miles from the nearest hospital?[9] Why is this form of basic health care such a large obstacle to so many, when most people live mere minutes from health-care distributors and the average driving distance to one is around 14 miles (20 minutes)?[10] The fact that the nearest hospital is orders of magnitude closer to most Americans than the average abortion provider means that a large number of hospitals simply do not perform the operation, despite the fact that abortions are needed medical care for many. People without a uterus can have their basic medical needs met close by, but people with a uterus are not so lucky.

So why do so many hospitals fail to provide complete health care to their patients? Hospitals anachronistically tending toward private status is not enough to explain the feature because private hospitals offer a range of needed services to all.[11] A large proportion of hospitals also happen to be religiously affiliated, have moral commitments, or constitute what Elizabeth Sepper calls "zombie religious institutions," in which a commercial transaction designates an institution as religious which otherwise has no connection to a church, place of worship, religious community, or mission.[12] These affiliations in turn lead to a number of ramifications for patients. According to an ACLU report, one in six hospital beds in the United States is in a Catholic hospital, and in some places that number is as high as 40%.[13] In 10 states, more than 30% of hospital beds are in Catholic hospitals.[14]

Religiously affiliated hospitals pose a problem for abortion access because many deny those services within their institutions for reasons pertaining to conscientious objection.[15] For example, "Conscientious objection is the refusal to participate in an activity that an individual considers incompatible with his/her religious, moral, philosophical, or ethical beliefs."[16] In this instance, an institution, rather than the traditionally claimed individual is the one claiming conscientious objector status.[17] However, these instances might more closely fall under what Douglas NeJaime and Reva B. Siegel call "complicity claims," in which "religious objections to being made complicit in the assertedly sinful conduct of others" outside the religion are in question.[18]

The United States Conference of Catholic Bishops (USCCB), which oversees Catholic hospitals, issues what are called the Ethical and Religious Directives for Catholic Health Care Services ("the Directives").[19] The broad number of Catholic hospitals under the Directives' mandate include:

> . . . hospitals that are owned by a Catholic health system or diocese, hospitals affiliated with a Catholic hospital or system through a business partnership (including some public hospitals that are managed by Catholic health systems), and historically Catholic hospitals that continue to follow the Directives despite now being owned by a secular non-profit or for-profit health care system.[20]

As the ACLU points out, "The Directives prohibit a range of reproductive health services, including contraception, sterilization, many infertility treatments, and abortion, even when a woman's health or life is jeopardized by a pregnancy."[21] These prohibitions restrict access to care, despite patients needing and requesting the services, despite employing doctors willing and able to perform them, and despite doctors and patients who do not share the religion or religious beliefs in question. As the ACLU meticulously catalogues, scores of women are denied lifesaving treatment,[22] such as when their water breaks months before their fetus's viability and the subsequent miscarriage of the fetus threatens sepsis, hemorrhaging, infection, and pain until it is removed.[23]

Other needed medical procedures are also in jeopardy within some religious institutions. For example, when a patient who is pregnant needs or wants a tubal ligation, it is safest to perform this directly after the delivery of a baby. Directive 53 governing Catholic hospitals, however, prohibits any sort of sterilization, meaning that patients cannot get access to the care they need.[24] Not all Catholic hospitals follow these exact mandates and not all hospitals that restrict lifesaving care are Catholic.[25] Some Catholic hospitals allow abortions and tubal ligations under some circumstances, while some publicly funded hospitals do not.

It is also relevant to keep in mind the significant distinction between doctors and hospitals. Although I argued that "the medical field" imposes restrictions on abortion access that go beyond judicial and legislative requirements, this language obscures the differences between a hospital guideline and a doctor preference. A conscientious objection usually refers to an individual. In that case, medical care providers refuse to provide reproductive health-care services to patients for conscience-based reasons and ask for accommodation.[26] In turn, fewer health care providers are willing to perform the procedures in question, and patients have reduced access as a result.[27] In fact, this reduction in accessible services can be viewed as the goal of the conscientious objection.[28]

A large proportion of hospitals may be antiabortion for religious reasons, but that does not mean that a particularly large proportion of doctors like or defend this antiabortion stance or that this type of objection is standard in professional fields.[29] Although all OB/GYN providers are taught abortion methods in training, an estimated 14% of OB/GYN doctors perform them.[30] As would be expected, the likelihood of a doctor performing an abortion depends on the doctor's religious affiliation, age, and gender.[31] However, a certain proportion of doctors who are willing to perform abortions will not, due to the restrictions of the hospitals where they are employed. Thus, the hospital administrators who make these decisions are not part of the class medical care providers. A religious board might be in charge of the restrictions, while the doctors employed there merely follow suit.

This distinction between doctors who are willing to provide an abortion and the hospitals they work for prohibiting abortion speaks to the broader problems in health care generally and lead to discrimination specifically. In the last chapter, I discussed the fact that a sexist outcome, behavior, or treatment does not necessarily mean any individuals hold sexist beliefs or are themselves sexist.[32] Structural sexism, and not sexism on the part of doctors, then, might be at stake when patients are denied needed care. For this reason, it is helpful to rely on a definition of sexism, as I do in the last chapter, that does not require insight into an individual's attitudes or beliefs; sometimes, they simply do not matter when structural bias is at play.

Of course, from the perspective of a patient denied needed medical care, it might not matter whether the doctor is personally against abortion, as is the case in conscientious objections, or finds abortion permissible and is prevented from offering it by a hospital policy for continued employment. Patients can suffer whatever the reason for the denial. And, since some evidence shows that "Ninety-seven percent of Ob-Gyns have encountered patients wanting an abortion, but only 14 percent of the doctors perform them," it is possible to conclude that a large number of patients face this trouble.[33]

In addition to the large proportion of hospitals that deny abortion and other reproductive care, a large proportion of doctors also work for hospitals.[34] More than half of all doctors work for hospitals overall, and that rate is increasing.[35] As a result, the fact that hospitals have discriminatory mandates takes on added significance; if one in six hospital beds was in a religious hospital, but the majority of doctors worked outside the hospital system, then religious policy would not have such a great impact on health care in the United States. But in reality, as the hospital goes, so does the health care: if your hospital does not provide a service, chances are, you cannot access that service anywhere.

Most doctors work at hospitals and a high proportion of hospitals do not allow abortion. The result is that many doctors simply will not provide abortions. In addition, the services religious hospitals refuse patients go beyond just offering abortions. Hormonal birth control, IUDs, tubal ligations, and other reproductive care are also at stake in such hospital guidelines.[36] I aim to distinguish between hospitals and doctors so as to acknowledge that doctors might be hindered by the Directives despite not believing in them. This distinction also helps identify where in the medical field the greatest problems arise for patients.

Since the existence of such hospitals is itself the result of granting exemptions to standing law,[37] the problem may be that too many discussions of abortion in hospital settings focus on such cases.[38] The religious freedom of someone who declines to perform an abortion is discussed at length, but the religious freedom of someone who wishes to perform an abortion is not similarly protected.[39] For example, as Sepper points out, legislation often protects some health-care professionals who want to refuse treatment to the detriment of others who want to offer it. She writes,

> Legislation in almost every state—known as "conscience clauses"—ensures that employers accommodate refusal and that refusing doctors and nurses face no adverse employment action for violating institutional policies (or professional discipline and liability for contravening acceptable medical standards). . . . First, conscience equally may compel a doctor or nurse to deliver a controversial treatment to a patient in need. But legislation meant to protect conscience, paradoxically, has undermined the consciences of these doctors and nurses. Second, endowing healthcare institutions with conscience via legislation is theoretically and practically problematic. By privileging the institutions' rights to refuse to provide certain treatments, legislation impinges on the rights of individual providers to provide care they feel obligated by conscience to deliver. Yet no theory of institutional conscience arrives at describing a concept akin to human conscience.[40]

The statistics given above suggest that at least some proportion of doctors are willing to provide abortion services but will not, due to hospital guidelines. In those cases, when both the doctor and the patient deem an abortion appropriate, but a bishop in charge prohibits it, both the doctor's and the patient's freedoms are curtailed.[41]

Doctors should not be left to fend for themselves in making such sacrifices in the face of massive institutional power. For example, larger medical institutions could provide support for doctors in these instances.[42] The American Medical Association actions include maintaining professional standards and preventing dilution of ethical standards, which theoretically could include the dilution of those ethical standards in the face of corporate religious pressure. This body has a Code of Medical Ethics,[43] which could theoretically prevent doctors from falling into this trap.[44] The AMA has specific safeguards in place to protect physician practices[45] and even has political and regulatory advocacy aims that include "protecting access to coverage" for patients.[46] But although these advocacy issues include protecting the Affordable Care Act, "Maintaining the strength of safety net programs like Medicaid and the Children's Health Insurance Program (CHIP)"; "Advocating to policymakers on state and federal levels to adequately fund Medicaid and ensure physician payment rates are sufficient to ensure meaningful access to care"; "Promoting Medicaid expansion to cover the uninsured"; and "Providing patient and physician advocates with the latest information and opportunities to take action in defense of their care," these advocacy priorities do not include legislative protections specifically for women, reproductive care, or attacks on access to OB/GYN services.[47] To the extent that the aims do include it, they should delineate the role the AMA could play in protecting doctors' rights to provide services.[48]

Other organizations failing to protect doctors and patients from nonmedical personnel imposing their religious beliefs on non-believers are states themselves. Laws in 40 states protect hospitals from liability when those hospitals deny needed care to women.[49] For example, Delaware's law states, "No hospital, hospital director or governing board shall be required to permit the termination of human pregnancies within its institution, and the refusal to permit such procedures shall not be grounds for civil liability to any person, nor a basis for any disciplinary or other recriminatory action against it by the State or any person."[50] What this law shows is that a hospital board can restrict the conduct of the individuals within it based on religious objections, even if no individual employed under the board or no patient seeking care in the institution shares the religious beliefs that would prevent access to care. These laws are also helpful in pointing out exactly which state laws hospitals likely would be violating when they deny care if they were not legislatively exempt. For example, civil liability, recriminatory action, claims for damages, discrimination, and others.[51]

These laws are also helpful in identifying the asymmetry in the legal framework. They exempt doctors who do not respect patients' constitutionally protected rights from legal ramifications on the one hand, and on the other hand, do not similarly exempt doctors who want to offer standard of care; whose conscience, religion, and inclination permit; and whose laws protect it, but whose employers do not. Considering both cases equally, would require the recognition that conscience can lead doctors to offer care as well as refuse it. Thus, conscience is not the determining factors in such cases; I argue moral evaluation of women can explain the perceived asymmetry where conscience cannot.

In fact, some case studies point in the other direction, such as convicting of involuntary manslaughter those Christian Science parents standing in the way of their children's care, or in other cases, doctors and hospitals suing for custody of Christian Science children so as to ensure care.[52] In those cases, religious reasons do not excuse a health-care provider from administering lifesaving care to a patient. Similarly, patients who do not stand to benefit from medical intervention and for whom medical intervention is neither clearly indicated nor requested sometimes receive it,[53] even as women who plead for it are denied.[54]

Once the meaning behind some abortion restrictions is identified, it does not just direct future responses and engagement with abortion opposition and help us aim toward a proper solution. It also more clearly identifies such denials as civil rights violations. If someone is denied medical care based on a protected class, then that denial could count as discrimination. The best explanation for denials of care is medical sexism.

I have already argued that morality does not permit discrimination against women, and that these denials of care amount to discrimination. Does the law permit discrimination against women?[55] Not until the passage of the Affordable Care Act (ACA) in 2010 was discrimination on the basis of sex prohibited by federal civil rights law in federally funded health programs or activities.[56] With the passage of the ACA, denying certain patients care by reference to their sex or on the basis of pregnancy is no longer permitted by law. According to Section 1557 of that law, sex discrimination includes pregnancy discrimination as well as contraception access.[57]

Since Catholic hospitals and other religious medical institutions that provide reproductive care treat their female and pregnant patients differently than other patients insofar as they do not follow standard of care for those subsets of patients, a strong case can be made that such actions are in violation of Section 1557 of the ACA. A Catholic hospital might stipulate that it is not discriminating against female patients because it also denies services to men. For example, Catholic hospitals refuse to perform vasectomies in addition to tubal ligations. But denial of a vasectomy does not put the patient's health at risk in the same way that a denial of a tubal ligation does. Because vasectomies cannot prevent against life-threatening conditions for the person receiving the procedure, and because vasectomies do not generally influence the health of the individual the way birth control services do, vasectomies are not standard of care for any particular condition. By contrast, abortions, tubal ligations, and other birth control services are standard of care for certain subsets of patients, primarily women. As a result, Catholic hospitals cannot lean on their mistreatment of male patients to justify their mistreatment of female patients because the cases are not analogous. Although they do not provide birth control services to anyone, they only violate medical standard of care for women. And although they do not provide abortions to men or women, for reasons described in chapter 5, the denial of abortions to men, such as trans men, can also constitute sexism.

Furthermore, it is essential to take into account the diversity of religion in the United States and not assume that all religious individuals are Christian, that all Christians seek these legislative exemptions, or that all permitted conscientious objectors fall into that category.[58] The religious freedom of the doctors who disproportionately wish to provide them is also relevant, especially if their religion or conscience not only permits, but also requires the action. If one's religion or conscience stipulates that abortion or contraception is permissible and even required in certain cases, then denial of one's wishes amounts to religious discrimination.[59] In other words, if it is religious discrimination to force a religious doctor to provide an abortion, then it might similarly be religious discrimination to force a religious doctor to cause the death of another through medical negligence.[60]

Non-Christian and atheist doctors are not the only relevant group of individuals whose freedom is at stake. Catholic and evangelical medical professionals have sometimes offered lifesaving abortions to their patients at great personal cost.[61] Restricting the free exercise of Catholic, evangelical, Jewish, atheist, and other religious and moral convictions by prohibiting them from performing a legally and constitutionally protected medical service in pursuit of their patients' health does not fully respect free exercise. In addition, the amount of control given to Catholic institutions to dictate their staff's actions is out of proportion with the amount of control federal law has to dictate citizens' actions. The only way to allow Catholic hospitals to dictate their staff's action on abortion is to give some people religious exemptions from the law of the land while denying others religious exemptions from institutional protocol when no legal exemption is even required. This double standard starts to look less like respect for religion and more like special treatment of antiabortion individuals in opposition to everyone else.[62]

RAPE AND INCEST EXCEPTIONS

Consider a common though not universal antiabortion position: that abortion restrictions should make exceptions for rape and incest.[63] The standard antiabortion position asserts that abortion is impermissible due to the moral status of the fetus, making abortion immoral and laws restricting it morally required. Abortion, according to this position, is murder: wrongful killing of persons or potential persons. However, as is sometimes acknowledged on both sides, if, in fact, fetuses have full moral personhood, then the circumstances under which they come to exist should have no bearing on their current set of moral rights, according to the genetic fallacy. The genesis of a thing does not establish its current moral evaluation. One does not inquire into the circumstances of adults' conception to determine their set of moral rights. Given the standard justification for abortion restriction, why, then, do some inquire into the circumstances of fetus' conceptions to determine their rights? How are the moderate views of abortion, which make these exceptions, justified? A standard understanding of the antiabortion position as focused on the moral personhood of the fetus cannot explain such views. To understand this particular moderate position on abortion, a look beyond the moral status of the fetus is required.

If the moral status of the fetus cannot explain rape and incest exceptions, then the moral status of the pregnant person comes into question. A reduced moral concern about certain pregnant women rather than a moral commitment to certain fetuses better explains the phenomenon. According to this explanation, special treatment in the cases of rape and incest is allowed not because the moral personhood of the fetus shifts depending on the circumstances of conception, but instead because the status of the pregnant person shifts depending on the circumstances of conception. In the case of rape, the woman does not choose to have sex and therefore her moral purity and even chastity are, from some perspectives, preserved. Thus, it is impermissible to override her right to bodily autonomy, even if an innocent bystander, the fetus, is sacrificed in protecting her rights. A victim of rape preserves her moral status by rejecting sexual intercourse and maintains her attendant rights as a result.[64]

Alternatively, those seeking abortion whose pregnancies are not the result of rape or incest implicitly chose to have sex. In the case of consensual sex, the pregnant woman's choice to have sex undermines her moral status. If a woman consents to sex, wants to have sex, or even seeks sex out, then according to this view, she is no longer worthy of the same moral rights to bodily autonomy, or, in some cases, even her right to life. More specifically, this position holds that a woman who chooses sex ought to face consequences. On this argument, the problem with abortion access is primarily that it allows for sex without the right sort of consequences.

These consequences hold not only a retributive role, ensuring that women receive punishment for sexual desire, but also a deterrent role, with the aim of altering women's behavior. If sex does not have negative consequences, then women cannot be trusted to curb their desire for sex. Female sexuality would thus be untethered.[65] Rape and incest exceptions do not preserve the consistent moral evaluation of fetuses across disparate cases; crucially, however, they preserve the consistent moral evaluation of women across disparate cases.

A byproduct of this view is that the pregnancy, the resulting baby, or the attendant motherhood is the negative consequence or punishment for the act of sex.[66] Far from lionizing motherhood, as some "family values" positions purport to do, this view takes pregnancy as an often burdensome, brutal, and life-threatening or life-effacing role that is a suitable and perhaps even required punishment for wanting to have sex.

Additionally, motherhood in the United States is sometimes viewed as a sexless role.[67] That means that motherhood can act as the appropriate form of restraint on the dangerous female sexuality at issue in a woman's choice to have sex; it imposes the chastity that preserves a woman's virtue. The implications of this view are broad. Iris Marion Young argues that, "The sex/gender system as we know it, then, enacts a border between motherhood and sexuality. . . . Freedom for women involves dissolving this separation."[68]

So, the standard antiabortion position views pregnancy, labor, delivery, and sometimes motherhood as an appropriate punishment for a woman taking control of her own sexuality. This position uses motherhood as a weapon against women. But that means that the standard antiabortion position not only views motherhood negatively, but also views the fetus itself negatively. Far from protecting the fetus and preserving its life, this argument primarily aims to use the baby as a bargaining chip in the control for women's sexuality, doling out babies as punishments for bad behavior. After the baby is born, its use for this purpose is diminished and the emphasis on its needs gets eliminated.[69]

In fact, policies to help young children once they are already born not only fail to serve the purpose of imposing a consequence of sex, but actually have the impact of helping new mothers, which would lessen their punishment. There might be other reasons for providing a social safety net that helps infants and children, making such a position have broad support. Still, views that withhold lifesaving help for babies and young children while also endorsing an antiabortion position are not contradictory or paradoxical, as sometimes claimed, but entirely consistent. If the difficulty in rearing children underlines the danger in having sex and giving birth, then withholding help to those who need it can serve as "just deserts" for undesirable behavior among those capable of pregnancy. This argument explains the connection between contraception and abortion. The idea that a woman ought to be punished or face consequences for sex means that both contraception and abortion are problematic because they both divorce sex from the "consequences" of motherhood and children.

This underlying view might be one reason why the high maternal mortality rate in the United States has been accepted for so long; gestation, labor, and delivery are not a sufficient punishment unless life threatening and preventable harm is possible.[70] Many causes might underlie a complex phenomenon like the maternal mortality rate and the corresponding failure of a large and urgent response, but sexism is also a sufficient explanatory factor. The United States does worse on measures of maternal mortality than any other developed nation in the world, with a rate that is triple that of Canada's and six times greater than the Scandinavian region's.[71] This comparison to other developed nations helps explain how unnecessary maternal morbidity is. Any explanation that does not incorporate sexism, such as statements on the state of the health delivery system in the United States or the overall declining health of the population, has to take into account the fact that the infant mortality rate reached its nadir just as the maternal mortality rate reached its zenith.[72]

Furthermore, intersectional feminism explains the ways in which different forms of oppression interact, amplifying the problem among some populations. That is, women of color do not just experience sexism and do not just experience racism; they also experience gendered forms of racism and racialized sexism. In this case, if the sexuality of women of color is perceived as more dangerous, a higher maternal mortality rate would be allowed to persist in that population, a fact that empirical evidence bears out. On this view, a high maternal mortality rate, especially as it exists currently, which is worse for already vulnerable populations like black and Latinx communities, is not unlike the demonization of such populations using racist and stigmatizing terms connected to uncontrolled sexuality.

For example, Patricia Hill Collins analyzes the term "welfare queen" as one not just connected to the politics of race and the attribution of pernicious and false stereotypes, but also a specifically gendered term, stating, "the welfare mother represents a woman of low morals and uncontrolled sexuality, factors identified as the cause of her impoverished state. . . . Black female control over sexuality and fertility is conceptualized as antithetical to elite White male interests."[73] According to Collins, the "welfare queen" must be demonized because she is not only threatening to White patriarchy due to the control she has over her sexuality and fertility; and is threatening not only because social safety nets like welfare, minimum wage, and child welfare programs make it possible to reject the kind of demeaning and exploitive jobs that fail to provide a living wage; but also because the welfare queen is defined as being a single mom, living without a male authority figure to oversee her and her children.[74] This particular type of misogynoir would then have a direct connection to the state of contraception and abortion services in the United States.

Thus, the antiabortion position that allows for exceptions for rape and incest aims to punish certain women, not protect certain fetuses. The type of woman being punished, or held accountable to certain avoidable consequences, is the type of woman who chooses, seeks out, or wants sex. Therefore, while the same act of abortion occurs in both instances, a woman who seeks an abortion after protected but consensual sex is a murderer, but a woman who seeks an abortion after rape is not. No moral difference between the fetuses or the acts can be observed. But large moral differences between the pregnant people are asserted.

One objection to this interpretation of some antiabortion views is that carrying a pregnancy to term after rape or incest is a bad outcome and that the bad outcome outweighs the value of the fetus. However, this reply is insufficient to explain the antiabortion position first, because it advocates a utilitarian calculus that weighs rights to life against other values, and is therefore no longer pro-life; second, because once it is agreed that the fetus's right to life is sometimes defeasible, it opens up the debate for other conditions that may override rights to life; and third, because it does not explain why an unwanted pregnancy after rape is worse than an unwanted pregnancy after consensual sex.

Another objection to this argument is that a woman who chooses sex does not lose her moral status but rather acquires new duties to the fetus.[75] In fact, perhaps parents acquire duties to their children in the same way.[76] However, this objection cannot explain the phenomenon because parents do not lose their bodily autonomy or rights to life when they have children, even if their duties to their children are very strong.[77] Only the lowering of moral status through erasure of rights, and not the existence of new duties, can explain antiabortion policies. Furthermore, acknowledging that the pregnant person acquires certain duties unique to her requires moving beyond moral commitments to the fetus, focusing instead on the moral evaluation of the person doing the gestating. Thus, the moral status of the fetus continues to distract from the real underlying reasons for the policies in question, which focus on the evaluation of the pregnant person.

A third objection is that abstinence is the only 100% effective method of preventing pregnancy, and therefore that people who engage in protected sex take on a certain amount of risk. However, this objection concedes the argument put forward in this chapter that the moral status of the fetus cannot explain abortion policy and only the actions of the prospective parents can. Once the abstinence-only proponent acknowledges that the individuals' actions create duties to the fetus, the discussion is no longer on the moral status of the fetus itself and instead is aimed at the pregnant individual.[78] This concession supports my view. Furthermore, since abstinence-only recommendations impose a chastity requirement to preserve a woman's bodily autonomy, this reply also supports the interpretation I defend.

This objection that abstinence can prevent the need for abortion is subject to another reply, which is the plausibility of avoiding pregnancy risk. Whether or not abstinence is very effective is itself subject to debate. If men rape about 20% of women in the United States, a woman merely choosing to abstain from sex is not sufficient to protect herself from the risk of pregnancy.[79] Due to the existence of men raping women, abstinence cannot be 100% effective at preventing pregnancy: some estimate 32,000 rape-related pregnancies in the United States every year.[80] Other data put the rate of pregnancy after rape at 5% nationally, while focusing on younger populations yields a rate of 12%, and other studies yield higher rates.[81] However, the antiabortion position in question already makes the exception for rape, so I can sidestep this problem with abstinence advocacy.

Whether or not abstinence is effective at preventing pregnancy, and therefore provides a method to avoid the risk of pregnancy, depends on what guidelines are used to measure effectiveness. Putting aside abstinence, take the example of the effectiveness of condoms. Condoms are 98% effective at preventing pregnancy if used correctly and every single time.[82] But looking instead at the effectiveness of condoms in actual use, condoms are only 85% effective at preventing pregnancy.[83] The 85% statistic is a much more accurate and realistic number to rely on when evaluating the effectiveness of condoms for health care.

What if we apply the same standard for abstinence? Although abstinence is often touted as being 100% effective,[84] this statistic should never be used in a society where men rape such a high percentage of women. However, as stipulated above, I am putting aside these cases of rape. Is abstinence effective among people who choose not to have sex and who men also do not rape? The answer, again, is no. In "perfect use" cases, the effectiveness of abstinence remains high. But looking at "typical use," as for condoms, the effectiveness of abstinence plummets.

Around 60% of college students who pledge abstinence break their vow.[85] And abstinence can yield another danger for those who choose it for moral reasons: like any crime, premeditation is morally worse than committing the crime in the heat of the moment. Similarly, premeditated sex is morally worse than sex that is unplanned, meaning that those who pledge abstinence might be less likely to take precautions against pregnancy when they do break their vows, since procuring protection is a form of premeditation. Those who pledge abstinence also may think they do not need any knowledge about protection against pregnancy, since they are not planning on taking on any risk, and may therefore be less informed than the general population. These are some of the many reasons abstinence does not reduce pregnancy rates in "typical use."[86] Depending on the standard used, then, abstinence is 2% more effective than condoms or 25% less effective than condoms in preventing pregnancy. Hormonal birth control pills are 99% effective in perfect use and 91% effective in typical use. They are also effective against pregnancy from rape in a way that abstinence and condoms are not, so are perhaps a better analog.[87] Abstinence is either 1% more effective than the pill or 31% less effective, depending on using a perfect use or typical use standard. It is not sufficiently realistic, then, to argue that someone can completely eliminate the risk for pregnancy.

Lastly, commitment to abstinence simply cannot explain abortion policy because abstinence-only recommendations are generally directed at children in the education system and not at all people susceptible to an unintended pregnancy. For example, no major religious or government-sponsored policies promote abstinence among married women. In fact, large-scale government and religious efforts sometimes recommend risky, unprotected sex among married populations like using the rhythm method or the withdrawal method, which have a 20% failure rate.[88]

Is the foreknowledge of possible pregnancy when choosing to have sex sufficient to justify the punishment of not having access to abortion? Others have addressed this point and ruled out its plausibility.[89] And, I have already argued that any such argument concedes that the debate is not about moral commitments to the fetus but instead about the actions of women.

Another related issue is that risk is not always treated this way in other contexts. For example, driving is a potentially dangerous act.[90]

When people get into motor accidents, states do not pass legislation to prevent motorists' access to health care because they accepted the risk of injury. If they end up at hospitals, doctors do not refrain from treating them due to the particular types of health care they need. Perhaps we find such people blameworthy, and even hold them financially responsible for the predicaments they find themselves in, just as people in need of reproductive care are financially responsible for any services provided to them. But no such case exists of preventing care entirely, preventing care for those who are willing to pay or preventing care from those who need it. People who take on risk generally do not lose their bodily autonomy, renounce their right to informed consent, lose their doctor-patient relationship, or get ignored in requests for help.[91]

What about types of illnesses that come about as the result of behavior that predictably leads to such consequences? In those cases, the risky activities individuals engage in that lead to illness also do not prevent them from getting care. For example, doctors do not withhold health care from patients who have cirrhosis of the liver as the result of alcoholism. In fact, among patients getting liver transplants, alcoholic liver disease (ALD) is one of the most common diagnoses.[92] States and courts do not prevent smokers from accessing pulmonary care and many lung transplant centers do not keep records on whether lung transplant recipients resume smoking.[93] Denials to patients who have voluntarily taken on added health risks are not universal. In fact, health care in our country tends to go in the opposite direction: a baby's congenital health problems are treated as pre-existing conditions and subject to higher financial penalties,[94] while an adult with cigarette smoke-induced pulmonary emphysema may have medical care covered by an insurance plan. At least in other contexts, we do not mete out health care based on the riskiness of the behavior that led to the need. But, we do it in abortion services.

The problem with both contraception and abortion, then, is not the moral personhood of the fetus, which does not exist in the first case and is not in question in the second case. I argue the problem instead is that women ought to face consequences for sex, and both abortion and contraception intervene. If a woman does have sex, presumably, she should be punished for it. Sexism is a better explanation of the phenomenon than the alternatives and can explain both where other explanations cannot. As Marlene Gerber Fried argues, "When pregnancy is finally viewed as a voluntary gift of life to another, not a woman's duty, the abortion debate will not turn on the question of when life begins."[95]

One might also object that because adoption is a possibility in the case of unwanted pregnancy, motherhood is not specifically maligned as a punishment for sex, even if pregnancy, labor, and delivery are. The burden on pregnant people created by banning abortion is not that people must raise children they do not want, but that they must carry fetuses up until the point—birth—that their bodies are no longer necessary for the fetuses' survival. However, pregnancy carries risks of mortality and morbidity,[96] whether or not the pregnant person rears the baby. In fact, adoption rates do shift with abortion law.[97]

Furthermore, focusing on the possibility of adoption as a consolation prize for an unwanted pregnancy turns the pregnant person into a breeder for others. It disregards bodily autonomy, whether or not it imposes duties after birth. Adoption is no more a solution to the problem of unwanted pregnancies than the illegal organ trade is a solution to the problem of kidney and liver failure. Using people's bodies against their consent to create more children would be impermissible, even if there were not hundreds of thousands of children in foster care in the United States.[98] Thus, abortion policy in this case is still reliant on sexism, rather than moral commitments to the fetus.

Even explanations that look to be about the moral status of the fetus actually undermine the moral status of the pregnant person and thus can be best explained by medical sexism in my view. For example, it is sometimes asserted that the growth of a fetus into a human being is a natural process, and interruption of that natural process is impermissible.[99] According to this argument, if we just leave the fetus alone, it has the resources within itself to grow into a person, and thus this predictable, natural, and inevitable personhood is threatened during abortion. This argument could be subject to the fallacy of the appeal to nature. However, even assuming that all that is natural is also good and all that is unnatural is also bad, this argument is still suspect. That is because the idea that a fetus will develop into a full, rational, autonomous being if we leave it alone only makes sense if the "we" in that clause does not include the pregnant person. A fetus will not develop into a competent adult if the pregnant person leaves it alone any more than a seed will turn into a plant if left in the dried goods bin of a supermarket. At least some people seeking abortion might even say the antiabortion activists can go ahead and take the fetus. Yet, the removal of a fetus from a pregnant person before the point of viability is called an abortion, and leaving it alone to let it develop with someone else's help would be restricted as such.

Furthermore, the view that a pregnant person contributes nothing to the development of a fetus, leaving it alone to grow, arises only when that view is compatible with control over her behavior. When a pregnant woman seeks an abortion, she is told that she contributes nothing to the fetus and need only leave it alone to ensure it grows into a person; this denial of an abortion undermines her autonomy. But when a pregnant woman seeks to consume drugs or alcohol, suddenly, her every behavior does influence the fetus and is accordingly blameworthy.[100] Even if people have children with higher IQs when they drink alcohol during pregnancy,[101] and even if using crack cocaine during pregnancy has no discernible impact on IQ,[102] according to this view, it is better to control women's behavior during pregnancy by criminalizing the use of recreational drugs than follow the scientific evidence.[103] Yet, when poverty has a lifelong negative impact on a fetus such that greater resources to support the pregnant person's autonomy could benefit the fetus greatly, no action needs to be taken to protect that fetus. Only when the same fetus is impacted by illicit substances is intervention needed, even if poverty has a greater impact than psychotropic drugs.[104] Thus, a pregnant person does contribute to a pregnancy with her actions, and a fetus cannot just develop on its own without her help, but these contributions are only highlighted when convenient. In fact, so long as it does not lead to birth control or abortion access, even telling women what to do when they are not pregnant—because they could become pregnant—makes sense.[105] According to the Preventative Services Task Force, it is better to recommend all women of childbearing age consume folic acid for the proper development of a fetus they do not want than to recommend all women of childbearing age consume birth control for the prevention of a fetus they do not want.[106] Thus, sexism better explains these broader policies toward women, of which abortion policy is only one part.

Thus far, I have argued that standard antiabortion policy and arguments are inconsistent and cannot rely on moral commitments to the fetus.[107] Instead, the best explanation references the moral status of the pregnant person. Without the underlying explanation of medical sexism, one possible avenue toward maintaining consistency, then, is to argue against the permissibility of abortion in cases of rape. Making abortion illegal in all cases with no exceptions could presumably improve the consistency of the position. However, this approach would treat the symptom and not the cause of antiabortion law. Only with the understanding of antiabortion law as a means to further sexist aims in controlling women's bodies does a successful resolution arise.

Furthermore, the point of this argument is not to praise those who achieve consistency by rejecting the moral status of women in all cases over those who only reject the moral status of women in some cases; it is to elucidate the underlying cause of antiabortion positions so as to better understand and respond to them. To someone whose reason for advocating pro-life positions is to ensure women who have sex face the proper consequences, no proof of the moral or biological features of a fetus will ever hold sway. Understanding the root cause of a position is the best way to address it. If sex-shaming and sexism at least partly underlie some attacks on women's health, then a proper response would be incomplete without addressing those issues.

And, focusing on the moral status of the fetus not only sidesteps the issue in abortion, since I have argued the pregnant person's moral status is actually in question, but also fails to protect women's moral status in other related scenarios. That is, if the moral status of the fetus is the reason that abortion is restricted, then there is no connection to other restrictions on women, from birth control to sex work. However, if, as I argue, sexism is a source of abortion restrictions, then abortion restrictions are related to these other forms of control. Understanding the common cause allows these issues to be addressed in a unified way and failing to understand the common cause splinters efforts to protect women's rights.

For example, sex work is a trope used to demean and undermine women in a variety of contexts. In the most obvious case, women in sex work face vicious attacks physically, legally, and emotionally, while men who hire sex workers do not.[108] However, the attack on status goes the other way, too. Epithets used to malign sex workers are utilized against women in other contexts as a way of demeaning them. According to bell hooks, epithets related to sex work even have been used when their literal meaning is absurd. For example, in talking about the systematic rape of black women during slavery, hooks states that,

> Because sexist religious doctrines had taught them that women were the seducers of men, they believed black women were not totally blameless. Frequently, they used the term "prostitution" to refer to the buying and selling of black women for sexually exploitative purposes. Since prostitutes are women and men who engage in sexual behavior for money or pay of some kind, it is a term inaccurately used when applied to enslaved black women who rarely received compensation for the use of their bodies as sexual latrines. Abolitionist women and men labeled black women "prostitutes" because they were trapped by the language of the Victorian ethos.[109]

In a case of a white man raping an enslaved black woman, blaming the victim as being a "prostitute," as if she could have chosen to have sex, let alone be paid for it, strains credibility to the point where the word seems to lose all meaning. In fact, use of the word only makes sense at all if the most degrading insult that could befall a woman is to be labeled someone who desires sex, actively seeks to control her access to it, benefits financially from it, and threatens accurate identification of paternity.

Feminists have argued that both the protection of celibate women and the degradation of sexual women under discussion in the abortion debate are sources of misogyny. Katherine Rogers makes this point in *Troublesome Helpmate: A History of Misogyny in Literature.* She states,

> Of the cultural causes of misogyny, rejection of or guilt about sex is the most obvious. It leads naturally to degradation of woman as the sexual object and projection onto her of the lust and desire to seduce which a man must repress in himself. At the same time that he denigrated woman's sexual function, the preoccupation with sex resulting from the attempt to repress desire is apt to make him see her exclusively as a sexual being, more lustful than man and not spiritual at all. . . . Misogyny can also develop as a result of the idealization with which men have glorified women as mistresses, wives, and mothers. This has led to a natural reaction, a desire to tear down what has been raised unduly high.[110]

According to Rogers, then, both the argument that women who are raped should be able to access abortion because they were raped, as well as the argument that women who have sexual intercourse voluntarily should not have access to abortion because they did so voluntarily, are both connected to misogyny.[111] bell hooks, who cites Rogers in the context of colonialism states that, "Colonial white men expressed their fear and hatred of womanhood by institutionalizing sexist discrimination and sexist oppression."[112] According to hooks, this twin cause of misogyny has a distinctly racial feature, which helps explain the sorts of misogynoir discussed above.[113]

OTHER EXCEPTIONS TO ANTIABORTION VIEWS

Holding up antiabortion views to added scrutiny demonstrates the lack of compelling justification for many common, yet seemingly unconnected positions. Another feature of antiabortion positions that seem inexplicable only when we view such restrictions as directed toward protecting the fetus, rather than controlling the pregnant person, are positions like spousal or parental permission, the doctrine of double effect, abortion bans after a certain point in a pregnancy, and failures to save the life of the mother.[114] In some such cases, saving the fetus is impossible, either because the fetus has life-threatening abnormalities that would make life excruciatingly painful and/or short, or because the fetus is already in the process of dying. If the fetus does not have hope of living, is in danger of facing a wrongful life, or is already dying, then protection of the fetus cannot logically justify the sort of abortion restrictions in question.

I argued that the moral status of the fetus cannot explain abortion policy, but the moral status of the pregnant person can. Laws aimed at requiring a pregnant person to get permission to abort fall under this explanation. For example, *Planned Parenthood v. Casey* struck down laws requiring spousal consent or notice to the husband of a person seeking an abortion, but such laws were and continued to be common.[115] Laws requiring parental notification perform a similar role: 37 states require parental involvement when a minor seeks an abortion.[116] These laws aim to subvert the decision of the person seeking an abortion to a father or husband. In those cases, patriarchal control over female decision-making, and not the status of the fetus, explain the laws.

Similarly, take laws aimed at prohibiting abortion after a certain point in the pregnancy.[117] Fetal pain is sometimes used to justify bans after 20 weeks, though no evidence suggests that fetuses can feel pain at that gestational age[118] and little evidence exists that fetuses feel pain until 29–34 weeks,[119] with greater evidence pointing to 40 weeks.[120] Pain is not the only consideration for killing, meaning that even utilitarians who place the utmost emphasis on pain are able to claim killing is sometimes permissible when causing pain is not.[121] But even if it were, I already argued that pointing to the fetus as an explanation for controlling female medical decisions is insufficient to explain the practice when the same attitudes and practices exist where no fetus is present, such as in the case of birth control discussed in chapters 1–5. In addition, though abortions occurring after 24 weeks of pregnancy make up a tiny proportion of all abortion, probably less than 1%, a significant portion of those seeking abortions later in a pregnancy face greater obstacles and wish they could have obtained an abortion earlier.[122] Around 60% of women report obstacles that delay access to abortion.[123] These obstacles are compounded as the pregnancy progresses, which is why evidence shows that "Later abortion recipients experienced logistical delays (e.g., difficulty finding a provider and raising funds for the procedure and travel costs), which compounded other delays in receiving care."[124] If abortions that come later in pregnancy are worse than abortions that come earlier in pregnancy, as these laws purport to assert, then those opposed to later abortions should seek to expand abortion access.

Another standard moderate position is to allow for the permissibility of abortion when the life of the mother is at stake.[125] Such exceptions for the life of the mother once again show that antiabortion restrictions are not about saving fetal lives, but rather about the pregnant person. After all, if the fetus is a full moral person worthy of protecting, and if the pregnant person contributes nothing to the existence of the fetus, which would live if left alone, then what difference would it make if allowing the fetus to live causes the byproduct of another's death? This discussion more closely resembles arguments concerning innocent threats than standard self-defense considerations. Utilitarian arguments notwithstanding, it is generally impermissible in U.S. law to kill one to save another, such as organ redistribution would accomplish.[126] Female freedom and martyrdom should not be under the purview of governmental operatives, but such restrictions make it so.

Or perhaps such exceptions to abortion restrictions have everything to do with the fetus. Perhaps exceptions for the life of the mother tacitly accept that the pregnant person's life does have more moral value than a fetus. In that case, the exception itself is no longer the problem. The exception accurately reflects the underlying position that fully autonomous, rational beings have greater moral worth than a fetus, which lacks autonomy, self-awareness or sentience. The problem, then, would only remain for the restrictions themselves: If fetuses are of lesser moral worth than the average adult, then the leftover restrictions outside the life-of-the-mother restrictions look to be much more about controlling female autonomy than about protecting fetal life already accepted as having lesser value. Understanding the common sexist strains underlying both birth control and abortion restrictions sheds light on each.

An objection to this argument is that it creates a false dichotomy: perhaps some views hold that the fetus has greater than zero value but less value than the life of the mother.[127] Would abortion restrictions then be consistent? I argue they would not. If the fetus has nonzero value but less value than the life of the mother, then this view opens the door to cost-benefit analyses that would allow certain very weighty reasons, when compounded, to move the scale toward the permissibility of abortion. In that case, however, the focus returns again to the moral status of the pregnant people: their reasons, character, outcomes, and decisions.

Other features of the standard antiabortion positions underline this explanation by reference to sexism. For example, a standard antiabortion position is to impose obstacles in obtaining abortion through legal means without going so far as to criminalize abortion with punishment like prison time.[128] If abortion is murder, what could justify this discrepancy? One explanation is that after the abortion has occurred, no benefits in forced pregnancy can accrue. Another is that women are not competent to make the choice in the first place, so cannot justifiably receive punishment for it.[129] Still, criminalization of women (not usually men)[130] who choose abortion has occurred in the past in the United States[131] and could be viewed as consistent with the position outlined by pro-life advocates today.[132] If holding back on criminalizing abortion is merely done out of political expediency and criminalization is the long-term goal, then sexism could still provide a consistent explanation of this view.[133]

Furthermore, once medical sexism is identified as an underlying cause of the antiabortion position, the parallels between practices on these disparate cases become more obvious. For example, implementing waiting periods for abortion is generally considered to be an obstacle to access, either explicitly by policies aiming to eliminate abortion, or in court decisions determining the permissibility of waiting periods.[134] TRAP laws (Targeted Restrictions on Abortion Providers) fall under this category as well.[135] While doctors may not generally accept that waiting periods imposed through testing requirements limit access to contraception, the similarities between abortion and contraception in reproductive health help illuminate the underlying issues and point to birth control restriction as a very powerful impact of waiting periods for birth control.

In addition, from a health perspective, very little similarity connects abortion access and birth control pill prescription renewals. They are different procedures, based on different patient needs, affecting the patients in different ways, with different side effects, requiring different health providers with differing specialties, and subject to different insurance coverage with different types of payouts. The understanding of medical sexism as the underlying cause of the similar treatment, then, helps offer a unifying explanation of what is going on in both otherwise divergent cases.

These restrictions have real impacts on access to abortion. Since some states impose waiting periods for abortion access like requiring a 24- to 72-hour wait after an initial consultation, at least some women will be unable to meet the requirements for abortion access even when dealing with medical staff who are willing to perform the procedure.[136] For example, 35 states require women receive counseling before an abortion, 27 states require a waiting period between 18 and 72 hours in between the consultation and the procedure, six states require that the person seeking an abortion be told that personhood begins at conception, and several require that factually inaccurate information be given to the patient on the risks or efficacy of the procedure.[137] Thus, even when abortion providers are available to patients, state and local laws can sometimes mean that the obstacles are insurmountable for the average patient.

Legal mandates for vaginal sonograms prior to abortion may also fit this model of overriding patient preference. No medical reason justifies the practice; medical sexism is instead a better explanation. Forcing a pregnant person to view an image of the fetus before abortion aims at changing patients' minds on their course of action through punitive measures. In other words, such practices do not take seriously the choices of those seeking abortion.[138] Counseling, which is a euphemism for undermining female choice and is not generally required for other medical procedures except in the case of consultation, is similarly inherently infantilizing because it displaces the state's decision for the patient's and uses the doctor as the mouthpiece for that violation of autonomy.[139]

ANTIABORTION AND ANTI-BIRTH CONTROL: WHAT PRO-CHOICE AND PRO-LIFE POLICIES DO NOT HAVE IN COMMON

Abortion policy is a hotly contested issue; those in favor of access and those opposed to access are perceived to be on opposite ends of the political spectrum in the United States.[140] Given the controversy surrounding it, one would not expect a lot of common ground between the two sides.[141] But one issue both sides should be able to agree on is birth control. If abortion is morally wrong, then preventing unwanted pregnancies should be the greatest priority of pro-life policy. If abortion is no different than murdering babies, then prevention, at any cost, should be the most urgent and primary concern. This explains why antiabortion extremists who are willing to kill abortion providers exist: they think they are killing one to save many.[142] Furthermore, from the pro-choice perspective, if abortion is permissible because choice must be protected, then birth control is as significant a priority as abortion. Thus, opposing sides on abortion could theoretically still work together to ensure everyone who wants birth control can obtain it, no matter what. And, since focusing on points of agreement is more likely to bring political change and have a greater impact, abortion in these circumstances could fade into the background of the political landscape. In this hypothetical, it does not lose its value entirely; it just loses its value in advancing one of the chief goals of either side.

Despite having the overlapping goals, despite having a unified mission, and despite being in agreement on one of the most central features of their views, pro-choice and pro-life policy are not aligned on this issue. Planned Parenthood prevents hundreds of thousands of unintended pregnancies every year.[143] That means it prevents at least some significant share of abortions.[144] If the organization serves such a great share of the total publicly funded contraceptive services offered in the United States, we might expect to see pro-life fundraisers for Planned Parenthood.[145] Or, if Planned Parenthood itself is tainted, pro-life policy could be created to set up clinics in every county to dispense birth control to anyone who wants it. Why are these policies still forthcoming? Do pro-life and pro-birth control access policy conflict? Is birth control so bad that it exceeds the moral wrong of abortion, justifying the limitations on it, despite its value in preventing abortion? If it were, that feature of birth control would explain why pro-life policies oppose it, even as it remains the single greatest factor in preventing abortion, and, with 99% of women relying on birth control,[146] also fairly pedestrian.

Why might policymakers not only overlook a successful means toward their goals, but also actively oppose it? Several possible answers are available. It is possible that every pro-lifer also believes that all sex must be procreative sex.[147] Several reasons make this possibility unlikely. The average American has around two children. That means a lot of non-procreative sex likely is occurring, especially given the high rates of contraception use in the United States. Of course, the people who oppose birth control and abortion because they believe sex should only be for procreation could merely be acting hypocritically at astonishingly high rates. However, this sort of selective hypocrisy would raise more questions than it answers. If sex ought to be for procreation only when deciding abortion and birth control law, but not when deciding whether heterosexual sex ought to be closely regulated by the government, then hypocrisy provides no added explanation to the phenomenon.

Second, no underlying theoretical position connects antiabortion views to views about procreative sex. It is possible that everyone who holds one view happens to hold the other, unconnected view, but is unlikely. Third, although religious justifications might be able to be given for both, this explanation also begs the question: If religions endorse both unrelated views, why do they do so? It is a separate question whether any Biblical justification can be found for either view.[148]

But, even if one could give a Biblical foundation for both claims, which is itself controversial,[149] it would still require cherry picking Biblical passages for the average American. For example, laws to uphold other Biblical rules like the prohibition in the Ten Commandments against graven images are uncommon. It would also require forcing others to follow one's own religious dictates in a way that is not generally accepted in other domains.[150] Thus, the question of sexism still arises.

Fourth, the emphasis on procreative sex could also beg the question, given that it has led to a great deal of control and regulation of women's behavior. For example, the oversight and regulation of birth control distribution is much more prevalent than the oversight and regulation of pornography distribution, male masturbation, sex with infertile men, or heterosexual sex. Other features of the law that seem to be regulating male behavior, such as historical prohibitions on sodomy,[151] could be explained better through sexism, since it is viewed to violate non-procreative sex, the "natural supremacy" of men,[152] place men in the "female role" of being penetrated, or connect to an intersecting axis of oppression.[153] In fact, prohibitions on non-procreative sex themselves could be viewed as a way to displace female sexuality and female sexual pleasure with a more acceptable desire for children.

For example, consider the view that all sex must be procreative sex and thus that contraception is therefore impermissible. But suppose some who hold this view also recommend the rhythm method, in which people capable of creating a pregnancy through sex choose certain days in a menstrual cycle to abstain from intercourse and instead have sex on "safe" days unlikely to coincide with ovulation.[154] The rhythm method relies on the notion that it is impossible to conceive during certain days of the menstrual cycle. However, having sex during days when it is impossible to conceive is not having procreative sex. In that case, some who defend the notion of sex as procreative are willing to recommend non-procreative sex. Thus, the common thread between advocating for some types of contraception and opposing others is not the preservation of procreative sex or the attitude toward the potential fetus but rather the social control of sex, specifically, female behavior.

Plenty of explanations exist for opposing both contraception and abortion, but I argue sexism is a plausible and compelling explanation and better fits at least some phenomena. According to the argument I have offered here, discrimination against people seeking birth control and discrimination against people seeking abortion exist along a continuum. They are, at their root, discriminatory against women and fearful of women's sexuality and therefore an attempt to control women's bodies and sexuality. If sexual intercourse can undermine the moral status of a woman to the point where her life and rights should only be protected if she does not want to have sex (e.g., rape), the sorts of restrictions that appear so commonly in birth control access have a fuller explanation. After all, the common feature between a pregnant person and a woman seeking birth control that would justify overriding autonomy in both cases is not a fetus; it is the fact that they are perceived of as having or planning to have consensual sex.

Sometimes, this fear of women wanting to have sex in the birth control debate is explicit. Parents worry that birth control access will mean their children will have sex;[155] Rush Limbaugh argued that Sandra Fluke, who was seeking birth control access for others, was herself seeking out sex, calling her names related to this assertion.[156] This sexism could explain the purported alignment of birth control with promiscuity, though the two have no relation.[157] Why would an increase in sexual partners, as Limbaugh attributed to Fluke in an attempt to discredit her, be relevant? Because, if removing the punishments of children and motherhood from sexual intercourse could result in altered sexual behavior on the part of women, even if only in theory, then access to birth control must be removed in all possible cases.[158] If people who use birth control are promiscuous, then people who do not use it are chaste. Denying birth control ensures the chastity of women; birth control policy succeeds in controlling women.

Another side effect of standard antiabortion policy that also maligns birth control is the double bind it creates for those aiming to control their reproduction. If you are criticized for seeking an abortion, but also cannot gain access to birth control, and pregnancy remains a life-threatening venture, then no permissible option to limit fertility remains. Lest abstinence seem like a possible alternative, note that some who hold this view believe sex with one's spouse is a moral duty, while others even believe spousal rape is not a crime, meaning that abstinence is not an available option, at least for married women who want to limit the number of children they have.[159] Of course, the double bind created by opposition to both birth control and abortion is a feature, not a bug, of the position. If the standard moderate antiabortion position has the goal to restrict women rather than protect fetuses, these seemingly contradictory positions come into alignment.

I already discussed attempts to advocate for ineffective means of birth control.[160] Other policies attempt to block access. In fact, in *Burwell v. Hobby Lobby Stores, Inc.*, antiabortion advocates falsely characterized hormonal birth control methods as abortifacients to better prevent access to them.[161] Even if the plaintiffs morally oppose birth control, they should at least be interested in the difference between birth control and abortion, instead of defying scientific consensus to call certain forms of birth control abortifacients. What it looks like the corporations are doing is making false claims about the scientific evidence to argue that there is no difference between birth control and abortion.[162] In other words, it appears as though they are ignoring the science and instead calling birth control that prevents implantation like IUDs an abortifacient.

In reality, their false equivalence may have nothing to do with the science. What they may actually be doing is making claims on the *moral* equivalence between birth control and abortion, which are both equally necessary to control women's bodies, though both do not have the same impact on fetuses. Focusing on the false characterization of the science in the case, then, misses the point: birth control is as bad as abortion not because it kills fetuses like abortion does but because it gives women control over their sexuality and freedom like abortion does. No amount of scientific literacy, then, would convince those who seek to control contraceptive access that an IUD is a morally permissible form of birth control, if the stance against birth control is essentially a moral one and not a scientific one.

THE PRO-CHOICE POSITION

Perhaps it is merely obvious that birth control and abortion restrictions are sexist, and therefore that this point is hardly worth making. If many—especially feminists—agree that restrictions on birth control and other forms of reproductive health are sexist, what value do I bring by making this argument? First, drawing attention to an issue helps identify it. Second, identifying the problem helps solve it through the proper channels. Third, the identification of sexism helps make sense of broader commonalities and themes in reproductive health specifically and medical care generally. Highlighting this pattern has its own value. Though many feminists would agree that restrictions on birth control and abortion are sexist, they nevertheless take their opponents at face value, and thus argue that fetuses do not have moral status; or do not have the same moral status as full, autonomous women; or that pregnant people have bodily autonomy to evacuate a fetus. These arguments fail to take into account that sexism must be addressed to protect reproductive rights. In addition, these arguments fail to take into account a proposed antiabortion view that women may lose their moral status as full, autonomous beings when they have sex.

For example, take the excerpt from a Supreme Court decision affirming rights to abortion access quoted in chapter 3: "The ability of women to participate equally in the economic and social life of the Nation has been facilitated by their ability to control their reproductive lives."[163] I do not argue against the truth of this claim or the import of a Supreme Court opinion citing it as a reason to strike down a law. It is valuable to point out the role that birth control plays in women's lives and that full citizenship requires reproductive autonomy. However, such arguments assume their opponents do not realize these facts and only accidentally restrict citizenship. In other words, such pro-choice arguments are premised on the idea that once the antiabortion advocates realize that equal participation in economic and social life are threatened by their proposals, they will rescind those proposals. But if the aim of these policies is to restrict citizenship, then pointing out that they restrict citizenship does not go far enough in addressing the underlying problem. If, instead, we fully grapple with the sexism in such proposals, it is insufficient to argue that abortion and birth control limitations are restrictive; that is the point. Calling out and addressing sexism would instead be a more effective response.

Thus, standard pro-choice arguments that aborted fetuses are not moral persons[164] and that unwanted pregnancy impermissibly violates pregnant people's rights[165] are incidental to the issues at hand. They are relevant only because antiabortion advocates rely on flawed arguments to achieve their real aims. Pro-choice policy, then, falls short of addressing the underlying issues. Rhetorically, legally, and politically, a more effective approach to the issue would be to identify the sexism in such proposals, call it out, and challenge it. Without mentioning sexism, an argument might be interesting or powerful, but it would not be complete. One cannot win an argument by attacking a smokescreen, leaving what is concealed untouched. Furthermore, too much emphasis on the smokescreen takes away from pro-choice policy. If antiabortion advocates only use abortion restrictions to achieve the aim of punishing women, they can easily alter or shift these concealment practices, giving the pro-choice position a moving target. By discussing the moral status of the fetus, pro-choice philosophers wrongly cede the terms of the argument to their opposition, leading them down unfruitful paths.

CONCLUSION

In chapters 1 through 3, I argued that birth control restrictions are physically damaging as well as illegal. But without acknowledging that they also violate autonomy and informed consent, infantilize the patient, and are sexist, as I argued in chapters 4 and 5, then it is difficult to address the problem. Doctors can untether birth control from Pap tests while still exerting control over patients by shifting their conduct to other restrictive practices or demeaning behavior, which I discuss in the next chapter. Addressing the symptom without addressing the cause ensures the expression of disrespect will take a different form instead of eliminating it altogether. Similarly, abortion restrictions can—and have—taken on different features to circumvent direct attacks. When courts rule certain abortion restrictions unconstitutional, antiabortion activists propose different restrictions rather than eliminating restrictions. It is my aim to give a correct account of reproductive and women's health issues so as to better address the problems surrounding them.

NOTES

1. "What happens when we think of being pregnant as an intrinsic value, and describe it less as a process of producing a baby and more as a way of being-in-the-world with uniquely interesting characteristics?" Young, *On Female Body Experience*, 10.

2. Chavkin et al., "Conscientious Objection and Refusal to Provide Reproductive Healthcare," S46.

3. Hartman and Werhane, *The Global Corporation*, 396.

4. Warren, "On the Moral and Legal Status of Abortion." Though note Kittay, "At the Margins of Moral Personhood."

5. "States Enact Record Number of Abortion Restrictions in First Half of 2011"; Iati and Paul, "Everything You Need to Know about the Abortion Ban News"; "State Bans on Abortion Throughout Pregnancy"; Wax-Thibodeaux and Cha, "Georgia Governor Signs 'Heartbeat Bill,' Giving the State One of the Most Restrictive Abortion Laws in the Nation."

6. Davis, *Women, Culture & Politics*, 55; Zaveri, "Mother of Dead Woman Says Medics Told Her She Could Not Afford Ambulance."

7. Bearak, Burke, and Jones, "Disparities and Change over Time in Distance Women Would Need to Travel to Have an Abortion in the USA."

8. Bearak, Burke, and Jones.

9. Bliss et al., "Estimating Proximity to Care."

10. Bliss et al.

11. Chavkin et al., "Conscientious Objection and Refusal to Provide Reproductive Healthcare," S43; Sepper, "Zombie Religious Institutions," 933.

12. Sepper, "Zombie Religious Institutions," 932.

13. Kaye et al., "Health Care Denied." American Civil Liberties Union. May 2016. https://www.aclu.org/report/report-health-care-denied.

14. Kaye et al., "Health Care Denied," 24.

15. Chavkin et al., "Conscientious Objection and Refusal to Provide Reproductive Healthcare," S43.

16. Chavkin et al., S41; International Covenant on Civil and Political Rights.

17. Chavkin et al., "Conscientious Objection and Refusal to Provide Reproductive Healthcare," S43.

18. NeJaime and Siegel, "Conscience Wars," 2518. See also The European Court of Human Rights, which decided that, "…the applicants cannot give precedence to their religious beliefs and impose them on others as justification for their refusal to sell such products, since they can manifest those beliefs outside the professional sphere." PICHON and SAJOUS v. FRANCE, Reports of Judgments and Decisions 2001-X.

19. United States Conference of Catholic Bishops, "Ethical and Religious Directives for Catholic Health Care Services, Fifth Edition."

20. Kaye et al., "Health Care Denied," 7.

21. Kaye et al., "Health Care Denied," 7.

22. Guiahi, "Catholic Health Care and Women's Health."

23. Kaye et al., "Health Care Denied," 7.

24. Kaye et al., "Health Care Denied," 19.

25. Guiahi, "Catholic Health Care and Women's Health."

26. Schuklenk, "Conscientious Objection in Medicine."

27. Chavkin et al., "Conscientious Objection and Refusal to Provide Reproductive Healthcare," S42, S45.

28. Delston, "When Doctors Deny Drugs"; Schuklenk, "Conscientious Objection in Medicine," 54. Schuklenk, "Accommodating Conscientious Objection in Medicine-Private Ideological Convictions Must Not Trump Professional Obligations," 229.

29. Schuklenk, "Conscientious Objection in Medicine," 55.

30. Gold, "Proportion Of OB-GYNs Offering Abortions May Be Lower Than Thought"; "Most U.S. Obstetrician-Gynecologists in Private Practice Do Not Provide Abortions and Many Also Fail to Provide Referrals," Guttmacher Institute, November 21, 2017, https://www.guttmacher.org/news-release/2017/most-us-obstetrician-gynecologists-private-practice-do-not-provide-abortions-and.

31. Gold, "Proportion Of OB-GYNs Offering Abortions May Be Lower Than Thought."

32. Tello, "Racism and Discrimination in Health Care"; Hardeman, Medina, and Kozhimannil, "Structural Racism and Supporting Black Lives—The Role of Health Professionals"; King and Redwood, "The Health Care Institution, Population Health and Black Lives"; US. Department of Health and Human Services, Centers for Disease Control and Prevention, and National Center for Health Statistics, "Health, United States, 2015: With Special Feature on Racial and Ethnic Health Disparities."

33. Gold, "Proportion Of OB-GYNs Offering Abortions May Be Lower Than Thought."

34. Gunderman, "Who Does Your Physician Work For?"

35. Gunderman.

36. Hope, "Woman Claims Doctor Refused to Remove IUD for Religious Reasons." Kaye et al., "Health Care Denied."

37. As opposed to countries like Finland and Sweden. Savulescu and Schuklenk, "Doctors Have No Right to Refuse Medical Assistance in Dying, Abortion or Contraception," 163.

38. "Conscience and Religious Freedom"; Office for Civil Rights, "Conscience Protections for Health Care Providers"; Thomson, "A Defense of Abortion."

39. Sepper, "Taking Conscience Seriously."

40. Sepper, 1505.

41. The Church Amendment to the Health Programs Extension Act of 1973, Pub. L. No. 93-45 is meant to protect medical staff working at a federally funded entity from discrimination on the basis of performing abortions. Feder, "The History and Effect of Abortion Conscience Clause Laws."

42. I thank Jeff Armel for this point.

43. American Medical Association, "AMA Code of Medical Ethics," 2016, https://www.ama-assn.org/delivering-care/ama-code-medical-ethics.

44. American Medical Association, "AMA Code of Medical Ethics."

45. American Medical Association, "AMA Advocacy Overview: Protecting Physician Practices."

46. American Medical Association, "What's Happening in 2018?: Top AMA Advocacy Issues."

47. American Medical Association. Though they originally opposed universal health care. Brownlee, *Overtreated*, 19.

48. Uttley, "State Oversight of Hospital Consolidation."

49. Kaye et al., "Health Care Denied," 30.

50. Del. Code Ann. tit. 24, § 1791(b)

51. Kaye et al., "Health Care Denied," 32.

52. May, "Challenging Medical Authority The Refusal of Treatment by Christian Scientists."

53. "Florida House of Representatives - HB 35E - Authority for the Governor to Issue a One-Time Stay to Prevent the Withholding of Nutrition and Hydration from a Patient."

54. Tamesha Means, Plaintiff–Appellant, v. United States Conference of Catholic Bishops; Stanley Urban; Robert Ladenburger; Mary Mollison, Defendants–Appellees.; "Tamesha Means v. United States Conference of Catholic Bishops."

55. Sepper, "The Role of Religion in State Public Accommodations Laws," 652. I also thank Liz Sepper for a discussion on this section.

56. Office for Civil Rights, "Section 1557 of the Patient Protection and Affordable Care Act."

57. Deutsch, "Expanding Conscience, Shrinking Care."

58. Savulescu and Schuklenk, "Doctors Have No Right to Refuse Medical Assistance in Dying, Abortion or Contraception," 165; Schuklenk, "Accommodating Conscientious Objection in Medicine-Private Ideological Convictions Must Not Trump Professional Obligations," 231.

59. Jütte, *Contraception*, 18. In some interpretations of religious law, such as Exodus 21:22–23 or Mishnah Oholot 7, the fetus does not attain full moral personhood until birth.

60. I am indebted to Rabbi Randy Fleisher for dialogues on these issues.

61. Sepper, "Not Only the Doctor's Dilemma," 385.

62. Sepper, "Taking Conscience Seriously"; NeJaime and Siegel, "Conscience Wars," 2542.

63. "An Overview of Abortion Laws"; "Public Funding for Abortion"; Luker, *Abortion and the Politics of Motherhood*, 69.

64. The pernicious terminology of "legitimate rape" complicates this issue further. Kozma and Schroer, "Purposeful Nonsense, Intersectionality and the Mission to Save Black Babies," 106.

65. Copelon, "From Privacy to Autonomy: The Conditions for Sexual and Reproductive Freedom," 32.

66. hooks, *Feminism Is for Everybody*, 85.

67. Young, *On Female Body Experience*, 87.

68. Young, 87–88.

69. Bapat, "How Can a 'Pro-Life' Legislator Fight to Gut SNAP?"; Dewey, "The Republican Plan to Tighten Food Stamp Work Requirements Is Advancing—without a Single Democrat's Vote."

70. Main et al., "Reduction of Severe Maternal Morbidity from Hemorrhage Using a State Perinatal Quality Collaborative."

71. "Health-Related SDGs | IHME Viz Hub."

72. National Center for Health Statistics, "Mortality in the United States, 2014"; Brait, "Infant Death Rate in US Drops to Historic Low, CDC Reports."

73. Collins, *Black Feminist Thought*, 84.

74. Collins, 78–79.

75. George and Lee, "The Wrong of Abortion," 44.

76. Watt, *The Ethics of Pregnancy, Abortion and Childbirth*, 67.

77. Copelon, "From Privacy to Autonomy: The Conditions for Sexual and Reproductive Freedom," 36; Boonin, *Beyond Roe*, 8–9.

78. Steinem, *Outrageous Acts and Everyday Rebellions*, 246.

79. NSVRC, "National Sexual Violence Resource Center Info & Stats for Journalists Statistics about Sexual Vioelnce"; Breiding et al., "Prevalence and Characteristics of Sexual Violence, Stalking, and Intimate Partner Violence Victimization — National Intimate Partner and Sexual Violence Survey, United States, 2011"; "The National Intimate Partner and Sexual Violence Survey: 2015 Data Brief — Updated Release."

80. Hamblin, "How Often Does Rape Lead to Pregnancy?"; Holmes et al., "Rape-Related Pregnancy."

81. Holmes et al., "Rape-Related Pregnancy"; Mulugeta, Kassaye, and Berhane, "Prevalence and Outcomes of Sexual Violence among High School Students"; Trussell, Rodríguez, and Ellertson, "New Estimates of the Effectiveness of the Yuzpe Regimen of Emergency Contraception."

82. "What Is the Effectiveness of Condoms?"
83. "What Is the Effectiveness of Condoms?"
84. "What Is the Effectiveness of Abstinence and Outercourse?"
85. "Understanding 'Abstinence.'"
86. Stanger-Hall and Hall, "Abstinence-Only Education and Teen Pregnancy Rates."
87. "What Is the Effectiveness of Birth Control Pills?"
88. Crary, "Lawsuits Target Trump Administration Family Planning Policy."
89. Thomson, "A Defense of Abortion."
90. Ahangari, "Why America's Roads Are so Much More Dangerous than Europe's."
91. Little, "The Moral Permissibility of Abortion."
92. Obed et al., "Six Month Abstinence Rule for Liver Transplantation in Severe Alcoholic Liver Disease Patients."
93. Vos et al., "Smoking Resumption after Lung Transplantation."
94. Greenberg, "Without Obamacare, What Happened to Kids like Kimmel's Son?"
95. Fried, *From Abortion to Reproductive Freedom*, 37.
96. CDC, "Severe Maternal Morbidity in the United States: Pregnancy: Reproductive Health: CDC."
97. Bitler and Zavodny, "Did Abortion Legalization Reduce the Number of Unwanted Children?"
98. "Adoptions in America Are Declining."
99. Kukla, *Mass Hysteria*, 6; George and Lee, "The Wrong of Abortion," 38.
100. Hendricks, "Even If the Fetus Is Not a Person, Abortion Is Immoral," 246.
101. Oster, *Expecting Better*, 47.
102. Michelle Martin, "Decades Later, Drugs Didn't Hold 'Crack Babies' Back," NPR.Org, July 31, 2013, sec. Tell Me More, https://www.npr.org/templates/story/story.php?storyId=207292639.
103. "How States Handle Drug Use During Pregnancy."
104. Michelle Martin, "Decades Later, Drugs Didn't Hold 'Crack Babies' Back," NPR.Org, July 31, 2013, sec. Tell Me More, https://www.npr.org/templates/story/story.php?storyId=207292639.
105. For example, Ayala and Freeman discuss the case of researchers recommending certain actions for periodontal disease in early reproductive years before individuals become pregnant and the dangers these recommendations pose without sufficient evidence or sufficient attention to sexist assumptions about women as primarily reproducers. Saray Ayala and Lauren Freeman, "The Placental Microbiome."
106. US Preventive Services Task Force, "Final Recommendation Statement: Folic Acid for the Prevention of Neural Tube Defects: Preventive Medication."

107. Marquis, "Why Abortion Is Immoral."

108. For example, Catharine A. MacKinnon argues, "At the same time, liberty for men is often construed in sexual terms and includes liberal access to women, including prostituted ones. So while, for men, liberty entails that women be prostituted, for women, prostitution entails loss of all that liberty means." MacKinnon, "Prostitution and Civil Rights," 14.

109. hooks, *Ain't I a Woman*.

110. Rogers, *The Troublesome Helpmate*.

111. Rogers.

112. hooks, *Ain't I a Woman*.

113. Using bell hooks' theoretical framework in application to this abortion is not meant to compare this case to her subject matter in *Ain't I a Woman*, and no comparison is necessary to take the claims she makes about sexism and misogyny in slavery and apply them to other cases. My purpose in using hooks is to rely on her insight and analysis rather than make comparisons, which she herself rightly argues against. Sexism can lead to big crimes like crimes against humanity (May, *Crimes Against Humanity*; "United Nations Office on Genocide Prevention and the Responsibility to Protect.") while it can also lead to smaller microagressions. (Swim and Cohen, "Overt, Covert, And Subtle Sexism.") The denial of birth control may not be as grave as the denial of a lifesaving abortion; the point is not to compare the gravity of the harms that result from sexism but rather to uncover sexism and reveal it for what it is as well as use that identification to come to a greater understanding.

114. Kaye et al., "Health Care Denied," 8–17.

115. O'Connor, *Planned Parenthood of Southeastern Pennsylvania, Et Al., Petitioners 91-744 v. Robert P. Casey, Et Al., Etc. Robert P. Casey, Et Al., Etc., Petitioners 91-902*, U.S.

116. "Parental Involvement in Minors' Abortions."

117. "State Bans on Abortion Throughout Pregnancy."

118. Sensenbrenner et al., "Committee on the Judiciary."

119. Lee et al., "Fetal Pain: A Systematic Multidisciplinary Review of the Evidence."

120. Sensenbrenner et al., "Committee on the Judiciary," 96.

121. Singer, *Practical Ethics*, 130.

122. Finer et al., "Timing of Steps and Reasons for Delays in Obtaining Abortions in the United States"; Jatlaoui, "Abortion Surveillance—United States, 2015."

123. Finer et al., "Timing of Steps and Reasons for Delays in Obtaining Abortions in the United States."

124. Foster and Kimport, "Who Seeks Abortions at or After 20 Weeks?"

125. For example, the decision in *Roe v. Wade* states, "For the stage subsequent to viability the State, in promoting its interest in the potentiality of human life, may, if it chooses, regulate, and even proscribe, abortion except where it is necessary, in appropriate medical judgment, for the preservation of the life or health of the mother." Roe v. Wade, 410 United States.

126. Harris, "The Survival Lottery."

127. Manninen, *Pro-Life, Pro-Choice*, 3.

128. Peck, "No Pro-Life American Advocates Punishment for Abortion."

129. Peck.

130. Greenhouse and Siegel, *Before Roe V. Wade*, 143.

131. Reagan, *When Abortion Was a Crime*.

132. Copelon, "From Privacy to Autonomy: The Conditions for Sexual and Reproductive Freedom," 32.

133. Tavernise and Hassan, "Missouri Lawmakers Pass Bill Criminalizing Abortion at About 8 Weeks of Pregnancy."

134. Whole Woman's Health et al. v. Hellerstedt, Commissioner, Texas Department of State Health Services, et al., 2016, 15–274. Supreme Court of the United States.

135. "Targeted Regulation of Abortion Providers."

136. Bearak, Burke, and Jones, "Disparities and Change over Time in Distance Women Would Need to Travel to Have an Abortion in the USA."

137. "Counseling and Waiting Periods for Abortion."

138. "Requirements for Ultrasound."

139. For example, Kristin Luker discusses a history of physicians taking themselves to have sole purview over abortion. Luker, *Abortion and the Politics of Motherhood*, 40; 66.

140. Manninen, "The Pro-Choice Pro-Lifer:"

141. Gutmann and Thompson, *Democracy and Disagreement*, 24; Manninen, *Pro-Life, Pro-Choice*, 4.

142. Stack, "A Brief History of Deadly Attacks on Abortion Providers."

143. CNN, "Planned Parenthood."

144. "Unintended Pregnancies and Abortions Averted by Planned Parenthood, 2015"; Specter, "Planned Parenthood Means Fewer Abortions."

145. "Publicly Funded Contraceptive Services at U.S. Clinics, 2015."

146. Daniels, Mosher, and Jones, "Contraceptive Methods Women Have Ever Used: United States, 1982–2010"; "Contraceptive Use in the United States."

147. NeJaime and Siegel, "Conscience Wars," 2546; George, George, and Colson, "Manhattan Declaration."

148. "CCAR Supports Contraceptive Coverage for All Women."

149. On the contrary, non-procreative sex is sometimes viewed as essential based on some interpretations of religious texts, and contraception is similarly subject to debate in religious interpretation. "ARR 486-499." I thank Rabbi Randy Fleisher for a conversation on a related point.

150. Delston, "Public Reason and Its Limits: The Role of Truth in Politics"; NeJaime and Siegel, "Conscience Wars," 2516.

151. Dailard, "What Lawrence v. Texas Says About the History and Future Of Reproductive Rights."

152. Sullivan, "Unnatural Law."

153. Calhoun, *Feminism, the Family, and the Politics of the Closet*, 15.

154. "Pope Says Church Is Making 'Profound' Birth Control Study."

155. Stein, "U.S. Campaign to Promote Abstinence Begins."

156. Fard, "Sandra Fluke, Georgetown Student Called a 'Slut' by Rush Limbaugh, Speaks Out."

157. McNicholas et al., "The Contraceptive CHOICE Project Round Up."

158. O'Neill, *Autonomy and Trust in Bioethics*, 51.

159. Mak, "How Michael Cohen Protects Trump By Making Legal Threats"; Carmon, "Meet the Marital Rape Deniers"; Sharman, "Bill to Outlaw Marital Rape Gets No Support from Ohio Republicans"; Rosenberg, "He's pro-Incest, Pedophilia, and Rape. He's Also Running for Congress from His Parents' House."; Bacarisse, "The Republican Lawmaker Who Secretly Created Reddit's Women-Hating 'Red Pill.'"

160. Strandberg and Hopkins, "New Title X Birth Control Rules Heed Conservatives, Ignore Women."

161. *Burwell v. Hobby Lobby*.

162. This reasoning falls under the definition of what Kozma and Schroer call, "purposeful nonsense." Kozma and Schroer, "Purposeful Nonsense, Intersectionality and the Mission to Save Black Babies," 108.

163. O'Connor, *Planned Parenthood of Southeastern Pennsylvania, Et Al., Petitioners 91-744 v. Robert P. Casey, Et Al., Etc. Robert P. Casey, Et Al., Etc., Petitioners 91-902*, U.S.

164. Warren, "On the Moral and Legal Status of Abortion"; Elizabeth Harman, "Creation Ethics: The Moral Status of Early Fetuses and the Ethics of Abortion"; Little, "The Moral Permissibility of Abortion"; Tooley, "Abortion and Infanticide," 37; Greasley and Kaczor, *Abortion Rights*, 5.

165. Thomson, "A Defense of Abortion"; Boonin, *Beyond Roe*.

7

THE TWO-BODY PROBLEM

Medical Sexism in Reproductive Health

In this chapter, I expand my thesis to show how medical sexism plays a role in other areas of reproductive health, especially those areas of reproductive health often directed at female patients. Identifying medical sexism as playing a role in overriding patient autonomy and fostering paternalism allows a greater understanding of other common abuses in the medical field. Identifying medical sexism as a contributing factor toward problematic behaviors towards certain patients, including violations of medical norms and standards of care, helps in identifying patterns and understanding that patient experience of medical sexism is systematic and not various unconnected violations. For example, I discussed how doctors routinely deny their patients access to IUDs, despite being the most effective form of birth control, because they worry about trusting patient choices and lifestyles. In chapter 6, I expanded that pursuit to abortion policy within the medical field. Yet the OB/GYN field is rife with violations of patient preference; patients routinely find their preferences overridden and their access to health care limited by the restrictions placed on them, especially when it comes to reproductive care like prenatal care. Furthermore, outside of reproductive and hormonal care, doctors also routinely treat female patients differently.

Often, what is occurring when such cases arise is under dispute. Why are patients given episiotomies and C-sections, while they are denied VBACs and compliance with their birthing decisions? Violations of patient preference are common, widespread, and can lead to consequences such as disability and death, as I discuss below. In general, doctors do follow patient preferences, especially in the case of invasive procedures like surgery. No standard doctor would perform surgery without asking or perform surgery on a competent and informed patient who explicitly and loudly refuses to undergo the treatment. Yet when it comes to C-sections and episiotomies, overriding patient choice is more common. Doctors seem to behave differently in this context, and it is helpful to investigate why.

One way to get to the bottom of why doctors override patient preference is to examine similarities between the cases in question. Abortion, discussed in the last chapter, along with C-sections, VBACs, episiotomies, and related pregnancy and birth related issues discussed below, have a similarity which could also explain the patient experience. In all such cases, a fetus exists which could justify overriding patient preference. After all, if two patients are at stake in such decisions—a fetus and a pregnant person—then choosing one over the other is not necessarily an example of overriding patient autonomy. Rather, conflicting rights and conflicting autonomy are at stake, and doctors make a call about which to follow without violating any moral dictates. Thus, the existence of the fetus could potentially be used to justify overriding the decisions of the pregnant person.

However, even if the fetus is the reason that doctors override patient rights and autonomy, medical sexism may still contribute to the relevant actions. It is impermissible to treat competent, informed and autonomous patients who have not consented to or have refused treatment. Doctors also may not engage in medical malpractice in which they violate standards of practice and cause demonstrable injury to the patient. In cases where a fetus's well-being is at odds with a pregnant person's well-being, some seeming conflicts of rights ignore the existence of the pregnant person's body. Because one cannot act on the fetus without acting or omitting to act on the pregnant person, it is impossible to consider the fetus's rights in a vacuum. Doctors may not violate one person's rights to maximize the health of another's. So, if a baby's health would be improved by a faster delivery via C-section or episiotomy (even though babies generally do not benefit from faster deliveries), a health-care professional may not violate the rights of a pregnant person to maximize the baby's health. If they do this, and if they do this regularly and systematically, even if they use the fetus as a justification for the treatment of the female patient, medical sexism may still be at root.

Furthermore, as in the last chapter, if the fetus is not the justification for overriding women's choices in abortion or contraception, and instead the moral status of the pregnant person is more properly the issue at stake, then a wide variety of restrictions exist for women and patients in every part of the medical profession make sense. In this chapter, I start with the OB/GYN field but expand the scope to consider a variety of obstacles that can plausibly be connected to discrimination in chapter 8.

First, some cases in which doctors override a pregnant woman's autonomy, such as in episiotomies, the husband stitch, C-sections, and other birth and labor decisions, they are not protecting the fetus at the expense of the mother. In many such cases, neither the fetus nor the pregnant person is better off. Second, if the fetus were the only justification for such actions, then we would not see the same treatment of female patients where no fetus exists, such as contraception, discussed in chapters 1–5 or in strokes, breast cancer, and autoimmune diseases, discussed in the next chapter. But we do. Thus, the fetus is not a plausible explanation. Third, if treating one patient (the fetus) can justify overriding another's autonomy (the pregnant person), then we would see the same trade-offs when women are not involved, such as doctors distributing organs of healthy patients to sick patients who need them, or cutting into some patients against their will to benefit others.[1] But we do not. Fourth, as discussed in chapter 5, no sexist attitudes or malicious intent is required to make the case for medical sexism as an explanatory feature of the current state of women's treatment. Instead, what is required is showing demonstrable harm to certain classes of patients. It is my goal in this chapter to make the case for systemic medical sexism in reproductive medicine.

PELVIC EXAMS

A pelvic exam generally includes a visual exam, a speculum exam, a Pap test, and a manual exam, in which doctors insert two fingers into the vagina and use the other hand to feel the abdomen for abnormalities.[2] The overarching dilemma of this book is unnecessary, harmful, and coercive pelvic exams and Pap tests. The primary case study discussed is the tying of Pap tests and pelvic exams to birth control prescriptions. But the moral concerns surrounding pelvic exams go beyond just using them as a means to withhold birth control. They also cover the policy by medical schools in the United States to allow students to perform pelvic exams on unconscious patients without first obtaining informed consent and without sufficiently informing patients.[3] Since the stated purpose of performing pelvic exams on unconscious patients is to improve medical training, it goes without saying that these exams do not benefit the patient. The purpose of the exam is to help the trainee, not to help the patient. Although illegal in four states, the practice is standard in the United States.[4]

One possible reason the practice of pelvic exams on non-consenting, unconscious patients continues without patient pushback is because, by its very nature, patients simply do not know it occurs.[5] After news coverage of a survey finding that 72% of Canadian doctors had performed pelvic exams on anesthetized patients without their consent in 2010, The Society of Obstetricians and Gynaecologists of Canada (SOGC) and The Association of Professors of Obstetrics and Gynaecology of Canada (APOG) updated their clinical practice guidelines to require consent for these examinations.[6]

The stated purpose of students performing exams on unconscious patients is educational practice. However, service to the profession is not a permissible justification for overriding patient consent. For example, if performing a controversial heart transplant would provide great service to the profession, but no patients were available to undergo the transplant, medical schools may not proceed with the procedure on unwilling patients. Furthermore, according to surveys, a significant portion of patients would provide consent for these exams if asked.[7] Thus, even if the benefit in training medical students somehow justified performing the exams against the wishes of the patient, performing exams on unwilling patients would still be impermissible given the availability of willing participants.

Service to the medical profession does not justify performing the exams, then. Yet it is worth noting that performing pelvic exams on unconscious patients does no service to the profession because after students finish their training, they will have to perform pelvic exams on conscious patients. Doctors who learn how to perform a pelvic exam on an unconscious patient do not learn how they might be hurting the patient, what they might be saying that offends the patient, or whether their bedside manner causes harm to patients.[8] Performing the exams on standardized, conscious, and consenting patients not only preserves moral legitimacy, then, but also ensures that the training is useful and beneficial to the medical professional.

Doctors sometimes balk at comparing vaginal penetration using a speculum or the insertion of two fingers into a patient's vagina without her consent to rape.[9] However, I have already argued that no good reason justifies the procedure to be nonconsensual and that the non-consensual version of the practice serves limited educational purposes. Some have argued that rape is different because it is sexual in nature.[10] However, since it is unknown whether the medical trainees get sexual gratification from the practice, that distinction does not settle the question. Furthermore, that distinction may misunderstand what rape and sexual harassment are. Rape can also dominate and assert power or control.[11] For example, the FBI defines rape as "Penetration, no matter how slight, of the vagina or anus with any body part or object, or oral penetration by a sex organ of another person, without the consent of the victim."[12] According to this definition, establishing sexual gratification on the part of the perpetrator is neither necessary nor sufficient to establish rape has occurred. Bioethicist Arthur Caplan compares the practice to Dr. Larry Nassar's molestation of women, for which he is now serving prison time.[13] Digital penetration of a person's vagina without consent falls under that definition of rape.

These moral evaluations would apply even where patients are informed in advance that conditional on an unrelated procedure, they must undergo pelvic exams by trainees during anesthesia. Based on the definition of informed consent given in chapter 4, this offer would still be coercive. Says O'Neill, "Patients are manipulated if they are 'made offers they cannot refuse', given their actual cognitive and volitional capacities. For example, patients who think they may be denied further care or discharged without recourse if they refuse proposed treatment may be unable to refuse it."[14] Patients in teaching hospitals may be subject to these restrictions, undermining their autonomy even where they are made aware of hospital practices.

CAESAREAN SECTIONS

About a third of all births in the United States are Caesarean section deliveries.[15] Yet C-section rates that exceed 10% do not decrease maternal or neonatal mortality.[16] In fact, C-sections are associated with higher rates of postpartum maternal morbidity and mortality as well as neonatal morbidity and mortality.[17] Maternal mortality is almost four times higher in C-section births than vaginal births,[18] and neonatal mortality is more than twice as high in C-section births than vaginal births.[19]

Furthermore, women sometimes feel alienated[20] from giving birth in C-section surgeries, even feeling as though they did not give birth.[21] Said one parent after a C-section, "It took me a long time even to be able to say that I gave birth to Avery. I felt like I didn't earn the right to say I gave birth to him, like it was taken from me somehow, like I hadn't done what I was supposed to do."[22] Perhaps for this reason, as well as the emphasis on "natural" childbirth,[23] a new phenomenon of "natural C-sections" or "gentle C-sections" is gaining popularity, which is meant to be more "woman-centered" or "family-centered."[24] These techniques include the pregnant patient more by allowing her to watch the surgery, push the baby out of the incision, or attempt immediate skin-to-skin contact with the infant, options that those giving birth vaginally generally already have.[25]

Many reasons might explain this alienation, including the cultural alignment of motherhood with suffering and martyrdom as well as pain in childbirth and adhering to a societal emphasis on doing what is "natural" in mothering. But another possible explanation for the alienation is that pregnant people feel pressured into these C-sections by their physicians, who justify them by emphasis on fetal life.

If, as I argued in chapter 6, too much emphasis on the moral personhood of the fetus has plagued discussions of abortions, one possible result is that what looks like respecting bodily autonomy in laws permitting abortion are actually just the representation of a view that early-stage fetuses are not moral persons and therefore have no great claim on rights to life. In that case, the right to bodily autonomy seems to disappear when the fetus is viable as in cases of labor and delivery, but actually never existed. This compromise, then, of allowing early abortions by ceding to the opposition that abortion was only ever about moral personhood and not bodily autonomy, ends up hurting women in labor and birth decisions. If bodily autonomy is asserted to be contingent on the status of the fetus, then it can be overridden when it is needed most. These compromises would then be Pyrrhic victories.

Thus, during labor and birth, the fetus, which is more clearly a moral person and definitely viable, is perceived as the highest moral consideration, while the consideration of the pregnant person's decisions over her own health care disappears. We can draw a line, then, from societal views on abortion to the alienation some women feel during C-sections.[26]

One possible explanation for this rise in C-sections is the corresponding rise in cardiotocography (CTG) or electronic fetal monitoring (EFM); after it was introduced in the 1960s, C-section rates climbed more than 450%.[27] The use of this sort of continuous monitoring is thought to increase the rate of C-section without any corresponding benefit.[28] The link between EFM and C-sections, as well as the lack of association with better outcomes for infants, was first established in the 1970s,[29] but it remains the most common obstetric intervention today, and more than 80% of births include it.[30] However, the readouts doctors receive from EFM are so unclear that only 22% of doctors agree on their meaning, leading ACOG to continue recommending its disuse over the last 30 years.[31] Furthermore, "women who have a C-section have an increased risk of hysterectomy, reshospitalization, and prolonged pain . . . infertility, troubles in future pregnancies, such as stillbirth, problems with the placenta, and uterine rupture," just to name a few dangers.[32] For babies, risks include respiration problems, injuries including skin lacerations from the scalpel, asthma, allergies, type 1 diabetes, obesity, and atopic disease generally, among others.[33]

This kind of empirical evidence on the rise of C-sections as causally connected to EFM, which focuses on the health of the fetus to the detriment of all involved, fits with the overall view discussed in this book that women's interests are sacrificed to their infants' interests. That is because EFM appears to and even purports to evaluate and prioritize fetal health. But, it is worth noting that C-section overuse does not benefit fetuses and in fact causes a wide array of problems discussed above, including a fivefold increase in difficulty breathing[34] and over 20 studies show at least a 20% increase in type 1 diabetes.[35] A more fitting explanation of the phenomena is sacrificing fetal interests to propagate coercive attitudes toward pregnant women.[36]

Although medical concerns about vaginal birth after Caesarean (VBAC) mean that 90% of those who have received a Caesarean once get it again, most of the rate of increase comes from primary C-sections.[37] Historically, the dangers of VBACs have been used to coerce women into repeat and unwanted C-sections, despite the risk of uterine rupture remaining under 1.5%, and despite the risk of perinatal death after a uterine rupture hovering around 6%.[38] For example, in 1999 a doctor won a court order to force Laura Pemberton to have a C-section when he found out she went into labor and was attempting a VBAC. When she sued after the forcible surgery,

> The court ruled that the cesarean section at the conclusion of a full-term pregnancy had been medically necessary to avoid a substantial risk that the child would die during delivery, and that a state's interest in preserving the life of an unborn child outweighed the mother's constitutional interest of bodily integrity.[39]

Unlike some who undergo forced C-sections, the surgery did not precipitate her death, but it did underline her lack of bodily autonomy.[40] Since most hospitals do not offer VBACs, women may feel pressured into C-sections today, even without a court order.[41]

Another possible explanation for the rise in C-sections is the increase in maternal health issues such as preeclampsia. However, some evidence suggests that C-section delivery rates are increasing much faster than preeclampsia rates; that explanation falls short. Similarly, arrest of dilation is sometimes cited as a reason for the rates of increase, but that indicator is subjective and varies across clinicians.[42]

Patient preference[43] has also been ruled out as an explanation for C-section rise, according to a number of studies.[44] The majority of patients report that the decision for a C-section was their doctor's, and most patients also report negative experiences with C-sections.[45] Patient preference is also an unlikely explanation because pregnant people often get C-sections without giving consent[46] and because they are misled on the medical reasons for having one.[47] Those who do give consent report being pressured into consenting at alarming rates.[48]

Doctor preference may explain the rise in C-sections.[49] If doctor preference for scheduling labor instead of having it occur on nights and weekends is the justification, then it fits the model of institutional medical sexism I have outlined above because the outcomes, independent of doctor intent, are sexist.[50] Similarly, doctor fears about malpractice or about following hospital guidelines could come into play.[51] In addition, while doctors themselves may not actively prefer C-sections, they may nevertheless fail to adhere to guidelines aimed at minimizing C-sections or rely on guidelines that themselves lag behind the scientific evidence, resulting in a rate that can be traced to physician action if not physician preference. For example, some have argued that compliance with organizational guidelines and insurance coverage could explain the rise in C-sections.[52] However, it is hard to justify a practice as protecting doctors, hospitals, and insurance companies from greater inconvenience, liability, or cost when that same practice is causing escalating costs and a massive epidemic of preventable death. C-sections cost 50–100% more than vaginal births.[53] Instead, medical sexism is a better explanation of the phenomenon.

This discussion of physician preference also rules out another possible, but implausible explanation for C-section rates: cost savings for insurance companies, doctors, patients, and institutions. C-sections are not cost-effective; but suppose they were. Any cost savings would still come at the cost of maternal mortality and preventable death. No amount of financial savings, then, can explain why organizations would accept a higher rate of mothers dying of preventable causes. And, if organizations were willing to choose financial savings over female life, the element of medical sexism would still be necessary to explain such a prioritization.

In the absence of medical indications, population health, physician or patient preference, and financial incentives explaining the phenomenon of C-sections, medical sexism is left as the best explanation. Medical sexism explains the cavalier treatment of maternal health; it explains why a developed nation would tolerate such a high rate of maternal mortality; it explains why women's labor and birth choices are not respected; it explains why institutional guidelines could advance policies on C-sections that do not privilege patient choice; it explains why medical professionals might think women take too long to give birth; it explains why medical guidelines and scientific evidence are not properly followed; and it explains why misguided views on fetal needs could underlie the rise of C-sections generally. In short, any explanation of C-section rates that does not take into account medical sexism is incomplete.

EPISIOTOMIES

As recently as 1979, more than half of all vaginal deliveries in the United States included episiotomies, roughly 61%.[54] The tipping point that led to reductions in these rates likely came in 2006, when ACOG came out against routine episiotomies.[55] However, ACOG did so because it found no evidence to recommend the practice, which means that doctors were performing episiotomies at high rates without any evidence indicating its use for decades. In other words, the scientific evidence did not point toward it and then reverse; rather, there was never any evidence to recommend it in the first place. Episiotomy rates have declined significantly from a quarter of all births in 2004 to half that rate in 2012,[56] with variations across hospitals today.[57] But that rate is still considered too high,[58] and even the lowest rates today are often two to three times the recommended guideline.[59] Some studies show no improvement in maternal health from episiotomies with clear evidence demonstrating harm and clear evidence pointing against routine episiotomies.[60] Differences in episiotomy rates also exist within those national numbers, with white women, women with traditional insurance, urban women, and patients of doctors practicing for a long time receiving more episiotomies overall.[61] Furthermore, the rates themselves mask the extent to which some patients receive episiotomies without asking,[62] against their expressed wishes, with some studies failing to report patient pain or even patient consent.[63] For example, according to one comprehensive survey, three out of four women said they had no choice in receiving their episiotomy.[64] These statistics suggest that doctors view the pregnant person as getting in the way during attempts to maximize the fetus's health.[65]

Episiotomy rates might mask other issues, such as whether or not they are being replaced with more invasive procedures. For example, as the episiotomy rate has gone down, the C-section rate has gone up in the United States.[66] In fact, C-section rates have increased so much in recent years that one study raises the possibility that the types of vaginal births that used to include episiotomies are now being performed via C-section.[67] In that case, medical outcomes would not necessarily improve for pregnant patients just because episiotomy rates are slowing down.

Episiotomies are often contrasted with perineal tearing, which doctors now consider to be a more manageable injury to the perineum and one that the patient can heal from easier. However, perineal injuries themselves are probably happening at rates that are too high, perhaps due to rushing a person in labor through the delivery.[68] Some studies also show that home births or births with midwives result in fewer perineal injuries than births that take place under the oversight of a physician at a hospital.[69] One possible reason for this difference is the higher incidence of midwives using warm packs, which some studies show leads to less perineal trauma and less severe perineal trauma.[70]

Associated with the episiotomy, though not limited to it, is what is sometimes called the "husband stitch" or "crown stitch," in which an extra stitch is added to the surgical repair of the perineum due to the perceived benefit in sexual pleasure for a male partner.[71] Though no major studies document the prevalence of this practice or the level of consent achieved in the patients who receive it,[72] the practice is fundamentally at odds with a doctor's role, since it is not for the patient's own benefit. On the contrary, it causes high rates of problems for the patients who receive it, such as increased pain, decreased sexual functioning, and problems healing.[73] Nevertheless, paternalism is explicitly at stake when doctors utilize the practice. For example, one euphemism used to describe the practice is "improving a woman's well-being."[74] The fact that patient consent is not always documented in reported cases of the husband stitch underlines the same misunderstanding of vaginal tearing and patient consent that may be behind the artificially high episiotomy rates.

BED REST

Confinement is a term we use to describe imprisonment and childbirth. Sometimes, however, the two definitions are closer than we think.[75] Doctors routinely prescribe bed rest to pregnant patients;[76] around 20% of pregnant women are prescribed bed rest yearly.[77] Nearly 90% of OB/GYN doctors are estimated to recommend bed rest during pregnancy when concerns about preterm birth arise.[78] In fact, some deem bed rest so critical that doctors are willing to enforce it by law and courts are willing to uphold their decisions. Like Laura Pemberton's C-section, Samantha Burton was also forced to have a C-section, but in this case, she was also forced to undergo bed rest against her will first.[79]

In 2009, the Circuit Court of Leon County effectively imprisoned Samantha Burton at Tallahasee Memorial Hospital, forcing her to stay in bed and putting her job and two toddlers at risk, ostensibly for the health of her fetus.[80] In its decision, the State explicitly appealed to the "parens patriae" best interest standard, paternalistically making Burton's health choices for herself and her children without her consent and against her explicit wishes. Like the case of tying birth control to yearly Pap tests, paternalism is used to justify a practice that provides no benefits to the patient and instead merely controls her bodily autonomy, health-care decisions, and behavior.

Four years earlier, in 2005, ACOG came out against precisely the type of "punitive and coercive legal approaches to maternal decision-making"[81] at stake in Burton's case due to the threat they pose to human health. Some of the reasons they listed for not acting as Burton's doctor did were the following:

> These approaches 1) fail to recognize that pregnant women are entitled to informed consent and bodily integrity, 2) fail to recognize that medical knowledge and predictions of outcomes in obstetrics have limitations, 3) treat addiction and psychiatric illness as if they were moral failings, 4) threaten to dissuade women from prenatal care, 5) unjustly single out the most vulnerable women, and 6) create the potential for criminalization of otherwise legal maternal behavior.[82]

Thus, in 2009, Burton's doctor violated standard of care and yet she was denied a request to see another doctor for a second opinion or be transferred to another functioning hospital. The fact that doctors were willing to perform an emergency C-section on her against her will fits with the evidence on coerced C-sections.[83] And the fact that the fetus had already died only underscores the point that no possible benefit to the fetus or the mother could be expected from the doctor, hospital, court, and state actions. The moral status of the fetus cannot explain these extreme decisions, but the desire to control a woman's behavior can explain them.

Ten years earlier, in 1999, *The Lancet* published an otherwise mundane meta-study on bed rest.[84] Its conclusion, that 39 studies found no evidence to support bed rest for any condition, was not surprising because bed rest was never an evidenced-based recommendation. For example, studies find no evidence of the benefit in bed rest to reduce preterm labor in singleton or multiple pregnancies.[85] In fact, as risky as preterm labor is, one reason ACOG has long rejected bed rest is that it is difficult to determine which patients are at risk for it.[86] Studies today confirm evidence from the 1940s:[87] bed rest increases risk for a number of dangers, from bone loss[88] to blood clots, but it yields no identifiable benefits.[89] In describing why bed rest "is typically no longer recommended," in pregnancy, the Mayo Clinic lists these side effects:

> A blood clot in a deep vein, such as a vein in your leg (venous thromboembolism); Decreased bone mass (bone demineralization); Musculoskeletal and cardiovascular deconditioning; Maternal weight loss or weight gain; Stress due to self-blame, child care issues, and concerns about job loss or finances; An increased risk of depression and anxiety.[90]

Several studies, meta-studies, and meta-analyses demonstrate that bed rest actually increases the risk of preterm birth, morbidity, and mortality.[91] To the contrary of most bed-rest prescriptions, the greater the physical activity, the greater the benefits in preventing preterm labor, with those engaging in competitive sports having a 66% reduced risk of preterm labor over those on bed rest.[92] ACOG recommends physical activity "in all phases of life, including pregnancy" with far reaching benefits while "there is no credible evidence to prescribe bed rest in pregnancy."[93] Again, in this example, no evidence ever supported the practice, as opposed to cases where the evidence reverses recommendations.

Although no evidence is forthcoming that doctors have any reason to recommend bed rest in pregnancy, bed rest likely fits societal expectations of pregnant women: they belong in the home, they ought not work outside of the home, they have no societal contributions to make besides gestation, their needs ought to be sacrificed to their fetus, they ought not engage in physical exertion, they are not strong, they should not be strong, they are delicate, they are helpless or in need of help. Bed rest literally keeps pregnant women barefoot. In fact, in the case of bed rest, the need to control a pregnant person's behavior outweighs the increased risk of death. In other words, as Hilde Lindemann puts it, "Women are not valued socially for themselves alone, but for something else: their fetuses, for example, or the care they give to their families and friends."[94] Like the case of doctors tying birth control to yearly Pap tests, these violations of women's rights are so routine that 90% of doctors override standards of care, patient preference, and bodily autonomy. And, like the Pap test case, no medical benefit for the policy has ever been found, including at the time the practice was originated. Instead, medical sexism is a better explanation for both practices.

FORCED PREGNANCY CARE, POLICING PREGNANCY, AND OBSTETRIC VIOLENCE

Forced bed rest, C-sections, and episiotomies are particular trends within the broader phenomenon of threatening pregnant women with court orders, jail time, or losing their parental rights for failing to comply with ill-informed or misguided physician dictates and for abuse of women before, during, or after pregnancy.[95] No medical association or medical governing body recommends these actions. They serve no medical or ethical purpose. And, since most states do not have laws on the books mandating compliance with interventions prescribed by doctors, physicians usually rely on courts to uphold their dictates. That means that without the cooperation of doctors, pregnant people would not face the sort of unprecedented violations of bodily autonomy they deal with today.

For example, in 1990, the Board of Trustees of the American Medical Association wrote that doctors "should not be responsible for policing the decisions that a pregnant woman makes that affect the health of herself and her fetus, nor should they be liable for respecting an informed, competent refusal of medical care"[96] Similarly, the Board writes that the "Society does not legally require parents to undergo a risk of life, health, or bodily invasion in order to carry out their moral obligations to provide medical care for their children. . . . Few, if any, medical procedures meant to benefit the fetus would entail no risk to a pregnant woman's health."[97] Furthermore, the broad documentation of abuse, including sexual abuse during labor and birth highlights the role doctors play in violating women's autonomy.[98]

Comparing doctor decisions to override patient preference in pregnancy to other informed refusals of care suggests that pregnancy is treated differently. Doctors may not permissibly examine patients without their consent, but routinely override the vocal refusals of patients when those patients are in labor.[99] For example, Ronald Munson and Ian Lague write,

> critics note that although society imposes some special obligations on parents, it does not force them to undergo risky medical procedures or give up their basic autonomy in order to preserve the life or health of their children. A father, for example, cannot be legally compelled to donate bone marrow to his child, even if he is the only compatible donor and the donation is necessary to preserve the child's health or life. Nor can physicians force a parent to donate blood to a child, even if it would save the child's life. (Pregnant women, by contrast, have on a number of occasions been forced to accept involuntary blood transfusions in the name of fetal interests.)[100]

Society places greater restrictions on potential mothers than actual mothers and offers greater protections for potential children—fetuses—than born ones. Or, as Rhonda Copelon puts it, "It burdens the pregnant woman with a duty to save fetal life at an enormous cost to herself—a cost that, as a society, we ask of no man, not even the parent of a child."[101]

Claiming that the fetus is a human being or a person cannot explain this disparity alone. As Howard Minkoff and Lynn M. Paltrow write, "But to take this stance is not merely to elevate the rights of the unborn to parity with those of born individuals. It is in fact to grant them rights previously denied to born individuals: courts have allowed forced surgery to benefit the unborn, but have precluded forced surgery to benefit born persons."[102] But the rights of the fetus, or the special status of the fetus, or even the higher status of the fetus over the pregnant woman cannot explain these acts of forcible care. After all, forcible care generally does not help the fetus, but harms it, and nobody besides the mother is expected to help the fetus in the same way. What explains the forcible treatment of women is not the higher status of the fetus, whose status, if it is higher, mysteriously impacts nobody but the mother. What explains the forcible treatment of women is the lower status of women. Medical sexism explains what medicine, biology, and ethics cannot.

For example, the health of a pregnant woman is considered only to the extent that she is making proper sacrifices. Says Hilde Lindemann, "Pregnant women do not get praised when they do all the things they are supposed to do to guard their fetuses' well-being—they just get demerits if they fail to do any of them."[103] And, whether or not these restrictions on the pregnant person are based in evidence misses the point. The restrictions persist because they have value independent of whether they promote the health of mother or child; the value they have is in the control and subordination of women.

BREASTFEEDING

Parents of babies need to feed those babies. And, just as doctors and those in the medical field tell the public about the benefits and harms of different foods for our own bodies—kale is good; processed meat is bad—they tell the public about the benefits and harms of the different foods our babies eat, namely, breast milk and formula. The American Academy of Pediatrics, the CDC, the NIH, UNICEF, and the World Health Organization number among the organizations that recommend exclusive breastfeeding as the healthiest option for babies zero to six months old.[104] In addition, more than a million babies in the United States, or 14%,[105] are born in "baby-friendly hospitals," which ensure that breastfeeding is encouraged and formula is discouraged.[106] Breastfeeding is thought to have significant benefits for both mother and child: on the one hand, some evidence shows breastfeeding can protect against breast cancer,[107] postpartum depression, and decreased blood loss postpartum for mothers; on the other hand, some evidence shows breastfeeding can reduce infections and sudden infant death syndrome in babies.[108] Parents ought to have full information when making a decision about how to feed their children.

However, the evidence on breastfeeding as beneficial for either the one breastfeeding or the one breastfed is mixed.[109] Organizations like ACOG only started recommending it in 2016, though this delay more likely is due to overlooking breastfeeding as a significant topic than remaining neutral on the evidence.[110] In fact, the only thing we know about breastfeeding is that we do not know enough.[111]

Furthermore, physicians' nutritional recommendations do not exist in a vacuum. For those who live in food deserts, getting access to fresh kale is not very easy; for those in certain types of jobs, getting access to a breast pump is not very easy. In a country where employers do not always respect the right to employee bathroom breaks,[112] additional breaks to breastfeed can be difficult.[113] In fact, nearly half of employees trying to breastfeed report being denied accommodations at work.[114] While most women initiate breastfeeding in the United States, most also do not breastfeed as long as they intend.[115] Presumably, these mothers faced obstacles they did not anticipate.[116] There is no federal requirement for paid parental leave in the United States, which is just one such major obstacle. In this context, recommendations that breastfeeding exclusively is best for a baby might start to sound like recommendations that growing up in a wealthy family is best for a baby. Scientific evidence might support the claim,[117] but that does not mean that parents can necessarily follow the recommendation to raise their child in a wealthy home.[118]

In addition, a variety of signals seemingly conflict in this context.[119] On the one hand, most women are told exclusive breastfeeding is the best option for their baby[120]; on the other hand, rights to breastfeeding are not always respected and public breastfeeding is stigmatized.[121] Women appear to be bombarded with conflicting messages, then.[122] On the one hand, they are told they ought to breastfeed; on the other hand, they are shamed, maligned, and denied the right to do so.[123]

But perhaps the signals that appear to conflict actually do not. Breastfeeding recommendations are, at their essence, dictating women's behavior, the common thread between much medical sexism. The apparent conflicting messages are compatible if we take into account the fact that breastfeeding recommendations tend to control or make invisible the breastfeeder. Recommending breastfeeding in a country that makes doing so possible only at home carries with it an implicit control over a woman's behavior: you ought to do something every two hours that cannot be done in public or at work;[124] therefore, you ought not leave the home or go to work. Breastfeeding defines our taxonomy in biological classification as mammals, but social norms and laws make exercising this bodily function difficult. Seemingly everyone agrees breastfeeding is great for an infant,[125] but if you use breasts to do it, you will face problems.

In fact, many reasons given for the health and safety of breastfeeding over formula sound odd if you take into account the person doing the breastfeeding. For example, breastfeeding is praised as being the best solution for infant health in cases where clean water may not be available, like disasters, emergencies, or in developing nations.[126] These recommendations only make sense if we do not consider the person nursing the infant. How long is one expected to produce breast milk without consuming water or while consuming dirty water? Presumably, if one cannot make formula because no clean water is available for mixing, then one also cannot safely drink enough water to replenish the breast milk produced.[127] Taking into account the health needs of the person breastfeeding makes meeting the health needs of the infant more difficult. Using a breastfeeding person as a filtration device to supply clean liquids to an infant only makes sense if the person breastfeeding is disposable.

Similarly, breastfeeding is described as free, while formula is expensive. But as Hanna Rosin points out, breastfeeding is "only free if a woman's time is worth nothing."[128] Time is not the only necessity for breastfeeding, however. We could build on Rosin's claim by taking into account other requirements: breastfeeding is only free if a woman's hydration is worth nothing; it is only free if a woman's nutrition is worth nothing; it is only free if a woman's employment, opportunity, motivation, desire, and energy are worth nothing. Perhaps breastfeeding is only free if the people doing the breastfeeding are worth nothing.

Baby-friendly hospitals, despite promoting a valuable action like breastfeeding, also face criticism.[129] First, one might question the very term "baby friendly," which highlights the health of the baby and makes invisible the person who gives birth. And when the person who gives birth is included, this inclusion still looks problematic because it creates a couple instead of individuals.[130] As Rebecca Kukla argues,

> During pregnancy, we treat the fetus as a primary and independent 'patient' or object of medical attention, and the mother's body becomes at best a medium of and at worst an obstacle to care for the fetus. Yet after birth we care for the 'maternal-child dyad' or the 'nursing couple.' . . . In neither case does the mother herself emerge as a coherent focus of medical care and attention.[131]

Similarly, the steps to becoming a baby friendly hospital themselves seem to eliminate choice. For example, one step is to, "Help mothers initiate breastfeeding within one half-hour of birth."[132] This policy does not incorporate the decision on the part of the mother on what to feed her child. A woman who is sedated, exhausted, HIV positive, or facing significant postpartum health problems does not enter into the consideration. Another step, "Give newborn infants no food or drink other than breastmilk [sic], unless medically indicated" also eliminates the subject, in this case the parent, from the equation.[133] What happens to the baby of a person who does not intend to breastfeed? Someone who anticipates needing to go back to work in several days due to a lack of paid parental leave and anticipates obstacles to pumping at work does not have a baby whose need for formula is "medically indicated," but may need access to formula nonetheless.[134] These policies may be less "baby friendly" and more "mother unfriendly."[135] In fact, some such policies, such as the removal of formula and pacifier access might inhibit breastfeeding success, cause maternal guilt and exhaustion, and cause harm to a baby.[136] These risks do not even include the current skepticism on whether breastfeeding is in fact significantly better than formula or better at all.[137] It may seem contradictory to advocate a policy that evidence suggests inhibits breastfeeding in order to better promote breastfeeding, but such a policy would not be contradictory if its aim was to control women rather than help babies.

What is the best action to take in this climate? Breastfeeding recommendations may be coercive and detrimental to the health of mothers and children. But touting the benefits of formula may hurt those who seek to breastfeed, since doing so may eliminate one critical reason to support paid parental leave, access to pumping breaks at work, public breastfeeding rights, and merely value corporate interests[138] over human health. Which recommendation, then, ought medical professionals to make?

Instead of taking a side in the so-called debate between breastfeeding and formula, or even endorsing the so-called existence of the two options as opposed, as if many parents do not rely on both, promoting choice would be better for all involved. Breastfeeding falls under the purview of bodily autonomy and thus is subject to the decision of the one breastfeeding. Doctors may have information about what health benefits breastfeeding generally brings, but may lack information about a mother's home life, work life, and emotional state that also bear on the benefits and risks of breastfeeding. That means doctors' expertise falls short of the knowledge needed to make a recommendation to a standard parent. Recommendations for or against breastfeeding that are either coercive toward women or make them invisible always will be at their essence problematic and fall under the umbrella of medical sexism. Instead, empowering women and parents to make informed choices should be a doctor's aim.

EUGENICS AND RACISM IN REPRODUCTIVE HEALTH

The American medical field's racist history is central to understanding the broader implications of women's health because racism and sexism intersect in this history.[139] Harriet A. Washington writes that the eugenicists of the early twentieth century targeted black women and women of color.[140] For example, Dr. Harry Haiselden, who engaged in "racial fear-mongering,"[141] killed babies he deemed unfit, and propagandized his views on eugenics with a film entitled *The Black Stork,* which promoted euthanizing black children as sanctioned by God.[142]

In fact, birth control as we know it today came about as the result of racially biased research.[143] Washington writes that,

> The Pill, Norplant, and the Depo-Provero shot were first tested in Mexico, Africa, Brazil, Puerto Rico, and India. Once approved, they were administered to large numbers of girls and women in U.S. venues that are disproportionately and, usually, overwhelmingly African American and Hispanic. . . . Thus, the immediately postapproval use of contraceptive methods in large numbers of closely monitored poor women of color constituted a final testing arm, so that they were unwittingly participating in a research study.[144]

As a result, women of color were injured and died disproportionately in the early stages of birth control and IUD use.[145]

It is incontrovertible that the United States has a long history of coercively sterilizing patients, especially women of color.[146] Although compulsory sterilization sometimes targeted the "mentally unfit," these targeted populations often were people of color. As Washington points out, "By 1983, when blacks constituted only 12 percent of the population, 43 percent of the women sterilized in federally funded family planning programs were African Americans."[147] California, where doctors performed tens of thousands of compulsory sterilizations late into the 1970s, was one of the worst offenders.[148] Some forced sterilization programs in the United States reached unfathomable levels. By the mid-1960s, a third of all women in Puerto Rico had been forcibly sterilized; by the late 1970s, doctors working for the United States government had forcibly sterilized half of all American Indian women.[149] In 1975, when a group of women joined a class action suit against L.A. County doctors for forcible sterilization targeting Mexican American women, the patients lost not because they failed to prove the sterilizations occurred but because the judge ruled that forcible tubal ligations could plausibly solve what doctors saw as an "overpopulation problem."[150] In none of these cases were the wishes of the women of color respected or even taken into account. Decisions about their own health were not perceived as falling under their purview; medical sexism explained mistreatment at the hands of doctors and government officials who thought they knew better.

In fact, this racist history had global influence; the Nazi genocide found roots in part in American eugenics.[151] Hitler's policies were connected not only to eugenics but also to broader issues related to this book. Nazi-era written works, policies, and laws often included antifeminist and antichoice ideas.[152]

These examples of racism and ethnocentrism in reproductive health take a distinctly gendered turn, demonstrating the intersection of various forms of oppression and the role of racism in medical sexism. Furthermore, discussing sexism in the medical field without addressing the distinct injustices perpetrated against women of color would run the risk not only of creating a distorted picture of sexist practices, as if medical sexism only affects white women, but would also fail to demonstrate the ways in which different forms of discrimination can bolster one another. As Kimberlé W. Crenshaw writes, "Because the intersectional experience is greater than the sum of racism and sexism, any analysis that does not take intersectionality into account cannot sufficiently address the particular manner in which Black women are subordinated."[153] Furthermore, pitting anti-racist and anti-sexist aims against one another has distinct benefits for white patriarchy.[154] Discussing these forms of oppression in conjunction, thus, allows for a deeper understanding of each mode of oppression.

CONCLUSION

Practices that override patient preference are endemic in reproductive health. Obstetrics and gynecology is a domain of the medical field rife with medical sexism, as evidenced by women's lack of control in abortion discussed in the last chapter, birth and labor choices discussed here, and even health recommendations on breastfeeding. Furthermore, it sheds light on other paternalistic practices in the profession. Paternalistic attitudes are found where doctors do not think their patients are fit to make decisions or are full agents—many are more willing to accept paternalism toward children. Infantilization of and medical sexism toward female patients is a better explanation for these practices.

Standard of care in the medical field is established by scientific research as well as physicians' interpretation of this research. It is also influenced by historical guidelines on treatment. Bias can infiltrate all of these factors; in the next chapter, I look specifically at the ways in which medical sexism impacts research on women. Thus, relying on standard of care in cases of women's health uncritically without engaging with the meaning behind those guidelines can be dangerous to women's health. Nevertheless, ignoring standard of care uncritically is also problematic and dangerous for patients. When doctors violate standards of care in their field because they recognize that the guidelines are lagging behind conclusive research or when they uncover bias in the research itself, they may be acting justifiably. But when doctors violate standards of care because those standards hold them to a higher bar in dealing with their patients, or because outmoded research they were taught in medical school makes them reluctant to change, they can create grave dangers for their patients.

In the examples presented in this chapter, I argue that doctors violate standards of care without compelling reasons. In each section, I discussed ways in which doctors routinely violate standards of care in ways that research suggests puts their patients in danger and which moral evaluation suggests is ultimately sexist. As discussed in chapter 3, routine violations of standards of care that result in patient harm fulfill the definition of medical malpractice and legal negligence. The cases discussed in this chapter meet that same definition. In many of the above cases, violations of standards of care are occurring and resultant harm to patients has ensued. These cases combine to make a stronger case for medical sexism. The fact that large-scale violations of standard of care persist and are tolerated in the medical community toward patients who have a uterus is itself problematic. I argue that it is not a coincidence that those who have wombs are ignored in a medical context; it is representative of society's attitudes toward those people. It would be impossible to understand why doctors ignore scientific research, the agreed upon guidelines of their profession, the moral obligations derived from their role as doctors, and the decisions of their patients within this population, without identifying medical sexism as a causal contributor.

This result has two further implications. First, medical recommendations are slightly better than practice. Second, equal treatment in hewing to standards of care and respecting bodily autonomy, and not special treatment, would redress many of the problems discussed here. Special treatment of historically oppressed populations might be warranted, but it is just not at issue here in the case studies discussed.[155]

As I have discussed throughout, women with privilege tend to do better on many health parameters and outcomes and tend to receive better treatment than women without privilege. This evaluation lends support to the idea that discrimination is at play when considering differential treatment. If some biological explanation justifies why those who have uteruses are treated differently than those without, then that biological explanation could not also explain the added instances of differential treatment found in communities facing discrimination. If we could come up with some plausible reason besides discrimination to explain why women face obstacles in treatment, health outcomes, autonomy, and health-care access, then we would not see the same factors alter when we take into account other axes of oppression. The fact that we do see the same factors lends credence to the claim that discrimination is at work. Furthermore, it means that solving the problem requires a feminist bioethics that is intersectional. The argument in this chapter thus calls for the end of all forms of discrimination and oppression.

NOTES

1. John Harris, "The Survival Lottery," *Philosophy* 50, no. 191 (January 1975): 81–87, https://doi.org/10.1017/S0031819100059118; Judith Jarvis Thomson, "A Defense of Abortion," *Philosophy & Public Affairs* 1, no. 1 (Fall 1997): 47–66.

2. David Heitz, "Pelvic Exam: Preparation, Process, and More," *Healthline*, November 21, 2013, https://www.healthline.com/health/pelvic-exam.

3. Phoebe Friesen, "Educational Pelvic Exams on Anesthetized Women: Why Consent Matters," *Bioethics* 32, no. 5 (June 1, 2018): 298–307, https://doi.org/10.1111/bioe.12441.

4. Arthur L. Caplan, "Pelvic Exams Done on Anesthetized Women Without Consent: Still Happening," *Medscape*, May 2, 2018, http://www.medscape.com/viewarticle/894693.

5. Avram Goldstein, "Practice vs. Privacy on Pelvic Exams," *The Washington Post*, May 10, 2003, https://www.washingtonpost.com/archive/politics/2003/05/10/practice-vs-privacy-on-pelvic-exams/4e9185c4-4b4c-4d6a-a132-b21b8471da58/; Paul Hsieh, "Pelvic Exams On Anesthetized Women Without Consent: A Troubling And Outdated Practice," *Forbes*, May 14, 2018, https://www.forbes.com/sites/paulhsieh/2018/05/14/pelvic-exams-on-anesthetized-women-without-consent-a-troubling-and-outdated-practice/; Friesen, "Educational Pelvic Exams on Anesthetized Women."

6. Andre Picard, "Time to End Pelvic Exams Done without Consent," *The Globe and Mail*, January 28, 2010, https://www.theglobeandmail.com/life/health-and-fitness/time-to-end-pelvic-exams-done-without-consent/article4325965/.

7. Sara Wainberg et al., "Teaching Pelvic Examinations Under Anaesthesia: What Do Women Think?," *Journal of Obstetrics and Gynaecology Canada* 32, no. 1 (January 1, 2010): 49–53, https://doi.org/10.1016/S1701-2163(16)34404-8.

8. Jami Kath Harrison, "It Happened To Me: I Teach Pelvic Exams to Med Students (On Myself)," *xoJane: Women's Lifestyle & Community Site*, October 17, 2012, https://www.xojane.com/it-happened-to-me/it-happened-to-me-i-teach-pelvic-exams-to-med-students-on-myself.

9. Goldstein, "Practice vs. Privacy on Pelvic Exams."

10. Goldstein; Arthur L. Caplan, "Med Students Still Do Pelvic Exams on Women Under Anesthesia," *Medscape*, May 25, 2018, http://www.medscape.com/viewarticle/896847; Caplan, "Pelvic Exams Done on Anesthetized Women Without Consent."

11. Susan Griffin, "Rape: The All-American Crime," *Ramparts* 10, no. 3 (1971); Susan Griffin, *Rape, The Power of Consciousness* (Harper & Row,

1979); Claudia Card, "Rape as a Weapon of War," *Hypatia* 11, no. 4 (1996): 5–18.

12. FBI, "Frequently Asked Questions about the Change in the UCR Definition of Rape," December 11, 2014, https://ucr.fbi.gov/recent-program-updates/new-rape-definition-frequently-asked-questions.

13. Caplan, "Pelvic Exams Done on Anesthetized Women Without Consent"; Caplan, "Med Students Still Do Pelvic Exams on Women Under Anesthesia."

14. Onora O'Neill, "Paternalism and Partial Autonomy," *Journal of Medical Ethics* 10 (1984): 176.

15. National Center for Health Statistics, "Births Method of Delivery," February 5, 2018, https://www.cdc.gov/nchs/fastats/delivery.htm.

16. J. Ye et al., "Association between Rates of Caesarean Section and Maternal and Neonatal Mortality in the 21st Century: A Worldwide Population-Based Ecological Study with Longitudinal Data," *BJOG: An International Journal of Obstetrics & Gynaecology* 123, no. 5 (August 24, 2015): 745–53, https://doi.org/10.1111/1471-0528.13592; Emma L. Barber et al., "Contributing Indications to the Rising Cesarean Delivery Rate," *Obstetrics & Gynecology* 118, no. 1 (July 2011): 29–38, https://doi.org/10.1097/AOG.0b013e31821e5f65.

17. Catherine Deneux-Tharaux et al., "Postpartum Maternal Mortality and Cesarean Delivery," *Obstetrics & Gynecology* 108, no. 3 Pt 1 (September 2006): 541–48, https://doi.org/10.1097/01.AOG.0000233154.62729.24; Theresa Morris, *Cut It Out: The C-Section Epidemic in America* (NYU Press, 2016), 14; José Villar et al., "Maternal and Neonatal Individual Risks and Benefits Associated with Caesarean Delivery: Multicentre Prospective Study," *BMJ (Clinical Research Ed.)* 335, no. 7628 (November 17, 2007): 1025, https://doi.org/10.1136/bmj.39363.706956.55; Marian F. MacDorman and T.J. Mathews, "The Challenge of Infant Mortality: Have We Reached a Plateau?" *Public Health Reports* 124, no. 5 (September 1, 2009): 670–81, https://doi.org/10.1177/003335490912400509.

18. Deneux-Tharaux et al., "Postpartum Maternal Mortality and Cesarean Delivery."

19. Marian F. MacDorman, Fay Menacker, and Eugene Declercq, "Cesarean Birth in the United States: Epidemiology, Trends, and Outcomes," *Clinics in Perinatology* 35, no. 2 (June 2008): 302, https://doi.org/10.1016/j.clp.2008.03.007; Morris, *Cut It Out*, 15.

20. Rebecca Kukla, *Mass Hysteria: Medicine, Culture, and Mothers' Bodies* (Rowman & Littlefield, 2005), 219. This alienation may occur despite strong preferences about gestational ties to offspring. Amy J. Ravin, Mary B. Mahowald, and Carol B. Stocking, "Genes or Gestation? Attitudes of Women and

Men about Biologic Ties to Children," *Journal of Women's Health* 6, no. 6 (December 1, 1997): 639–47, https://doi.org/10.1089/jwh.1997.6.639.

21. Claudia Malacrida and Tiffany Boulton, "Women's Perceptions of Childbirth 'Choices': Competing Discourses of Motherhood, Sexuality, and Selflessness," *Gender & Society* 26, no. 5 (October 1, 2012): 748–72, https://doi.org/10.1177/0891243212452630.

22. Jennifer Schmidt, "The Gentle Cesarean: More Like A Birth Than An Operation," NPR.org, March 9, 2015, sec. Shots Health News, https://www.npr.org/sections/health-shots/2015/03/09/390977656/the-gentle-cesarean-more-like-a-birth-than-an-operation.

23. Kukla, *Mass Hysteria*, 223.

24. Eleanor Tucker, "I Had A Natural C-Section," HuffPost UK, August 14, 2014, http://www.huffingtonpost.co.uk/2014/08/14/i-had-a-natural-c-section_n_7367200.html; Susan Scutti, "'Gentle' C-Sections Are Growing in Popularity," CNN, June 13, 2017, https://www.cnn.com/2017/06/13/health/gentle-natural-c-section/index.html; Schmidt, "The Gentle Cesarean: More Like A Birth Than An Operation"; J Smith, F Plaat, and NM Fisk, "The Natural Caesarean: A Woman-Centred Technique," *BJOG* 115, no. 8 (July 2008): 1037–42, https://doi.org/10.1111/j.1471-0528.2008.01777.x.

25. Daniel Mallory Ortberg, "Help! My Idiot Husband Gave My Heirloom Jewelry to His Mistress.," *Slate*, July 24, 2018, https://slate.com/human-interest/2018/07/my-husband-gave-his-mistress-my-jewelry-and-more-advice-from-dear-prudence.html; Schmidt, "The Gentle Cesarean: More Like A Birth Than An Operation."

26. Rhonda Copelon, "From Privacy to Autonomy: The Conditions for Sexual and Reproductive Freedom," in *From Abortion to Reproductive Freedom: Transforming a Movement*, ed. Marlene Gerber Fried (Boston, MA: South End Press, 1999), 36.

27. Jacqueline H. Wolf, "Risk and Reputation: Obstetricians, Cesareans, and Consent," *Journal of the History of Medicine and Allied Sciences* 73, no. 1 (January 5, 2018): 7–28.

28. Declan Devane et al., "Cardiotocography versus Intermittent Auscultation of Fetal Heart on Admission to Labour Ward for Assessment of Fetal Wellbeing," *The Cochrane Database of Systematic Reviews* 1 (26 2017): CD005122, https://doi.org/10.1002/14651858.CD005122.pub5; Z. Alfirevic et al., "Continuous Cardiotocography (CTG) as a Form of Electronic Fetal Monitoring (EFM) for Fetal Assessment during Labour" (Cochrane Library, February 3, 2017), https://doi.org/10.1002/14651858.CD006066.pub3.

29. Warren E. Leary, "Routine Electronic Monitoring Of Fetuses Is Challenged in Study," *The New York Times*, October 25, 1995, sec. U.S., https://www.nytimes.com/1995/10/25/us/routine-electronic-monitoring-of-fetuses-is-

challenged-in-study.html; Morris, *Cut It Out*, 8; Tamar Lewin, "Despite Criticism, Fetal Monitors Are Likely to Remain in Wide Use," *The New York Times*, March 27, 1988, sec. U.S., https://www.nytimes.com/1988/03/27/us/despite-criticism-fetal-monitors-are-likely-to-remain-in-wide-use.html.

30. Brenda A. Bucklin, David R. Gambling, and David Wlody, *A Practical Approach to Obstetric Anesthesia* (Lippincott Williams & Wilkins, 2008), 94–95; Morris, *Cut It Out*, 8; Noah Berlatsky, "The Most Common Childbirth Practice in America Is Unnecessary and Dangerous," *The New Republic*, August 13, 2015, https://newrepublic.com/article/122532/most-common-childbirth-practice-us-unnecessary-dangerous.

31. The American College of Obstetricians and Gynecologists, "ACOG Practice Bulletin Number 106: Intrapartum Fetal Heart Rate Monitoring: Nomenclature, Interpretation, and General Management Principles," July 2009, 106, https://www.mnhospitals.org/Portals/0/Documents/patientsafety/Perinatal/3a_ACOG%20Bulletin%20106.pdf.

32. Morris, *Cut It Out*, 15.

33. Jan Blustein and Jianmeng Liu, "Time to Consider the Risks of Caesarean Delivery for Long Term Child Health," *BMJ* 350 (June 10, 2015): h2410, https://doi.org/10.1136/bmj.h2410; Morris, *Cut It Out*, 16; Anne Kirkeby Hansen et al., "Risk of Respiratory Morbidity in Term Infants Delivered by Elective Caesarean Section: Cohort Study," *BMJ (Clinical Research Ed.)* 336, no. 7635 (January 12, 2008): 85–87, https://doi.org/10.1136/bmj.39405.539282.BE; Muhammad T. Salam et al., "Mode of Delivery Is Associated with Asthma and Allergy Occurrences in Children," *Annals of Epidemiology* 16, no. 5 (May 2006): 341–46, https://doi.org/10.1016/j.annepidem.2005.06.054; James M. Alexander et al., "Fetal Injury Associated with Cesarean Delivery," *Obstetrics and Gynecology* 108, no. 4 (October 2006): 885–90, https://doi.org/10.1097/01.AOG.0000237116.72011.f3.

34. Hansen et al., "Risk of Respiratory Morbidity in Term Infants Delivered by Elective Caesarean Section."

35. Blustein and Liu, "Time to Consider the Risks of Caesarean Delivery for Long Term Child Health."

36. Given that preventative care has a bigger influence on the very conditions C-sections and other interventions are meant to protect, "invading women's bodies to impose last-minute, heroic care is stupid, mean, and unfair." Laura M. Purdy, *Reproducing Persons: Issues in Feminist Bioethics* (Cornell University Press, 1996), 100.

37. Barber et al., "Contributing Indications to the Rising Cesarean Delivery Rate," 6.

38. Marja Vääräsmäki and Tytti Raudaskoski, "Pregnancy and Delivery after a Cesarean Section," *Duodecim; Laaketieteellinen Aikakauskirja* 133, no. 4

(2017): 345–52; "Vaginal Birth After Cesarean: New Insights. Evidence Report/Technology Assessment, No. 191," 397; Carrie Murphy, "Why Do So Many U.S. Hospitals Prohibit Vaginal Birth After a C-Section?," *ELLE*, December 7, 2016, https://www.elle.com/life-love/a41109/vbac-vaginal-birth-after-c-section/.

39. Pemberton v. TALLAHASSEE MEMORIAL REGIONAL MEDICAL, 66 F. Supp. 2d 1247 (N.D. Fla. 1999), No. ID09-1958 (United States District Court, N.D. Florida, Tallahassee Division October 13, 1999).

40. "Coercive and Punitive Governmental Responses to Women's Conduct During Pregnancy," American Civil Liberties Union, accessed November 2, 2016, https://www.aclu.org/other/coercive-and-punitive-governmental-responses-womens-conduct-during-pregnancy.

41. Sumathi Reddy, "A Type of Childbirth Some Women Will Fight For," *Wall Street Journal*, December 8, 2014, sec. Health and Wellness, http://www.wsj.com/articles/a-type-of-childbirth-some-women-will-fight-for-1418081344; Morris, *Cut It Out*, 28.

42. Barber et al., "Contributing Indications to the Rising Cesarean Delivery Rate," 6.

43. Eugene R. Declercq et al., "Listening to Mothers II: Report of the Second National U.S. Survey of Women's Childbearing Experiences," *The Journal of Perinatal Education* 16, no. 4 (2007): 9–14, https://doi.org/10.1624/105812407X244769; Eugene R. Declercq et al., "Major Survey Findings of Listening to Mothers SM III: Pregnancy and Birth," *The Journal of Perinatal Education* 23, no. 1 (2014): 9–16, https://doi.org/10.1891/1058-1243.23.1.9; Morris, *Cut It Out*, 19; Chris McCourt et al., "Elective Cesarean Section and Decision Making: A Critical Review of the Literature," *Birth* (Berkeley, Calif.) 34, no. 1 (March 2007): 65–79, https://doi.org/10.1111/j.1523-536X.2006.00147.x.

44. Barber et al., "Contributing Indications to the Rising Cesarean Delivery Rate," 7; MacDorman, Menacker, and Declercq, "Cesarean Birth in the United States"; Blustein and Liu, "Time to Consider the Risks of Caesarean Delivery for Long Term Child Health"; Morris, *Cut It Out*, 19.

45. Sezer Kisa and Simge Zeyneloğlu, "Opinions of Women towards Cesarean Delivery and Priority Issues of Care in the Postpartum Period," *Applied Nursing Research* 30 (May 1, 2016): 70–75, https://doi.org/10.1016/j.apnr.2015.11.004.

46. Molly Redden, "New York Hospital's Secret Policy Led to Woman Being given C-Section against Her Will," *The Guardian*, October 5, 2017, sec. US news, http://www.theguardian.com/us-news/2017/oct/05/new-york-staten-island-university-hospital-c-section-ethics-medicine.

47. American College of Obstetricians and Gynecologists, "ACOG Releases New Guidance Aimed at Making VBAC Available to More Women," October 24, 2017, https://www.acog.org/About-ACOG/News-Room/News-Releases/2017/ACOG-Releases-New-Guidance-Aimed-at-Making-VBAC-Available-to-More-Women; Kristine Hopkins, "Are Brazilian Women Really Choosing to Deliver by Cesarean?," *Social Science & Medicine* 51, no. 5 (September 1, 2000): 725–40, https://doi.org/10.1016/S0277-9536(99)00480-3; Sarah Munro et al., "Do Women Have a Choice? Care Providers' and Decision Makers' Perspectives on Barriers to Access of Health Services for Birth after a Previous Cesarean," *Birth* 44, no. 2 (December 2016): 153–60, https://doi.org/10.1111/birt.12270; Tara Haelle, "Your Biggest C-Section Risk May Be Your Hospital," *Consumer Reports*, May 10, 2018, https://www.consumerreports.org/c-section/biggest-c-section-risk-may-be-your-hospital/.

48. Declercq et al., "Major Survey Findings of Listening to Mothers(SM) III."

49. Lewin, "Despite Criticism, Fetal Monitors Are Likely to Remain in Wide Use"; Gilbert W. Gimm, "The Impact of Malpractice Liability Claims on Obstetrical Practice Patterns," *Health Services Research* 45, no. 1 (February 2010): 195–211, https://doi.org/10.1111/j.1475-6773.2009.01062.x; Hopkins, "Are Brazilian Women Really Choosing to Deliver by Cesarean?"; Munro et al., "Do Women Have a Choice?"; Haelle, "Your Biggest C-Section Risk May Be Your Hospital."

50. Alejandro Arrieta and Ariadna García Prado, "Non-Elective C-Sections in Public Hospitals: Capacity Constraints and Doctor Incentives," *Applied Economics* 48, no. 49 (October 19, 2016): 4719–31, https://doi.org/10.1080/00036846.2016.1164820.

51. Redden, "New York Hospital's Secret Policy Led to Woman Being given C-Section against Her Will."

52. Morris, *Cut It Out*, 21.

53. Elizabeth O'Brien and Pratheek Rebala, "Find Out How Much It Costs to Give Birth in Every State," *Time*, October 30, 2017, http://time.com/money/4995922/how-much-costs-give-birth-state/.

54. Elizabeth A. Frankman et al., "Episiotomy in the United States: Has Anything Changed?," *American Journal of Obstetrics and Gynecology* 200, no. 5 (May 2009): 573.e1-7, https://doi.org/10.1016/j.ajog.2008.11.022; Chin-Shyan Chen et al., "The Failure of Financial Incentive? The Seemingly Inexorable Rise of Cesarean Section," *Social Science & Medicine* 101 (January 1, 2014): 47–51, https://doi.org/10.1016/j.socscimed.2013.11.010.

55. "ACOG Practice Bulletin No. 71: Episiotomy," *Obstetrics & Gynecology* 107, no. 4 (April 2006): 956.

56. Frankman et al., "Episiotomy in the United States"; Alexander M. Friedman et al., "Variation in and Factors Associated with Use of Episiotomy," *JAMA* 313, no. 2 (January 13, 2015): 197–99, https://doi.org/10.1001/jama.2014.14774.

57. Alison Young and John Kelly, "Episiotomies Are Painful, Risky and Not Routinely Recommended. Dozens of Hospitals Are Doing Too Many.," *USA Today*, May 21, 2019, https://www.usatoday.com/in-depth/news/investigations/deadly-deliveries/2019/05/21/episiotomy-vs-tearing-moms-cut-in-childbirth-despite-guidelines/3668035002/.

58. Inês Melo et al., "Selective Episiotomy vs. Implementation of a Non Episiotomy Protocol: A Randomized Clinical Trial," *Reproductive Health* 11 (August 14, 2014): 66, https://doi.org/10.1186/1742-4755-11-66.

59. Young and Kelly, "Episiotomies Are Painful, Risky and Not Routinely Recommended. Dozens of Hospitals Are Doing Too Many."

60. Janet Burlingame et al., "166: Episiotomies: Who Does Them and Do They Help?," *American Journal of Obstetrics & Gynecology* 212, no. 1 (January 1, 2015): S98, https://doi.org/10.1016/j.ajog.2014.10.212; Hong Jiang et al., "Selective versus Routine Use of Episiotomy for Vaginal Birth," *The Cochrane Database of Systematic Reviews* 2 (08 2017): CD000081, https://doi.org/10.1002/14651858.CD000081.pub3; Carrie Armstrong, "Practice Guidelines," *American Family Physician* 74, no. 11 (December 1, 2006): 1970.

61. Friedman et al., "Variation in and Factors Associated with Use of Episiotomy."

62. Morris, *Cut It Out*, 2.

63. Jocelyn Wiener, "Episiotomies Still Common During Childbirth Despite Advice To Do Fewer," NPR.org, July 4, 2016, https://www.npr.org/sections/health-shots/2016/07/04/483945168/episiotomies-still-common-during-childbirth-despite-advice-to-do-fewer; Greenfield, "Woman Forced Into Violent Episiotomy Settles With Doctor," Yahoo News, March 15, 2017, https://www.yahoo.com/news/woman-forced-into-violent-episiotomy-settles-with-doctor-182947205.html; Jiang et al., "Selective versus Routine Use of Episiotomy for Vaginal Birth."

64. Declercq et al., "Listening to Mothers II."

65. Kukla, *Mass Hysteria*, 221.

66. Barber et al., "Contributing Indications to the Rising Cesarean Delivery Rate."

67. Frankman et al., "Episiotomy in the United States."

68. Helena E. Lindgren, Åsa Brink, and Marie Klinberg-Allvin, "Fear Causes Tears - Perineal Injuries in Home Birth Settings. A Swedish Interview Study," *BMC Pregnancy and Childbirth* 11 (January 18, 2011): 6, https://doi.org/10.1186/1471-2393-11-6.

69. Patricia A. Janssen et al., "Outcomes of Planned Home Birth with Registered Midwife versus Planned Hospital Birth with Midwife or Physician," *CMAJ : Canadian Medical Association Journal* 181, no. 6–7 (September 2009): 377–83, https://doi.org/10.1503/cmaj.081869.

70. Hannah G. Dahlen et al., "'Soothing the Ring of Fire': Australian Women's and Midwives' Experiences of Using Perineal Warm Packs in the Second Stage of Labour," *Midwifery* 25, no. 2 (April 2009): e39-48, https://doi.org/10.1016/j.midw.2007.08.002; Hannah G. Dahlen et al., "Perineal Outcomes and Maternal Comfort Related to the Application of Perineal Warm Packs in the Second Stage of Labor: A Randomized Controlled Trial," *Birth* (Berkeley, Calif.) 34, no. 4 (December 2007): 282–90, https://doi.org/10.1111/j.1523-536X.2007.00186.x; V. Aasheim et al., "Perineal Techniques during the Second Stage of Labour for Reducing Perineal Trauma," Cochrane, June 13, 2017, https://doi.org/10.1002/14651858.CD006672.pub3.

71. Carmen Maria Machado, "The Husband Stitch," *Granta* (blog), October 28, 2014, https://granta.com/the-husband-stitch/; "The 'Husband Stitch' Is Real, And It's Horrifying," *Scary Mommy* (blog), July 8, 2016, https://www.scarymommy.com/husband-stitch/; Jane Dykema, "What I Don't Tell My Students About 'The Husband Stitch,'" Electric Literature, October 10, 2017, https://electricliterature.com/what-i-dont-tell-my-students-about-the-husband-stitch-690899157394; Heather Rupe, "An OB Weighs in on the 'Husband Stitch,'" *WebMD* (blog), March 16, 2018, sec. Women's Health, https://blogs.webmd.com/womens-health/2018/03/an-ob-weighs-in-on-the-husband-stitch.html; Carrie Murphy, "The Husband Stitch Isn't Just a Horrifying Childbirth Myth," Healthline, January 24, 2018, https://www.healthline.com/health-news/husband-stitch-is-not-just-myth.

72. Julie M.L.C.L. Dobbeleir, Koenraad Van Landuyt, and Stan J. Monstrey, "Aesthetic Surgery of the Female Genitalia," *Seminars in Plastic Surgery* 25, no. 2 (May 2011): 130–41, https://doi.org/10.1055/s-0031-1281482.

73. "The 'Husband Stitch' Is Real, And It's Horrifying"; Murphy, "The Husband Stitch Isn't Just a Horrifying Childbirth Myth."

74. Fiona J. Green, "From Clitoridectomies to 'Designer Vaginas': The Medical Construction of Heteronormative Female Bodies and Sexuality through Female Genital Cutting," *Sexualities, Evolution & Gender* 7, no. 2 (August 2005): 170.

75. Wu Lili, "For Chinese Moms, Birth Means 30 Days In Pajamas," NPR.org, July 20, 2011, https://www.npr.org/2011/07/20/138536998/for-chinese-moms-birth-means-30-days-in-pajamas.

76. "Bed Rest," American Pregnancy Association, April 26, 2012, http://americanpregnancy.org/pregnancy-complications/bed-rest/; Christina McCall, David Grimes, and Anne Lyerly, "'Therapeutic' Bed Rest in Pregnancy: Un-

ethical and Unsupported by Data," *Obstetrics & Gynecology* 121, no. 6 (June 1, 2013): 1305–8, https://doi.org/10.1097/AOG.0b013e318293f12f.

77. "Reasons For Bed Rest During Pregnancy & More," Cleveland Clinic, accessed July 31, 2018, https://my.clevelandclinic.org/health/articles/9757-pregnancy-bed-rest.

78. Judith A. Maloni, "Lack of Evidence for Prescription of Antepartum Bed Rest," *Expert Review of Obstetrics & Gynecology* 6, no. 4 (July 1, 2011): 385–93, https://doi.org/10.1586/eog.11.28.

79. Samantha Burton, Appellant, v. State of Florida, Appellee, No. 1DO9-1958 (FL Dist. Ct. App. August 12, 2010); Randall C. Marshall, Maria Kayanan, and Diana Kasdan, "Burton v. State of Florida - ACLU Amicus Brief," accessed July 26, 2018, https://www.aclu.org/legal-document/burton-v-state-florida-aclu-amicus-brief.

80. Lisa Belkin, "Is Refusing Bed Rest a Crime?," *Motherlode* (blog), January 12, 2010, https://parenting.blogs.nytimes.com/2010/01/12/is-refusing-bed-rest-a-crime/.

81. ACOG Committee on Ethics, "ACOG Committee Opinion #321: Maternal Decision Making, Ethics, and the Law," *Obstetrics & Gynecology* 106, no. 5 Pt 1 (November 2005): 1127–37.

82. ACOG Committee on Ethics, 321.

83. Theresa Morris and Joan H. Robinson, "Forced and Coerced Cesarean Sections in the United States," *Contexts* 16, no. 2 (May 1, 2017): 24–29, https://doi.org/10.1177/1536504217714259.

84. Chris Allen, Paul Glasziou, and Chris Del Mar, "Bed Rest: A Potentially Harmful Treatment Needing More Careful Evaluation," *The Lancet* 354, no. 9186 (October 9, 1999): 1229–33, https://doi.org/10.1016/S0140-6736(98)10063-6.

85. C. Sosa et al., "Bed Rest in Singleton Pregnancies for Preventing Preterm Birth," *The Cochrane Database of Systematic Reviews*, no. 1 (2004): CD003581, https://doi.org/10.1002/14651858.CD003581.pub2; Crowther and Han, "Hospitalisation and Bed Rest for Multiple Pregnancy," Cochrane, July 7, 2010, https://doi.org/10.1002/14651858.CD000110.pub2.

86. American College of Obstetricians and Gynecologists and Committee on Practice Bulletins—Obstetrics, "ACOG Practice Bulletin No. 127: Management of Preterm Labor," *Obstetrics & Gynecology* 119, no. 6 (June 2012): 1308–17, https://doi.org/10.1097/AOG.0b013e31825af2f0.

87. Maloni, "Lack of Evidence for Prescription of Antepartum Bed Rest."

88. Joanne H. E. Promislow et al., "Bed Rest and Other Determinants of Bone Loss during Pregnancy," *American Journal of Obstetrics and Gynecology* 191, no. 4 (October 1, 2004): 1077–83, https://doi.org/10.1016/j.ajog.2004.05.058.

89. Allen, Glasziou, and Mar, "Bed Rest."

90. Mayo Clinic Staff, "Coping with Bed Rest and Pelvic Rest during Pregnancy," Mayo Clinic, March 31, 2017, http://www.mayoclinic.org/healthy-lifestyle/pregnancy-week-by-week/in-depth/pregnancy/art-20048007; Samantha Brennan and Tracy Isaacs, "Feminist Fitness Is for Everyone," in *Fit at Mid-Life: A Feminist Fitness Journey* (Greystone Books Ltd, 2018); Helen Watt, *The Ethics of Pregnancy, Abortion and Childbirth: Exploring Moral Choices in Childbearing* (Routledge, 2016), 66.

91. Maloni, "Lack of Evidence for Prescription of Antepartum Bed Rest."

92. Maloni.

93. The American College of Obstetricians and Gynecologists Committee on Obstetric Practice, "ACOG Committee Opinion Number 650: Physical Activity and Exercise During Pregnancy and the Postpartum Period," *Obstet Gynecol* 126 (December 2015): 650.

94. Hilde Lindemann, "The Woman Question in Medicine: An Update," *Hastings Center Report* 42, no. 3 (2012): 43, https://doi.org/10.1002/hast.34.

95. "Prevention and Elimination of Disrespect and Abuse during Childbirth," World Health Organization, 2015, http://www.who.int/reproductivehealth/topics/maternal_perinatal/statement-childbirth-govnts-support/en/; Purdy, *Reproducing Persons*, 89; Annette Dula, "Bioethics: The Need for a Dialogue with African Americans," in *"It Just Ain't Fair": The Ethics of Health Care for African Americans* (ABC-CLIO, 1994), 18.

96. "Legal Interventions During Pregnancy: Court-Ordered Medical Treatments and Legal Penalties for Potentially Harmful Behavior by Pregnant Women," *JAMA* 264, no. 20 (November 28, 1990): 2663–70, https://doi.org/10.1001/jama.1990.03450200071034.

97. "Legal Interventions During Pregnancy," 2664.

98. Sarah Yahr Tucker, "There Is a Hidden Epidemic of Doctors Abusing Women in Labor, Doulas Say," Broadly, May 8, 2018, https://broadly.vice.com/en_us/article/evqew7/obstetric-violence-doulas-abuse-giving-birth?utm_campaign=interest&utm_source=broadlyfbusads.

99. Maria TR Borges, "A Violent Birth: Reframing Coerced Procedures During Childbirth as Obstetric Violence," *Duke Law Journal* 67, no. 4 (January 2018): 827–62.

100. Ronald Munson and Ian Lague, *Intervention and Reflection: Basic Issues in Bioethics*, 10 edition (Boston, MA: Cengage Learning, 2016), 744.

101. Copelon, "From Privacy to Autonomy: The Conditions for Sexual and Reproductive Freedom," 36.

102. Howard Minkoff and Lynn M. Paltrow, "The Rights of 'Unborn Children' and the Value of Pregnant Women," *Hastings Center Report* 36, no. 2 (March 4, 2006): 27, https://doi.org/10.1353/hcr.2006.0031.

103. Lindemann, "The Woman Question in Medicine," 41.

104. "What Are the Recommendations for Breastfeeding?," http://www.nichd.nih.gov/, January 21, 2017, http://www.nichd.nih.gov/health/topics/breastfeeding/conditioninfo/recommendations.

105. CDC, "Hospital Support for Breastfeeding," Centers for Disease Control and Prevention, October 6, 2015, https://www.cdc.gov/vitalsigns/breastfeeding2015/index.html.

106. "Baby-Friendly USA," accessed July 16, 2018, https://www.babyfriendlyusa.org/get-started/the-guidelines-evaluation-criteria.

107. Erica H. Anstey et al., "Breastfeeding and Breast Cancer Risk Reduction: Implications for Black Mothers," *American Journal of Preventive Medicine* 53, no. 3 (September 1, 2017): S40–46, https://doi.org/10.1016/j.amepre.2017.04.024.

108. Section On Breastfeeding, "Breastfeeding and the Use of Human Milk," *Pediatrics* 129, no. 3 (March 1, 2012): e827–41, https://doi.org/10.1542/peds.2011-3552; Saad S. Al-Shehri et al., "Breastmilk-Saliva Interactions Boost Innate Immunity by Regulating the Oral Microbiome in Early Infancy," *PLOS ONE* 10, no. 9 (September 1, 2015): e0135047, https://doi.org/10.1371/journal.pone.0135047.

109. Hanna Rosin, "The Case Against Breast-Feeding," *The Atlantic*, April 1, 2009, https://www.theatlantic.com/magazine/archive/2009/04/the-case-against-breast-feeding/307311/; M. L. Hediger et al., "Association between Infant Breastfeeding and Overweight in Young Children," *JAMA* 285, no. 19 (May 16, 2001): 2453–60; M. Kramer et al., "Does Breastfeeding Help Prevent Asthma and Allergy? Evidence from a Randomized Trial in Belarus," *American Journal of Epidemiology* 163, no. suppl_11 (June 1, 2006): S85–S85, https://doi.org/10.1093/aje/163.suppl_11.S85-d; Eirik Evenhouse and Siobhan Reilly, "Improved Estimates of the Benefits of Breastfeeding Using Sibling Comparisons to Reduce Selection Bias," *Health Services Research* 40, no. 6 Pt 1 (December 2005): 1781–1802, https://doi.org/10.1111/j.1475-6773.2004.00453.x; S. M. Filteau, "Role of Breast-Feeding in Managing Malnutrition and Infectious Disease," *The Proceedings of the Nutrition Society* 59, no. 4 (November 2000): 565–72; "Breast Cancer and Breastfeeding: Collaborative Reanalysis of Individual Data from 47 Epidemiological Studies in 30 Countries, Including 50 302 Women with Breast Cancer and 96 973 Women without the Disease," *The Lancet* 360, no. 9328 (July 20, 2002): 187–95, https://doi.org/10.1016/S0140-6736(02)09454-0.

110. Allison Yarrow, "Why Do We Understand so Little about Breast-Feeding?," *The Washington Post*, February 21, 2018, sec. Perspective, https://www.washingtonpost.com/news/posteverything/wp/2018/02/21/why-do-we-understand-so-little-about-breastfeeding/; American College of Obstetricians

and Gynecologists Committee Opinion, "Optimizing Support for Breastfeeding as Part of Obstetric Practice," February 2016, https://www.acog.org/-/media/Committee-Opinions/Committee-on-Obstetric-Practice/co658.pdf?dmc=1&ts=20180125T1846099708.

111. Allison Yarrow, "Why Do We Understand so Little about Breast-Feeding?"

112. "Restroom Break Laws," United States Department of Labor Occupational Safety and Health Administration Education Center, 2019, https://www.oshaeducationcenter.com/articles/restroom-breaks.aspx.

113. Tara Haelle, "Employers Routinely Break The Law When It Comes To Breastfeeding Moms," *Forbes*, October 20, 2015, https://www.forbes.com/sites/tarahaelle/2015/10/20/less-than-half-of-breastfeeding-mothers-have-legally-required-pumping-accommodations-at-work/.

114. Katy B. Kozhimannil et al., "Access to Workplace Accommodations to Support Breastfeeding after Passage of the Affordable Care Act," Women's Health Issues 26, no. 1 (January 1, 2016): 6–13, https://doi.org/10.1016/j.whi.2015.08.002.

115. CDC, "Hospital Support for Breastfeeding."

116. Office of the Surgeon General (US), Centers for Disease Control and Prevention (US), and Office on Women's Health (US), *Barriers to Breastfeeding in the United States* (Office of the Surgeon General (US), 2011), https://www.ncbi.nlm.nih.gov/books/NBK52688/.

117. Paula A. Braveman et al., "Socioeconomic Disparities in Health in the United States: What the Patterns Tell Us," *American Journal of Public Health* 100, no. Suppl 1 (April 2010): S186–96, https://doi.org/10.2105/AJPH.2009.166082.

118. Ben Johnson, "Science Communication: The Dangers of Oversimplifying Microbiome Studies," npj Biofilms and Microbiomes Community, October 7, 2016, https://npjbiofilmscommunity.nature.com/users/17778-ben-johnson/posts/12600-q-a-with-lauren-freeman-and-saray-ayala-the-dangers-of-oversimplification-in-microbiome-research.

119. "If women are allegedly passive and fragile, then why are Black women treated as 'mules' and assigned heavy cleaning chores? If good mothers are supposed to stay at home with their children, then why are U.S. Black women on public assistance forced to find jobs and leave their children in day care? If women's highest calling is to become mothers, then why are Black teen mothers pressured to use Norplant and Depo Provera?" Patricia Collins, *Black Feminist Thought: Knowledge, Consciousness, and the Politics of Empowerment* (New York: Routledge, 2008), 14.

120. Breastfeeding, "Breastfeeding and the Use of Human Milk."

121. General (US), Prevention (US), and Health (US), *Barriers to Breastfeeding in the United States*.

122. Gloria Steinem, *Outrageous Acts and Everyday Rebellions: Second Edition* (New York: Holt Paperbacks, 1995), 11.

123. General (US), Prevention (US), and Health (US), *Barriers to Breastfeeding in the United States*.

124. "Public Opinions About Breastfeeding," Centers for Disease Control, December 1, 2017, https://www.cdc.gov/breastfeeding/data/healthstyles_survey/index.htm.

125. Rebecca Schuman, "Is a Kid Who's 'Old Enough to Ask for It' Too Old to Breast-Feed?," *Slate*, July 18, 2016, https://slate.com/human-interest/2016/07/how-old-is-too-old-to-breast-feed.html.

126. American Academy of Pediatrics, "Infant Feeding in Disasters and Emergencies" (2015), https://www.aap.org/en-us/advocacy-and-policy/aap-health-initiatives/Breastfeeding/Documents/InfantNutritionDisaster.pdf.

127. Mike Muller, "Nestlé Baby Milk Scandal Has Grown up but Not Gone Away," *The Guardian*, February 13, 2013, sec. Guardian Sustainable Business, http://www.theguardian.com/sustainable-business/nestle-baby-milk-scandal-food-industry-standards.

128. Rosin, "The Case Against Breast-Feeding."

129. Joel L. Bass, Tina Gartley, and Ronald Kleinman, "Unintended Consequences of Current Breastfeeding Initiatives," *JAMA Pediatrics* 170, no. 10 (October 1, 2016): 923–24, https://doi.org/10.1001/jamapediatrics.2016.1529.

130. Watt, *The Ethics of Pregnancy, Abortion and Childbirth*, 3, 8.

131. Kukla, *Mass Hysteria*, 221.

132. UNICEF, "The Baby-Friendly Hospital Initiative," accessed July 16, 2018, https://www.unicef.org/programme/breastfeeding/baby.htm#10.

133. UNICEF.

134. Kukla, *Mass Hysteria*, 226.

135. Abigail Howe-Heyman and Melanie Lutenbacher, "The Baby-Friendly Hospital Initiative as an Intervention to Improve Breastfeeding Rates: A Review of the Literature," *Journal of Midwifery & Women's Health* 61, no. 1 (January 22, 2016): 77–102, https://doi.org/10.1111/jmwh.12376; Schulte, "More U.S. Hospitals Adopting 'Baby-Friendly' Policies," *The Washington Post*, accessed September 10, 2014, https://www.washingtonpost.com/local/more-us-hospitals-adopting-baby-friendly-policies/2014/09/10/49a86998-34c4-11e4-a723-fa3895a25d02_story.html; Jessica Grose and Christina Cauterucci, "No Nursery, No Formula, No Pacifier: Are 'Baby-Friendly' Hospitals Unfriendly to New Mothers?," *Slate*, October 9, 2014, http://www.slate.com/articles/double_x/doublex/2014/10/

baby_friendly_hospitals_promoting_breast_feeding_at_the_expense_of_the_new.html.

136. Juliana Bunim, "Early Formula Use Helps Some Mothers Breastfeed Longer," UC San Francisco, May 13, 2013, https://www.ucsf.edu/news/2013/05/105831/early-formula-use-helps-some-mothers-breastfeed-longer; "Researchers Question Pulling Plug on Pacifiers," American Academy of Pediatrics, April 30, 2012, https://www.aap.org/en-us/about-the-aap/aap-press-room/Pages/Researchers-Question-Pulling-Plug-on-Pacifiers.aspx; Elissa Strauss and Jean-Marie Pottier, "Baby-Friendly Hospitals May Not Be So Baby-Friendly After All," *Slate*, February 25, 2016, http://www.slate.com/blogs/xx_factor/2016/02/25/baby_friendly_hospitals_may_not_be_so_baby_friendly_after_all.html; Michelle Goldberg and Willa Paskin, "Breast-Feeding Extremists Are Even Worse Than You Thought," *Slate*, December 4, 2015, http://www.slate.com/articles/double_x/doublex/2015/12/the_breast_feeding_extremists_who_put_lactivism_ahead_of_protecting_babies.html; "It Happened to Me: Problems with Breastfeeding Triggered My Postpartum Depression," *xoJane: Women's Lifestyle & Community Site*, November 21, 2014, https://www.xojane.com/it-happened-to-me/breastfeeding-postpartum-depression; Rebecca Kukla, "Measuring Mothering," *International Journal of Feminist Approaches to Bioethics* 1, no. 1 (2008): 67–90.

137. Courtney Jung, "Overselling Breast-Feeding," *The New York Times*, January 19, 2018, sec. Opinion, https://www.nytimes.com/2015/10/18/opinion/sunday/overselling-breast-feeding.html; Rosin, "The Case Against Breast-Feeding"; Cynthia G. Colen and David M. Ramey, "Is Breast Truly Best? Estimating the Effects of Breastfeeding on Long-Term Child Health and Wellbeing in the United States Using Sibling Comparisons," *Social Science & Medicine* 109 (May 1, 2014): 55–65, https://doi.org/10.1016/j.socscimed.2014.01.027; Strauss and Pottier, "Baby-Friendly Hospitals May Not Be So Baby-Friendly After All"; Hediger et al., "Association between Infant Breastfeeding and Overweight in Young Children."

138. Rebecca Schuman, "Formula Advertising Has Always Gone Straight for the New-Mother Jugular," *Slate*, June 4, 2015, https://slate.com/human-interest/2015/06/a-century-of-formula-advertising-its-always-gone-straight-for-the-new-mother-jugular.html.

139. Alice Walker, "What Can the White Man Say to the Black Woman?," *The Nation*, May 22, 1989, https://www.thenation.com/wp-content/uploads/2015/05/whitemanblackwoman.pdf; Patricia Hill Collins, "It's All In the Family: Intersections of Gender, Race, and Nation," *Hypatia* 13, no. 3 (August 1, 1998): 76, https://doi.org/10.1111/j.1527-2001.1998.tb01370.x.

140. Harriet A. Washington, *Medical Apartheid: The Dark History of Medical Experimentation on Black Americans from Colonial Times to the Present*, 1st pbk. ed (New York: Harlem Moon, 2006), 191.

141. Martin S. Pernick, *The Black Stork: Eugenics and the Death of "Defective" Babies in American Medicine and Motion Pictures since 1915*, 1 edition (New York: Oxford University Press, 1999), 57.

142. Washington, *Medical Apartheid*, 192–93.

143. Washington, 201.

144. Washington, 202.

145. Washington, 201.

146. Loretta Ross and Rickie Solinger, *Reproductive Justice: An Introduction*, First edition (Oakland, California: University of California Press, 2017), 118; Collins, "It's All In the Family," 77.

147. Washington, *Medical Apartheid*, 203.

148. Lisa Ko, "Unwanted Sterilization and Eugenics Programs in the United States," PBS.org, *Independent Lens* (blog), January 29, 2016, http://www.pbs.org/independentlens/blog/unwanted-sterilization-and-eugenics-programs-in-the-united-states/; Estrada, "The Politics of Female Biology and Reproduction," The UCSB Current, April 26, 2015, http://www.news.ucsb.edu/2015/015287/politics-female-biology-and-reproduction; Gregory W. Rutecki, "Forced Sterilization of Native Americans: Late Twentieth Century Physician Cooperation with National Eugenic Policies," October 8, 2010, https://cbhd.org/content/forced-sterilization-native-americans-late-twentieth-century-physician-cooperation-national-; Saudi Garica, "8 Shocking Facts About Sterilization in U.S. History," Mic, July 10, 2013, https://mic.com/articles/53723/8-shocking-facts-about-sterilization-in-u-s-history; Matthew Wills, "When Forced Sterilization Was Legal in the U.S.," *JSTOR Daily*, August 3, 2017, https://daily.jstor.org/when-forced-sterilization-was-legal-in-the-u-s/; Alexandra Minna Stern, "That Time The United States Sterilized 60,000 Of Its Citizens," *Huffington Post*, January 8, 2016, sec. Politics, https://www.huffingtonpost.com/entry/sterilization-united-states_us_568f35f2e4b0c8beacf68713.

149. Garcia, "8 Shocking Facts About Sterilization in U.S. History"; Ko, "Unwanted Sterilization and Eugenics Programs in the United States"; Rutecki, "Forced Sterilization of Native Americans."

150. Ko, "Unwanted Sterilization and Eugenics Programs in the United States"; Marcela Valdes, "When Doctors Took 'Family Planning' Into Their Own Hands," *The New York Times*, December 21, 2017, sec. Magazine, https://www.nytimes.com/2016/02/01/magazine/when-doctors-took-family-planning-into-their-own-hands.html.

151. Washington, *Medical Apartheid*, 195.

152. Gloria Steinem, "If Hitler Were Alive, Whose Side Would He Be On?," in *Outrageous Acts and Everyday Rebellions: Second Edition* (New York: Holt Paperbacks, 1995), 337.

153. Kimberlé Williams Crenshaw, "Demarginalizing the Intersection of Race and Sex: A Black Feminist Critique of Antidiscrimination Doctrine, Feminist Theory and Antiracist Politics," *University of Chicago Legal Forum*, no. 1 (1989): 140.

154. bell hooks, *Ain't I a Woman: Black Women and Feminism* (Boston, Mass: South End Press, 1999), 171.

155. Iris Marion Young, *Justice and the Politics of Difference* (Princeton University Press, 1990), 158.

8

LOSING PATIENTS

Broader Implications for Medical Sexism

Women may get more procedures overall and have greater interaction with the medical field, but receive fewer diagnostic tools and other interventions.[1] Women live five to six years longer than men on average, 95% of supercentenarians are women, and they have greater resistance to most major causes of death, including disease and infection. But women are not healthier than men.[2] Susan Sherwin argues that what she calls women's oppressed status contributes to their harm.[3] She states that,

> . . . women constitute an oppressed group, which is at a clear disadvantage in the health system. Women are the primary consumers of health care, but the care they receive does not always serve their overall health interests. . . . Although they receive a great deal of medical treatment, the relevant research data are frequently missing, and specific treatment decisions seem to be biased against them.[4]

In a context that oppresses women, medical care does not successfully preserve health for women.

So far, I have looked at contraception, abortion, and other forms of reproductive health through the lens of medical sexism and argued that policies, procedures, and treatment of patients cannot properly be understood without identifying medical sexism at play. In this chapter, my aim is to identify other areas of medicine in which sexism could be contributing to the mistreatment of patients.[5] Audre Lorde reports that, "Battling racism and battling heterosexism and battling apartheid share the same urgency inside me as battling cancer. None of these struggles is ever easy, and even the smallest victory must be applauded, because it is so easy not to battle at all, to just accept, and to call that acceptance inevitable."[6] Misdiagnosing strokes, underestimating pain, and over or undertreating breast cancer all exemplify the types of problems arising from the same root cause. Only by mistrusting patients, minimizing their symptoms, overriding their decisions, and infantilizing them can we properly explain these and other related phenomena in the medical field. Therefore, I argue sexism is a component part of treating women and identify it as playing a role in a variety of problematic patient outcomes. Women consume more health care on average than men.[7] Thus, if health care is not in their best interests, these broader issues in the medical field can have severe impacts.

TRANSPLANTS

Sexist medical care is no different in cases of organ transplants. For that reason, researchers are calling the status quo a public health crisis, saying, for example, "Gender inequity in access to hemodialysis and kidney transplantation has created a public health crisis in the US."[8] Why does gender inequity play such a large role in transplantation cases like kidney transplants?

Women have equal or greater survival rates than men after a kidney transplant, but according to more than 20 studies, are significantly less likely to have access to transplants.[9] Older women have even lower access[10] and discrimination against older women extends to other areas of organ transplantation; 45% of men receiving heart transplants are over 60 years of age, while only 24% of women receiving heart transplants are over 60.[11] These results are constant across races, with doctors roughly 25% less likely to evaluate black women for a kidney transplant than black men.[12] And, these numbers are consistent with historical data showing that black men received living donor kidney transplants at rates 20% higher than black women.[13] Discrepancies persist even though women are more likely to both give and receive offers of living organ donation.[14] Nevertheless, most living donors are women even as most recipients are men.[15] To date, men in the United States have received more than one and a half times as many organ transplants as women.[16] For lung transplants, the difference is even greater, with more than twice as many men receiving lung transplants than women.[17]

Women suffer at each stage of the process: diagnosis, referral, time spent on a waiting list, and post-transplantation care.[18] For example, when women are referred for an organ transplant, they spend longer on waiting lists than men, sometimes five times as long.[19] That means higher numbers of women than men die on the waiting list.[20] And, although I have focused on the United States, the gender disparity in the U.S. holds across the world generally, from Nepal to France.[21]

Furthermore, strong evidence supports the idea that skewed and inaccurate physician perceptions of women explain the gender disparity.[22] Race also exacerbates the inequalities in organ transplantation, but whereas racial differences are decreasing in organ transplantation access over the last decade, gender disparities are increasing.[23] And, since women receive worse care overall, but men who receive transplants are more likely to be older and have greater numbers of comorbidities, the survival rates do not significantly differ.[24]

TRANS PATIENTS

In chapter 5, I discussed Julia Serano's analysis of oppositional sexism. Oppositional sexism is also one part of the complex story that leads to denials of care for trans patients as a class.[25] Trans patients face significant obstacles in health-care access.[26] In fact, even research documenting the discrimination trans people face in the medical field includes terminology often not accepted in the trans community.[27] Yet, failing to see the relevance of trans issues in gender inequity, discrimination, and physician bias is an oversight that can compound these wrongs. Thus, researchers fail trans patients both when they include trans issues in their work and when they ignore trans issues, making invisible the demonstrable needs of whole communities.

Just as traditional sexism helps explain certain forms of bias against trans individuals, oppositional sexism also helps explain some of this prejudice.[28] It might not be obvious how someone's subconscious sex can possibly threaten another's concept of self. But in the context of oppositional sexism, if one's identity is defined by being the opposite of another's, then anyone crossing that imagined barrier and demonstrating the two identities are not actually mutually exclusive seemingly does pose a threat. Similarly, if doctors view attributes and characteristics of women as opposites of attributes and characteristics of men, then a man with a vagina seeking treatment, or a woman with a penis seeking treatment, may seem to violate preconceived notions of patients, leading to denials of treatment. Serano states, "on a societal level, we purposefully ignore the variation that exists in sex characteristics and create the illusion that there is absolutely no overlap between the physical sexes. . . . Thus, we assume that people can only be attracted to women or men (not both), they can only be feminine or masculine (not both), and they can only identify as female or male (not both)."[29] Confirmation bias may lead physicians to deny the existence of people who challenge their beliefs about sex and gender, leading them to ignore or discriminate against women and men who seek treatment for basic medical needs.

Similarly, from clinical pathology, to medical records, to using the correct pronouns with patients, doctors fail trans people systematically.[30] Discrimination toward trans patients and erasure is well documented.[31] For example, some studies show health-care providers have mistreated 70% of trans patients.[32] Doctors often refuse to treat trans patients, relying on sexist attitudes either to prevent access to needed medical care or to require unnecessary testing.[33] One in five trans patients report health-care providers refusing care.[34] Even receptive doctors are often ignorant of trans issues, to the detriment of their patients. Between a third and half of all transgender people surveyed report needing to teach their health-care provider about transgender health care.[35]

For example, trans individuals face significant difficulties gaining access to hormones, from finding a doctor and getting an appointment, to dealing with specialists and special testing, to getting prescriptions and getting pharmacists to fill those prescriptions.[36] Yet, cis men can get access to hormones with relative ease without seeing specialists, without a psychological workup, and without invasive testing. In fact, "T-clinics" that freely dispense testosterone to cis men are gaining popularity for this purpose.[37] Similarly, cis women do not have to engage in significant talk therapy to access hormones.[38] This gatekeeping on the part of doctors ensures that doctors and therapists have unique control over patient lives.[39] Even without well-documented discrimination and abuse in health-care settings, these double standards demonstrate the types of traditional sexism, cissexism, oppositional sexism, and medical sexism in the treatment of trans patients seeking health-care access.[40]

RESEARCH ON WOMEN

Many diseases have sex and gender differences with respect to prevalence, severity, comorbidity, mortality, age of onset, symptom presentation, responsiveness to treatment, and unmet need for treatment, from Alzheimer's[41] to asthma.[42] Research on women can help identify these differences, establish best practices in treatment, and improve women's health. However, research on women faces a number of obstacles.[43] Forced participation in research is one such issue discussed above.

Another obstacle is the exclusion of women in research.[44] In "The Woman Question in Medicine," Hilde Lindemann discusses a Rockefeller University study that looked at the impact of obesity on breast and uterine cancer but only enrolled men.[45] Of course, men can get breast and uterine cancer, but the prevalence of these diseases are orders of magnitude less common in men than women, and a study that enrolls only men overlooks a significant population subject to these diseases.[46] As a result, Dr. Janine Austin Clayton points out, "We literally know less about every aspect of female biology compared to male biology."[47] In fact, the state of research on women is a vicious cycle. As Maya Dusenbery writes, "Women's symptoms are not taken seriously because medicine doesn't know as much about their bodies and health problems. And medicine doesn't know as much about their bodies and health problems because it doesn't take their symptoms seriously."[48] We might add that women's symptoms are not taken seriously due to medical sexism, that medicine does not know as much about their bodies due to medical sexism, and that treatments are seen as less urgent due to medical sexism.

The problem of excluding women from clinical trials and research is longstanding. Decades ago, Congress passed the National Institutes of Health Revitalization Act of 1993 mandating the inclusion of women and minorities in trials.[49] Mandating the NIH to include these populations by law led to great successes, though the need to mandate itself demonstrates the severity of the problem.[50] However, today, compliance remains incomplete.[51]

Understanding why women are left out of medical research can help counteract the problem.[52] According to Lindemann, "Androcentrism is the view that man is the paradigmatic human being, the most basic and obvious example of the species . . . "[53] If men are paradigmatic members of the species, then focusing research on them makes sense.[54] If women are aberrations or even just more complex and more difficult, then excluding them makes sense. In other words, the invisibility of women is the direct result of prejudice.

Some researchers might say that hormone changes make studying women more expensive.[55] This claim is odd given that the purpose of research is to understand and uncover biology. If the assumption underlying this claim is that hormonal changes impact drug efficacy and dosage, for example, then we would expect scientists to seek more information on what relationship that is, not less. After all, they know a relationship is likely, and they want to find out about the drug, so they have every reason to investigate the interaction of hormones and pharmaceuticals. Since any research that excludes that relationship is, by their own lights, incomplete, research that excludes it would not be justified. In fact, one wonders whether, if men experienced the same hormonal changes posited in women, not only would we have full information about the relationship but also whether all drug dosages and recommendations would include a timeline of when to take it in their cycle.

The problems with including minorities in research help underscore this claim. If no prejudice governed the inclusion of all populations in research, then populations historically subject to prejudice would not be left out. If biological gender differences and not oppression explained exclusion, then minority men would be included in the research where women are missing; if perceived biological racial differences somehow explained exclusion,[56] then white women would be included in studies where racial minorities were missing. Instead, multiple axes of oppression exist in society and in research enrollments.

One possible solution to minorities, women, and especially minority women systematically excluded from clinical trials is to fund and promote research by these groups. Says Lindemann, "If you want to find out about women, you have to ask them—it's no use counting on men to do the necessary research because, by and large, they seem to be indifferent to the woman question."[57] Women and minorities are themselves subject to societal prejudice, and can perpetuate that prejudice, so this answer is not complete. But in a later section, I consider discrimination against female doctors as itself a problem in the medical field generally.

These systemic problems fit within a broader historical pattern in contraceptive work. For example, as Onora O'Neill points out,

> Historical work on the development of contraceptives reminds us that even scientific research on human reproduction and contraception, let alone making effective contraceptive advice and technology widely available, was opposed by many who feared that once it was available women would achieve greater independence, and so greater individual autonomy. Often the fear was that this independence would include sexual independence, that contraception would remove one of the great sanctions of women's marital fidelity and premarital chastity.[58]

The sexist and racist origins of so much work in reproductive health suggests that this type of behavior is part of a larger pattern and not able to be fully understood out of the context of its history.

For example, the "Father of American Gynecology," as Dr. James Marion Sims is sometimes called, created the first hospital for women in the United States on a slave farm in which experimental procedures were performed on enslaved women.[59] His enslaved patients became enslaved nurses as he trained and utilized their labor to contribute to hospital surgical procedures and medical treatment. Although these women were patients, nurses, and gynecological experts with knowledge that surpassed most doctors at the time, they were never recognized as contributors to gynecology nor freed from slavery and were summarily sent back to plantations when their labor was deemed complete.[60] Besides the fact that informed consent on an enslaved individual is by its nature a contradiction in terms, the patients were also not asked permission to undergo the procedures.[61] The fact that the patients' lives were threatened by the procedures, did not receive anesthesia, had to work as part of their hospitalization, and often endured more than a dozen procedures, also makes Dr. Sims's project unethical.[62]

An objector might say that we can ignore these features of the origin of gynecology because they fall prey to the genetic fallacy; perhaps medical advances were made in unfortunate ways, but we can put that history aside in understanding gynecology more generally. Had Dr. Sims and his team made these advances using informed consent on a different population of patients, the same findings would be above reproach. However, the problems with the origins of gynecology go deeper than just accidental features of medical breakthroughs. Gynecology relied on slavery and slavery relied on gynecology: "reproductive medicine was essential to the maintenance and success of southern slavery, especially during the antebellum era, when the largest migration and sale of black women occurred in the nation's young history."[63] The prices for enslaved women depended on medical evaluations, and medical evaluations depended on slave women to use as guinea pigs. In fact, the impetus for solving problems in women's health was not the avoidance of suffering, as would be evident from the fact that women underwent multiple, horrifically painful surgeries, but instead to preserve the reproductive capacity of a person whose sole worth to society was deemed dependent on her ability to birth more slaves. So, technology was advanced not by medicine but by agriculture and privately supported by organizations like Rockefeller Foundation instead of publicly supported in recognition of its necessity for public health.[64]

Historically, advocates of women's health who aimed to spread what little information existed, or who aimed to advance our understandings of birth control were attacked in the United States. For example, Margaret Sanger, the founder of what we now call the Planned Parenthood Federation of America and the person who coined the term "birth control,"[65] herself a problematic figure in this history of contraception, faced incredible obstacles in distributing information about contraception. Inspired by the women she visited as a nurse who begged for the information that would prevent further pregnancies, and who died without it,[66] Sanger commenced work on a project to collect the existing information on contraception, give it to the women who needed it, and advance medical research on it. A variety of laws hampered her efforts, as she describes in her autobiography:

> The younger druggists usually refused to give advice because, if it were to be known, they would come under the law; midwives were

> even more fearful. The doomed women implored me to reveal the "secret" rich people had, offering to pay me extra to tell them; many really believed I was holding back information for money. They asked everybody and tried anything, but nothing did them any good. On Saturday nights I have seen groups of from fifty to one hundred with their shawls over their heads waiting outside the office of a five-dollar abortionist.[67]

The Comstock Law of 1873 prohibited any mailing that was "lewd, lascivious, indecent, or obscene," as defined by the post office.[68] Sanger's work, which mentioned concepts like sexually transmitted diseases and was distributed through the mail when published in pamphlets, newspapers, or letters, was therefore subject to censorship. According to Sanger, she was prosecuted as violating the law before she ever actually did, since she openly discussed the plan to distribute contraception information at a future date, which she argued itself should have been legal.[69] The case against her, *The People vs. Margaret Sanger*, led her to leave the United States for a significant portion of time. Sanger's own sister Ethel was sentenced to a workhouse and went on a hunger strike that nearly killed her.[70] These obstacles underline the fact that, historically, the research done on reproductive health could not possibly help women, since doctors, nurses, pharmacists, reporters, writers, and activists were prohibited from sharing it.

BREAST CANCER

Tens of thousands of women die every year from breast cancer in the United States alone.[71] Furthermore, while it is the second most deadly cancer for American women, it hits some populations harder than others: non-Hispanic black women are 39% more likely to die from it than non-Hispanic white women.[72] And yet, despite the high death rate, testing and treatment options remain controversial.[73] Like the overtesting that occurs when patients receive yearly Pap tests, evidence indicates that the general populace receives too many mammograms.[74] For decades, experts have questioned whether evidence supports mammography, though mammograms continue at high rates to this day.[75] Some go as far as to recommend that breast cancer screening end altogether,[76] with a prominent critic arguing that they are "one of the greatest deceptions perpetrated on the women of the Western world."[77] Evidence about mammography is complicated, due to what is called "lead-time bias," in which early detection suggests that women live longer when in fact they just know about their condition longer; "length bias," in which the sorts of cancers one finds by self-examination are more aggressive cancers than the sorts of cancers one finds by yearly mammograms; and "selection bias," in which study subjects differ from the general populace.[78] In fact, even if mammography saves lives, it is not necessarily the most valuable emphasis for breast cancer progress from a public health perspective. Focus on awareness and on mammograms through "pinkwashing" might distract from broader issues such as improved research, and from systemic causes of breast cancer.[79] Breast cancer treatment can also kill, maim, and debilitate, meaning that a cost-benefit analysis must take into account all the effects of testing and not just the good effects.[80]

The concern is that mammograms lead to a collection of problems familiar from chapter 2: overdiagnosis from false positives, overtreatment, stress, worry, and financial problems, to name a few. And, just as in Pap testing, individuals considering mammograms may not be informed on the risks.[81] In fact, doctors may be misleading the public on the risks of mammograms.[82] This possibility raises the concern that testing and treatment might itself include too much paternalism, which extends into the entire edifice surrounding breast cancer. As Barbara Ehrenreich puts it,

> And although we may imagine ourselves to be well past the era of patriarchal medicine, obedience is the message behind the infantilizing theme in breast-cancer culture, as represented by the teddy bears, the crayons, and the prevailing pinkness. You are encouraged to regress to a little-girl state, to suspend critical judgment, and to accept whatever measures the doctors, as parent surrogates, choose to impose.[83]

The result of this paternalism can be damaging for many patients: they will receive chemotherapy, surgery, and radiation for cancers that are harmless.[84] According to some data, a third of all breast cancer diagnoses are faulty.[85] Some go further, arguing that, "Most women with screen-detected breast cancer have not had their life saved by screening. They are instead either diagnosed early (with no effect on their mortality) or overdiagnosed."[86] These studies call into question the common beliefs about breast cancer diagnoses.

Too much mammography leads to too much chemotherapy, which in turn harms patients. New studies show that many patients receive chemotherapy who do not need it.[87] In fact, it is possible that up to 70% of patients who are recommended to receive chemotherapy, especially those older than 50, can avoid it.[88]

If women are harmed by breast-cancer testing, diagnosis, and treatment, why does it persist? Financial considerations are one possibility, especially keeping in mind that $6 billion a year is raised for breast cancer, if we include federal, state, and local contributions. Yet financial considerations are not a plausible explanation, since not all cancers face the same problems. Without putting breast cancer in context, it might not seem that different than many other cancers that are overdiagnosed and overtreated, like thyroid cancer and prostate cancer.[89] In the context of larger issues covered in this book, however, overtreatment in this arena starts to look like part of a larger pattern. Barbara Ehrenreich cites Cindy Pearson, executive director at the National Women's Health Network who has said that, "Breast cancer provides a way of doing something for women, without being feminist."[90] In other words, medical sexism is at root.

CARDIOVASCULAR DISEASE AND HEART DISEASE

In 1991, Dr. Bernadine Healy coined the term "Yentl Syndrome" in the *New England Journal of Medicine* to describe the disparate treatment women receive for heart disease.[91] She named it after an Isaac Bashevis Singer character who pretended to be a boy so she could study the Talmud.[92] Healy then called for "a general awakening."[93] Unequal treatment of women, and especially women of color in heart disease is a serious matter.[94] Twenty-five percent of all deaths among women in the United States are due to heart disease.[95] Doctors do not hew to standards of care for women when it comes to cardiovascular disease (CVD).[96] Young women are regularly sent home from the hospital during a heart attack, at rates seven times more often than men.[97] In fact, physicians are not even informed on what disease kills most women: "Fewer than 1 in 5 physicians knew that more women than men die each year from CVD."[98] These factors are related: women may die at higher rates because they receive worse care.[99] They are less likely to get referred for diagnostic care; historically, women were 10% as likely to get cardiac catheterization than a man despite getting more health-care procedures overall.[100] And, they receive worse care in turn because the research focuses on men: "For several decades, the male model of coronary disease . . . constituted the basis for most diagnostic and treatment strategies for both sexes. As a result, many women who did not have classic obstructive coronary atherosclerosis were not diagnosed with ischemic heart disease and did not receive appropriate treatment."[101] For example, the use of aspirin as a preventative measure against coronary heart disease resulted from research done exclusively on men.[102] Ignoring the existence of women succeeds in harming them.[103] Dr. Sharonne Hayes points out that, "guidelines are less likely to be applied to women compared to men. We know that when hospitals have systems in place to ensure they provide care according to the guidelines, women's outcomes improve, even more than men's."[104] But even as scientific studies examine the differences in research, the characteristic symptoms, the treatment of patients, the suffering, the mortality rates, and the gravity of heart disease and CVD, medical sexism continues to be a contributing factor.[105] Recent studies continue to identify the Yentl Syndrome as playing a significant role in health outcomes.[106]

PAIN

In general, pain is often not taken seriously enough, either from the perspective of doctors giving diagnoses or from the perspective of research budgets and public health initiatives.[107] But pain is also an area where doctors tend to dismiss women,[108] do so at higher rates,[109] and give women different care, such as sedatives rather than pain relief medication when they do respond.[110] Women even wait 25% longer in an emergency room when they have abdominal pain than men do.[111] The gap in diagnoses and treatment can lead to a variety of problems for women in particular ranging from greater and longer suffering, to the psychological trauma of gaslighting,[112] to the harms that arise from delay of treatment. Furthermore, since women are primarily the ones who are affected by chronic pain, this differential treatment has an impact on the lives of millions of women.[113] Bias in pain management can take many forms.[114] But over 90% of women who experience chronic pain report that they have experienced discrimination at the hands of the health-care system.[115] And, some conditions that primarily afflict women, like period pain, are dismissed as untreatable or unmanageable;[116] conditions that might be causing period pain like endometriosis can take an average of 10 years for doctors to accurately diagnose,[117] while others are chalked up to catch-all conditions like hysteria.[118] In fact, dangers in dismissing women's pain can take us full circle to Pap testing, since denying women care who report being in pain has led to death from cervical cancer.[119]

If women's pain is stereotyped as not existing, then it would be no surprise that, "Doctors gaslighting women in real pain isn't the exception. It's the status quo."[120] It is why doctors may tell their female patients that, "All your symptoms are your imagination."[121] The attention necessary to treat and manage pain, when it is found in women, is viewed as self-indulgence.[122] However, women do feel pain intensely.[123] And, if they are misdiagnosed at higher rates, discriminated against, and receive worse treatment, these problems are exacerbated.[124] More research is unlikely to help: "To return to the issue of chronic pain, 70% of the people it impacts are women. And yet, 80% of pain studies are conducted on male mice or human men."[125] When men are viewed as the norm or default, that perception persists even in the face of problems primarily affecting women, resulting in medical sexism.

AUTOIMMUNE DISORDERS

Millions of Americans have autoimmune disorders, with estimates ranging from 25 to 50 million. At the upper range, that means that the number of Americans with autoimmune disorders would surpass heart disease and cancer combined.[126] Furthermore, the majority—about 75%—of those that suffer from autoimmune diseases are women.[127] For example, 90% of those with lupus are women, and lupus disproportionately affects women of color.[128] One hypothesis for this difference is that women have better immune systems overall.[129] In fact, the number of naturally occurring autoantibodies in an individual, useful for fighting inflammation, disease, and promoting healing, also predicts the likelihood of an individual developing an autoimmune disorder.[130] An autoimmune disorder occurs when those strong immune systems backfire, attacking healthy cells instead of actual diseases. Thus, it may be that the stronger the immune system, the more dangerous an autoimmune disorder becomes.[131]

Sex differences influence the treatment of autoimmune disorders at every level, and many of these problems are interlocking. From research to diagnosis, treatment, and cures, autoimmune disorders lag behind other diseases. For example, research on autoimmune diseases is not proportionate to other major threats to health in the United States, with smaller budgets, less coordination, fewer scientists working on the issues, and less doctor training.[132] In addition, women are more likely to have autoimmune disorders, but take longer to get a diagnosis than men.[133] Women's pain, symptoms, and the sorts of diseases that tend to afflict women are taken less seriously in the medical community, which means that a successful diagnosis is less likely, but even if it occurs, is more likely to result in a referral to a psychological workup than a physical one. Meanwhile, mistreatment can continue well after an accurate diagnosis.[134] Life expectancy for women with autoimmune disorders is lower than that for men, even as severity of several autoimmune diseases, as measured by age of onset, disability progression, relapses, and comorbidities, can be worse in males.[135] As Dusenbery points out, "women make up more than three-quarters of those with autoimmune diseases, while they constitute less than a third of practicing doctors in a medical system that has, until recently, been even more overwhelmingly male dominated."[136] If a male-dominated field ignores diseases primarily afflicting women, and to the extent that it does recognize them, mistreats those patients, then a discussion of those diseases that leaves out medical sexism will be incomplete. In fact, treating, curing, or researching a disease without believing the patients who have it seems so farfetched that we can expect little progress on the underlying scientific issues without combating or eliminating medical sexism.

DISCRIMINATION AGAINST FEMALE DOCTORS

Historically, women have never made up an equal share of doctors, those that do enter the profession have never seen a proportionate share of highly ranked positions, and those that do make it to highly ranked positions have never seen pay commensurate with their skill. One news report puts it pointedly: "Since 1970, women have grown from 9.7 percent of physicians to 32.4 percent in 2010. In law careers, women have gone from 4.9 percent to 33.4. But wages have remained significantly lower for women than men. . . ."[137] Since 2010, evidence suggests the pay gap has persisted, even growing from 2016 to 2017. Comparing numbers across studies with different methods creates difficulties, but suggests that the pay gap has decreased from roughly 40% less in 2007 to roughly 30% less in 2017.[138] This pay gap amounts to women making tens of thousands of dollars less every year than their male counterparts.[139]

Differences in specialties could explain this phenomenon. Dusenbery reports, "There remain large segments of medicine where women are vastly outnumbered: women make up about a quarter of emergency medicine physicians, neurologists, and anesthesiologists; less than 20 percent of general surgeons; 12 percent of cardiologists; 7 percent of urologists; and less than 5 percent of orthopedic surgeons."[140] However, the pay gap remains high, and a "significant gender gap that cannot be explained by specialty choice, practice setting, work hours, or other characteristics" between salaries persists, suggesting that sexism is the best explanation.[141] For example, female doctors seem to be better than male doctors, if patient outcomes and patient interactions are any indication.[142] Similarly, other features besides sexism cannot explain the failure to promote female physicians to tenured positions: "Among physicians with faculty appointments at US medical schools, there were sex differences in academic faculty rank, with women substantially less likely than men to be full professors, after accounting for age, experience, specialty, and measures of research productivity."[143]

Furthermore, while the high share of female medical students and trainees has been widely reported for years,[144] it has not translated into a higher proportion of female doctors overall. In 2018, the percentage of female physicians was no better than it was in 2010.[145] This lag time is no surprise. Women made up the majority of medical school applicants for the first time in 2004, while they made up the majority of medical school students actually enrolled for the first time in 2017.[146]

In fact, there is the problem of hierarchy in the medical field generally. Here is Lindemann writing in 2012: "Women's advancement to leadership positions in academic medicine has been unduly slow. Only 17 percent of tenured professors, 16 percent of full professors, 10 percent of department chairs, and 11 percent of deans in U.S. medical schools are women."[147] A 2018 report identifies similar trends and assessments: "But the top leadership positions in medicine remain predominantly male. Only 15% of department chairs are women, and 16% of medical school deans are female. For the past 10 years, according to an Association of American Medical Colleges report, women in academic medicine have received only 30% of new tenured positions."[148] If the methodology of the studies can be compared, the numbers may be improving, but the much-touted influx of female leaders that would be expected from high shares of medical students being women has yet to manifest. Considering all health-care workers, the majority are women. But breaking down the numbers by organizational hierarchy, the majority of executives, directors, and other upper-level positions are male.

Given the sexism belied by lower salary for better work; more difficulty getting into medical school; more difficulty getting tenure track jobs; more difficulty getting tenure; as well as more difficulty being promoted to chair, dean, and other leadership positions, it is no surprise women in the medical field face discrimination at extremely high rates.[149] For example, while only 5% of men in the medical field report having experienced sexual harassment, nearly a third of women in the medical field have.[150] Studies that look at female physicians who are also mothers found even starker numbers: four out of five physicians who are mothers report experiencing discrimination in the work place.[151] The examples of maternal discrimination most often reported were pregnancy and maternity leave (nearly 90%) and discrimination about breastfeeding (nearly half).[152] The effects are broad: work-family conflict results in a 36% increase of depression among women in the medical field over men.[153]

Increasing the number, status, and salaries of women in the medical field will not solve the problems documented in this book. On the contrary, both are symptoms of the same root problem of medical sexism. However, we should not ignore that organization structures that include primarily individuals from one segment of society tend to serve primarily individuals from that segment of society. Says Sherwin,

> It should come as no surprise, then, that the health care system is least effective at providing for the needs of people who are multiply oppressed in society. Such consequences might be unconscious and wholly unintended. It is part of the very nature of oppression that those with the power to set the social agenda and define the realms of knowledge view the world from their own perspective. Hence in the realm of health care, the professionals who make the decisions about policies and priorities are most attuned to needs that arise among the types of people they know best—other people with power and privilege in society.[154]

Hierarchical organizations, then, support sexist, racist and classist values, which compound each other.[155] These structures in turn support the paternalism of white men toward those seeking health care, who are predominantly women, and keep health-care decisions out of the reach of patients and safely ensconced in the purview of the doctor.[156] Sexism does not start or end in the medical field, but recognizing and understanding medical sexism within it helps focus the problem.[157]

DOCTOR DISENCHANTMENT

When sexism or racism pervades an industry, people get hurt because it leads to mistrust of the medical establishment, as evidenced by the so-called "Tuskegee effect."[158] The Tuskegee effect was the result of the Tuskegee Experiment, a study performed by the Public Health Service to evaluate the effects of syphilis in African Americans.[159] It ostensibly had the goal to improve the health of black men, but experimenters withheld both the diagnoses and the eventual cure. The study violated the Nuremberg Code, and after journalists published an exposé in 1972, the *Belmont Report* on ethical principles governing research with human subjects was created. One result of the ethical and legal violations in the Tuskegee Experiment is that the medical establishment was viewed with mistrust by millions of people in the United States, especially African Americans.[160] Before the experiment came to light, differences in health outcomes by race were slowly narrowing. After the news coverage, those differences grew and the life expectancy of black men over the age of 45 declined, likely through the avoidance of health care and refusal of treatments.[161]

Something similar to the Tuskegee effect might be happening among women. For example, there has been a persistent movement of people resisting basic medical care due to mistrust of doctors, including preventative care, such as the group of people come to be known as "anti-vaxxers."[162] Perhaps it is not surprising that anti-vaccine views could appear in contemporary society. Since some parents think vaccines cause autism and therefore reject them, anti-vaccine sentiment could be due to ableism and discrimination against neurodiversity. The United States also has a history of opposing scientific advancement in the form of conspiracy theories.[163] Additionally, the United States has a problematic model of public education generally and poor scientific literacy specifically.[164] Vaccination rates are roughly stable over time and the lowest rates are in populations that lack health insurance.[165] But to the extent that some with access still reject vaccines, many such views occur in educated, urban communities that are otherwise characterized by privilege.[166] The view also seems to be the purview of female voices.[167]

What if the reason that anti-vaccine beliefs arise in these populations is that they feel disempowered specifically by those within the medical community? Perhaps patients who feel their autonomy overridden by their doctors in birth and labor choices aim to reassert it when they become mothers of young children.[168] For example, Mark Navin writes that,

> . . . it is well documented that childcare—and parental care for children's health—is gendered feminine, and that mothers are usually the primary decision-makers surrounding their children's healthcare. Relatedly, the epistemic practices of physicians are gendered masculine, even though many physicians are women. Therefore, the interactions between parents and pediatricians surrounding vaccination decisions take place against the background of gender inequalities and gendered conceptions of the reasoning of physicians and parents.[169]

As a result, he argues that "facts about gender oppression provide parents (and especially mothers) with good reason to be skeptical of physicians' assurances regarding the safety and efficacy of vaccines."[170] In fact, he elsewhere attributes a parents' reasonable denial of trust in pediatricians directly to paternalism, saying that "Parents may be aware of physicians' historical and ongoing abuse of their (epistemic) power, and they may have been treated paternalistically by pediatricians."[171] Understanding the power dynamics at play in the doctor's office and the gendered treatment parents often receive permits a better understanding of this growing epidemic of vaccine refusals.[172]

If some of the people who feel their rights being denied are educated and wealthy, and if such people have more time and opportunity to redress those wrongs, then distrust of the medical establishment could be more popular among that community. In addition, the sort of "me-first" mentality that attends these wealthy communities who often make choices that help their own children to the detriment of society is compatible with a view on vaccines that would rely on others to maintain a herd immunity while free-riding on the supposed risks others take.

Anti-vaccination attitudes, then, would be of a piece with general distrust of medicine and explain alternative medical treatments generally. They would also be consistent with the popularity of midwives and doulas, who allow pregnant people to safely give birth outside the medical OB/GYN context. In a society where wellness is viewed as an individual pursuit rather than a public health issue, the rejection of vaccines fits right in. People subscribing to this constellation of views might be anti-medicine or in search of alternative medicine without being anti-science. And, this distinction between medicine and science, especially with regard to the trustworthiness of the surrogates of those fields, explains how a highly educated and wealthy individual who subscribes to the scientific method could also reject the trappings of the medical field when those trappings seem to override her autonomy, disempower her, and generally take away the control she has over her body.

The identification of medical sexism as a contributing factor to the denial of birth control and the mandating of Pap testing has given us broader insights into gendered health. First, it allows us to reject the notion that political institutions, like legislation and court cases, and financial institutions, like insurance companies and employers, are primarily to blame for the injustices occurring against people in need of hormonal birth control. The sort of sexism that leads to restrictions on reproductive health from these institutions pervades the medical sphere as well, meaning that doctors are not immune to society's hierarchies in permitting and perpetuating medical sexism. Second, this argument shows that sexism is a pervasive and powerful force in women's lives, affecting not only their standing in society, income, wealth, and risks, but also their health and health care in medical sexism. This view shows that often explicit rules undermine women's equity but go unnoticed, and that medical sexism influences women's lives in meaningful ways.

CONCLUSION

While I cannot address every area or instance of medical sexism, or sexism that people face in the medical field, I can build up a stronger case for the position that sexism underlies crucial interactions some populations of patients have with their doctors by using pragmatic examples. It can be dangerous to overlook medical sexism in health care. If gender discrimination, inequity, bias, and negligent harm characterize health care, then we should identify it, mention it, discuss it, and work to end it. If we do not, then we can end up perpetuating an unjust system. Just as in the last chapter, where I argued that doctors violate standards of care in ways that kill their patients in reproductive care, in this chapter, I argue the same problems occur outside of reproductive health.

NOTES

1. McMurray et al., "Gender Disparities in Clinical Decision Making."
2. Saini, *Inferior*, 36.
3. Sherwin, *No Longer Patient*, 72.
4. Sherwin, 223–25.
5. Wolf, "Gender, Feminism, and Death."
6. Lorde, *A Burst of Light*, 115. Also quoted in Davis, *Women, Culture & Politics*, 64–65.
7. Bertakis et al., "Gender Differences in the Utilization of Health Care Services."
8. Jindal et al., "Kidney Transplantation and Gender Disparity."

9. Segev et al., "Age and Comorbidities Are Effect Modifiers of Gender Disparities in Renal Transplantation."
10. Segev et al.
11. Hickey et al., "Clinical and Gender Differences in Heart Transplant Recipients in the NEW HEART Study."
12. Gillespie et al., "Sex Differences and Attitudes toward Living Donor Kidney Transplantation among Urban Black Patients on Hemodialysis."
13. Ojo and Port, "Influence of Race and Gender on Related Donor Renal Transplantation Rates."
14. Gillespie et al., "Sex Differences and Attitudes toward Living Donor Kidney Transplantation among Urban Black Patients on Hemodialysis"; Thompson, Robinson, and Kenny, "Gender Differences in Family Communication About Organ Donation."
15. Jindal et al., "Kidney Transplantation and Gender Disparity."
16. Organ Procurement and Transplantation Network (OPTN), "National Data: Transplants in the U.S. by Recipient Gender, January 1,1988-June 30, 2018."
17. Heubner et al., "Gender Differences in Access to Lung Transplant in the US After LAS Implementation."
18. Young and Little, "Women and Heart Transplantation."
19. Magoon, "Women Are More Likely To Die Waiting For An Organ."
20. Mindikoglu et al., "Gender Disparity in Liver Transplant Waiting-List Mortality"; Myers et al., "Gender, Renal Function, and Outcomes on the Liver Transplant Waiting List."
21. Gordon and Ladner, "Gender Inequities Pervade Organ Transplantation Access"; Rasmussen et al., "Gender Bias and Organ Transplantation in Nepal"; Couchoud et al., "A New Approach for Measuring Gender Disparity in Access to Renal Transplantation Waiting Lists"; Puoti et al., "Organ Transplantation and Gender Differences"; Magoon, "Women Are More Likely To Die Waiting For An Organ."
22. Pabst et al., "Physician Reported Adherence to Immunosuppressants in Renal Transplant Patients"; Myers et al., "Gender, Renal Function, and Outcomes on the Liver Transplant Waiting List."
23. Wille et al., "Disparities In Lung Transplantation Before And After Introduction Of The Lung Allocation Score."
24. Hickey et al., "Clinical and Gender Differences in Heart Transplant Recipients in the NEW HEART Study"; Young and Little, "Women and Heart Transplantation."
25. Office for Civil Rights, "HHS Proposes to Revise ACA Section 1557 Rule to Enforce Civil Rights in Healthcare, Conform to Law, and Eliminate Billions in Unnecessary Costs"; "ACLU Responds to Proposed Changes to

Health Care Rights Law," American Civil Liberties Union, May 24, 2019, https://www.aclu.org/press-releases/aclu-responds-proposed-changes-health-care-rights-law.

26. Safer et al., "Barriers to Health Care for Transgender Individuals"; McKinnon, "Gender Transition Isn't a Whim, so Why the Mistrust?"; McKinnon, "Trouble Making the Change."

27. Gupta, Imborek, and Krasowski, "Challenges in Transgender Healthcare"; "GLAAD Media Reference Guide - Transgender."

28. Serano, *Whipping Girl*, 108.

29. Serano, *Whipping Girl*, 102.

30. "Study"; Gupta, Imborek, and Krasowski, "Challenges in Transgender Healthcare"; Krasowski and Imborek, "Obstacles in Transgender Healthcare"; White Hughto et al., "Barriers to Gender Transition-Related Healthcare."

31. Bradford et al., "Experiences of Transgender-Related Discrimination and Implications for Health"; Bauer et al., "I Don't Think This Is Theoretical; This Is Our Lives"; "About The TransAdvocate"; "Victim Issues: Mistrust of Professionals | Responding to Transgender Victims of Sexual Assault"; cárdenas, "Pregnancy: Reproductive Futures in Trans of Color Feminism."

32. "Addressing the Challenges of Transgender Health Care."

33. Sanchez, Sanchez, and Danoff, "Health Care Utilization, Barriers to Care, and Hormone Usage among Male-to-Female Transgender Persons in New York City"; Hembree et al., "Endocrine Treatment of Transsexual Persons."

34. Grant et al., "Injustice at Every Turn: A Report of the National Transgender Discrimination Survey," 6.

35. White Hughto et al., "Barriers to Gender Transition-Related Healthcare"; Dupere, "6 Ways the Health Care System Fails Transgender Patients"; "Victim Issues: Mistrust of Professionals | Responding to Transgender Victims of Sexual Assault"; Grant et al., "Injustice at Every Turn: A Report of the National Transgender Discrimination Survey," 6.

36. Budge, "Psychotherapists as Gatekeepers"; Urquhart, "Gatekeepers vs. Informed Consent"; Grinberg, "CVS Apologizes after Pharmacist Refused to Fill Transgender Woman's Prescription - CNN."

37. Varney, "Testosterone, The Biggest Men's Health Craze Since Viagra, May Be Risky."

38. Urquhart, "Gatekeepers vs. Informed Consent"; Hembree et al., "Endocrine Treatment of Transsexual Persons"; Committee on Health Care for Underserved Women, "Committee Opinion No. 512," 512.

39. Bockting et al., "Patient Satisfaction with Transgender Health Services"; Gardner and Safer, "Progress on the Road to Better Medical Care for Trans-

gender Patients"; Budge, "Psychotherapists as Gatekeepers"; McKinnon, "Gender Transition Isn't a Whim, so Why the Mistrust?"

40. Serano, *Excluded*, 254.

41. Carter et al., "Sex and Gender Differences in Alzheimer's Disease." 75% of people with Alzheimer's are women. Dusenbery, *Doing Harm*, 3.

42. Disorders, *Studying Sex Differences in Health and Disease*.

43. Saini, *Inferior*, 43.

44. Kibbe, "Sex Bias in Surgical Research."

45. Kibbe, "Female Trouble."

46. Morillo-Cucci and German, "Males with a Uterus and Fallopian Tubes, a Rare Disorder of Sexual Development"; American Cancer Society, "Key Statistics for Breast Cancer in Men"; Flanagin, "WHO: Risk of Certain Cancers Is Higher in Transgender Communities"

47. Rabin, "Health Researchers Will Get $10.1 Million to Counter Gender Bias in Studies."

48. Dusenbery, *Doing Harm*, 12.

49. "Text of S. 1 (103rd)."

50. Mazure and Jones, "Twenty Years and Still Counting."

51. Chen et al., "Twenty Years Post-NIH Revitalization Act."

52. The idea that, "Woman is a pair of ovaries with a human being attached, whereas man is a human being furnished with a pair of testes" is perhaps not as prevalent today as it once was, but disrespect toward women and minorities should not be overlooked as a contributing factor. Rudolph Virchow as quoted in Lindemann, "The Woman Question in Medicine," 39; Sagan, "Special Section: Gender Specifics: Why Women Aren't Men."

53. Lindemann, "The Woman Question in Medicine," 43.

54. Miner et al., "Smartphone-Based Conversational Agents and Responses to Questions About Mental Health, Interpersonal Violence, and Physical Health"; Chemaly, "Why Is New Technology Designed Primarily for Men?"

55. Rabin, "Health Researchers Will Get $10.1 Million to Counter Gender Bias in Studies."

56. Though both are social constructs. Zack, *Philosophy of Science and Race*.

57. Lindemann, "The Woman Question in Medicine," 44.

58. O'Neill, *Autonomy and Trust in Bioethics*, 51–52.

59. Owens, "Medical Bondage: Race, Gender, and the Origins of American Gynecology," 1 edition (Athens, GA: University of Georgia Press, 2017); Zhang, "The Surgeon Who Experimented on Slaves."

60. Owens, "Medical Bondage," 2.

61. Ojanuga, "The Medical Ethics of the 'Father of Gynaecology', Dr J. Marion Sims."

62. Ojanuga.

63. Owens, "Medical Bondage," 4.

64. O'Neill, *Autonomy and Trust in Bioethics*, 52.

65. Sanger, *The Autobiography of Margaret Sanger*, 107.

66. Sanger, 55. For example, Sanger states, "Night after night the wistful image of Mrs. Sachs appeared before me. I made all sorts of excuses to myself for not going back. I was busy on other cases; I really did not know what to say to her or how to convince her of my own ignorance; I was helpless to avert such monstrous atrocities. Time rolled by and I did nothing...Its pains and griefs crowded in upon me, a moving picture rolled before my eyes with photographic clearness: women writhing in travail to bring forth little babies; the babies themselves naked and hungry, wrapped in newspapers to keep them from the cold; six-year-old children with pinched, pale, wrinkled faces, old in concentrated wretchedness, pushed into gray and fetid cellars, crouching on stone floors, their small scrawny hands scuttling through rags, making lamp shades, artificial flowers; white coffins, black coffins, coffins, coffins interminably passing in never-ending succession. The scenes piled one upon another on another. I could bear it no longer. As I stood there the darkness faded. The sun came up and threw its reflection over the house tops. It was the dawn of a new day in my life also. The doubt and questioning, the experimenting and trying, were now to be put behind me. I knew I could not go back merely to keeping people alive. I went to bed, knowing that no matter what it might cost, I was finished with palliatives and superficial cures; I was resolved to seek out the root of evil, to do something to change the destiny of mothers whose miseries were vast as the sky." Sanger, 92.

67. Sanger, *The Autobiography of Margaret Sanger*, 89.

68. Sanger, 77.

69. Sanger, 110.

70. Sanger, 227.

71. DeSantis et al., "Breast Cancer Statistics, 2017, Racial Disparity in Mortality by State."

72. DeSantis et al.

73. Welch, Schwartz, and Woloshin, *Overdiagnosed*, 74.

74. Aschwanden, "What If Everything Your Doctors Told You About Breast Cancer Was Wrong?"; Bleyer and Welch, "Effect of Three Decades of Screening Mammography on Breast-Cancer Incidence"; Autier et al., "Breast Cancer Mortality in Neighbouring European Countries with Different Levels of Screening but Similar Access to Treatment"; Welch, Schwartz, and Woloshin, *Overdiagnosed*, 82.

75. "NCI Adopts New Mammography Screening Guidelines For Women."

76. Baum, "Breast Screening Should Be Scrapped"; Welch, Schwartz, and Woloshin, *Overdiagnosed*, 89.

77. Ehrenreich, "Welcome to Cancerland."

78. Plotkin, "Good News and Bad News About Breast Cancer."

79. "Think Before You Pink: About Us."

80. Baum, "Harms from Breast Cancer Screening Outweigh Benefits If Death Caused by Treatment Is Included."

81. Domenighetti et al., "Women's Perception of the Benefits of Mammography Screening."

82. Jørgensen and Gøtzsche, "Content of Invitations for Publicly Funded Screening Mammography"; Baum, "Breast Screening Should Be Scrapped."

83. Ehrenreich, "Welcome to Cancerland."

84. Bleyer and Welch, "Effect of Three Decades of Screening Mammography on Breast-Cancer Incidence."

85. Bleyer and Welch.

86. Welch and Frankel, "Likelihood That a Woman with Screen-Detected Breast Cancer Has Had Her 'Life Saved' by That Screening."

87. Sparano et al., "Adjuvant Chemotherapy Guided by a 21-Gene Expression Assay in Breast Cancer."

88. Grady, "Good News for Women With Breast Cancer: Many Don't Need Chemo."

89. Or just overtreatment in general. Welch, Schwartz, and Woloshin, *Overdiagnosed*, 61; Brownlee, *Overtreated*, 277–78.

90. Quoted in, Ehrenreich, "Welcome to Cancerland."

91. Healy, "The Yentl Syndrome."

92. Singer and Frasconi, *Yentl the Yeshiva Boy*.

93. Healy, "The Yentl Syndrome."

94. Davis, *Women, Culture & Politics*, 58.

95. "Women and Heart Disease Fact Sheet."

96. Mosca et al., "National Study of Physician Awareness and Adherence to Cardiovascular Disease Prevention Guidelines"; Kim, Hofer, and Kerr, "Review of Evidence and Explanations for Suboptimal Screening and Treatment of Dyslipidemia in Women"; Sueta et al., "Analysis of the Degree of Undertreatment of Hyperlipidemia and Congestive Heart Failure Secondary to Coronary Artery Disease"; Pearson et al., "The Lipid Treatment Assessment Project (L-TAP)"; Ford et al., "Serum Total Cholesterol Concentrations and Awareness, Treatment, and Control of Hypercholesterolemia Among US Adults"; Jha et al., "Differences in Medical Care and Disease Outcomes Among Black and White Women With Heart Disease"; Mosca et al., "Evidence-Based Guidelines for Cardiovascular Disease Prevention in Women"; Lichtman et al., "Symptom Recognition and Healthcare Experiences of Young

Women With Acute Myocardial Infarction"; Vaccarino et al., "Sex-Based Differences in Early Mortality after Myocardial Infarction. National Registry of Myocardial Infarction 2 Participants"; Vaccarino et al., "Sex Differences in Mortality After Acute Myocardial Infarction."

97. Dusenbery, *Doing Harm*, 4.

98. Mosca et al., "National Study of Physician Awareness and Adherence to Cardiovascular Disease Prevention Guidelines."

99. Mosca et al.

100. Sherwin, *No Longer Patient*, 224.

101. June 16th and Comment, "First Set of Recommendations in a Decade Advocate Gender-Specific Approach for Women." Note also Mahowald, *Women and Children in Health Care*, viii.

102. McMurray et al., "Gender Disparities in Clinical Decision Making."

103. Chiaramonte and Friend, "Medical Students' and Residents' Gender Bias in the Diagnosis, Treatment, and Interpretation of Coronary Heart Disease Symptoms"; Chiaramonte, "Physicians' Gender Bias in the Diagnosis, Treatment, and Interpretation of Coronary Heart Disease Symptoms"; Maserejian et al., "Disparities in Physicians' Interpretations of Heart Disease Symptoms by Patient Gender"; Adams et al., "The Influence of Patient and Doctor Gender on Diagnosing Coronary Heart Disease"; "Is Medicine's Gender Bias Killing Young Women?"

104. Thomas, "Heart Disease – Not Just a Man's Disease Anymore."

105. Canto et al., "Association of Age and Sex With Myocardial Infarction Symptom Presentation and In-Hospital Mortality."

106. Merz, "The Yentl Syndrome Is Alive and Well"; Merz, "The Yentl Syndrome and Gender Inequality in Ischemic HD."

107. Institute of Medicine (US) Committee on Advancing Pain Research, Care, and Education, *Relieving Pain in America*; Norlock, "Can't Complain."

108. Fassler, "How Doctors Take Women's Pain Less Seriously."

109. Dusenbery, "When Doctors Dismiss Women's Pain."

110. Hoffmann and Tarzian, "The Girl Who Cried Pain."

111. Dusenbery, *Doing Harm*, 4.

112. Wilson, "Doctors, Stop Gaslighting Women In Pain."

113. Foreman, "Why Women Are Living in the Discomfort Zone."

114. Hadjistavropoulos, McMurtry, and Craig, "Beautiful Faces in Pain."

115. Anson, "Women in Pain Report Significant Gender Bias."

116. Sanghani, "Period Pain Can Feel 'as Bad as a Heart Attack' - so Why Is It Being Ignored?"; Fenton, "Period Pain Is Officially as Bad as a Heart Attack - so Why Have Doctors Ignored It?"

117. Ellin, "Endometriosis Is Often Ignored in Teenage Girls."

118. Tasca et al., "Women And Hysteria In The History Of Mental Health."

119. Sanghani, "'It's Just Lady Pains.'"
120. Wilson, "Doctors, Stop Gaslighting Women In Pain."
121. Culp-Ressler, "When Gender Stereotypes Become A Serious Hazard To Women's Health."
122. Leslie Jamison, "Grand Unified Theory of Female Pain."
123. Fillingim et al., "Sex, Gender, and Pain"; MyHealthNewsDaily, "Women Feel Pain More Intensely Than Men Do."
124. *Chronic Pain.*
125. Kiesel, "Women and Pain."
126. Dusenbery, *Doing Harm*, 138.
127. Dusenbery, 138; Fairweather, Frisancho-Kiss, and Rose, "Sex Differences in Autoimmune Disease from a Pathological Perspective."
128. Dusenbery, *Doing Harm*, 138; Sullivan, "Lupus: The Silent Killer," 26.
129. Saini, *Inferior*, 37; Fairweather, Frisancho-Kiss, and Rose, "Sex Differences in Autoimmune Disease from a Pathological Perspective"; Fairweather and Rose, "Women and Autoimmune Diseases."
130. Fairweather, Frisancho-Kiss, and Rose, "Sex Differences in Autoimmune Disease from a Pathological Perspective."
131. Other theories may complement or offer alternatives to this one: Wilhelmson et al., "Testosterone Is an Endogenous Regulator of BAFF and Splenic B Cell Number"; Nelson, "HLA Relationships of Pregnancy, Microchimerism and Autoimmune Disease"; Lleo et al., "Is Autoimmunity a Matter of Sex?"; Pessach and Notarangelo, "X-Linked Primary Immunodeficiencies as a Bridge to Better Understanding X-Chromosome Related Autoimmunity"; Billi et al., "The Female-Biased Factor VGLL3 Drives Cutaneous and Systemic Autoimmunity," 3; Natri et al., "The Pregnancy Pickle."
132. Dusenbery, *Doing Harm*, 144.
133. Dusenbery, 148.
134. Dusenbery, 147; Esser, "Story"; Ernst, "Miss Treated: Fighting Misogyny in the Medical Profession One Story at a Time."
135. Ngo, Steyn, and McCombe, "Gender Differences in Autoimmune Disease"; Fairweather and Rose, "Women and Autoimmune Diseases."
136. Dusenbery, *Doing Harm*, 2.
137. Strasser, "Despite Growing Number Of Female Doctors And Lawyers, Women's Pay Still Lags Behind."
138. Kavilanz, "The Gender Pay Gap for Women Doctors Is Big—and Getting Worse"; Strasser, "Despite Growing Number Of Female Doctors And Lawyers, Women's Pay Still Lags Behind"; Lo Sasso et al., "The $16,819 Pay Gap For Newly Trained Physicians."
139. Dusenbery, *Doing Harm*, 10; Oaklander, "Women Doctors Are Paid $20,000 Less Than Male Doctors"; Jena, Olenski, and Blumenthal, "Sex Dif-

ferences in Physician Salary in US Public Medical Schools"; Parks and Redberg, "Women in Medicine and Patient Outcomes"; Arora, "It Is Time for Equal Pay for Equal Work for Physicians—Paging Dr Ledbetter"; Lo Sasso et al., "The $16,819 Pay Gap For Newly Trained Physicians"; "Second Annual Physician Compensation Report: March 2018."

140. Dusenbery, *Doing Harm*, 9.

141. Lo Sasso et al., "The $16,819 Pay Gap For Newly Trained Physicians."

142. Parks and Redberg, "Women in Medicine and Patient Outcomes"; Cruickshank, "Are Women Better Doctors Than Men?"; Tsugawa et al., "Comparison of Hospital Mortality and Readmission Rates for Medicare Patients Treated by Male vs Female Physicians."

143. Jena et al., "Sex Differences in Academic Rank in US Medical Schools in 2014."

144. Wells, "The Good and Bad Statistics on Women in Medicine"; Contorno, "Rand Paul Says More than Half of Students at Medical, Dental and Law Schools Are Females"; Wang, "For the First Time Ever, More Women than Men Are Going to Med School."

145. "Professionally Active Physicians by Gender."

146. Lindemann, "The Woman Question in Medicine," 42; Wang, "For the First Time Ever, More Women than Men Are Going to Med School"; "More Women Than Men Enrolled in U.S. Medical Schools in 2017"; Chandler, "Women Are Now a Majority of Entering Medical Students Nationwide."

147. Lindemann, "The Woman Question in Medicine," 42–43.

148. Poorman, "Why Does America Still Have so Few Female Doctors?"

149. Khullar, "Being a Doctor Is Hard. It's Harder for Women."

150. Jagsi et al., "Sexual Harassment and Discrimination Experiences of Academic Medical Faculty."

151. Adesoye et al., "Perceived Discrimination Experienced by Physician Mothers and Desired Workplace Changes"; Fernandez, "Physician Moms Are Often Subject to Workplace Discrimination."

152. Adesoye et al., "Perceived Discrimination Experienced by Physician Mothers and Desired Workplace Changes."

153. Guille et al., "Work-Family Conflict and the Sex Difference in Depression Among Training Physicians."

154. Sherwin, *No Longer Patient*, 232.

155. Sherwin, 235.

156. Sherwin, 139.

157. Shapiro and Bramer, "Gender Issues in Corporate Leadership."

158. II, "A Generation of Bad Blood."

159. "Tuskegee Study - Timeline."

160. Dula, "African American Suspicion of the Healthcare System Is Justified." Gamble, "Under the Shadow of Tuskegee." While this distrust existed before the Tuskegee Experiment, the experiments seem to have confirmed this distrust.

161. And, of course, the ethical safeguards put in place after Tuskegee were insufficient to prevent the medical experimentation on black and brown people without their consent, as a 1989 vaccination study on 900 black and Latino infants in the United States shows. Gamble, "Under the Shadow of Tuskegee," 1776.

162. Norman, *Ask Me About My Uterus*.

163. Oreskes and Conway, *Merchants of Doubt*, 136; Goertzel, "Conspiracy Theories in Science."

164. Pew Research Center, "What Americans Know and Don't Know about Science."

165. Hill, "Vaccination Coverage Among Children Aged 19–35 Months — United States, 2016."

166. Yang et al., "Sociodemographic Predictors of Vaccination Exemptions on the Basis of Personal Belief in California."

167. Navin, *Values and Vaccine Refusal*, 21.

168. Navin, 22.

169. Navin, "Competing Epistemic Spaces," 246–47.

170. Navin, 249–50.

171. Navin, *Values and Vaccine Refusal*, 22.

172. Navin, 23.

9

GRACE PERIOD

Solutions and Conclusions

Doctors routinely deny requests from patients to refill birth control prescriptions and instead use these requests as bargaining chips to elicit compliance with unnecessary and ultimately harmful cancer testing. I argued this behavior on the part of doctors is morally wrong. Using the case of doctors denying drugs as a wedge, we can break apart larger issues in the medical field, primarily sexism toward female patients. Audre Lorde argues that, "There is no such thing as a single-issue struggle because we do not lead single-issue lives."[1] What, then, ought to be done to solve the issues raised in the foregoing chapters? What solution can we provide to ensure the elimination of the practice? In this chapter, I catalog and discuss potential solutions and argue for a focus on medical sexism as an inextricable component of a sufficient response to doctor behavior.

ELIMINATING DOCTORS FROM THE EQUATION

More than half of American women use birth control for reasons besides contraception.[2] Like condoms, birth control can protect against pregnancy and even cancer. Unlike condoms, however, birth control can also treat health conditions beyond any prophylactic benefits it offers. Understanding what medical needs people have is central to choosing the right drug to treat it, and doctors can provide guidance. Furthermore, many of the conditions birth control treats, like endometriosis, are serious health issues that require medical oversight. For the two-thirds of women who use birth control to treat medical conditions, serious or not, the ability to visit a doctor is a necessity.

Hormonal birth control is a serious medication and carries health risks like blood clots and liver failure. Adrenal disease, acetaminophen use, and alcohol consumption can all pose added dangers from hormonal birth control use. Choosing which birth control method is best for a patient could often benefit from medical expertise in part because not all patients know either of the attendant risks or of related conditions that could impact their health while using birth control.

We require prescriptions for drugs when those medications can cause potential harm to the patient. Most hormonal birth control prescriptions can be used as emergency contraception if taken in higher doses. Unlike the insertion of a copper IUD, which changes the chemical makeup of the uterus making the environment inhospitable for sperm and preventing fertilization, higher doses of hormonal birth control can merely prevent ovulation. In addition, the recommended procedure when a patient misses a pill is to take two. So while overdose on hormonal birth control is uncommon and not likely to be serious, it can happen and can include symptoms like nausea and vomiting.[3]

Next, changes in health impact birth control choice. Breastfeeding not only requires different hormonal birth control pills without estrogen, but also the need to know that those pills are less effective. Similarly, antibiotics like rifampin might undermine the efficacy of birth control, meaning that interactions between medications might need oversight.[4] Even aging can impact the effectiveness and need for birth control over time, as can changes in weight. The medical knowledge required is detailed and complex. Some individuals may not have the relevant medical knowledge to navigate these variables.

Many reasons, then, suggest that doctors could be needed for the dispensing of birth control prescriptions, which underlines the status quo. However, the damage done to patients when doctors withhold birth control from them yields an obvious reply: eliminate the need for doctors, and no patient will be harmed by the attendant abuse of power.

States like California and Oregon are making changes that allow for pharmacists to prescribe birth control.[5] Patients would fill out a short survey and receive their prescriptions directly from their pharmacist. Doctors are overwhelmingly in favor of such advances.[6] Such policies are merely a stopgap measure until the Food and Drug Administration moves to make the drugs more widely available.[7] However, pharmacists tend not to have private offices, making conversations with patients difficult. Additionally, pharmacists may not have full knowledge of a patient's medical history. One could make the case that since birth control is very safe, a pharmacist actually is qualified to prescribe it. But if hormonal birth control really were safe enough for anyone to take, then we should not add in an extra hoop for patients to jump through like a discussion with a pharmacist, especially one that can violate a need for privacy.

Making birth control available over the counter (OTC), as it is in other countries, might address many of the problems listed in the first five chapters.[8] OTC birth control pills eliminate the intermediaries, making doctors unnecessary in patient access. Thus, this proposal addresses many of the problems I raise and circumvents doctor-instigated obstructionism. It is thus a viable option to address to some of the problems raised thus far. Other benefits could attend this policy: prices could go down, patients could gain privacy from their parents and partners, and people could access birth control without insurance.[9]

OTC birth control can do a lot of good.[10] It can give people immediate bodily autonomy and protect them from threats to their welfare. It can reduce the power the medical field holds over a significant proportion of patients. And, it can send a signal to doctors that far from doing their patients good by withholding birth control, their denials are serious threats to autonomy.

Although some medical reasons may justify requiring a prescription for birth control, many other unrelated OTC medications are themselves life threatening, and that fact does not prevent them from remaining widely available. For example, acetaminophen can be dangerous despite being available over the counter. It can cause serious liver damage, and much more readily than an overdose on birth control. In fact, many drugs available over the counter are much more dangerous than birth control when taken in large quantities, including vitamins and supplements, which can be lethal in an overdose.

Other OTC drugs also treat ongoing conditions, like drugs that treat acid reflux, allergies, and chronic pain. Just like the underlying conditions birth control treats, these conditions are subject to change over time, interact with other conditions and medications, and are sometimes serious and in need of management by a doctor. Thus, making birth control over the counter would not significantly differentiate it from other similar OTC drugs.

Around 102 countries offer birth control OTC, including China, India, and Mexico.[11] No significant negative health outcomes have occurred from these practices from a public health perspective. Women tend to do a good job of screening for potential health risks, choosing the same medication doctors recommend for them 90% of the time.[12] Birth control is so safe and effective that making it OTC does not raise serious medical concerns.

The proposal to make hormonal birth control OTC paradoxically does raise issues with access, however. Making birth control over the counter does not increase patient access if it would increase costs for patients and eliminate the Affordable Care Act's gains in covering preventative medicine at zero cost to consumers.[13] Hormonal birth control was developed more than 50 years ago, giving ample time to make it OTC. Making it OTC now, after the implementation of the ACA mandating that insurance companies offer it for free, could harm some patients to a significant degree. To people who paid $30–$60 a month for years or decades, and who have started receiving it without a copay relatively recently, changing the law now could reverse gains in accessibility.

Two potential compromises, then, could ensure that patients can use birth control without facing financial obstacles or losing access to doctors' expertise. First, birth control could be offered both OTC and with a doctor's prescription. Heartburn medication, prenatal vitamins, pain medication, and numerous other drugs occupy this dual status. If it remains a responsibility of doctors to discuss these issues with patients, and it remains a responsibility of insurance companies to cover this needed medical care, then making it OTC for those patients who either do not have health insurance or face obstacles from their doctors would be a net benefit. Second, modifying the Affordable Care Act to mandate health insurance companies cover hormonal birth control whether or not it is prescribed could circumvent this problem. Since hormonal birth control fulfills a serious medical need for a large proportion of the population, a new mandate to cover OTC birth control would ensure patients have access to affordable health care.

Of course, it turns out that when cost is not a factor and when offered true freedom of choice, women do not tend to choose the pill at the same rates. Two-thirds choose a much safer form of contraception which is 10 times more effective than pills: IUDs.[14] Women are obviously balancing a range of different considerations.

Nevertheless, one of these relevant solutions might do a good job in increasing access to birth control. Patients would not have to receive yearly Pap tests, unnecessary doctor's appointments, or painful and harmful screenings for unrelated diseases. However, the solution to remove doctors entirely from the process of using birth control has another problem: the practice is merely a symptom of an underlying disease in medicine of medical sexism. Eliminating the symptom without addressing its cause runs the risk of leaving patients open to other attacks on their autonomy and rights to refusal of care. These solutions to circumvent doctors or medical professionals generally let sexist attitudes continue unchecked.

If, as discussed above, sexism explains current practices, then removing physicians from the calculus helps patients without requiring doctors to change their problematic values and behaviors. In fact, doing so could be seen as a way of protecting sexist attitudes from receiving any opposition whatsoever. Any solution to the problem of birth control access that elides or even preserves sexism is going to circumvent some problems while leaving others intact. In such cases, patients may gain autonomy in one sphere—hormonal birth control—while continuing to lose ground in other spheres. Patients would continue to face discrimination and infantilization in birth and labor decisions as well as the other issues discussed in chapters 6, 7, and 8. Birthing centers, midwives, and doulas can help eliminate doctors from the sphere of birth and labor but do so without addressing the underlying reasons why patients seek them out. That means that while they are a significant component of addressing the choices of pregnant people, they cannot be the end of the story. Similarly, OTC birth control would fail to give patients comprehensive protections when they inevitably do enter the medical context.

Having unqualified or underqualified medical professionals prescribe medicine simply because the qualified parties do not, or having laypeople self-medicate, cannot entirely fix the problem. We can reduce the role of doctors' decisions in individuals' lives only so much. If doctors continue to treat female and female-associated patients differently, then finding alternatives to doctors in some instances without addressing the systemic problem is like cutting off one head of the Hydra only to have two more grow in its place.

OTC birth control, midwives and birthing centers, and Planned Parenthood facilities do demonstrable good in improving patient choice and self-determination and we should support them as such. Furthermore, anything that empowers women can itself be a tool to oppose sexism. But upholding these as solutions to the problems raised in this book ultimately misunderstands those problems. As effective as it may be in giving women control over their fertility, fertility is just one aspect of bodily autonomy. The answer to the problem of sexism in the medical field is not to circumvent the medical field but to confront the medical field, disrupt it, and ultimately change it. The first step toward doing that is to identify sexism where it exists. I have spent the last eight chapters arguing that some patients receive differential treatment and that the best explanation for this treatment is sexism. Acknowledging sexism and medical sexism where they exist is undoubtedly the first step toward eradication, because we cannot solve a problem whose existence we do not face. However, it is also not the end of the story.

RECKONING

When doctors engage in discriminatory practices that override the autonomy and consent of their patients, they are not just doing what I take to be immoral actions. They are also engaging in bad medicine and bad science. The unifying feature of most problematic practices discussed thus far is that these practices violate standards of care. Denying a patient birth control prescription refills in light of her Pap test status violates standards of care set by the profession. Planned C-sections without a demonstrated medical need violate standards of care. Routine episiotomies violate standards of care. Allowing a patient to die from sepsis as the result of a miscarriage violates standards of care.[15] In other words, when doctors deviate from the standards set by their profession, they act wrongly not just from the perspective of morality, but also from the perspective of medicine. When best practices in morality and medicine diverge, a significant tension must be reconciled through complex philosophical analyses.[16] However, when morality and medicine align, as they do in the cases I cover here, I am on stronger ground to advocate for change from a consensus standpoint. The practitioners, not the principles of medicine, are subject to criticism.

In many cases covered in this book, doctors violate medical recommendations for reasons that they probably would not endorse upon reflection and for reasons that are subject to human error and bias. But doctors may not realize that they are engaging in activity that they would not endorse upon reflection if they do not take time to reflect. So, the first step on the path toward a just medical field must be reflection.

Assuming that doctors have already recognized that they deviate from the standards of care and that they disproportionately treat female patients differently from male ones, doctors ought to think about why they give themselves permission to do this. Are they being less careful because they do not recognize a moral situation when they face one or do not recognize the principles of justice as applicable to the dispensing of medical care? Asking how to empower patients to achieve their health goals can help doctors in this respect. This attitude of empowering patients can also improve patient outcomes and reduce overtreatment, all the while allowing doctors to reckon with the systemic problems in their field. It can also help doctors avoid the difficult moral questions that can arise in a medical context without imposing their own worldview on the patient or making decisions for the patient that are not theirs to make. Even if doctors need to ask further questions about a patient's health goals, such as whether they are realistic, what kind of cost-benefit analysis is needed to attain them, or whether they should actually stand in the way of those goals (such as a psychiatrist acting as a mandatory reporter for a patient's expressed desire to commit violence), asking how to empower patients can be a good starting point.

For example, Susan Sherwin argues against the authoritarian model of medicine, in which the only expertise that is relevant for successful health care is the doctor's.[17] Experiential knowledge is essential, political and moral understanding is necessary, and physiological knowledge is significant, but not the only or even most central sets of knowledge.

Thus, Sherwin argues that patients also bring a level of expertise to the table. Once we acknowledge the expertise patients have in their own care, the authoritarian model that places doctors over patients is upended. It also prevents us from tolerating unequal distribution of positions within this hierarchy.[18] Sherwin argues that upending the hierarchy brings about a net benefit for health.[19]

It is tempting to explain the continuation of this practice and other problematic practices I have labeled sexist by reference to a good doctor vs. bad doctor dichotomy; only bad doctors and sexist ones engage in the practice, and they constitute merely a few bad apples. But labeling the doctors who engage in discriminatory practices as bad is not a helpful method of addressing the problem.

First, performing bad actions does not necessarily make someone a bad person, in part because we can distinguish between behavior and character.[20] Conflating the two does not help and can cause people to be defensive or shut down. Second, labeling some doctors as bad is reflective of a fixed mindset, when in fact a growth mindset might be more productive.[21] Third, demonizing those people who make mistakes can make it harder for us to recognize our shortcomings when we make those same mistakes, since noticing those mistakes in ourselves would therefore lead to the uncomfortable conclusion that we are morally bad and not merely flawed individuals seeking to improve. In fact, recognizing that wrongdoing can be normalized and banal can help counteract the idea that all violations of rights are necessarily violent and therefore help us identify more subtle forms of discrimination. Fourth, we can do wrong without wrong intentions, as evidenced by our roles in institutional injustice discussed in chapter 5. Fifth, the idea can lead to complacency by letting us wrongly assume that the next generation of doctors will not make the same mistakes, when in reality, much more comprehensive reflection and reform is required to eradicate wrongdoing.

A reckoning is required to improve the medical field and reduce injustice. This reckoning, however, must be done with the aim of improvement and not self-flagellation, defensiveness, or complacency. Education and continuing education would therefore be a crucial component of this avenue.[22]

ACCOUNTABILITY

A variety of consequences can be used to hold medical professionals accountable to ethical standards.[23] One avenue is a legal remedy. If the paternalistic and sexist behaviors discussed in this book run afoul of state medical malpractice laws, then lawsuits against doctors who engage in them are one way to ensure protection of patient rights. Some evidence suggests that medical malpractice law can improve health quality[24] and some does not.[25] However, this method is not necessarily likely to be successful. First, patients may be disinclined to sue their doctors. Second, doctors win most cases.[26] Third, malpractice cases in one state may not impact activities in another.

If the legal avenue of medical malpractice suits is not successful, another judicial avenue is to pursue constitutional rights.[27] I have argued that denials of birth control, abortion, and other patient needs can fall under the category of human rights violations. Of course, the fact that some actions are unconstitutional does not necessarily mean they will happen less, but underlining the gravity of the claim can make some progress toward protecting rights. Furthermore, the Supreme Court could potentially reverse some of these protections rather than enforce them.

Legislative remedies are another possibility to addressing these concerns, such as the Affordable Care Act enshrining the protection from gender discrimination in law.[28] Further efforts to protect patients from discriminatory behavior and outline specific violations could make a difference in patient lives. For example, California's health insurance marketplace set up under the Affordable Care Act has already established standards to revoke "in-network" status to hospitals that perform too many C-sections and violate standards of care in other ways.[29] This legislative remedy to hospitals engaging in activity likely to lead to poor health outcomes for patients is easily replicable elsewhere.

As helpful as legal remedies can be to achieve greater protections against discriminatory and paternalistic behavior, self-regulation within the medical field is another significant step toward justice for patients. The American Medical Association already sets codes of ethics that rule out many of the actions I argued against thus far. Taking a more active approach to disseminating information on policy, reducing noncompliant activities, and prioritizing women's health in public policy intervention can do more to ensure that patients receive the care that they need.

Furthermore, merely tracking and publishing these practices can have a significant impact on physician behavior.[30] For example, recording and publishing C-section rates by doctors itself can lower those rates with no further intervention required.[31] This sort of "name and shame,"[32] "social pressure," or, more positively, "normative influence" practice has found success in other areas, from energy use[33] to voting in elections.[34] Showing individuals the way their actions deviate from the norm can be an inexpensive and less litigious solution to a problem, so long as we successfully identify the targeted behavior as undesirable and are motivated to change it.

International institutions can also contribute to improving local decision-making. For example, the World Health Organization (WHO) has outlined best practices for labor and delivery, including increased emphasis on the rights of women.[35] By setting standards and engaging in advocacy, international organizations can influence local attitudes in positive ways.

A variety of judicial, legislative, training, and regulatory methods are possible for redress. Accountability may not combat sexist values and behaviors, but it can combat sexist outcomes. However, nothing short of ending sexism itself is called for in response to the issues outlined in this book. When doctors start to see themselves as part of a larger systematic framework that is capable of oppressing or lifting up individuals in the face of discriminatory attitudes, they can make greater progress to achieving their goals of improving human health.[36] Discriminatory practices do not arise in a vacuum; problematic medical practices are reflective of the values and perceptions of the world around us. Medicine cannot exist outside of social justice and social justice cannot exist outside of medicine.

These approaches are not mutually exclusive; they overlap and build on one another to provide greater protections for patients against discriminatory and paternalistic practices in the medical field. There is not one catch-all solution to eliminate the problem nor is there necessarily one best way to achieve that goal.

INTERSECTIONALITY

Drawing on the themes of intersectionality discussed in chapter 5 and throughout the book, we can use these discussions to help point toward a better goal. Patricia Hill Collins has argued that, "Rather than examining gender, race, class, and nation as distinctive social hierarchies, intersectionality examines how they mutually construct one another."[37] And, what makes discrimination based on sex and gender wrong is that it is discrimination, not that it is based on sex and gender. Eliminating all forms of injustice through liberation is central to achieving feminist aims.[38] According to Lindemann,

> What makes feminist bioethics feminist is its primary focus on gender. But because women come in various races, classes, degrees of poverty, degrees of disability, and degrees of queerness, we feminist bioethicists could address the woman question in medicine and bioethics considerably more fully if we joined forces with the colleagues who theorize those other imbalances of power. Everyone—doctors, other health care professionals, bioethicists, patients, and society as a whole—might benefit from the result.[39]

Furthermore, due to intersectional injustice, it is impossible to achieve feminist aims without also eliminating racism, ableism, and other forms of discrimination because, as discussed in earlier chapters, sexism interlocks with other forms of injustice.[40] In fact, any attempt to do so runs the risk of focusing on certain subsets of marginalized communities to the exclusion of others.[41] Martin Luther King, Jr.'s precept that "Injustice anywhere is a threat to justice everywhere" underscores this point.[42] Many of the injustices documented in this book have been injustices that occur in a medical setting, a medical setting which itself is indicative of a patient's time, wealth, resources, and privilege.[43] Ensuring greater access to medical care means both respecting the reproductive autonomy of those who receive medical care as well as expanding access.

CONCLUSION

Sexism explains systemic denials of birth control refills for patients when no medical evidence can justify the practice. Understanding this point and spreading its message can serve to protect patients. However, once we recognize that sexism is at stake in birth control access, we can bring that insight to a variety of different medical practices in which sex and gender can explain differential treatment at the hands of doctors. After that analysis, a variety of crucial issues in the medical field have a more accurate and comprehensive explanation. Drawing attention to problems in reproductive health and health more generally can make the medical field less sexist and a safer place for patients. When we uncover these underlying reasons for physician behavior, we are better suited to find efficient and successful solutions. Identifying discrimination, rejecting discrimination, and working toward ending discrimination in practice can not only improve health but also create a more just world. Advancing feminism requires applying principles from biomedical ethics and advancing biomedical ethics requires applying the principles of feminism. Reducing injustice improves health care, and improving health care reduces injustice.

NOTES

1. Audre Lorde, *Sister Outsider: Essays and Speeches*, Reprint edition (Berkeley, Calif: Crossing Press, 2007), 138.
2. "Many American Women Use Birth Control Pills for Noncontraceptive Reasons," Guttmacher Institute, November 15, 2011, https://www.guttmacher.org/news-release/2011/many-american-women-use-birth-control-pills-noncontraceptive-reasons.
3. "Birth Control Pill Overdose: MedlinePlus Medical Encyclopedia," https://medlineplus.gov/ency/article/002599.htm.
4. Elizabeth Enochs, "How To Keep Your Birth Control Effective," *Bustle*, February 3, 2016, https://www.bustle.com/articles/139434-11-ways-you-might-be-decreasing-the-effectiveness-of-your-birth-control; "Rifampin: MedlinePlus Drug Information," April 15, 2019, https://medlineplus.gov/druginfo/meds/a682403.html.
5. Pam Belluck, "Birth Control Without Seeing a Doctor: Oregon Now, More States Later," *The New York Times*, January 4, 2016, http://

www.nytimes.com/interactive/2016/01/04/health/birth-control-oregon-contraception.html.

6. Sally Rafie et al., "Provider Opinions Regarding Expanding Access to Hormonal Contraception in Pharmacies," *Women's Health Issues: Official Publication of the Jacobs Institute of Women's Health* 26, no. 2 (April 2016): 153–60, https://doi.org/10.1016/j.whi.2015.09.006.

7. Belluck, "Birth Control Without Seeing a Doctor."

8. Kate Grindlay, Bridgit Burns, and Daniel Grossman, "Prescription Requirements and Over-the-Counter Access to Oral Contraceptives: A Global Review," *Contraception* 88, no. 1 (July 1, 2013): 91–96, https://doi.org/10.1016/j.contraception.2012.11.021.

9. Currently, Planned Parenthood already fulfills these concerns: they subsidize birth control, do not require insurance, and give minors privacy from their parents. However, Planned Parenthood is itself under attack in our current political climate, and many patients no longer have easy access to Planned Parenthood itself.

10. The American College of Obstetricians and Gynecologists, "Committee Opinion, Number 544 Over-the-Counter Access to Oral Contraceptives," *Committee on Gynecologic Practice*, December 2012, https://www.acog.org/-/media/Committee-Opinions/Committee-on-Gynecologic-Practice/co544.pdf?dmc=1&ts=20150125T0334021611.

11. Anna Almendrala, "What You Need to Know about 'Over-the-Counter' Birth Control Pills," *Huffington Post*, January 6, 2016, http://www.huffingtonpost.com/entry/over-the-counter-birth-control_us_568c5fdae4b0a2b6fb6dc14a.

12. Solmaz Shotorbani et al., "Agreement between Women's and Providers' Assessment of Hormonal Contraceptive Risk Factors," *Contraception* 73, no. 5 (May 2006): 501–6, https://doi.org/10.1016/j.contraception.2005.12.001.

13. "Preventive Care Benefits," HealthCare.gov, accessed May 28, 2015, https://www.healthcare.gov/preventive-care-benefits/.

14. Gina M. Secura et al., "The Contraceptive CHOICE Project: Reducing Barriers to Long-Acting Reversible Contraception," *American Journal of Obstetrics and Gynecology* 203, no. 2 (August 2010): 115.e1-115.e7, https://doi.org/10.1016/j.ajog.2010.04.017. OB/GYNs impose added obstacles to women seeking IUDs, often refusing access to unmarried patients or patients who are not monogamous and patients who plan on having children in the future.

15. Kathryn Norlock, Miscarriage, Pregnancy Loss, and Death, interview by Matthews Beth, 3CR Community Radio, July 19, 2018, https://drive.google.com/file/d/1DM6mhrJS-LXJ3RCKGVdcVNKOG5okjHEV/view.

16. John Harris, "The Survival Lottery," *Philosophy* 50, no. 191 (January 1975): 81–87, https://doi.org/10.1017/S0031819100059118.

17. Susan Sherwin, *No Longer Patient: Feminist Ethics and Health Care* (Temple University Press, 1992).

18. Susan Sherwin, *No Longer Patient: Feminist Ethics and Health Care* (Temple University Press, 1992), 235.

19. Sherwin, 234.

20. For example, T. H. Irwin, "Theory and Common Sense in Greek Philosophy," in *How Should One Live?: Essays on the Virtues*, ed. Roger Crisp (Oxford University Press, USA, 1998), 46; Rosalind Hursthouse, *On Virtue Ethics* (Oxford University Press US, 1999), 17.

21. Carol S. Dweck, *Self-Theories: Their Role in Motivation, Personality, and Development*, Essays in Social Psychology (Philadelphia, PA: Psychology Press, 1999); Carol S .Dweck, *Self-Theories: Their Role in Motivation, Personality, and Development*, 1 edition (Philadelphia, PA: Psychology Press, 2000); Carol S. Dweck, "Messages That Motivate: How Praise Molds Students' Beliefs, Motivation, and Performance (in Surprising Ways)," *Improving Academic Achievement: Impact of Psychological Factors on Education*, 2002, 37–60; Carol S. Dweck, *Mindset: The New Psychology of Success*, Reprint edition (New York: Ballantine Books, 2007); A. Cimpian et al., "Subtle Linguistic Cues Affect Children's Motivation," *Psychological Science* 18, no. 4 (2007): 314.

22. Ranit Mishori, "Why Doctors Should Study Human Rights," *The Washington Post*, December 10, 2014. https://www.washingtonpost.com/posteverything/wp/2014/12/10/why-doctors-should-study-human-rights/?utm_term=.cad71603ff0b.

23. Amy Gutmann and Dennis Thompson, *Democracy and Disagreement* (Harvard University Press, 2009), 129.

24. Michael Frakes and Anupam B. Jena, "Does Medical Malpractice Law Improve Health Care Quality?," *Journal of Public Economics* 143 (November 2016): 142–58, https://doi.org/10.1016/j.jpubeco.2016.09.002.

25. Karl Y. Bilimoria et al., "Association Between State Medical Malpractice Environment and Surgical Quality and Cost in the United States," *Annals of Surgery* 263, no. 6 (June 2016): 1126, https://doi.org/10.1097/SLA.0000000000001538; Christina A. Minami et al., "Association Between State Medical Malpractice Environment and Postoperative Outcomes in the United States," *Journal of the American College of Surgeons* 224, no. 3 (March 1, 2017): 310-318.e2, https://doi.org/10.1016/j.jamcollsurg.2016.12.012.

26. Anupam B. Jena et al., "Malpractice Risk According to Physician Specialty," *New England Journal of Medicine* 365, no. 7 (August 18, 2011): 629–36, https://doi.org/10.1056/NEJMsa1012370.

27. B. Jessie Hill, "The Constitutional Right to Make Medical Treatment Decisions: A Tale of Two Doctrines," *Texas Law Review* 86 (December 2007): 70.

28. Elizabeth B. Deutsch, "Expanding Conscience, Shrinking Care: The Crisis in Access to Reproductive Care and the Affordable Care Act's Nondiscrimination Mandate" *Yale Law Journal*, 124, no. 7 (May 2015), https://www.yalelawjournal.org/note/reproductive-care-and-the-acas-nondiscrimination-mandate.

29. April Dembosky, "California's Message To Hospitals: Shape Up Or Lose 'In-Network' Status," NPR.org, May 23, 2018, https://www.npr.org/sections/health-shots/2018/05/23/611975420/californias-message-to-hospitals-shape-up-or-lose-in-network-status.

30. Jason N. Doctor et al., "Opioid Prescribing Decreases after Learning of a Patient's Fatal Overdose," *Science* 361, no. 6402 (August 10, 2018): 588–90, https://doi.org/10.1126/science.aat4595.

31. Kaiser Health News, "How One Hospital Brought Its C-Section Rate Down Fast," US News & World Report, May 9, 2015, https://health.usnews.com/health-news/hospital-of-tomorrow/articles/2015/05/09/how-one-hospital-brought-its-c-section-rate-down-fast.

32. J. B. Delston, "The Criminalization of Money Laundering and Terrorism in Global Contexts: A Hybrid Solution," *Journal of Global Ethics* 10, no. 3 (September 2, 2014): 327, https://doi.org/10.1080/17449626.2014.971854.

33. Amy J. C. Cuddy, Kyle T. Doherty, and Maarten W. Bos, "OPOWER: Increasing Energy Efficiency through Normative Influence (A)," September 14, 2010, https://hbr.org/product/OPOWER--Increasing-Energy/an/911016-PDF-ENG.

34. Donald P. Green and Alan S. Gerber, *Get Out the Vote: How to Increase Voter Turnout* (Brookings Institution Press, 2015), 147.

35. World Health Organization, "WHO Recommendations: Intrapartum Care for a Positive Childbirth Experience" (Geneva, 2018), http://apps.who.int/iris/bitstream/handle/10665/260178/9789241550215-eng.pdf;jsessionid=BE701325C5A41B3C92634F86E2E2BD46?sequence=1.

36. Dorothy Roberts writes that, "True reproductive freedom requires a living wage, universal health care, and the abolition of prisons." Dorothy Roberts, *Killing the Black Body: Race, Reproduction, and the Meaning of Liberty* (Vintage, 2014), xxi.

37. Patricia Hill Collins, "It's All In the Family: Intersections of Gender, Race, and Nation," *Hypatia* 13, no. 3 (August 1, 1998): 62, https://doi.org/10.1111/j.1527-2001.1998.tb01370.x.

38. Ann E. Cudd, "The Paradox of Liberal Feminism: Preference, Rationality, and Oppression," in *Varieties of Feminist Liberalism*, ed. Amy R. Baehr (Lanham, MD: Rowman & Littlefield Publishers, 2004), 57; Samantha Brennan, "Feminist Ethics and Everyday Inequalities," *Hypatia* 24, no. 1 (February 1, 2009): 141–59, https://doi.org/10.1111/j.1527-2001.2009.00011.x.

39. Hilde Lindemann, "The Woman Question in Medicine: An Update," *Hastings Center Report* 42, no. 3 (2012): 44, https://doi.org/10.1002/hast.34.

40. Kimberlé Williams Crenshaw, "Demarginalizing the Intersection of Race and Sex: A Black Feminist Critique of Antidiscrimination Doctrine, Feminist Theory and Antiracist Politics," *University of Chicago Legal Forum*, no. 1 (1989): 140; Kimberlé Williams Crenshaw, "Mapping the Margins: Intersectionality, Identity Politics, and Violence against Women of Color," *Stanford Law Review* 43, no. 6 (1991): 1244, https://doi.org/10.2307/1229039; Shay Welch, *Existential Eroticism: A Feminist Approach to Understanding Women's Oppression-Perpetuating Choices* (Lexington Books, 2017), 4; Collins, "It's All In the Family," 78; Connie S. Chan, "Reproductive Issues Are Essential Survival Issues for the Asian-American Communities," in *From Abortion to Reproductive Freedom: Transforming a Movement*, ed. Marlene Gerber Fried (Boston, MA: South End Press, 1999), 178.

41. Crenshaw states, "Despite the narrow scope of this dominant conception of discrimination and its tendency to marginalize those whose experiences cannot be described within its tightly-drawn parameters, this approach has been regarded as the appropriate framework for addressing a range of problems. In much of feminist theory and, to some extent, in antiracist politics, this framework is reflected in the belief that sexism or racism can be meaningfully discussed without paying attention to the lives of those other than the race-, gender- or class-privileged. As a result, both feminist theory and antiracist politics have been organized, in part, around the equation of racism with what happens to the Black middle-class or to Black men, and the equation of sexism with what happens to white women." Crenshaw, "Demarginalizing the Intersection of Race and Sex: A Black Feminist Critique of Antidiscrimination Doctrine, Feminist Theory and Antiracist Politics," 152.

42. Dr. Martin Luther King, Jr., "Letter from the Birmingham Jail," April 16, 1963; Meena Krishnamurthy, "Featured Philosopher: Meena Krishnamurthy," *Philosopher* (blog), June 3, 2016, https://politicalphilosopher.net/2016/06/03/meenakrishnamurthy/.

43. Loretta Ross and Rickie Solinger, *Reproductive Justice: An Introduction*, First edition (Oakland, California: University of California Press, 2017), 121.

BIBLIOGRAPHY

215 ILCS 134/ Managed Care Reform and Patient Rights Act. (2000). http://www.ilga.gov/legislation/ilcs/ilcs3.asp?ActID=1265&ChapterID=22.

Aasheim, V., A. Nilsen, L. Reinar, and M. Lukasse. "Perineal Techniques during the Second Stage of Labour for Reducing Perineal Trauma." Cochrane, June 13, 2017. https://doi.org/10.1002/14651858.CD006672.pub3.

Abadir, Anna Maria, Ariella Lang, Talia Klein, and Haim Arie Abenhaim. "Influence of Qualitative Research on Women's Health Screening Guidelines." *American Journal of Obstetrics and Gynecology* 210, no. 1 (January 1, 2014): 44.e1-44.e6. https://doi.org/10.1016/j.ajog.2013.09.021.

"About The TransAdvocate." *The TransAdvocate* (blog), November 16, 2006. http://transadvocate.com/about-2.

Ackerman, T. F. "Why Doctors Should Intervene." *The Hastings Center Report* 12, no. 4 (August 1982): 14–17.

"ACOG Committee Opinion. Recommendations on Frequency of Pap Test Screening. Number 152—March 1995. Committee on Gynecologic Practice. American College of Obstetricians and Gynecologists." *International Journal of Gynaecology and Obstetrics: The Official Organ of the International Federation of Gynaecology and Obstetrics* 49, no. 2 (May 1995): 210–11.

"ACOG Practice Bulletin No. 71: Episiotomy." *Obstetrics & Gynecology* 107, no. 4 (April 2006): 956.

Adams, Ann, Christopher D. Buckingham, Antje Lindenmeyer, John B. McKinlay, Carol Link, Lisa Marceau, and Sara Arber. "The Influence of Patient and Doctor Gender on Diagnosing Coronary Heart Disease." *Sociology of Health & Illness* 30, no. 1 (August 2007): 1–18. https://doi.org/10.1111/j.1467-9566.2007.01025.x.

Adesoye, Taiwo, Christina Mangurian, Esther K. Choo, Christina Girgis, Hala Sabry-Elnaggar, and Eleni Linos. "Perceived Discrimination Experienced by Physician Mothers and Desired Workplace Changes: A Cross-Sectional Survey." *JAMA Internal Medicine* 177, no. 7 (July 1, 2017): 1033–36. https://doi.org/10.1001/jamainternmed.2017.1394.

"Adoptions in America Are Declining." *The Economist*, June 24, 2017. https://www.economist.com/united-states/2017/06/24/adoptions-in-america-are-declining.

Ahangari, Norman Garrick, Carol Atkinson-Palombo, and Hamed. "Why America's Roads Are so Much More Dangerous than Europe's." *Vox*, November 30, 2016. https://www.vox.com/the-big-idea/2016/11/30/13784520/roads-deaths-increase-safety-traffic-us.

Alexander, James M., Kenneth J. Leveno, John Hauth, Mark B. Landon, Elizabeth Thom, Catherine Y. Spong, Michael W. Varner, et al. "Fetal Injury Associated with Cesarean

Delivery." *Obstetrics & Gynecology* 108, no. 4 (October 2006): 885–90. https://doi.org/10.1097/01.AOG.0000237116.72011.f3.
Alexander, Larry. "The Ontology of Consent." *Analytic Philosophy* 55, no. 1 (2014): 102–13. https://doi.org/10.1111/phib.12035.
Alfirevic, Z., D. Devane, G. M. L. Gyte, and A. Cuthbert. "Continuous Cardiotocography (CTG) as a Form of Electronic Fetal Monitoring (EFM) for Fetal Assessment during Labour." *Cochrane Library*, February 3, 2017. https://doi.org/10.1002/14651858.CD006066.pub3.
Allen, Chris, Paul Glasziou, and Chris Del Mar. "Bed Rest: A Potentially Harmful Treatment Needing More Careful Evaluation." *The Lancet* 354, no. 9186 (October 9, 1999): 1229–33. https://doi.org/10.1016/S0140-6736(98)10063-6.
Almendrala, Anna. "What You Need to Know about 'Over-the-Counter' Birth Control Pills." *Huffington Post*, January 6, 2016. http://www.huffingtonpost.com/entry/over-the-counter-birth-control_us_568c5fdae4b0a2b6fb6dc14a.
Al-Shehri, Saad S., Christine L. Knox, Helen G. Liley, David M. Cowley, John R. Wright, Michael G. Henman, Amitha K. Hewavitharana, et al. "Breastmilk-Saliva Interactions Boost Innate Immunity by Regulating the Oral Microbiome in Early Infancy." *PLOS ONE* 10, no. 9 (September 1, 2015): e0135047. https://doi.org/10.1371/journal.pone.0135047.
American Academy of Pediatrics. "Infant Feeding in Disasters and Emergencies." 2015. https://www.aap.org/en-us/advocacy-and-policy/aap-health-initiatives/Breastfeeding/Documents/InfantNutritionDisaster.pdf.
———. "Researchers Question Pulling Plug on Pacifiers." April 30, 2012. https://www.aap.org/en-us/about-the-aap/aap-press-room/Pages/Researchers-Question-Pulling-Plug-on-Pacifiers.aspx.
American Cancer Society. "Can Cervical Cancer Be Prevented?," January 23, 2019. http://www.cancer.org/cancer/cervicalcancer/detailedguide/cervical-cancer-prevention.
———. "Key Statistics for Breast Cancer in Men." April 27, 2018. https://www.cancer.org/cancer/breast-cancer-in-men/about/key-statistics.html.
American Civil Liberties Union. "ACLU Responds to Proposed Changes to Health Care Rights Law," May 24, 2019, https://www.aclu.org/press-releases/aclu-responds-proposed-changes-health-care-rights-law.
———. "Coercive and Punitive Governmental Responses to Women's Conduct During Pregnancy." Accessed November 2, 2016. https://www.aclu.org/other/coercive-and-punitive-governmental-responses-womens-conduct-during-pregnancy.
American Civil Liberties Union. "Tamesha Means v. United States Conference of Catholic Bishops." June 30, 2015. https://www.aclu.org/cases/tamesha-means-v-united-states-conference-catholic-bishops.
The American College of Obstetricians and Gynecologists. "Abnormal Cervical Cancer Screening Test Results: FAQ187," January 2016. http://www.acog.org/Patients/FAQs/Abnormal-Cervical-Cancer-Screening-Test-Results#difference.
American College of Obstetricians and Gynecologists, "ACOG Releases New Guidance Aimed at Making VBAC Available to More Women," October 24, 2017. https://www.acog.org/About-ACOG/News-Room/News-Releases/2017/ACOG-Releases-New-Guidance-Aimed-at-Making-VBAC-Available-to-More-Women.
American College of Obstetricians and Gynecologists, and Committee on Practice Bulletins—Obstetrics. "ACOG Practice Bulletin No. 127: Management of Preterm Labor." *Obstetrics & Gynecology* 119, no. 6 (June 2012): 1308–17. https://doi.org/10.1097/AOG.0b013e31825af2f0.
American College of Obstetricians and Gynecologists Committee on Ethics. "ACOG Committee Opinion #321: Maternal Decision Making, Ethics, and the Law." *Obstetrics & Gynecology* 106, no. 5 Pt 1 (November 2005): 1127–37.
American College of Obstetricians and Gynecologists Committee Opinion. "Optimizing Support for Breastfeeding as Part of Obstetric Practice," February 2016. https://www.acog.org/-/media/Committee-Opinions/Committee-on-Obstetric-Practice/co658.pdf?dmc=1&ts=20180125T1846099708.

American College of Physicians. "American College of Physicians Recommends against Screening Pelvic Examination in Adult, Asymptomatic, Average Risk, Non-Pregnant Women." acponline.org, July 1, 2014. https://www.acponline.org/acp-newsroom/american-college-of-physicians-recommends-against-screening-pelvic-examination-in-adult-asymptomatic.

American Heart Association News Archive. "First Set of Recommendations in a Decade Advocate Gender-Specific Approach for Women." June 16, 2014. https://news.heart.org/first-set-of-recommendations-in-a-decade-advocate-gender-specific-approach-for-women/.

American Medical Association. "AMA Advocacy Overview: Protecting Physician Practices." www.ama-assn.org, 2017. https://www.ama-assn.org/sites/default/files/media-browser/specialty%20group/arc/protecting-physician-practices.pdf.

———. "Code of Medical Ethics: Genetics & Reproductive Medicine." Accessed June 12, 2018. https://www.ama-assn.org/delivering-care/code-medical-ethics-genetics-reproductive-medicine.

———. "AMA Code of Medical Ethics," 2016. https://www.ama-assn.org/delivering-care/ama-code-medical-ethics.

———. "What's Happening in 2018?: Top AMA Advocacy Issues." www.ama-assn.org, 2018. https://www.ama-assn.org/sites/default/files/media-browser/public/arc-public/advocacy-dashboard.pdf.

American Pregnancy Association. "Bed Rest," April 26, 2012. http://americanpregnancy.org/pregnancy-complications/bed-rest/.

"An Overview of Abortion Laws." Guttmacher Institute, August 1, 2019. https://www.guttmacher.org/state-policy/explore/overview-abortion-laws.

Andersen, Kip, and Keegan Kuhn. *What the Health*. Documentary. A.U.M. Films & Media, 2017. www.whatthehealthfilm.com.

Andrews, Michelle. "Health Insurance Prices For Women Set To Drop." NPR.org, July 17, 2012. https://www.npr.org/sections/health-shots/2012/07/17/156895577/leveling-the-playing-field-for-women-s-premiums.

Anson, Pat. "Women in Pain Report Significant Gender Bias." National Pain Report (blog), September 12, 2014. http://nationalpainreport.com/women-in-pain-report-significant-gender-bias-8824696.html.

Anstey, Erica H., Meredith L. Shoemaker, Chloe M. Barrera, Mary Elizabeth O'Neil, Ashley B. Verma, and Dawn M. Holman. "Breastfeeding and Breast Cancer Risk Reduction: Implications for Black Mothers." *American Journal of Preventive Medicine* 53, no. 3 (September 1, 2017): S40–46. https://doi.org/10.1016/j.amepre.2017.04.024.

Aristotle. *Nicomachean Ethics*. Translated by Terence Irwin. 2nd ed. Hackett Publishing Company, Inc., 1999.

Armstrong, Carrie. "Practice Guidelines." *American Family Physician* 74, no. 11 (December 1, 2006): 1970.

Arora, Vineet M. "It Is Time for Equal Pay for Equal Work for Physicians—Paging Dr Ledbetter." *JAMA Internal Medicine* 176, no. 9 (September 1, 2016): 1305–6. https://doi.org/10.1001/jamainternmed.2016.3289.

Arrieta, Alejandro, and Ariadna García Prado. "Non-Elective C-Sections in Public Hospitals: Capacity Constraints and Doctor Incentives." *Applied Economics* 48, no. 49 (October 19, 2016): 4719–31. https://doi.org/10.1080/00036846.2016.1164820.

Arvizo, Cynthia, and Haider Mahdi. "Disparities in Cervical Cancer in African American Women: What Primary Care Physicians Can Do." *Cleveland Clinica Journal of Medicine* 84, no. 10 (October 2017): 788–94.

Aschwanden, Christie. "What If Everything Your Doctors Told You About Breast Cancer Was Wrong?" *Mother Jones*, October 6, 2015. https://www.motherjones.com/politics/2015/10/faulty-research-behind-mammograms-breast-cancer/.

Autier, Philippe, Mathieu Boniol, Anna Gavin, and Lars J. Vatten. "Breast Cancer Mortality in Neighbouring European Countries with Different Levels of Screening but Similar Access to Treatment: Trend Analysis of WHO Mortality Database." *BMJ* 343 (July 28, 2011): d4411. https://doi.org/10.1136/bmj.d4411.

Ayala, Saray, and Lauren Freeman. “The Placental Microbiome: A New Site for Policing Women’s Bodies.” *IJFAB: International Journal of Feminist Approaches to Bioethics*, March 3, 2016. https://doi.org/10.3138/ijfab.9.1.121.

Azidah, A. K., N. H. Nik Hazlina, and M. N. Aishah. “Swyer Syndrome in a Woman with Pure 46, XY Gonadal Dysgenesis and a Hypoplastic Uterus.” *Malaysian Family Physician : The Official Journal of the Academy of Family Physicians of Malaysia* 8, no. 2 (August 31, 2013): 58–61.

“Baby-Friendly USA.” Accessed July 16, 2018. https://www.babyfriendlyusa.org/get-started/the-guidelines-evaluation-criteria.

Bacarisse, Bonnie. “The Republican Lawmaker Who Secretly Created Reddit’s Women-Hating ‘Red Pill.’” *The Daily Beast*, April 25, 2017, sec. politics. https://www.thedailybeast.com/articles/2017/04/25/the-republican-lawmaker-who-secretly-created-reddit-s-women-hating-red-pill.

Bal, B. Sonny. “An Introduction to Medical Malpractice in the United States.” *Clinical Orthopaedics and Related Research* 467, no. 2 (February 2009): 339–47. https://doi.org/10.1007/s11999-008-0636-2.

Balmer, Dorene F., David A. Hirsh, Daphne Monie, Henry Weil, and Boyd F. Richards. “Caring to Care: Applying Noddings’ Philosophy to Medical Education.” *Academic Medicine* 91, no. 12 (December 2016): 1618–21. https://doi.org/10.1097/ACM.0000000000001207.

Bapat, Sheila. “How Can a ‘Pro-Life’ Legislator Fight to Gut SNAP?” *Rewire*. July 8, 2013. https://rewire.news/article/2013/07/08/how-can-a-pro-life-legislator-fight-to-gut-snap/.

Barber, Emma L., Lisbet Lundsberg, Kathleen Belanger, Christian M. Pettker, Edmund F. Funai, and Jessica L. Illuzzi. “Contributing Indications to the Rising Cesarean Delivery Rate.” *Obstetrics & Gynecology* 118, no. 1 (July 2011): 29–38. https://doi.org/10.1097/AOG.0b013e31821e5f65.

Bass, Joel L., Tina Gartley, and Ronald Kleinman. “Unintended Consequences of Current Breastfeeding Initiatives.” *JAMA Pediatrics* 170, no. 10 (October 1, 2016): 923–24. https://doi.org/10.1001/jamapediatrics.2016.1529.

Battersby, Christine. *The Phenomenal Woman: Feminist Metaphysics and the Patterns of Identity*. John Wiley & Sons, 2016.

Battin, Margaret P. Sex & Consequences: World Population Growth vs. Reproductive Rights. 54th Annual Frederick William Reynolds Lecture. Salt Lake City, Utah: Frederick William Reynolds Association, 1994. http://catalog.hathitrust.org/Record/002958488.

Bauer, Greta R., Rebecca Hammond, Robb Travers, Matthias Kaay, Karin M. Hohenadel, and Michelle Boyce. “‘I Don’t Think This Is Theoretical; This Is Our Lives’: How Erasure Impacts Health Care for Transgender People.” *The Journal of the Association of Nurses in AIDS Care: JANAC* 20, no. 5 (October 2009): 348–61. https://doi.org/10.1016/j.jana.2009.07.004.

Baum, Michael. “Breast Screening Should Be Scrapped.” *The Guardian*, August 2, 2011, sec. Opinion. http://www.theguardian.com/commentisfree/2011/aug/02/breast-cancer-screening.

———. “Harms from Breast Cancer Screening Outweigh Benefits If Death Caused by Treatment Is Included.” *BMJ* 346 (January 23, 2013): f385. https://doi.org/10.1136/bmj.f385.

Bearak, Jonathan M., Kristen Lagasse Burke, and Rachel K. Jones. “Disparities and Change over Time in Distance Women Would Need to Travel to Have an Abortion in the USA: A Spatial Analysis.” *The Lancet Public Health* 2, no. 11 (November 1, 2017): e493–500. https://doi.org/10.1016/S2468-2667(17)30158-5.

Beauchamp, Tom L., and James F. Childress. *Principles of Biomedical Ethics*. Oxford University Press, 2001.

Belkin, Lisa. “Is Refusing Bed Rest a Crime?” *Motherlode* (blog), January 12, 2010. https://parenting.blogs.nytimes.com/2010/01/12/is-refusing-bed-rest-a-crime/.

Belluck, Pam. “Birth Control Without Seeing a Doctor: Oregon Now, More States Later.” *The New York Times*, January 4, 2016. http://www.nytimes.com/interactive/2016/01/04/health/birth-control-oregon-contraception.html.

Belluz, Julia. "Why Doctors Overprescribe Antibiotics — Even in Cases Where They're Useless." *Vox*, November 27, 2015. https://www.vox.com/2015/11/27/9802108/doctors-abuse-overprescribe-antibiotics.

Benen, Steve. "Senate Republicans Return to Controversial Contraception Posture." MSNBC, May 26, 2015. http://www.msnbc.com/rachel-maddow-show/senate-republicans-return-controversial-contraception-posture.

Bentham, Jeremy. *The Collected Works of Jeremy Bentham: An Introduction to the Principles of Morals and Legislation*. Clarendon Press, 1996.

Berlatsky, Noah. "The Most Common Childbirth Practice in America Is Unnecessary and Dangerous." *The New Republic*, August 13, 2015. https://newrepublic.com/article/122532/most-common-childbirth-practice-us-unnecessary-dangerous.

Bertakis, K. D., R. Azari, L. J. Helms, E. J. Callahan, and J. A. Robbins. "Gender Differences in the Utilization of Health Care Services." *The Journal of Family Practice* 49, no. 2 (February 2000): 147–52.

Bilimoria, Karl Y., Min-Woong Sohn, Jeanette W. Chung, Christina A. Minami, Elissa H. Oh, Emily S. Pavey, Jane L. Holl, Bernard S. Black, Michelle M. Mello, and David J. Bentrem. "Association Between State Medical Malpractice Environment and Surgical Quality and Cost in the United States." *Annals of Surgery* 263, no. 6 (June 2016): 1126. https://doi.org/10.1097/SLA.0000000000001538.

Bill Of Rights. Vol. 9501. https://www.law.cornell.edu/uscode/text/42/9501: Legal Information Institute.

Billi, Allison C., Mehrnaz Gharaee-Kermani, Joseph Fullmer, Lam C. Tsoi, Brett D. Hill, Dennis Gruszka, Jessica Ludwig, et al. "The Female-Biased Factor VGLL3 Drives Cutaneous and Systemic Autoimmunity." *JCI Insight* 4, no. 8 (April 18, 2019). https://doi.org/10.1172/jci.insight.127291.

"Birth Control Pill Overdose: MedlinePlus Medical Encyclopedia." Accessed July 3, 2018. https://medlineplus.gov/ency/article/002599.htm.

Bitler, Marianne, and Madeline Zavodny. "Did Abortion Legalization Reduce the Number of Unwanted Children? Evidence from Adoptions." *Perspectives on Sexual and Reproductive Health* 34, no. 1 (2002): 25–33. https://doi.org/10.2307/3030229.

Bleyer, Archie, and H. Gilbert Welch. "Effect of Three Decades of Screening Mammography on Breast-Cancer Incidence." *New England Journal of Medicine* 367, no. 21 (November 22, 2012): 1998–2005. https://doi.org/10.1056/NEJMoa1206809.

Bliss, Robin L., Jeffrey N. Katz, Elizabeth A. Wright, and Elena Losina. "Estimating Proximity to Care: Are Straight Line and Zipcode Centroid Distances Acceptable Proxy Measures?" *Medical Care* 50, no. 1 (January 2012): 99–106. https://doi.org/10.1097/MLR.0b013e31822944d1.

Blustein, Jan, and Jianmeng Liu. "Time to Consider the Risks of Caesarean Delivery for Long Term Child Health." *BMJ* 350 (June 10, 2015): h2410. https://doi.org/10.1136/bmj.h2410.

Bockting, W., B. Robinson, A. Benner, and K. Scheltema. "Patient Satisfaction with Transgender Health Services." *Journal of Sex & Marital Therapy* 30, no. 4 (September 2004): 277–94. https://doi.org/10.1080/00926230490422467.

Bolam v. Friern Hospital Management Committee, No. 1 *WLR* 582 (1957).

Bonevski, B., R. Sanson-Fisher, A. Girgis, and J. Perkins. "Women's Experiences of Having a Colposcopic Examination: Self-Reported Satisfaction with Care, Perceived Needs and Consequences." *Journal of Obstetrics and Gynaecology: The Journal of the Institute of Obstetrics and Gynaecology* 18, no. 5 (September 1998): 462–70. https://doi.org/10.1080/01443619866804.

Boonin, David. *Beyond Roe: Why Abortion Should Be Legal—Even If the Fetus Is a Person*. Oxford University Press, 2019.

Borges, Maria T. R. "A Violent Birth: Reframing Coerced Procedures During Childbirth as Obstetric Violence." *Duke Law Journal* 67, no. 4 (January 2018): 827–62.

Bradford, Judith, Sari L. Reisner, Julie A. Honnold, and Jessica Xavier. "Experiences of Transgender-Related Discrimination and Implications for Health: Results from the Virginia Transgender Health Initiative Study." *American Journal of Public Health* 103, no. 10 (October 2013): 1820–29. https://doi.org/10.2105/AJPH.2012.300796.

Brady, James B. "Recklessness, Negligence, Indifference, and Awareness." *The Modern Law Review* 43, no. 4 (July 1, 1980): 381–99. https://doi.org/10.1111/j.1468-2230.1980.tb01599.x.

Brait, Ellen. "Infant Death Rate in US Drops to Historic Low, CDC Reports." *The Guardian*, December 9, 2015, sec. US news. http://www.theguardian.com/us-news/2015/dec/09/us-infant-death-rate-drops-historic-low-cdc-reports.

Brake, Elizabeth. *The Marriage Promise: Is Divorce Promise-Breaking?* Oxford University Press, 2012.

Braveman, Paula A., Catherine Cubbin, Susan Egerter, David R. Williams, and Elsie Pamuk. "Socioeconomic Disparities in Health in the United States: What the Patterns Tell Us." *American Journal of Public Health* 100, no. Suppl 1 (April 2010): S186–96. https://doi.org/10.2105/AJPH.2009.166082.

Brawley, Otis. "No More Annual Pap Smear: New Cervical Cancer Screening Guidelines." CNN, March 15, 2012. http://www.cnn.com/2012/03/14/health/brawley-cervical-cancer-screenings/index.html.

"Breast Cancer and Breastfeeding: Collaborative Reanalysis of Individual Data from 47 Epidemiological Studies in 30 Countries, Including 50 302 Women with Breast Cancer and 96 973 Women without the Disease." *The Lancet* 360, no. 9328 (July 20, 2002): 187–95. https://doi.org/10.1016/S0140-6736(02)09454-0.

"Breastfeeding and the Use of Human Milk." *Pediatrics* 129, no. 3 (March 1, 2012): e827–41. https://doi.org/10.1542/peds.2011-3552.

Breiding, Matthew J., Sharon G. Smith, Kathleen C. Basile, Mikel L. Walters, Jieru Chen, and Melissa T. Merrick. "Prevalence and Characteristics of Sexual Violence, Stalking, and Intimate Partner Violence Victimization—National Intimate Partner and Sexual Violence Survey, United States, 2011." CDC, September 2014. https://www.cdc.gov/mmwr/preview/mmwrhtml/ss6308a1.htm?s_cid=ss6308a1_e.

Brennan, Samantha. "Feminist Ethics." In *The Routledge Companion to Ethics*, 514–24, 2010. https://doi.org/10.4324/9780203850701-53.

———. "Feminist Ethics and Everyday Inequalities." *Hypatia* 24, no. 1 (February 1, 2009): 141–59. https://doi.org/10.1111/j.1527-2001.2009.00011.x.

———. "Recent Work in Feminist Ethics." *Ethics* 109, no. 4 (1999): 858–93. https://doi.org/10.1086/233951.

Brennan, Samantha, and Tracy Isaacs. "Feminist Fitness Is for Everyone." In *Fit at Mid-Life: A Feminist Fitness Journey*. Greystone Books Ltd, 2018.

Brogaard, Berit. "12 Ways to Spot a Misogynist." *Psychology Today*. Accessed July 19, 2018. https://www.psychologytoday.com/blog/the-mysteries-love/201502/12-ways-spot-misogynist.

———. "Bias-Driven Attention, Cognitive Penetration and Epistemic Downgrade." In *Philosophy of Perception*, edited by Christoph Limbeck and Friedrich Stadler. Publications of the Austrian Ludwig Wittgenstein Society. De Gruyter, 2018.

———. "Sex By Deception." In *Oxford Handbook of Moral Psychology*, edited by John Doris and Manuel Vargas. Oxford University Press, Forthcoming.

Brown, Jennifer. "Women Pay up to 50% More for Health Insurance Premiums." *The Denver Post* (blog), October 24, 2009. http://www.denverpost.com/2009/10/24/women-pay-up-to-50-more-for-health-insurance-premiums/.

Brown, Sara S., and Dana Hughes. *The Medical Malpractice Crisis and Poor Women*. Edited by Institute of Medicine (US) Committee to Study Outreach for Prenatal Care. National Academies Press (US), 1988. https://www.ncbi.nlm.nih.gov/books/NBK217698/.

Brownlee, Shannon. *Overtreated: Why Too Much Medicine Is Making Us Sicker and Poorer*. 1 edition. Bloomsbury USA, 2008.

Buchanan, Alec. "Mental Capacity, Legal Competence and Consent to Treatment." *Journal of the Royal Society of Medicine* 97, no. 9 (September 2004): 415–20.

Buchanan, Allen, Dan W. Brock, Norman Daniels, and Daniel Wikler. From *Chance to Choice: Genetics and Justice*. Cambridge: Cambridge University Press, 2001.

Bucklin, Brenda A., David R. Gambling, and David Wlody. *A Practical Approach to Obstetric Anesthesia*. Lippincott Williams & Wilkins, 2008.

Budge, Stephanie L. "Psychotherapists as Gatekeepers: An Evidence-Based Case Study Highlighting the Role and Process of Letter Writing for Transgender Clients." *Psychotherapy* 52, no. 3 (2015): 287–97. https://doi.org/10.1037/pst0000034.

Bunch, Charlotte. "Women's Rights as Human Rights: Toward a Re-Vision of Human Rights." *Human Rights Quarterly* 12, no. 4 (November 1, 1990): 486–98. https://doi.org/10.2307/762496.

Bunim, Juliana. "Early Formula Use Helps Some Mothers Breastfeed Longer." *UC San Francisco*, May 13, 2013. https://www.ucsf.edu/news/2013/05/105831/early-formula-use-helps-some-mothers-breastfeed-longer.

Bureau of Labor Statistics. "Obstetricians and Gynecologists." May 2018. http://www.bls.gov/oes/current/oes291064.htm.

Burlingame, Janet, Chieko Kimata, Kelly Yamasato, Bruce Huegel, Marsha Durbin, and Melinda Ashton. "166: Episiotomies: Who Does Them and Do They Help?" *American Journal of Obstetrics and Gynecology* 212, no. 1 (January 1, 2015): S98. https://doi.org/10.1016/j.ajog.2014.10.212.

Burt, Robert A., and Dax Cowart. "Confronting Death: Who Chooses? Who Controls? A Dialogue between Dax Cowart and Robert Burt." Yale Law School Faculty Scholarship Series 706 (January 1, 1998). https://pdfs.semanticscholar.org/d478/88dce40390296abca7c13d6f9e0aec304264.pdf.

Burwell, Secretary of Health and Human Services, Et Al. v. Hobby Lobby Stores, Inc., Et Al., No. 13–354 (Supreme Court of the United States October 2013).

Calhoun, Cheshire. *Feminism, the Family, and the Politics of the Closet: Lesbian and Gay Displacement*. Oxford: Oxford University Press, 2002.

California Health and Safety Code - HSC, 1262.6(a)(3) § (2001). https://leginfo.legislature.ca.gov/faces/codes_displaySection.xhtml?lawCode=HSC&sectionNum=1262.6.

Canavan, Timothy. "Appropriate Use of the Intrauterine Device." *American Family Physician* 58, no. 9 (December 1, 1998): 2077–84.

Canto, John G., William J. Rogers, Robert J. Goldberg, Eric D. Peterson, Nanette K. Wenger, Viola Vaccarino, Catarina I. Kiefe, et al. "Association of Age and Sex With Myocardial Infarction Symptom Presentation and In-Hospital Mortality." *JAMA* 307, no. 8 (February 22, 2012): 813–22. https://doi.org/10.1001/jama.2012.199.

Caplan, Arthur L. "Med Students Still Do Pelvic Exams on Women Under Anesthesia." *Medscape*, May 25, 2018. http://www.medscape.com/viewarticle/896847.

———. "Pelvic Exams Done on Anesthetized Women Without Consent: Still Happening." *Medscape*, May 2, 2018. http://www.medscape.com/viewarticle/894693.

Card, Claudia. "Rape as a Weapon of War." *Hypatia* 11, no. 4 (1996): 5–18.

cárdenas, micha. "Pregnancy: Reproductive Futures in Trans of Color Feminism." *TSQ: Transgender Studies Quarterly* 3, no. 1–2 (May 1, 2016): 48–57. https://doi.org/10.1215/23289252-3334187.

Carey, Mary Agnes. "Hobby Lobby Ruling Cuts Into Contraceptive Mandate." NPR.org. June 30, 2014, sec. Shots Health News. http://www.npr.org/sections/health-shots/2014/06/30/327065968/hobby-lobby-ruling-cuts-into-contraceptive-mandate.

Carmon, Irin. "Meet the Marital Rape Deniers." MSNBC, July 28, 2015. http://www.msnbc.com/msnbc/meet-the-marital-rape-deniers.

Carney, Robert J., and Donald W. Hardigree. "The Economic Impact of Gender-Neutral Insurance Rating on Women." *The Journal of Insurance Issues and Practices* 13, no. 2 (1990): 1–23.

Carter, Christine L., Eileen M. Resnick, Monica Mallampalli, and Anna Kalbarczyk. "Sex and Gender Differences in Alzheimer's Disease: Recommendations for Future Research." *Journal of Women's Health* 21, no. 10 (October 2012): 1018–23. https://doi.org/10.1089/jwh.2012.3789.

Carvalho, Cláudia, Joaquim Machado Caetano, Lidia Cunha, Paula Rebouta, Ted J. Kaptchuk, and Irving Kirsch. "Open-Label Placebo Treatment in Chronic Low Back Pain: A

Randomized Controlled Trial." *Pain* 157, no. 12 (2016): 2766–72. https://doi.org/10.1097/j.pain.0000000000000700.

Cassad, Bettina J., Abdiel J. Flores, Andrew S. Cheli, and Drake A. Anderson. "How Sexism Undermines the Advancement of Women in Science, Technology, Engineering, and Mathematics." In *Sexism: Past, Present and Future Perspectives*, edited by Gemma Sáez and Inmaculada Valor Segura. Social Issues, Justice and Status. Hauppauge, New York: Nova Science Publishers, Inc, 2018.

Cendejas, Blanca R., Karen K. Smith-Mccune, and Michelle J. Khan. "Does Treatment for Cervical and Vulvar Dysplasia Impact Women's Sexual Health?" *American Journal of Obstetrics and Gynecology* 212, no. 3 (March 2015): 291–97. https://doi.org/10.1016/j.ajog.2014.05.039.

Center for Disease Control. "Effectiveness of Family Planning Methods." 2014. http://www.cdc.gov/reproductivehealth/contraception/unintendedpregnancy/pdf/family-planning-methods-2014.pdf.

———. "Hospital Support for Breastfeeding." October 6, 2015. https://www.cdc.gov/vitalsigns/breastfeeding2015/index.html.

———. "Public Opinions About Breastfeeding," December 1, 2017. https://www.cdc.gov/breastfeeding/data/healthstyles_survey/index.htm.

———. "Severe Maternal Morbidity in the United States: Pregnancy: Reproductive Health." January 17, 2019. https://www.cdc.gov/reproductivehealth/maternalinfanthealth/severematernalmorbidity.html.

———. "US Selected Practice Recommendations for Contraceptive Use, 2016 Appendix C: Examinations and Tests Needed Before Initiation of Contraceptive Methods," December 25, 2017. https://www.cdc.gov/reproductivehealth/contraception/mmwr/spr/appendixc.html.

———. "What Should I Know about Screening?," August 23, 2018. http://www.cdc.gov/cancer/cervical/basic_info/screening.htm.

Center for Infectious Disease Research and Policy. "Overuse and Overprescribing of Antibiotics." Accessed April 6, 2018. http://www.cidrap.umn.edu/asp/overuse-overprescribing-of-antibiotics.

Centers for Disease Control and Prevention. "Heart Disease Facts & Statistics." August 24, 2017. https://www.cdc.gov/heartdisease/facts.htm.

———. "Tuskegee Study - Timeline," October 3, 2018. https://www.cdc.gov/tuskegee/timeline.htm.

———. "Women and Heart Disease Fact Sheet." May 3, 2017. https://www.cdc.gov/dhdsp/data_statistics/fact_sheets/fs_women_heart.htm.

Central Conference of American Rabbis. "CCAR Responsa: American Reform Responsa Birth Control." 1927. https://www.ccarnet.org/ccar-responsa/arr-486-499/.

———. "CCAR Supports Contraceptive Coverage for All Women." October 6, 2017. https://www.ccarnet.org/ccar-supports-contraceptive-coverage-women/.

Chan, Connie S. "Reproductive Issues Are Essential Survival Issues for the Asian-American Communities." In *From Abortion to Reproductive Freedom: Transforming a Movement*, edited by Marlene Gerber Fried. Boston, MA: South End Press, 1999.

Chandler, Michael Alison. "Women Are Now a Majority of Entering Medical Students Nationwide." *The Washington Post*, January 22, 2018. https://www.washingtonpost.com/local/social-issues/women-are-now-a-majority-of-entering-medical-students-nationwide/2018/01/22/b2eb00e8-f22e-11e7-b3bf-ab90a706e175_story.html.

Charlton, Brittany M., Janet W. Rich-Edwards, Graham A. Colditz, Stacey A. Missmer, Bernard A. Rosner, Susan E. Hankinson, Frank E. Speizer, and Karin B. Michels. "Oral Contraceptive Use and Mortality after 36 Years of Follow-up in the Nurses' Health Study: Prospective Cohort Study." *BMJ* (Clinical Research Ed.) 349 (October 31, 2014): g6356.

Chavkin, Wendy, Liddy Leitman, Kate Polin, and for Global Doctors for Choice. "Conscientious Objection and Refusal to Provide Reproductive Healthcare: A White Paper Examining Prevalence, Health Consequences, and Policy Responses." *International Journal of Gynaecology and Obstetrics: The Official Organ of the International Federation of Gy-*

naecology and Obstetrics 123 Suppl 3 (December 2013): S41-56. https://doi.org/10.1016/S0020-7292(13)60002-8.

Chemaly, Soraya. "Why Is New Technology Designed Primarily for Men?" *World Economic Forum*. March 18, 2016. https://www.weforum.org/agenda/2016/03/why-is-new-technology-designed-primarily-for-men/.

Chen, Chin-Shyan, Tsai-Ching Liu, Bradley Chen, and Chung-Liang Lin. "The Failure of Financial Incentive? The Seemingly Inexorable Rise of Cesarean Section." *Social Science & Medicine* 101 (January 1, 2014): 47–51. https://doi.org/10.1016/j.socscimed.2013.11.010.

Chen, Moon S., Primo N. Lara, Julie H.T. Dang, Debora A. Paterniti, and Karen Kelly. "Twenty Years Post-NIH Revitalization Act: Renewing the Case for Enhancing Minority Participation in Cancer Clinical Trials." *Cancer* 120, no. 0 7 (April 1, 2014): 1091–96. https://doi.org/10.1002/cncr.28575.

Chiaramonte, Gabrielle R., and Ronald Friend. "Medical Students' and Residents' Gender Bias in the Diagnosis, Treatment, and Interpretation of Coronary Heart Disease Symptoms." *Health Psychology* 25, no. 3 (2006): 255–66. https://doi.org/10.1037/0278-6133.25.3.255.

Chiaramonte, Gabrielle Rosina. "Physicians' Gender Bias in the Diagnosis, Treatment, and Interpretation of Coronary Heart Disease Symptoms." Stony Brook University, 2007.

Childers, Christopher P., Jill Q. Dworsky, Gerald Kominski, and Melinda Maggard-Gibbons. "A Comparison of Payments to a For-Profit Dialysis Firm From Government and Commercial Insurers." *JAMA Internal Medicine*, May 13, 2019. https://doi.org/10.1001/jamainternmed.2019.0431.

Chiu, Allyson. "'Unintended Pregnancy': Nearly 170,000 Allergan Birth Control Packs Recalled." *The Washington Post*, May 30, 2018, sec. Morning Mix. https://www.washingtonpost.com/news/morning-mix/wp/2018/05/30/nearly-170000-allergan-birth-control-packs-recalled-after-error-leaves-pills-out-of-order/.

Cimpian, A., H. M.C. Arce, E. M. Markman, and C. S. Dweck. "Subtle Linguistic Cues Affect Children's Motivation." *Psychological Science* 18, no. 4 (2007): 314.

Cleland, John G., Robert P. Ndugwa, and Eliya M. Zulu. "Family Planning in Sub-Saharan Africa: Progress or Stagnation?" *World Health Organization*. November 4, 2010. http://www.who.int/bulletin/volumes/89/2/10-077925/en/.

Colen, Cynthia G., and David M. Ramey. "Is Breast Truly Best? Estimating the Effects of Breastfeeding on Long-Term Child Health and Wellbeing in the United States Using Sibling Comparisons." *Social Science & Medicine* 109 (May 1, 2014): 55–65. https://doi.org/10.1016/j.socscimed.2014.01.027.

Collaborative Group on Epidemiological Studies on Endometrial Cancer. "Endometrial Cancer and Oral Contraceptives: An Individual Participant Meta-Analysis of 27 276 Women with Endometrial Cancer from 36 Epidemiological Studies." *The Lancet*. Oncology 16, no. 9 (September 2015): 1061–70. https://doi.org/10.1016/S1470-2045(15)00212-0.

Collins, Patricia Hill. *Black Feminist Thought: Knowledge, Consciousness, and the Politics of Empowerment*. New York: Routledge, 2008.

———. "It's All In the Family: Intersections of Gender, Race, and Nation." *Hypatia* 13, no. 3 (August 1, 1998): 62–82. https://doi.org/10.1111/j.1527-2001.1998.tb01370.x.

Committee on Adolescent Care: Long-Acting Reversible Contraception Working Group. "Adolescents and Long-Acting Reversible Contraception: Implants and Intrauterine Devices." *The American College of Obstetricians and Gynecologists* 539 (October 2012). http://www.acog.org/-/media/Committee-Opinions/Committee-on-Adolescent-Health-Care/co539.pdf?dmc=1&ts=20170330T1452030170.

Committee on Health Care for Underserved Women. "Committee Opinion No. 512: Health Care for Transgender Individuals." *Obstetrics & Gynecology* 118, no. 6 (December 2011): 1454–58. https://doi.org/10.1097/AOG.0b013e31823ed1c1.

Conly, Sarah. *Against Autonomy: Justifying Coercive Paternalism*. Cambridge University Press, 2013.

Contorno, Steve. "Rand Paul Says More than Half of Students at Medical, Dental and Law Schools Are Females." @politifact, January 28, 2014. //www.politifact.com/truth-o-meter/statements/2014/jan/28/rand-paul/rand-paul-says-more-half-students-medical-dental-a/.

Cooper, Anna Julia. *A Voice from the South*. Aldine Printing House, 1892.

Copelon, Rhonda. "From Privacy to Autonomy: The Conditions for Sexual and Reproductive Freedom." In *From Abortion to Reproductive Freedom: Transforming a Movement*, edited by Marlene Gerber Fried. Boston, MA: South End Press, 1999.

Corliss, Julie. "New Mammography Guidelines Call for Starting Later and Screening Less Often." Harvard Health Publishing. October 21, 2015. https://www.health.harvard.edu/blog/new-mammography-guidelines-call-for-starting-later-and-screening-less-often-201510218466.

Couchoud, Cécile, Sahar Bayat, Emmanuel Villar, Christian Jacquelinet, and René Ecochard. "A New Approach for Measuring Gender Disparity in Access to Renal Transplantation Waiting Lists." *Transplantation* 94, no. 5 (September 15, 2012): 513–19. https://doi.org/10.1097/TP.0b013e31825d156a.

"Counseling and Waiting Periods for Abortion." Guttmacher Institute, March 14, 2016. https://www.guttmacher.org/state-policy/explore/counseling-and-waiting-periods-abortion.

Cowart, Donald, Concern for Dying (Association), inc Filmakers Library, and Unicorn Media. Dax's Case. New York: Filmakers Library, 1984.

Crary, David. "Lawsuits Target Trump Administration Family Planning Policy." AP News. May 2, 2018. https://apnews.com/68cf3416b80441c8bcbc33905584c77d/Lawsuits-target-Trump-administration-family-planning-policy.

Crawford, Chris. "AAFP Recommends Against Pelvic Exams in Asymptomatic Women," April 25, 2017. https://www.aafp.org/news/health-of-the-public/20170425aafppelvicexam.html.

Crenshaw, Kimberlé Williams. "Mapping the Margins: Intersectionality, Identity Politics, and Violence against Women of Color." *Stanford Law Review* 43, no. 6 (1991): 1241–99. https://doi.org/10.2307/1229039.

———. "Beyond Racism and Misogyny: Black Feminism and 2 Live Crew." In *Words That Wound: Critical Race Theory, Assaultive Speech, And The First Amendment*. Westview Press, 1993.

———. "Demarginalizing the Intersection of Race and Sex: A Black Feminist Critique of Antidiscrimination Doctrine, Feminist Theory and Antiracist Politics." *University of Chicago Legal Forum*, no. 1 (1989): 31.

Crowther, Caroline A. and Shanshan Han. "Hospitalisation and Bed Rest for Multiple Pregnancy." *Cochrane*, July 7, 2010. https://doi.org/10.1002/14651858.CD000110.pub2.

Cruickshank, Heather. "Are Women Better Doctors Than Men?" *Healthline*, April 12, 2018. https://www.healthline.com/health-news/women-doctors-better-patient-interactions.

Cruzan v. Director, Missouri Department of Health. 497 U.S. 261, 88-1503 (1990). Supreme Court of the United States.

Cudd, Ann E. "The Paradox of Liberal Feminism: Preference, Rationality, and Oppression." In *Varieties of Feminist Liberalism*, edited by Amy R. Baehr and Anita Allen, 37–61. Rowman & Littlefield Publishers, 2004.

Cudd, Ann E., and Leslie E. Jones. "Sexism." In *A Companion to Applied Ethics*, edited by R. G. Frey and Christopher Heath Wellman, 1 edition. Malden, Mass.: Wiley-Blackwell, 2005.

Cuddy, Amy J. C., Kyle T. Doherty, and Maarten W. Bos. "OPOWER: Increasing Energy Efficiency through Normative Influence (A)," September 14, 2010. https://hbr.org/product/OPOWER--Increasing-Energy/an/911016-PDF-ENG.

Cullen, Susan, and Margaret Klein. "Respect for Patients, Physicians, and the Truth." In *Intervention and Reflection: Basic Issues in Medical Ethics*, edited by Ronald Munson, 8 edition. Belmont, CA: Cengage Learning, 2007.

Culp-Ressler, Tara. "When Gender Stereotypes Become A Serious Hazard To Women's Health." May 11, 2015. https://thinkprogress.org/when-gender-stereotypes-become-a-serious-hazard-to-womens-health-f1f130a5e79/.

Cunningham, Shayna D., Deanna L. Kerrigan, Jacky M. Jennings, and Jonathan M. Ellen. "Relationships Between Perceived STD-Related Stigma, STD-Related Shame and STD Screening Among a Household Sample of Adolescents." *Perspectives on Sexual and Reproductive Health* 41, no. 4 (December 2009): 225–30. https://doi.org/10.1363/4122509.

Dahlen, Hannah G., Caroline S. E. Homer, Margaret Cooke, Alexis M. Upton, Rosalie A. Nunn, and Belinda S. Brodrick. "'Soothing the Ring of Fire': Australian Women's and Midwives' Experiences of Using Perineal Warm Packs in the Second Stage of Labour." *Midwifery* 25, no. 2 (April 2009): e39-48. https://doi.org/10.1016/j.midw.2007.08.002.

Dahlen, Hannah G., Caroline S. E. Homer, Margaret Cooke, Alexis M. Upton, Rosalie Nunn, and Belinda Brodrick. "Perineal Outcomes and Maternal Comfort Related to the Application of Perineal Warm Packs in the Second Stage of Labor: A Randomized Controlled Trial." *Birth* (Berkeley, Calif.) 34, no. 4 (December 2007): 282–90. https://doi.org/10.1111/j.1523-536X.2007.00186.x.

Dailard, Cynthia. "What Lawrence v. Texas Says About the History and Future Of Reproductive Rights." Guttmacher Institute, September 22, 2004. https://www.guttmacher.org/gpr/2003/10/what-lawrence-v-texas-says-about-history-and-future-reproductive-rights.

Daniels, Kimberly, William Mosher, and Jo Jones. "Contraceptive Methods Women Have Ever Used: United States, 1982-2010." *National Health Statistics Reports*, February 14, 2013. http://www.cdc.gov/nchs/data/nhsr/nhsr062.pdf.

Daniels, Norman. "Health-Care Needs and Distributive Justice." *Philosophy & Public Affairs* 10, no. 2 (1981): 146–79.

———. "Justice, Health, and Healthcare." *American Journal of Bioethics* 1, no. 2 (2001): 2–16.

Davis, Angela Y. *Women, Culture & Politics*. Reprint edition. New York: Vintage, 1990.

———. *Women, Race, & Class*. 1st Vintage Books ed edition. New York: Vintage, 1983.

De Craemer, Willy. "A Cross-Cultural Perspective on Personhood." The Milbank Memorial Fund Quarterly. *Health and Society* 61, no. 1 (1983): 19–34. https://doi.org/10.2307/3349814.

Declercq, Eugene R., Carol Sakala, Maureen P. Corry, and Sandra Applebaum. "Listening to Mothers II: Report of the Second National U.S. Survey of Women's Childbearing Experiences." *The Journal of Perinatal Education* 16, no. 4 (2007): 9–14. https://doi.org/10.1624/105812407X244769.

Declercq, Eugene R., Carol Sakala, Maureen P. Corry, Sandra Applebaum, and Ariel Herrlich. "Major Survey Findings of Listening to Mothers SM III: Pregnancy and Birth." *The Journal of Perinatal Education* 23, no. 1 (2014): 9–16. https://doi.org/10.1891/1058-1243.23.1.9.

Delston, Jill B. "Gutmann, Amy." In *Encyclopedia of the Philosophy of Law and Social Philosophy*, 1–5. Springer, Dordrecht, 2017. https://doi.org/10.1007/978-94-007-6730-0_43-2.

———. "Public Reason and Its Limits: The Role of Truth in Politics." In *Ethics in Politics: The Rights and Obligations of Individual Political Agents*, edited by Emily Crookston, David Killoren, and Jonathan Trerise. Routledge, 2016.

———. "The Criminalization of Money Laundering and Terrorism in Global Contexts: A Hybrid Solution." *Journal of Global Ethics* 10, no. 3 (September 2, 2014): 326–38. https://doi.org/10.1080/17449626.2014.971854.

———. "When Doctors Deny Drugs: Sexism and Contraception Access in the Medical Field." *Bioethics* 31, no. 9 (November 2017): 703–10. https://doi.org/10.1111/bioe.12373.

Dembosky, April. "California's Message To Hospitals: Shape Up Or Lose 'In-Network' Status." NPR.org, May 23, 2018. https://www.npr.org/sections/health-shots/2018/05/23/611975420/californias-message-to-hospitals-shape-up-or-lose-in-network-status.

Dempsey, Patrick P., Alexandra C. Businger, Lauren E. Whaley, Joshua J. Gagne, and Jeffrey A. Linder. "Primary Care Clinicians' Perceptions about Antibiotic Prescribing for Acute Bronchitis: A Qualitative Study." *BMC Family Practice* 15, no. 1 (December 12, 2014): 194. https://doi.org/10.1186/s12875-014-0194-5.

Deneux-Tharaux, Catherine, Elodie Carmona, Marie-Hélene Bouvier-Colle, and Gérard Bréart. "Postpartum Maternal Mortality and Cesarean Delivery." *Obstetrics & Gynecolo-*

gy 108, no. 3 Pt 1 (September 2006): 541–48. https://doi.org/10.1097/01.AOG.0000233154.62729.24.

Department of Health & Human Services. "Medicare Coverage of Kidney Dialysis & Kidney Transplant Services." Medicare.gov. 2018. https://www.medicare.gov/Pubs/pdf/10128-Medicare-Coverage-ESRD.pdf.

DeRossi, Scott S., and Elliot V. Hersh. "Antibiotics and Oral Contraceptives." *Dental Clinics of North America* 46, no. 4 (October 2002): 653–64.

DeSantis, Carol E., Jiemin Ma, Ann Goding Sauer, Lisa A. Newman, and Ahmedin Jemal. "Breast Cancer Statistics, 2017, Racial Disparity in Mortality by State." *CA: A Cancer Journal for Clinicians* 67, no. 6 (October 3, 2017): 439–48. https://doi.org/10.3322/caac.21412.

Deutsch, Elizabeth B. "Expanding Conscience, Shrinking Care: The Crisis in Access to Reproductive Care and the Affordable Care Act's Nondiscrimination Mandate" *The Yale Law Journal* 124, no. 7 (May 2015). https://www.yalelawjournal.org/note/reproductive-care-and-the-acas-nondiscrimination-mandate.

Devane, Declan, Joan G. Lalor, Sean Daly, William McGuire, Anna Cuthbert, and Valerie Smith. "Cardiotocography versus Intermittent Auscultation of Fetal Heart on Admission to Labour Ward for Assessment of Fetal Wellbeing." *The Cochrane Database of Systematic Reviews* 1 (26 2017): CD005122. https://doi.org/10.1002/14651858.CD005122.pub5.

Dewey, Caitlin. "The Republican Plan to Tighten Food Stamp Work Requirements Is Advancing — without a Single Democrat's Vote." *The Washington Post*, April 18, 2018. https://www.washingtonpost.com/news/wonk/wp/2018/04/18/the-republican-plan-to-tighten-food-stamp-work-requirements-is-advancing-without-a-single-democrats-vote/.

Diekema, Douglas S. "Parental Refusals of Medical Treatment: The Harm Principle as Threshold for State Intervention." *Theoretical Medicine and Bioethics* 25, no. 4 (2004): 243–64.

Disorders, Institute of Medicine (US) Forum on Neuroscience and Nervous System. *Studying Sex Differences in Health and Disease*. National Academies Press (US), 2011. https://www.ncbi.nlm.nih.gov/books/NBK53393/.

Dobbeleir, Julie M.L.C.L., Koenraad Van Landuyt, and Stan J. Monstrey. "Aesthetic Surgery of the Female Genitalia." *Seminars in Plastic Surgery* 25, no. 2 (May 2011): 130–41. https://doi.org/10.1055/s-0031-1281482.

Doctor, Jason N., Andy Nguyen, Roneet Lev, Jonathan Lucas, Tara Knight, Henu Zhao, and Michael Menchine. "Opioid Prescribing Decreases after Learning of a Patient's Fatal Overdose." *Science* 361, no. 6402 (August 10, 2018): 588–90. https://doi.org/10.1126/science.aat4595.

Domenighetti, Gianfranco, Barbara D'Avanzo, Matthias Egger, Franco Berrino, Thomas Perneger, Paola Mosconi, and Marcel Zwahlen. "Women's Perception of the Benefits of Mammography Screening: Population-Based Survey in Four Countries." *International Journal of Epidemiology* 32, no. 5 (October 2003): 816–21.

Donner, Wendy. "Mill's Theory of Value." In *The Blackwell Guide to Mill's Utilitarianism*, edited by Henry West, 1st ed., 117–38. Wiley-Blackwell, 2006.

Driver, Julia. "Consequentialism and Feminist Ethics." *Hypatia* 20, no. 4 (Fall 2005): 183–99.

Drolet, Mélanie, Marc Brisson, Elizabeth Maunsell, Eduardo L. Franco, François Coutlée, Alex Ferenczy, William Fisher, and James A. Mansi. "The Psychosocial Impact of an Abnormal Cervical Smear Result." *Psycho-Oncology* 21, no. 10 (October 2012): 1071–81. https://doi.org/10.1002/pon.2003.

Dula, Annette. "African American Suspicion of the Healthcare System Is Justified: What Do We Do about It?" *Cambridge Quarterly of Healthcare Ethics* 3, no. 3 (ed 1994): 347–57. https://doi.org/10.1017/S0963180100005168.

———. "Bioethics: The Need for a Dialogue with African Americans." In *"It Just Ain't Fair": The Ethics of Health Care for African Americans*. ABC-CLIO, 1994.

Dupere, Katie. "6 Ways the Health Care System Fails Transgender Patients." *Mashable*, August 5, 2015. https://mashable.com/2015/08/05/transgender-health-care/.

Dusenbery, Maya. *Doing Harm: The Truth About How Bad Medicine and Lazy Science Leave Women Dismissed, Misdiagnosed, and Sick*. 1 edition. New York, NY: HarperOne, 2018.

———. "Is Medicine's Gender Bias Killing Young Women?" *Pacific Standard*, March 23, 2015. https://psmag.com/social-justice/is-medicines-gender-bias-killing-young-women.

———. "When Doctors Dismiss Women's Pain." *Lenny Letter*. April 24, 2018. https://www.lennyletter.com/story/when-doctors-dismiss-womens-pain.

Dweck, Carol S. "Messages That Motivate: How Praise Molds Students' Beliefs, Motivation, and Performance (in Surprising Ways)." In *Improving Academic Achievement: Impact of Psychological Factors on Education*, 2002, 37–60.

———. *Mindset: The New Psychology of Success*. Reprint edition. New York: Ballantine Books, 2007.

———. *Self-Theories: Their Role in Motivation, Personality, and Development*. 1 edition. Philadelphia, PA: Psychology Press, 2000.

Dworkin, Ronald. *Life's Dominion: An Argument About Abortion, Euthanasia, and Individual Freedom*. Knopf Doubleday Publishing Group, 2011.

Dworkin, Ronald, Thomas Nagel, Robert Nozick, John Rawls, Thomas Scanlon, and Judith Jarvis Thomson. "Assisted Suicide: The Philosophers' Brief." *The New York Review of Books*, March 27, 1997, 41–47.

Dykema, Jane. "What I Don't Tell My Students About 'The Husband Stitch.'" *Electric Literature*, October 10, 2017. https://electricliterature.com/what-i-dont-tell-my-students-about-the-husband-stitch-690899157394.

Eastman, Peggy. "NCI Adopts New Mammography Screening Guidelines For Women." *JNCI: Journal of the National Cancer Institute* 89, no. 8 (April 16, 1997): 538–40. https://doi.org/10.1093/jnci/89.8.538.

Eastman-Mueller, Heather P., and Sara B. Oswalt. "Trends in Pap Test Practices and Results: An 11-Year Review of the Annual ACHA Pap Test and STI Survey." *Journal of American College Health* 65, no. 7 (October 3, 2017): 474–81. https://doi.org/10.1080/07448481.2017.1341898.

Edmonds, Jillian. "Transgender People Are Facing Incredibly High Rates of Poverty." *NWLC* (blog), December 9, 2016. https://nwlc.org/blog/income-security-is-elusive-for-many-transgender-people-according-to-u-s-transgender-survey/.

Ehrenreich, Barbara. "Welcome to Cancerland." *Harper's Magazine*, November 2001. https://harpers.org/archive/2001/11/welcome-to-cancerland/.

Eisenstadt v. Baird, United States (Supreme Court 1972).

Elizabeth Harman. "Creation Ethics: The Moral Status of Early Fetuses and the Ethics of Abortion." *Philosophy & Public Affairs* 28, no. 4 (1999): 310–24.

Ellin, Abby. "Endometriosis Is Often Ignored in Teenage Girls." *Well* (blog), March 30, 2015. https://well.blogs.nytimes.com/2015/03/30/endometriosis-is-often-ignored-in-teenage-girls/.

Elliott, Carl. *White Coat, Black Hat: Adventures on the Dark Side of Medicine*. Beacon Press, 2010.

Emanuel, Ezekiel J., and Linda L. Emanuel. "Four Models of the Physician-Patient Relationship." *The Journal of the American Medical Association* 267, no. 16 (April 22, 1992). http://www.antoniocasella.eu/salute/Emanuel_1992.pdf.

Engelhardt, Jr., H. Tristram. "Rights to Health Care, Social Justice, and Fairness in Health Care Allocations: Frustrations in the Face of Finitude." In *The Foundations of Bioethics*, 375–410. Oxford University Press, USA, 1996.

Enochs, Elizabeth. "How To Keep Your Birth Control Effective." *Bustle*. February 3, 2016. https://www.bustle.com/articles/139434-11-ways-you-might-be-decreasing-the-effectiveness-of-your-birth-control.

Epstein, David. "When Evidence Says No, But Doctors Say Yes." *ProPublica*, March 16, 2017. https://web.archive.org/web/20170316151510/https://www.propublica.org/article/when-evidence-says-no-but-doctors-say-yes.

Erdely, Sabrina Rubin. "Doctors' Beliefs Can Hinder Patient Care." msnbc.com, June 22, 2007. http://www.nbcnews.com/id/19190916/ns/health-womens_health/t/doctors-beliefs-can-hinder-patient-care/.

Ernst, Katie. "Miss Treated: Fighting Misogyny in the Medical Profession One Story at a Time." *Miss•Treated*. Accessed July 17, 2018. http://www.misstreated.org/about/.

Esser, Rachel. "Story: Even after Diagnosis Doctors Can Still MissTreat You." *Miss•Treated*, May 24, 2018. http://www.misstreated.org/blog/2018/5/24/story-even-after-diagnosis-doctors-can-still-misstreat-you.

Estlund, David M. *Democratic Authority: A Philosophical Framework*. Princeton, NJ: Princeton University Press, 2009.

Estrada, Andrea. "The Politics of Female Biology and Reproduction." *The UCSB Current*. April 6, 2015. http://www.news.ucsb.edu/2015/015287/politics-female-biology-and-reproduction.

Evenhouse, Eirik, and Siobhan Reilly. "Improved Estimates of the Benefits of Breastfeeding Using Sibling Comparisons to Reduce Selection Bias." *Health Services Research* 40, no. 6 Pt 1 (December 2005): 1781–1802. https://doi.org/10.1111/j.1475-6773.2004.00453.x.

Faden, Ruth R., Tom L. Beauchamp, and Nancy M. P. King. *A History and Theory of Informed Consent*. 1 edition. New York: Oxford University Press, 1986.

Fairweather, DeLisa, Sylvia Frisancho-Kiss, and Noel R. Rose. "Sex Differences in Autoimmune Disease from a Pathological Perspective." *The American Journal of Pathology* 173, no. 3 (September 2008): 600–609. https://doi.org/10.2353/ajpath.2008.071008.

Fairweather, DeLisa, and Noel R. Rose. "Women and Autoimmune Diseases." *Emerging Infectious Diseases* 10, no. 11 (November 2004): 2005–11. https://doi.org/10.3201/eid1011.040367.

"Family Planning/Contraception." World Health Organization. February 8 2018. http://www.who.int/mediacentre/factsheets/fs351/en/.

Fard, Maggie Fazeli. "Sandra Fluke, Georgetown Student Called a 'Slut' by Rush Limbaugh, Speaks Out." *The Washington Post* (blog), March 2, 2012. https://www.washingtonpost.com/blogs/the-buzz/post/rush-limbaugh-calls-georgetown-student-sandra-fluke-a-slut-for-advocating-contraception/2012/03/02/gIQAvjfSmR_blog.html.

Fassler, Joe. "How Doctors Take Women's Pain Less Seriously." *The Atlantic*, October 15, 2015. https://www.theatlantic.com/health/archive/2015/10/emergency-room-wait-times-sexism/410515/.

FBI. "Frequently Asked Questions about the Change in the UCR Definition of Rape," December 11, 2014. https://ucr.fbi.gov/recent-program-updates/new-rape-definition-frequently-asked-questions.

Feder, Jody. "The History and Effect of Abortion Conscience Clause Laws," CRS Report for Congress, January 14, 2005, 5.

Feldman, Henry A., Irwin Goldstein, Dimitrios G. Hatzichristou, Robert J. Krane, and John B. McKinlay. "Impotence and Its Medical and Psychosocial Correlates: Results of the Massachusetts Male Aging Study." *The Journal of Urology* 151, no. 1 (January 1, 1994): 54–61. https://doi.org/10.1016/S0022-5347(17)34871-1.

Fenton, Siobhan. "Period Pain Is Officially as Bad as a Heart Attack - so Why Have Doctors Ignored It?" *The Independent*, February 19, 2016. http://www.independent.co.uk/voices/period-pain-is-officially-as-bad-as-a-heart-attack-so-why-have-doctors-ignored-it-the-answer-is-a6883831.html.

Fernandez, Elizabeth. "Physician Moms Are Often Subject to Workplace Discrimination." *UC San Francisco*, May 8, 2017. https://www.ucsf.edu/news/2017/05/406921/physician-moms-are-often-subject-workplace-discrimination.

Ferrara, Jeanette. "The Top Five Most Effective Methods of Birth Control." *Scienceline*, January 30, 2016. http://scienceline.org/2016/01/the-top-five-most-effective-methods-of-birth-control/.

Fetters, K. Aleisha. "Pap Smear FAQs." *Women's Health*, January 11, 2012. http://www.womenshealthmag.com/health/pap-smear-faqs.

Fillingim, Roger B., Christopher D. King, Margarete C. Ribeiro-Dasilva, Bridgett Rahim-Williams, and Joseph L. Riley. "Sex, Gender, and Pain: A Review of Recent Clinical and

Experimental Findings." *The Journal of Pain: Official Journal of the American Pain Society* 10, no. 5 (May 2009): 447–85. https://doi.org/10.1016/j.jpain.2008.12.001.

Filteau, S. M. "Role of Breast-Feeding in Managing Malnutrition and Infectious Disease." *The Proceedings of the Nutrition Society* 59, no. 4 (November 2000): 565–72.

US Preventative Services Task Force, "Final Recommendation Statement: Folic Acid for the Prevention of Neural Tube Defects: Preventative Medication." January 2017. https://www.uspreventiveservicestaskforce.org/Page/Document/RecommendationStatementFinal/folic-acid-for-the-prevention-of-neural-tube-defects-preventive-medication.

Finer, Lawrence B., Lori F. Frohwirth, Lindsay A. Dauphinee, Susheela Singh, and Ann M. Moore. "Timing of Steps and Reasons for Delays in Obtaining Abortions in the United States." *Contraception* 74, no. 4 (October 2006): 334–44. https://doi.org/10.1016/j.contraception.2006.04.010.

Fisher, Sue. *In the Patient's Best Interest: Women and the Politics of Medical Decisions*. Rutgers University Press, 1986.

Flanagin, Jake. "WHO: Risk of Certain Cancers Is Higher in Transgender Communities." *Quartz* (blog). July 23, 2015. https://qz.com/461575/who-risk-of-certain-cancers-is-higher-in-transgender-communities/.

Florida House of Representatives. HB 35E. "Authority for the Governor to Issue a One-Time Stay to Prevent the Withholding of Nutrition and Hydration from a Patient." October 21, 2003. http://www.myfloridahouse.gov/Sections/Bills/billsdetail.aspx?BillId=12713.

Flynn, Trisha. "Female Trouble." *Chicago Tribune*. October 29, 1986. http://articles.chicagotribune.com/1986-10-29/entertainment/8603210488_1_male-body-male-model-moral.

Foot, Philippa. "The Problem of Abortion and the Doctrine of Double Effect." *Oxford Review* 5 (1967): 5–15.

Ford, Earl S., Ali H. Mokdad, Wayne H. Giles, and George A. Mensah. "Serum Total Cholesterol Concentrations and Awareness, Treatment, and Control of Hypercholesterolemia Among US Adults: Findings From the National Health and Nutrition Examination Survey, 1999 to 2000." *Circulation* 107, no. 17 (May 6, 2003): 2185–89. https://doi.org/10.1161/01.CIR.0000066320.27195.B4.

Foreman, Judy. "Why Women Are Living in the Discomfort Zone." *The Wall Street Journal*, February 1, 2014, sec. Life and Style. https://www.wsj.com/articles/escape-from-the-chronic-pain-trap-1391220523.

Foster, Diana Greene, and Katrina Kimport. "Who Seeks Abortions at or After 20 Weeks?" *Perspectives on Sexual and Reproductive Health* 45, no. 4 (December 2013): 210–18. https://doi.org/10.1363/4521013.

Fowler, Kevin John. "Accountability of Dialysis Facilities in Transplant Referral: CMS Needs to Collect National Data on Dialysis Facility Kidney Transplant Referrals." *Clinical Journal of the American Society of Nephrology* 13, no. 2 (February 7, 2018): 193–94. https://doi.org/10.2215/CJN.13741217.

Frakes, Michael, and Anupam B. Jena. "Does Medical Malpractice Law Improve Health Care Quality?" *Journal of Public Economics* 143 (November 2016): 142–58. https://doi.org/10.1016/j.jpubeco.2016.09.002.

Frankfurt, Harry G. *Necessity, Volition, and Love*. Cambridge, UK; New York: Cambridge University Press, 1998.

Frankman, Elizabeth A., Li Wang, Clareann H. Bunker, and Jerry L. Lowder. "Episiotomy in the United States: Has Anything Changed?" *American Journal of Obstetrics and Gynecology* 200, no. 5 (May 2009): 573.e1-7. https://doi.org/10.1016/j.ajog.2008.11.022.

Freeman, Lauren, and Saray Ayala López. "Sex Categorization in Medical Contexts: A Cautionary Tale." *Kennedy Institute of Ethics Journal* 28, no. 3 (October 25, 2018): 243–80. https://doi.org/10.1353/ken.2018.0017.

Fried, Marlene Gerber, ed. *From Abortion to Reproductive Freedom: Transforming a Movement*. Boston, MA: South End Press, 1999.

Friedman, Alexander M., Cande V. Ananth, Eri Prendergast, Mary E. D'Alton, and Jason D. Wright. "Variation in and Factors Associated with Use of Episiotomy." *JAMA* 313, no. 2 (January 13, 2015): 197–99. https://doi.org/10.1001/jama.2014.14774.

Friedman, Marilyn. *Autonomy, Gender, Politics*. Oxford University Press, 2003.

Friesen, Phoebe. "Educational Pelvic Exams on Anesthetized Women: Why Consent Matters." *Bioethics* 32, no. 5 (June 1, 2018): 298–307. https://doi.org/10.1111/bioe.12441.

Frye, Marilyn. *Politics of Reality: Essays in Feminist Theory*. Trumansburg, NY: Crossing Press, 1983.

Gamble, V N. "Under the Shadow of Tuskegee: African Americans and Health Care." *American Journal of Public Health* 87, no. 11 (November 1997): 1773–78.

Garcia, Saudi. "8 Shocking Facts About Sterilization in U.S. History." *Mic*, July 10, 2013. https://mic.com/articles/53723/8-shocking-facts-about-sterilization-in-u-s-history.

Gardner, Ivy H., and Joshua D. Safer. "Progress on the Road to Better Medical Care for Transgender Patients." *Current Opinion in Endocrinology, Diabetes, and Obesity* 20, no. 6 (December 2013): 553–58. https://doi.org/10.1097/01.med.0000436188.95351.4d.

Garrett, Danielle. "Turning to Fairness: Insurance Discrimination Against Women Today and the Affordable Care Act." *NWLC* (blog), March 2012. https://www.nwlc.org/sites/default/files/pdfs/nwlc_2012_turningtofairness_report.pdf.

Gauthier, David P. *Morals by Agreement*. Oxford: Clarendon Press, 1986.

George, Robert, Timothy George, and Chuck Colson. "Manhattan Declaration." November 20, 2009. https://www.manhattandeclaration.org/.

George, Robert P., and Patrick Lee. "The Wrong of Abortion." In *Contemporary Debates in Applied Ethics*, edited by Andrew I. Cohen and Christopher Heath Wellman. John Wiley & Sons, 2014.

Gierisch, Jennifer M., Remy R. Coeytaux, Rachel Peragallo Urrutia, Laura J. Havrilesky, Patricia G. Moorman, William J. Lowery, Michaela Dinan, et al. "Oral Contraceptive Use and Risk of Breast, Cervical, Colorectal, and Endometrial Cancers: A Systematic Review." *Cancer Epidemiology*, Biomarkers & Prevention: A Publication of the American Association for Cancer Research, Cosponsored by the American Society of Preventive Oncology 22, no. 11 (November 2013): 1931–43. https://doi.org/10.1158/1055-9965.EPI-13-0298.

Gillespie, Avrum, Heather Hammer, Stanislav Kolenikov, Athanasia Polychronopoulou, Vladimir Ouzienko, Zoran Obradovic, Megan A. Urbanski, Teri Browne, and Patricio Silva. "Sex Differences and Attitudes toward Living Donor Kidney Transplantation among Urban Black Patients on Hemodialysis." *Clinical Journal of the American Society of Nephrology* 9, no. 10 (October 7, 2014): 1764–72. https://doi.org/10.2215/CJN.12531213.

Gillespie, Duff, Saifuddin Ahmed, Amy Tsui, and Scott Radloff. "Unwanted Fertility among the Poor: An Inequity?" *Bulletin of the World Health Organization* 85, no. 2 (February 2007): 100–107. https://doi.org/10.1590/S0042-96862007000200007.

Gimm, Gilbert W. "The Impact of Malpractice Liability Claims on Obstetrical Practice Patterns." *Health Services Research* 45, no. 1 (February 2010): 195–211. https://doi.org/10.1111/j.1475-6773.2009.01062.x.

Gines, Kathryn T. "Race Women, Race Men, and Early Expressions of Proto-Intersectionality, 1830s-1930s." *In Why Race and Gender Still Matter: An Intersectional Approach*, edited by Maeve M. O'Donovan, Namita Goswami, and Lisa Yount. Routledge, 2015.

GLAAD. "GLAAD Media Reference Guide - Transgender." September 9, 2011. https://www.glaad.org/reference/transgender.

Goertzel, Ted. "Conspiracy Theories in Science." *EMBO Reports* 11, no. 7 (July 2010): 493–99. https://doi.org/10.1038/embor.2010.84.

Gold, Jenny. "Proportion Of OB-GYNs Offering Abortions May Be Lower Than Thought." NPR.org. August 22, 2011, sec. Shots Health News from NPR. https://www.npr.org/sections/health-shots/2011/08/22/139859979/proportion-of-ob-gyns-offering-abortions-may-be-lower-than-thought.

Goldberg, Michelle, and Willa Paskin. "Breast-Feeding Extremists Are Even Worse Than You Thought." *Slate*, December 4, 2015. http://www.slate.com/articles/double_x/doublex/2015/12/
the_breast_feeding_extremists_who_put_lactivism_ahead_of_protecting_babies.html.

Goldman, Alan H. *The Moral Foundations of Professional Ethics*. Rowman & Littlefield, 1980.

Goldschmidt, Debra, and Ashley Strickland. "Planned Parenthood: Fast Facts and Revealing Numbers." CNN, August 1, 2017. https://www.cnn.com/2015/08/04/health/planned-parenthood-by-the-numbers/index.html.

Goldstein, Avram. "Practice vs. Privacy on Pelvic Exams." *The Washington Post*, May 10, 2003. https://www.washingtonpost.com/archive/politics/2003/05/10/practice-vs-privacy-on-pelvic-exams/4e9185c4-4b4c-4d6a-a132-b21b8471da58/.

Gordon, Elisa, and Daniela Ladner. "Gender Inequities Pervade Organ Transplantation Access." *Transplantation* 94 (September 15, 2012): 447–48. https://doi.org/10.1097/TP.0b013e31825d15a1.

Grady, Denise. "Good News for Women With Breast Cancer: Many Don't Need Chemo." *The New York Times*, June 3, 2018. https://www.nytimes.com/2018/06/03/health/breast-cancer-chemo.html.

Grant, Jaime M., Lisa A. Mottet, Justin Tanis, Jack Harrison, Jody L. Herman, and Mara Keisling. "Injustice at Every Turn: A Report of the National Transgender Discrimination Survey." Washington: National Center for Transgender Equality and National Gay and Lesbian Task Force, 2011. http://www.thetaskforce.org/static_html/downloads/reports/reports/ntds_full.pdf.

Gray, Frances. "Original Habitation." In *Coming to Life: Philosophies of Pregnancy, Childbirth and Mothering*, 71–87. Fordham University Press, 2013. http://www.jstor.org.ezproxy.umsl.edu/stable/j.ctt1c5ck2p.8.

Greasley, Kate, and Christopher Kaczor. *Abortion Rights: For and Against*. Cambridge University Press, 2017.

Green, Donald P., and Alan S. Gerber. *Get Out the Vote: How to Increase Voter Turnout*. Brookings Institution Press, 2015.

Green, Fiona J. "From Clitoridectomies to 'Designer Vaginas': The Medical Construction of Heteronormative Female Bodies and Sexuality through Female Genital Cutting." *Sexualities*, Evolution & Gender 7, no. 2 (August 2005): 153–87.

Greenberg, Beth. "Woman Forced Into Violent Episiotomy Settles With Doctor." Yahoo News, March 15, 2017. https://www.yahoo.com/news/woman-forced-into-violent-episiotomy-settles-with-doctor-182947205.html.

Greenberg, Jon. "Without Obamacare, What Happened to Kids like Kimmel's Son?" *PolitiFact*. May 3, 2017. http://www.politifact.com/truth-o-meter/article/2017/may/03/without-obamacare-what-happened-kids-jimmy-kimmels/.

Greenhouse, Linda, and Reva B. Siegel. *Before Roe V. Wade: Voices That Shaped the Abortion Debate Before the Supreme Court's Ruling: With a New Afterword*. Yale Law School, 2012.

Griffin, Susan. "Rape: The All-American Crime." Ramparts 10, no. 3 (1971).

———. *Rape, The Power of Consciousness*. Harper & Row, 1979.

Grinberg, Emanuella. "CVS Apologizes after Pharmacist Refused to Fill Transgender Woman's Prescription," CNN, July 22, 2018. https://www.cnn.com/2018/07/20/health/arizona-trans-woman-cvs-pharmacist-prescription-trnd/index.html.

Grindlay, Kate, Bridgit Burns, and Daniel Grossman. "Prescription Requirements and Over-the-Counter Access to Oral Contraceptives: A Global Review." *Contraception* 88, no. 1 (July 1, 2013): 91–96. https://doi.org/10.1016/j.contraception.2012.11.021.

Grindlay, Kate, and Daniel Grossman. "Prescription Birth Control Access Among U.S. Women at Risk of Unintended Pregnancy." *Journal of Women's Health* 25, no. 3 (December 14, 2015): 249–54. https://doi.org/10.1089/jwh.2015.5312.

Griswold v. Connecticut, United States (Supreme Court 1965).

Grose, Jessica, and Christina Cauterucci. "No Nursery, No Formula, No Pacifier: Are 'Baby-Friendly' Hospitals Unfriendly to New Mothers?" *Slate*, October 9, 2014. http://www.slate.com/articles/double_x/doublex/2014/10/baby_friendly_hospitals_promoting_breast_feeding_at_the_expense_of_the_new.html.

Guiahi, Maryam. "Catholic Health Care and Women's Health." *Obstetrics & Gynecology* 131, no. 3 (March 2018): 534. https://doi.org/10.1097/AOG.0000000000002477.

Guille, Constance, Elena Frank, Zhuo Zhao, David A. Kalmbach, Paul J. Nietert, Douglas A. Mata, and Srijan Sen. "Work-Family Conflict and the Sex Difference in Depression

Among Training Physicians." *JAMA Internal Medicine* 177, no. 12 (December 1, 2017): 1766–72. https://doi.org/10.1001/jamainternmed.2017.5138.

Guldi, Melanie. "Fertility Effects of Abortion and Birth Control Pill Access for Minors." *Demography* 45, no. 4 (November 2008): 817–27. https://doi.org/10.1353/dem.0.0026.

Gunderman, Richard. "Who Does Your Physician Work For?" *The Atlantic*, November 22, 2013. https://www.theatlantic.com/health/archive/2013/11/who-does-your-physician-work-for/281724/.

Gunter, Jen. "Do You Need a Pap Smear to Get Birth Control?" *The New York Times*, October 18, 2018, sec. Well. https://www.nytimes.com/2018/10/18/well/do-you-need-a-pap-smear-to-get-birth-control.html.

Gupta, Sarika, Katherine L. Imborek, and Matthew D. Krasowski. "Challenges in Transgender Healthcare: The Pathology Perspective." *Laboratory Medicine* 47, no. 3 (August 2016): 180–88. https://doi.org/10.1093/labmed/lmw020.

Gutmann, Amy. *Democratic Education*. Princeton University Press, 1999.

———, ed. "Distributing Public Education in a Democracy." In *Democracy and the Welfare State*. Princeton, NJ: Princeton University Press, 1988.

———. *Liberal Equality*. CUP Archive, 1980.

Gutmann, Amy, and Dennis Thompson. *Democracy and Disagreement*. Harvard University Press, 2009.

Guttmacher Institute. "Contraceptive Use in the United States." July 2018. https://www.guttmacher.org/fact-sheet/contraceptive-use-united-states.

Guttmacher Institute. "Most U.S. Obstetrician-Gynecologists in Private Practice Do Not Provide Abortions and Many Also Fail to Provide Referrals." November 21, 2017. https://www.guttmacher.org/news-release/2017/most-us-obstetrician-gynecologists-private-practice-do-not-provide-abortions-and.

Hadjistavropoulos, Thomas, Bruce McMurtry, and Kenneth D. Craig. "Beautiful Faces in Pain: Biases and Accuracy in the Perception of Pain." *Psychology & Health* 11, no. 3 (March 1, 1996): 411–20. https://doi.org/10.1080/08870449608400268.

Haelle, Tara. "Employers Routinely Break The Law When It Comes To Breastfeeding Moms." *Forbes*. October 20, 2015. https://www.forbes.com/sites/tarahaelle/2015/10/20/less-than-half-of-breastfeeding-mothers-have-legally-required-pumping-accommodations-at-work/.

———. "Your Biggest C-Section Risk May Be Your Hospital." *Consumer Reports*, May 10, 2018. https://www.consumerreports.org/c-section/biggest-c-section-risk-may-be-your-hospital/.

Hamblin, James. "How Often Does Rape Lead to Pregnancy?" *The Atlantic*, August 20, 2012. https://www.theatlantic.com/health/archive/2012/08/how-often-does-rape-lead-to-pregnancy/261307/.

Hampton, Jean. *Hobbes and the Social Contract Tradition*. Cambridge University Press, 1988.

Hansen, Anne Kirkeby, Kirsten Wisborg, Niels Uldbjerg, and Tine Brink Henriksen. "Risk of Respiratory Morbidity in Term Infants Delivered by Elective Caesarean Section: Cohort Study." *BMJ* (Clinical Research Ed.) 336, no. 7635 (January 12, 2008): 85–87. https://doi.org/10.1136/bmj.39405.539282.BE.

Hardeman, Rachel R., Eduardo M. Medina, and Katy B. Kozhimannil. "Structural Racism and Supporting Black Lives — The Role of Health Professionals." *New England Journal of Medicine* 375, no. 22 (December 1, 2016): 2113–15. https://doi.org/10.1056/NEJMp1609535.

Harper, Cynthia C., Laura Stratton, Tina R. Raine, Kirsten Thompson, Jillian T. Henderson, Maya Blum, Debbie Postlethwaite, and J. Joseph Speidel. "Counseling and Provision of Long-Acting Reversible Contraception in the US: National Survey of Nurse Practitioners." *Preventive Medicine* 57, no. 6 (December 2013): 883–88. https://doi.org/10.1016/j.ypmed.2013.10.005.

Harris, John. "The Survival Lottery." *Philosophy* 50, no. 191 (January 1975): 81–87. https://doi.org/10.1017/S0031819100059118.

Harrison, Jami Kath. "It Happened To Me: I Teach Pelvic Exams to Med Students (On Myself)." *xoJane: Women's Lifestyle & Community Site*, October 17, 2012. https://www.xojane.com/it-happened-to-me/it-happened-to-me-i-teach-pelvic-exams-to-med-students-on-myself.

Harrison-Hohner, Jane. "How Accurate Is My Pap Smear Result?" *WebMD* (blog). June 6, 2011. http://blogs.webmd.com/womens-health/2011/06/how-accurate-is-my-pap-smear-result.html.

Harris-Perry, Melissa Victoria. *Sister Citizen: Shame, Stereotypes, and Black Women in America*. Yale University Press, 2011.

Hartman, Laura P., and Patricia H. Werhane, eds. *The Global Corporation: Sustainable, Effective and Ethical Practices, A Case Book*. Routledge, 2009.

Havrilesky, Laura J., Patricia G. Moorman, William J. Lowery, Jennifer M. Gierisch, Remy R. Coeytaux, Rachel Peragallo Urrutia, Michaela Dinan, et al. "Oral Contraceptive Pills as Primary Prevention for Ovarian Cancer: A Systematic Review and Meta-Analysis." *Obstetrics & Gynecology* 122, no. 1 (July 2013): 139–47. https://doi.org/10.1097/AOG.0b013e318291c235.

Hawthorne, Susan. *Accidental Intolerance: How We Stigmatize ADHD and How We Can Stop*. Oxford University Press, 2013.

"Health-Related SDGs." 2017. http://vizhub.healthdata.org/sdg.

Healy, B. "The Yentl Syndrome." *The New England Journal of Medicine* 325, no. 4 (July 25, 1991): 274–76. https://doi.org/10.1056/NEJM199107253250408.

Hediger, M. L., M. D. Overpeck, R. J. Kuczmarski, and W. J. Ruan. "Association between Infant Breastfeeding and Overweight in Young Children." *JAMA* 285, no. 19 (May 16, 2001): 2453–60.

Heinonen, Annu, Anna-Maija Tapper, Arto Leminen, Harri Sintonen, and Risto P. Roine. "Health-Related Quality of Life and Perception of Anxiety in Women with Abnormal Cervical Cytology Referred for Colposcopy: An Observational Study." *European Journal of Obstetrics, Gynecology, and Reproductive Biology* 169, no. 2 (July 2013): 387–91. https://doi.org/10.1016/j.ejogrb.2013.03.033.

Heitz, David. "Pelvic Exam: Preparation, Process, and More." *Healthline*, November 21, 2013. https://www.healthline.com/health/pelvic-exam.

Hellsten, C., P. G. Lindqvist, and K. Sjöström. "A Longitudinal Study of Sexual Functioning in Women Referred for Colposcopy: A 2-Year Follow Up." *BJOG: An International Journal of Obstetrics & Gynaecology* 115, no. 2 (September 28, 2007): 205–11. https://doi.org/10.1111/j.1471-0528.2007.01503.x.

Hembree, Wylie C., Peggy Cohen-Kettenis, Henriette A. Delemarre-van de Waal, Louis J. Gooren, Walter J. Meyer, Norman P. Spack, Vin Tangpricha, Victor M. Montori, and Endocrine Society. "Endocrine Treatment of Transsexual Persons: An Endocrine Society Clinical Practice Guideline." *The Journal of Clinical Endocrinology and Metabolism* 94, no. 9 (September 2009): 3132–54. https://doi.org/10.1210/jc.2009-0345.

Henderson, Jillian T., George F. Sawaya, Maya Blum, Laura Stratton, and Cynthia C. Harper. "Pelvic Examinations and Access to Oral Hormonal Contraception:" *Obstetrics & Gynecology* 116, no. 6 (December 2010): 1257–64. https://doi.org/10.1097/AOG.0b013e3181fb540f.

Hendricks, Aart. "UN Convention on the Rights of Persons with Disabilities." *European Journal of Health Law* 14 (2007): 273.

Hendricks, Perry. "Even If the Fetus Is Not a Person, Abortion Is Immoral: The Impairment Argument." *Bioethics* 33, no. 2 (2019): 245–53. https://doi.org/10.1111/bioe.12533.

Heubner, B., M. Skeans, M. Hertz, J. Snyder, B. Kasiske, A. Israni, and M. Valapour. "Gender Differences in Access to Lung Transplant in the US After LAS Implementation.: Abstract# C2016." *Transplantation* 98 (July 2014): 803. https://doi.org/10.1097/00007890-201407151-02745.

Hickey, Kathleen T., Lynn V. Doering, Belinda Chen, Erik V. Carter, Robert R. Sciacca, David Pickham, Carmen Castillo, Nicole R. Hauser, and Barbara J. Drew. "Clinical and Gender Differences in Heart Transplant Recipients in the NEW HEART Study." *European Journal of Cardiovascular Nursing: Journal of the Working Group on Cardiovascu-*

lar Nursing of the European Society of Cardiology 16, no. 3 (2017): 222–29. https://doi.org/10.1177/1474515116651178.

Hill, B. Jessie. "The Constitutional Right to Make Medical Treatment Decisions: A Tale of Two Doctrines." *Texas Law Review* 86 (December 2007): 70.

Hill, Holly A. "Vaccination Coverage Among Children Aged 19–35 Months — United States, 2016." *MMWR. Morbidity and Mortality Weekly Report* 66 (2017). https://doi.org/10.15585/mmwr.mm6643a3.

Hoffman, Jan. "Estimate of U.S. Transgender Population Doubles to 1.4 Million Adults." *The New York Times*, June 30, 2016, sec. Health. https://www.nytimes.com/2016/07/01/health/transgender-population.html.

Hoffmann, Diane E., and Anita J. Tarzian. "The Girl Who Cried Pain: A Bias Against Women in the Treatment of Pain." SSRN Scholarly Paper. Rochester, NY: Social Science Research Network, 2001. https://papers.ssrn.com/abstract=383803.

Holmes, M. M., H. S. Resnick, D. G. Kilpatrick, and C. L. Best. "Rape-Related Pregnancy: Estimates and Descriptive Characteristics from a National Sample of Women." *American Journal of Obstetrics and Gynecology* 175, no. 2 (August 1996): 320–24; discussion 324-325.

hooks, bell. *Ain't I a Woman: Black Women and Feminism*. South End Press, 1999.

———. *Feminism Is for Everybody: Passionate Politics*. South End Press, 2000.

Hope, Leah. "Woman Claims Doctor Refused to Remove IUD for Religious Reasons." ABC7 Chicago, August 22, 2016. http://abc7chicago.com/1480333/.

Hopkins, Kristine. "Are Brazilian Women Really Choosing to Deliver by Cesarean?" *Social Science & Medicine* 51, no. 5 (September 1, 2000): 725–40. https://doi.org/10.1016/S0277-9536(99)00480-3.

Howard, Dana. "The Medical Surrogate as Fiduciary Agent." *The Journal of Law, Medicine & Ethics* 45, no. 3 (September 1, 2017): 402–20. https://doi.org/10.1177/1073110517737541.

Howe-Heyman, Abigail, and Melanie Lutenbacher. "The Baby-Friendly Hospital Initiative as an Intervention to Improve Breastfeeding Rates: A Review of the Literature." *Journal of Midwifery & Women's Health* 61, no. 1 (January 22, 2016): 77–102. https://doi.org/10.1111/jmwh.12376.

Hsieh, Paul. "Pelvic Exams On Anesthetized Women Without Consent: A Troubling And Outdated Practice." *Forbes*, May 14, 2018. https://www.forbes.com/sites/paulhsieh/2018/05/14/pelvic-exams-on-anesthetized-women-without-consent-a-troubling-and-outdated-practice/.

Humer, Caroline, and Caroline Copley. "FOCUS-U.S. Seeks to Cut Dialysis Costs with More Home Care versus Clinics." CNBC, March 4, 2019. https://www.cnbc.com/2019/03/04/reuters-america-focus-u-s-seeks-to-cut-dialysis-costs-with-more-home-care-versus-clinics.html.

Hurd, Heidi M. "The Moral Magic of Consent." *Legal Theory* 2, no. 2 (June 1996): 121–46. https://doi.org/10.1017/S1352325200000434.

Hursthouse, Rosalind. *On Virtue Ethics*. Oxford University Press US, 1999.

Iati, Marisa, and Deanna Paul. "Everything You Need to Know about the Abortion Ban News." *The Washington Post*, May 17, 2019, sec. Health. https://www.washingtonpost.com/health/2019/05/17/havent-been-following-abortion-ban-news-heres-everything-you-need-know/.

II, Vann R. Newkirk. "A Generation of Bad Blood." *The Atlantic*, June 17, 2016. https://www.theatlantic.com/politics/archive/2016/06/tuskegee-study-medical-distrust-research/487439/.

Ingall, Marjorie. *Mamaleh Knows Best: What Jewish Mothers Do to Raise Successful, Creative, Empathetic, Independent Children*. Harmony, 2016.

Institute of Medicine (US) Committee on Advancing Pain Research, Care, and Education. *Relieving Pain in America: A Blueprint for Transforming Prevention, Care, Education, and Research*. The National Academies Collection: Reports Funded by National Institutes of Health. Washington (DC): National Academies Press (US), 2011. http://www.ncbi.nlm.nih.gov/books/NBK91497/.

Institute of Medicine (US) Committee on Unintended Pregnancy, Sarah S. Brown, and Leon Eisenberg, editors. *Consequences of Unintended Pregnancy*. National Academies Press (US), 1995. https://www.ncbi.nlm.nih.gov/books/NBK232137/.

International Collaboration of Epidemiological Studies of Cervical Cancer, Paul Appleby, Valerie Beral, Amy Berrington de González, Didier Colin, Silvia Franceschi, Adrian Goodhill, et al. "Cervical Cancer and Hormonal Contraceptives: Collaborative Reanalysis of Individual Data for 16,573 Women with Cervical Cancer and 35,509 Women without Cervical Cancer from 24 Epidemiological Studies." *The Lancet* (London, England) 370, no. 9599 (November 10, 2007): 1609–21. https://doi.org/10.1016/S0140-6736(07)61684-5.

International Covenant on Civil and Political Rights, G.A. Res. 2200A (XXI), U.N. GAOR, 21st Sess., Supp. No. 16, at 52, U.N. Doc.A/6316 (1966), 999 U.N.T.S. 171 § (1966). https://www.un.org/en/development/desa/population/migration/generalassembly/docs/globalcompact/A_RES_2200A(XXI)_civil.pdf.

Iodice, S., M. Barile, N. Rotmensz, I. Feroce, B. Bonanni, P. Radice, L. Bernard, P. Maisonneuve, and S. Gandini. "Oral Contraceptive Use and Breast or Ovarian Cancer Risk in BRCA1/2 Carriers: A Meta-Analysis." *European Journal of Cancer* (Oxford, England: 1990) 46, no. 12 (August 2010): 2275–84. https://doi.org/10.1016/j.ejca.2010.04.018.

Irwin, T. H. "Theory and Common Sense in Greek Philosophy." In *How Should One Live?: Essays on the Virtues*, edited by Roger Crisp. Oxford University Press, USA, 1998.

Isaacs, Tracy. "Feminism and Agency." *Canadian Journal of Philosophy* 32, no. sup1 (January 2002): 129–54. https://doi.org/10.1080/00455091.2002.10717585.

"It Happened to Me: Problems with Breastfeeding Triggered My Postpartum Depression." *xoJane: Women's Lifestyle & Community Site*, November 21, 2014. https://www.xojane.com/it-happened-to-me/breastfeeding-postpartum-depression.

Iversen, Lisa, Selvaraj Sivasubramaniam, Amanda J. Lee, Shona Fielding, and Philip C. Hannaford. "Lifetime Cancer Risk and Combined Oral Contraceptives: The Royal College of General Practitioners' Oral Contraception Study." *American Journal of Obstetrics and Gynecology* 216, no. 6 (2017): 580.e1-580.e9. https://doi.org/10.1016/j.ajog.2017.02.002.

Jafari, Mahtab, Ramin Ebrahimi, Mastaneh Ahmadi-Kashani, Harry Balian, and Mohammad Bashir. "Efficacy of Alternate-Day Dosing versus Daily Dosing of Atorvastatin." *Journal of Cardiovascular Pharmacology and Therapeutics* 8, no. 2 (June 2003): 123–26. https://doi.org/10.1177/107424840300800205.

Jagsi, Reshma, Kent A. Griffith, Rochelle Jones, Chithra R. Perumalswami, Peter Ubel, and Abigail Stewart. "Sexual Harassment and Discrimination Experiences of Academic Medical Faculty." *JAMA* 315, no. 19 (May 17, 2016): 2120–21. https://doi.org/10.1001/jama.2016.2188.

Jamison, Leslie. "Grand Unified Theory of Female Pain." *VQR Online*, Spring 2014. http://www.vqronline.org/essays-articles/2014/04/grand-unified-theory-female-pain.

Janssen, Patricia A., Lee Saxell, Lesley A. Page, Michael C. Klein, Robert M. Liston, and Shoo K. Lee. "Outcomes of Planned Home Birth with Registered Midwife versus Planned Hospital Birth with Midwife or Physician." *CMAJ: Canadian Medical Association Journal* 181, no. 6–7 (September 2009): 377–83. https://doi.org/10.1503/cmaj.081869.

Jatlaoui, Tara C. "Abortion Surveillance — United States, 2015." *MMWR*. Surveillance Summaries 67 (2018). https://doi.org/10.15585/mmwr.ss6713a1.

Jefferson, Thomas. "Thomas Jefferson to Edward Carrington," January 16, 1787.

Jena, Anupam B., Dhruv Khullar, Oliver Ho, Andrew R. Olenski, and Daniel M. Blumenthal. "Sex Differences in Academic Rank in US Medical Schools in 2014." *JAMA* 314, no. 11 (September 15, 2015): 1149–58. https://doi.org/10.1001/jama.2015.10680.

Jena, Anupam B., Andrew R. Olenski, and Daniel M. Blumenthal. "Sex Differences in Physician Salary in US Public Medical Schools." *JAMA Internal Medicine* 176, no. 9 (September 1, 2016): 1294–1304. https://doi.org/10.1001/jamainternmed.2016.3284.

Jena, Anupam B., Seth Seabury, Darius Lakdawalla, and Amitabh Chandra. "Malpractice Risk According to Physician Specialty." *New England Journal of Medicine* 365, no. 7 (August 18, 2011): 629–36. https://doi.org/10.1056/NEJMsa1012370.

Jha, Ashish K., Paul D. Varosy, Alka M. Kanaya, Donald B. Hunninghake, Mark A. Hlatky, David D. Waters, Curt D. Furberg, and Michael G. Shlipak. "Differences in Medical Care and Disease Outcomes Among Black and White Women With Heart Disease." *Circulation* 108, no. 9 (September 2, 2003): 1089–94. https://doi.org/10.1161/01.CIR.0000085994.38132.E5.

Jiang, Hong, Xu Qian, Guillermo Carroli, and Paul Garner. "Selective versus Routine Use of Episiotomy for Vaginal Birth." *The Cochrane Database of Systematic Reviews* 2 (08 2017): CD000081. https://doi.org/10.1002/14651858.CD000081.pub3.

Jindal, Rahul M., John J. Ryan, Imran Sajjad, Madhukiran H. Murthy, and Lyndsay S. Baines. "Kidney Transplantation and Gender Disparity." *American Journal of Nephrology* 25, no. 5 (October 2005): 474–83. https://doi.org/10.1159/000087920.

Joelving, Frederik. "Doctors Don't Always Take Their Own Advice: Survey." Reuters, April 12, 2011. http://www.reuters.com/article/us-doctors-advice-life-idUSTRE73B0IZ20110412.

Johnson, Ben. "Science Communication: The Dangers of Oversimplifying Microbiome Studies." npj Biofilms and Microbiomes Community, October 7, 2016. https://npjbiofilmscommunity.nature.com/users/17778-ben-johnson/posts/12600-q-a-with-lauren-freeman-and-saray-ayala-the-dangers-of-oversimplification-in-microbiome-research.

Jones, Jo, William Mosher, and Kimberly Daniels. "Current Contraceptive Use in the United States, 2006–2010, and Changes in Patterns of Use Since 1995." *National Health Statistics Reports* 60 (October 18, 2012).

Jones, Rachel K. "Beyond Birth Control: The Overlooked Benefits Of Oral Contraceptive Pills." Guttmacher Institute, February 25, 2011. https://www.guttmacher.org/report/beyond-birth-control-overlooked-benefits-oral-contraceptive-pills.

Jørgensen, Karsten Juhl, and Peter C Gøtzsche. "Content of Invitations for Publicly Funded Screening Mammography." *BMJ : British Medical Journal* 332, no. 7540 (March 4, 2006): 538–41.

Jung, Courtney. "Overselling Breast-Feeding." *The New York Times*, January 19, 2018, sec. Opinion. https://www.nytimes.com/2015/10/18/opinion/sunday/overselling-breast-feeding.html.

Jütte, Robert. *Contraception: A History*. 1 edition. Cambridge ; Malden, MA: Polity, 2008.

Kahn, Samantha. "The End of Gender Rating: Women's Insurance Under the ACA." *Wharton Public Policy Initative*, August 4, 2015. https://publicpolicy.wharton.upenn.edu/live/news/819-the-end-of-gender-rating-womens-insurance-under.

Kaiser Health News. "How One Hospital Brought Its C-Section Rate Down Fast." US News & World Report. May 9, 2015. https://health.usnews.com/health-news/hospital-of-tomorrow/articles/2015/05/09/how-one-hospital-brought-its-c-section-rate-down-fast.

Kant, Immanuel. *Groundwork of the Metaphysics of Morals*. Edited by Mary Gregor. Cambridge University Press, 1998.

Kaptchuk, Ted J., Elizabeth Friedlander, John M. Kelley, M. Norma Sanchez, Efi Kokkotou, Joyce P. Singer, Magda Kowalczykowski, Franklin G. Miller, Irving Kirsch, and Anthony J. Lembo. "Placebos without Deception: A Randomized Controlled Trial in Irritable Bowel Syndrome." *PLOS ONE* 5, no. 12 (December 22, 2010): e15591. https://doi.org/10.1371/journal.pone.0015591.

Katz, Jay. "Informed Consent - Must It Remain a Fairy Tale?" *Journal of Contemporary Health Law and Policy* 10 (1994): 69.

Kavilanz, Parija. "The Gender Pay Gap for Women Doctors Is Big—and Getting Worse." CNN Money, March 14, 2018. https://money.cnn.com/2018/03/14/news/economy/gender-pay-gap-doctors/index.html.

Kaye, Julia, Brigitte Amiri, Louise Melling, and Jennifer Dalven. "Health Care Denied." American Civil Liberties Union. May 2016. https://www.aclu.org/report/report-health-care-denied.

Kazley, Abby S, Kit N. Simpson, Kenneth D. Chavin, and Prabhakar Baliga. "Barriers Facing Patients Referred for Kidney Transplant Cause Loss to Follow-Up." *Kidney International* 82, no. 9 (November 2012): 1018–23. https://doi.org/10.1038/ki.2012.255.

Kenagy, Gretchen P. "Transgender Health: Findings from Two Needs Assessment Studies in Philadelphia." *Health & Social Work* 30, no. 1 (February 1, 2005): 19–26. https://doi.org/10.1093/hsw/30.1.19.

Kiesel, Laura. "Women and Pain: Disparities in Experience and Treatment." *Harvard Health Blog*, October 9, 2017. https://www.health.harvard.edu/blog/women-and-pain-disparities-in-experience-and-treatment-2017100912562.

Kim, Catherine, Timothy P. Hofer, and Eve A. Kerr. "Review of Evidence and Explanations for Suboptimal Screening and Treatment of Dyslipidemia in Women." *Journal of General Internal Medicine* 18, no. 10 (October 1, 2003): 854–63. https://doi.org/10.1046/j.1525-1497.2003.20910.x.

King, Christopher J., and Yanique Redwood. "The Health Care Institution, Population Health and Black Lives." *Journal of the National Medical Association* 108, no. 2 (June 1, 2016): 131–36. https://doi.org/10.1016/j.jnma.2016.04.002.

King, Jr., Martin Luther. "Letter from the Birmingham Jail." April 16, 1963.

Kisa, Sezer, and Simge Zeyneloğlu. "Opinions of Women towards Cesarean Delivery and Priority Issues of Care in the Postpartum Period." *Applied Nursing Research* 30 (May 1, 2016): 70–75. https://doi.org/10.1016/j.apnr.2015.11.004.

Kittay, Eva Feder. "At the Margins of Moral Personhood." *Ethics* 116, no. 1 (2005): 100–131. https://doi.org/10.1086/454366.

Kling, Juliana M., Suneela Vegunta, Mina Al-Badri, Stephanie S. Faubion, Heather E. Fields, Amit A. Shah, Mark R. Wallace, et al. "Routine Pelvic Examinations: A Descriptive Cross-Sectional Survey of Women's Attitudes and Beliefs after New Guidelines." *Preventive Medicine* 94 (January 1, 2017): 60–64. https://doi.org/10.1016/j.ypmed.2016.11.007.

Ko, Lisa. "Unwanted Sterilization and Eugenics Programs in the United States." PBS.org, *Independent Lens* (blog). January 29, 2016. http://www.pbs.org/independentlens/blog/unwanted-sterilization-and-eugenics-programs-in-the-united-states/.

Kola, Susanna, and Jane C. Walsh. "Patients' Psychological Reactions to Colposcopy and LLETZ Treatment for Cervical Intraepithelial Neoplasia." *European Journal of Obstetrics, Gynecology, and Reproductive Biology* 146, no. 1 (September 2009): 96–99. https://doi.org/10.1016/j.ejogrb.2009.05.005.

Koliopoulos, George, Victoria N. Nyaga, Nancy Santesso, Andrew Bryant, Pierre P. L. Martin-Hirsch, Reem A. Mustafa, Holger Schünemann, Evangelos Paraskevaidis, and Marc Arbyn. "Cytology versus HPV Testing for Cervical Cancer Screening in the General Population." *Cochrane Database of Systematic Reviews*, no. 8 (2017). https://doi.org/10.1002/14651858.CD008587.pub2.

Kozhimannil, Katy B., Judy Jou, Dwenda K. Gjerdingen, and Patricia M. McGovern. "Access to Workplace Accommodations to Support Breastfeeding after Passage of the Affordable Care Act." *Women's Health Issues* 26, no. 1 (January 1, 2016): 6–13. https://doi.org/10.1016/j.whi.2015.08.002.

Kozma, Melissa M., and Jeanine Weekes Schroer. "Purposeful Nonsense, Intersectionality and the Mission to Save Black Babies." In *Why Race and Gender Still Matter: An Intersectional Approach*. Routledge, 2015.

Kramer, M., L. Matush, I. Vanilovich, R. Piatt, and B. Mazer. "Does Breastfeeding Help Prevent Asthma and Allergy? Evidence from a Randomized Trial in Belarus." *American Journal of Epidemiology* 163, no. suppl_11 (June 1, 2006): S85–S85. https://doi.org/10.1093/aje/163.suppl_11.S85-d.

Krasowski, Matthew D., and Katie L. Imborek. "Obstacles in Transgender Healthcare." *OUPblog*, August 22, 2016. https://blog.oup.com/2016/08/obstacles-transgender-healthcare/.

Krishnamurthy, Meena. "Featured Philosopher: Meena Krishnamurthy." *Philosopher* (blog), June 3, 2016. https://politicalphilosopher.net/2016/06/03/meenakrishnamurthy/.

Krogstad, Jens Manuel. "More Women than Men Earn the Federal Minimum Wage." *Pew Research Center* (blog), May 5, 2014. http://www.pewresearch.org/fact-tank/2014/05/05/more-women-than-men-earn-the-federal-minimum-wage/.

Kucirka, Lauren M, Tanjala S Purnell, and Dorry L Segev. "Improving Access to Kidney Transplantation: Referral Is Not Enough." *JAMA* 314, no. 6 (August 11, 2015): 565–67. https://doi.org/10.1001/jama.2015.8932.

Kukla, Rebecca. *Mass Hysteria: Medicine, Culture, and Mothers' Bodies*. Rowman & Littlefield, 2005.

———. "Measuring Mothering." *International Journal of Feminist Approaches to Bioethics* 1, no. 1 (2008): 67–90.

Laqueur, Thomas Walter. *Making Sex: Body and Gender from the Greeks to Freud*. Harvard University Press, 1992.

Leary, Warren E. "Routine Electronic Monitoring Of Fetuses Is Challenged in Study." *The New York Times*, October 25, 1995, sec. U.S. https://www.nytimes.com/1995/10/25/us/routine-electronic-monitoring-of-fetuses-is-challenged-in-study.html.

Lee Mortensen, Gitte, and Anny Lisbeth Adeler. "Qualitative Study of Women's Anxiety and Information Needs after a Diagnosis of Cervical Dysplasia." *Journal of Public Health* 18, no. 5 (October 1, 2010): 473–82. https://doi.org/10.1007/s10389-010-0330-1.

Lee, Susan J., Henry J. Peter Ralston, Eleanor A. Drey, John Colin Partridge, and Mark A. Rosen. "Fetal Pain: A Systematic Multidisciplinary Review of the Evidence." *JAMA Network* 294, no. 8 (August 24, 2005): 947–54. https://doi.org/doi:10.1001.

"Legal Interventions During Pregnancy: Court-Ordered Medical Treatments and Legal Penalties for Potentially Harmful Behavior by Pregnant Women." *JAMA* 264, no. 20 (November 28, 1990): 2663–70. https://doi.org/10.1001/jama.1990.03450200071034.

Leonard, Kimberly. "Obama Administration: Insurance Companies Must Cover Birth Control." *US News & World Report*. May 11, 2015. http://www.usnews.com/news/articles/2015/05/11/obama-administration-insurance-companies-must-cover-birth-control.

Lewin, Tamar. "Despite Criticism, Fetal Monitors Are Likely to Remain in Wide Use." *The New York Times*, March 27, 1988, sec. U.S. https://www.nytimes.com/1988/03/27/us/despite-criticism-fetal-monitors-are-likely-to-remain-in-wide-use.html.

Lichtman, Judith H., Erica C. Leifheit-Limson, Emi Watanabe, Norrina B. Allen, Brian Garavalia, Linda S. Garavalia, John A. Spertus, Harlan M. Krumholz, and Leslie A. Curry. "Symptom Recognition and Healthcare Experiences of Young Women With Acute Myocardial Infarction." *Circulation: Cardiovascular Quality and Outcomes*, January 1, 2015, CIRCOUTCOMES.114.001612. https://doi.org/10.1161/CIRCOUTCOMES.114.001612.

Lili, Wu. "For Chinese Moms, Birth Means 30 Days In Pajamas." NPR.org, July 20, 2011. https://www.npr.org/2011/07/20/138536998/for-chinese-moms-birth-means-30-days-in-pajamas.

Lindemann, Hilde. "The Woman Question in Medicine: An Update." *Hastings Center Report* 42, no. 3 (April 23, 2012): 38–45. https://doi.org/10.1002/hast.34.

Linder, Jeffrey A., Jason N. Doctor, Mark W. Friedberg, Harry Reyes Nieva, Caroline Birks, Daniella Meeker, and Craig R. Fox. "Time of Day and the Decision to Prescribe Antibiotics." *JAMA Internal Medicine* 174, no. 12 (December 1, 2014): 2029–31. https://doi.org/10.1001/jamainternmed.2014.5225.

Linder, Jeffrey A, and Daniel E Singer. "Desire for Antibiotics and Antibiotic Prescribing for Adults with Upper Respiratory Tract Infections." *Journal of General Internal Medicine* 18, no. 10 (October 2003): 795–801. https://doi.org/10.1046/j.1525-1497.2003.21101.x.

Lindgren, Helena E, Åsa Brink, and Marie Klinberg-Allvin. "Fear Causes Tears - Perineal Injuries in Home Birth Settings. A Swedish Interview Study." *BMC Pregnancy and Childbirth* 11 (January 18, 2011): 6. https://doi.org/10.1186/1471-2393-11-6.

Little, Margaret Olivia. "The Moral Permissibility of Abortion." In *Contemporary Debates in Applied Ethics*, eds. Andrew Cohen and Christopher Wellman (Blackwell Publishing, 2005)

Lleo, Ana, Pier Maria Battezzati, Carlo Selmi, M. Eric Gershwin, and Mauro Podda. "Is Autoimmunity a Matter of Sex?" *Autoimmunity Reviews*, Special Issue: Predictive and diagnostic autoantibodies, 7, no. 8 (September 1, 2008): 626–30. https://doi.org/10.1016/j.autrev.2008.06.009.

Lo Sasso, Anthony T., Michael R. Richards, Chiu-Fang Chou, and Susan E. Gerber. "The $16,819 Pay Gap For Newly Trained Physicians: The Unexplained Trend Of Men Earn-ing More Than Women." *Health Affairs* 30, no. 2 (February 1, 2011): 193–201. https://doi.org/10.1377/hlthaff.2010.0597.

Locke, John. *Second Treatise of Government*. Edited by C. B. Macpherson. Indianapolis, Ind: Hackett Publishing Company, Inc., 1980.

Lorde, Audre. *A Burst of Light: And Other Essays*. Mineola, New York: Ixia Press, 2017.

———. *Sister Outsider: Essays and Speeches*. Reprint edition. Berkeley, Calif: Crossing Press, 2007.

Luchowski, Alicia T., Britta L. Anderson, Michael L. Power, Greta B. Raglan, Eve Espey, and Jay Schulkin. "Obstetrician–Gynecologists and Contraception: Long-Acting Reversible Contraception Practices and Education." *Contraception* 89, no. 6 (June 1, 2014): 578–83. https://doi.org/10.1016/j.contraception.2014.02.004.

Luker, Kristin. *Abortion and the Politics of Motherhood*. University of California Press, 1985.

Lyons, David. *Forms and Limits of Utilitarianism*. Clarendon Press, 1965.

MacDorman, Marian F., and T.J. Mathews. "The Challenge of Infant Mortality: Have We Reached a Plateau?" *Public Health Reports* 124, no. 5 (September 1, 2009): 670–81. https://doi.org/10.1177/003335490912400509.

MacDorman, Marian F., Fay Menacker, and Eugene Declercq. "Cesarean Birth in the United States: Epidemiology, Trends, and Outcomes." *Clinics in Perinatology* 35, no. 2 (June 2008): 293–307, v. https://doi.org/10.1016/j.clp.2008.03.007.

Machado, Carmen Maria. "The Husband Stitch." *Granta* (blog), October 28, 2014. https://granta.com/the-husband-stitch/.

MacKinnon, Catharine A. "Prostitution and Civil Rights." *Michigan Journal of Gender and Law* 1, no. 1 (1993): 21.

Magoon, Christopher. "Women Are More Likely To Die Waiting For An Organ." *The Huffington Post*, May 10, 2018. https://www.huffingtonpost.com/entry/women-organ-transplants-disparity_us_5aec8975e4b0c4f193223b87.

Mahowald, Mary Briody. *Women and Children in Health Care: An Unequal Majority*. Oxford University Press, 1996.

Main, Elliott K., Valerie Cape, Anisha Abreo, Julie Vasher, Amanda Woods, Andrew Carpenter, and Jeffrey B. Gould. "Reduction of Severe Maternal Morbidity from Hemorrhage Using a State Perinatal Quality Collaborative." *American Journal of Obstetrics and Gynecology* 216, no. 3 (March 2017): 298.e1-298.e11. https://doi.org/10.1016/j.ajog.2017.01.017.

Mak, Tim. "How Michael Cohen Protects Trump By Making Legal Threats." NPR.org. May 31, 2018. https://www.npr.org/2018/05/31/615843930/listen-how-michael-cohen-protects-trump-by-making-legal-threats.

Malacrida, Claudia, and Tiffany Boulton. "Women's Perceptions of Childbirth 'Choices': Competing Discourses of Motherhood, Sexuality, and Selflessness." *Gender & Society* 26, no. 5 (October 1, 2012): 748–72. https://doi.org/10.1177/0891243212452630.

Maloni, Judith A. "Lack of Evidence for Prescription of Antepartum Bed Rest." *Expert Review of Obstetrics & Gynecology* 6, no. 4 (July 1, 2011): 385–93. https://doi.org/10.1586/eog.11.28.

Mangan, Joseph T. "An Historical Analysis of the Principle of Double Effect." *Theological Studies* 10, no. 1 (1949): 41–61.

Manninen, Bertha. *Pro-Life, Pro-Choice: Shared Values in the Abortion Debate*. Vanderbilt University Press, 2014.

———. *"The Pro-Choice Pro-Lifer:" In Coming to Life: Philosophies of Pregnancy, Childbirth and Mothering*, 171–92. Fordham University Press, 2013. http://www.jstor.org.ezproxy.umsl.edu/stable/j.ctt1c5ck2p.13.

Marquis, Don. "Why Abortion Is Immoral." *The Journal of Philosophy* 86, no. 4 (April 1989): 183–202.

Marshall, Randall C., Maria Kayanan, and Diana Kasdan. "Burton v. State of Florida - ACLU Amicus Brief." July 31, 2009. https://www.aclu.org/legal-document/burton-v-state-florida-aclu-amicus-brief.

Martin, Michelle. "Decades Later, Drugs Didn't Hold 'Crack Babies' Back." NPR.org, July 31, 2013, sec. Tell Me More. https://www.npr.org/templates/story/story.php?

storyId=207292639.
Maserejian, Nancy N., Carol L. Link, Karen L. Lutfey, Lisa D. Marceau, and John B. McKinlay. "Disparities in Physicians' Interpretations of Heart Disease Symptoms by Patient Gender: Results of a Video Vignette Factorial Experiment." *Journal of Women's Health* 18, no. 10 (October 2009): 1661–67. https://doi.org/10.1089/jwh.2008.1007.
Maslow, A. H. "A Theory of Human Motivation." *Psychological Review* 50, no. 4 (1948): 370–96.
May, Larry. "Challenging Medical Authority The Refusal of Treatment by Christian Scientists." *Hastings Center Report* 25, no. 1 (1995): 15–21. https://doi.org/10.2307/3562485.
———. *Crimes Against Humanity: A Normative Account*. Cambridge University Press, 2005.
Mayo Clinic. "Addressing the Challenges of Transgender Health Care." September 7, 2016. http://www.mayoclinic.org/medical-professionals/clinical-updates/endocrinology/addressing-the-challenges-of-transgender-health-care.
———. "Pap Smear," July 25, 2019. http://www.mayoclinic.org/tests-procedures/pap-smear/basics/why-its-done/prc-20013038.
Mayo Clinic Staff. "Coping with Bed Rest and Pelvic Rest during Pregnancy." Mayo Clinic, March 31, 2017. http://www.mayoclinic.org/healthy-lifestyle/pregnancy-week-by-week/in-depth/pregnancy/art-20048007.
Mazure, Carolyn M., and Daniel P. Jones. "Twenty Years and Still Counting: Including Women as Participants and Studying Sex and Gender in Biomedical Research." *BMC Women's Health* 15 (October 26, 2015). https://doi.org/10.1186/s12905-015-0251-9.
McCall, Christina, David Grimes, and Anne Lyerly. "'Therapeutic' Bed Rest in Pregnancy: Unethical and Unsupported by Data." *Obstetrics & Gynecology* 121, no. 6 (June 1, 2013): 1305–8. https://doi.org/10.1097/AOG.0b013e318293f12f.
McClung, Nancy M., Julia W. Gargano, Nancy M. Bennett, Linda M. Niccolai, Nasreen Abdullah, Marie R. Griffin, Ina U. Park, et al. "Trends in Human Papillomavirus Vaccine Types 16 and 18 in Cervical Precancers, 2008–2014." *Cancer Epidemiology and Prevention Biomarkers*, February 21, 2019. https://doi.org/10.1158/1055-9965.EPI-18-0885.
McCourt, Chris, Jane Weaver, Helen Statham, Sarah Beake, Jenny Gamble, and Debra K. Creedy. "Elective Cesarean Section and Decision Making: A Critical Review of the Literature." *Birth* (Berkeley, Calif.) 34, no. 1 (March 2007): 65–79. https://doi.org/10.1111/j.1523-536X.2006.00147.x.
McKinnon, Rachel. "Gender Transition Isn't a Whim, so Why the Mistrust?" *The Conversation*, November 4, 2013. http://theconversation.com/gender-transition-isnt-a-whim-so-why-the-mistrust-19783.
———. "Trouble Making the Change: My Transgender Experience." *The Conversation*, September 26, 2013. http://theconversation.com/trouble-making-the-change-my-transgender-experience-18527.
McLaren, Margaret A. "Feminist Ethics: Care as a Virtue." In *Feminists Doing Ethics*, edited by Peggy DesAutels and JoAnne Waugh, 101–118. Rowman & Littlefield, 2001.
McLeod, Carolyn. "How to Distinguish Autonomy from Integrity." *Canadian Journal of Philosophy* 35, no. 1 (March 2005): 107–33.
McMurray, Richard J., Oscar W. Clarke, John A. Barrasso, Dexanne B. Clohan, Charles H. Epps, John Glasson, Robert McQuillan, et al. "Gender Disparities in Clinical Decision Making." *JAMA* 266, no. 4 (July 24, 1991): 559–62. https://doi.org/10.1001/jama.1991.03470040123034.
McNicholas, Colleen, Madden Tessa, Gina Secura, and Jeffrey F. Peipert. "The Contraceptive CHOICE Project Round Up: What We Did and What We Learned." *Clinical Obstetrics and Gynecology* 57, no. 4 (December 2014): 635–43. https://doi.org/10.1097/GRF.0000000000000070.
"Medscape OB/GYN Compensation Report: 2011 Results." *Medscape*, 2011. http://www.medscape.com/features/slideshow/compensation/2011/womenshealth.
Melnick, Meredith. "Are Doctors' Exams a Barrier to Birth Control?" *Time*. December 6, 2010. http://healthland.time.com/2010/12/06/why-annual-exams-shouldnt-be-required-to-get-birth-control-pills/.

Melo, Inês, Leila Katz, Isabela Coutinho, and Melania Maria Amorim. "Selective Episiotomy vs. Implementation of a Non Episiotomy Protocol: A Randomized Clinical Trial." *Reproductive Health* 11 (August 14, 2014): 66. https://doi.org/10.1186/1742-4755-11-66.

Mencimer, Stephanie. "Holding Birth Control Hostage." *Mother Jones*, April 30, 2012. http://www.motherjones.com/politics/2012/04/doctors-holding-birth-control-hostage.

Merz, C. Noel Bairey. "The Yentl Syndrome Is Alive and Well." *European Heart Journal* 32, no. 11 (June 1, 2011): 1313–15. https://doi.org/10.1093/eurheartj/ehr083.

Merz, C. Noel Bairey. "The Yentl Syndrome and Gender Inequality in Ischemic HD." August 2011. https://www.healio.com/cardiology/news/print/cardiology-today/%7B7cff01d6-0b82-4d2e-a3c9-aea61a5c61ad%7D/the-yentl-syndrome-and-gender-inequality-in-ischemic-hd.

Michels, Kara A., Ruth M. Pfeiffer, Louise A. Brinton, and Britton Trabert. "Modification of the Associations Between Duration of Oral Contraceptive Use and Ovarian, Endometrial, Breast, and Colorectal Cancers." *JAMA Oncology* 4, no. 4 (April 1, 2018): 516–21. https://doi.org/10.1001/jamaoncol.2017.4942.

Mill, John Stuart. *On Liberty*. Edited by Elizabeth Rapaport. Hackett Pub Co, 1978.

———. *Utilitarianism*. Edited by George Sher. 2nd ed. Hackett Publishing Company, Inc., 2002.

Miller, Claire Cain. "As Women Take Over a Male-Dominated Field, the Pay Drops." *The New York Times*, March 18, 2016, sec. Economic View. https://www.nytimes.com/2016/03/20/upshot/as-women-take-over-a-male-dominated-field-the-pay-drops.html.

Minami, Christina A., Catherine R. Sheils, Emily Pavey, Jeanette W. Chung, Jonah J. Stulberg, David D. Odell, Anthony D. Yang, David J. Bentrem, and Karl Y. Bilimoria. "Association Between State Medical Malpractice Environment and Postoperative Outcomes in the United States." *Journal of the American College of Surgeons* 224, no. 3 (March 1, 2017): 310-318.e2. https://doi.org/10.1016/j.jamcollsurg.2016.12.012.

Mindikoglu, Ayse L., Arie Regev, Stephen L. Seliger, and Laurence S. Magder. "Gender Disparity in Liver Transplant Waiting-List Mortality: The Importance of Kidney Function." *Liver Transplantation: Official Publication of the American Association for the Study of Liver Diseases and the International Liver Transplantation Society* 16, no. 10 (October 2010): 1147–57. https://doi.org/10.1002/lt.22121.

Miner, Adam S., Arnold Milstein, Stephen Schueller, Roshini Hegde, Christina Mangurian, and Eleni Linos. "Smartphone-Based Conversational Agents and Responses to Questions About Mental Health, Interpersonal Violence, and Physical Health." *JAMA Internal Medicine* 176, no. 5 (May 1, 2016): 619–25. https://doi.org/10.1001/jamainternmed.2016.0400.

Minkoff, Howard, and Lynn M. Paltrow. "The Rights of 'Unborn Children' and the Value of Pregnant Women." *Hastings Center Report* 36, no. 2 (March 4, 2006): 26–28. https://doi.org/10.1353/hcr.2006.0031.

Miranda, Leticia, Vince Dixon, and Cecilia Reyes. "How States Handle Drug Use During Pregnancy." *ProPublica*. September 30, 2015. https://projects.propublica.org/graphics/maternity-drug-policies-by-state.

Mishori, Ranit. "Why Doctors Should Study Human Rights." *The Washington Post*, December 10, 2014. https://www.washingtonpost.com/posteverything/wp/2014/12/10/why-doctors-should-study-human-rights/?utm_term=.cad71603ff0b.

Moravcsik, Julius M. "The Role of Virtue in Alternatives to Kantian and Utilitarian Ethics." *Philosophia* 20, no. 1–2 (July 1990): 33–48. https://doi.org/10.1007/BF02382583.

"More Women Than Men Enrolled in U.S. Medical Schools in 2017." December 18, 2017. https://news.aamc.org/press-releases/article/applicant-enrollment-2017/.

Moreno, Victor, F. Xavier Bosch, Nubia Muñoz, Chris J. L. M. Meijer, Keerti V. Shah, Jan M. M. Walboomers, Rolando Herrero, and Silvia Franceschi. "Effect of Oral Contraceptives on Risk of Cervical Cancer in Women with Human Papillomavirus Infection: The IARC Multicentric Case-Control Study." *The Lancet* 359, no. 9312 (March 2002): 1085–92. https://doi.org/10.1016/S0140-6736(02)08150-3.

Morillo-Cucci, G., and J. German. "Males with a Uterus and Fallopian Tubes, a Rare Disorder of Sexual Development." *Birth Defects* Original Article Series 7, no. 6 (May 1971): 229–31.

Morris, Jessica L., Sheri A. Lippman, Susan Philip, Kyle Bernstein, Torsten B. Neilands, and Marguerita Lightfoot. "Sexually Transmitted Infection Related Stigma and Shame Among African American Male Youth: Implications for Testing Practices, Partner Notification, and Treatment." *AIDS Patient Care and STDs* 28, no. 9 (September 1, 2014): 499–506. https://doi.org/10.1089/apc.2013.0316.

Morris, Theresa. *Cut It Out: The C-Section Epidemic in America*. NYU Press, 2016.

Morris, Theresa, and Joan H. Robinson. "Forced and Coerced Cesarean Sections in the United States." *Contexts* 16, no. 2 (May 1, 2017): 24–29. https://doi.org/10.1177/1536504217714259.

Mosca, Lori, Lawrence J. Appel, Emelia J. Benjamin, Kathy Berra, Nisha Chandra-Strobos, Rosalind P. Fabunmi, Deborah Grady, et al. "Evidence-Based Guidelines for Cardiovascular Disease Prevention in Women." *Circulation* 109, no. 5 (February 10, 2004): 672–93. https://doi.org/10.1161/01.CIR.0000114834.85476.81.

Mosca, Lori, Allison H. Linfante, Emelia J. Benjamin, Kathy Berra, Sharonne N. Hayes, Brian W. Walsh, Rosalind P. Fabunmi, Johnny Kwan, Thomas Mills, and Susan Lee Simpson. "National Study of Physician Awareness and Adherence to Cardiovascular Disease Prevention Guidelines." *Circulation* 111, no. 4 (February 1, 2005): 499–510. https://doi.org/10.1161/01.CIR.0000154568.43333.82.

Muller, Mike. "Nestlé Baby Milk Scandal Has Grown up but Not Gone Away." *The Guardian*, February 13, 2013, sec. Guardian Sustainable Business. http://www.theguardian.com/sustainable-business/nestle-baby-milk-scandal-food-industry-standards.

Mulugeta, E., M. Kassaye, and Y. Berhane. "Prevalence and Outcomes of Sexual Violence among High School Students." *Ethiopian Medical Journal* 36, no. 3 (July 1998): 167–74.

Munro, Sarah, Jude Kornelsen, Kitty Corbett, Elizabeth Wilcox, Nick Bansback, and Patricia Janssen. "Do Women Have a Choice? Care Providers' and Decision Makers' Perspectives on Barriers to Access of Health Services for Birth after a Previous Cesarean." *Birth* 44, no. 2 (December 2016): 153–60. https://doi.org/10.1111/birt.12270.

Munson, Ronald. *Intervention and Reflection*. 8th ed. Belmont, California: Thomas Wadsworth, 2008.

Munson, Ronald, and Ian Lague. *Intervention and Reflection: Basic Issues in Bioethics*. 10 edition. Boston, MA: Cengage Learning, 2016.

Murphy, Carrie. "The Husband Stitch Isn't Just a Horrifying Childbirth Myth." *Healthline*, January 24, 2018. https://www.healthline.com/health-news/husband-stitch-is-not-just-myth.

———. "Why Do So Many U.S. Hospitals Prohibit Vaginal Birth After a C-Section?" *ELLE*, December 7, 2016. https://www.elle.com/life-love/a41109/vbac-vaginal-birth-after-c-section/.

Myers, Robert P., Abdel Aziz M. Shaheen, Alexander I. Aspinall, Robert R. Quinn, and Kelly W. Burak. "Gender, Renal Function, and Outcomes on the Liver Transplant Waiting List: Assessment of Revised MELD Including Estimated Glomerular Filtration Rate." *Journal of Hepatology* 54, no. 3 (March 1, 2011): 462–70. https://doi.org/10.1016/j.jhep.2010.07.015.

Nash, Elizabeth, Rachel Benson Gold, Gwendolyn Rathbun, and Zohra Ansari-Thomas. "Laws Affecting Reproductive Health and Rights: 2015 State Policy Review." Guttmacher Institute, January 1, 2016. https://www.guttmacher.org/laws-affecting-reproductive-health-and-rights-2015-state-policy-review.

Nash, Elizabeth, Rachel Benson Gold, Lizamarie Mohammed, Zohra Ansari-Thomas, and Olivia Cappello. "Laws Affecting Reproductive Health and Rights: State Policy Trends at Midyear, 2018." Guttmacher Institute, July 31, 2018. https://www.guttmacher.org/article/2018/07/laws-affecting-reproductive-health-and-rights-state-policy-trends-midyear-2018.

National Alliance for Caregiving. "Caregiving in the U.S. 2015." *AARP Research*, June 2015. https://doi.org/10.26419/res.00062.001.

National Center for Health Statistics. "Births—Method of Delivery," February 5, 2018. https://www.cdc.gov/nchs/fastats/delivery.htm.

———. "Mortality in the United States, 2014." *Data Briefs* Number 229, December 2015. https://www.cdc.gov/nchs/data/databriefs/db229.htm.

Natri, Heini, Angela R. Garcia, Kenneth H. Buetow, Benjamin C. Trumble, and Melissa A. Wilson. "The Pregnancy Pickle: Evolved Immune Compensation Due to Pregnancy Underlies Sex Differences in Human Diseases." *Trends in Genetics* 35, no. 7 (July 1, 2019): 478–88. https://doi.org/10.1016/j.tig.2019.04.008.

Navin, Mark. "Competing Epistemic Spaces: How Social Epistemology Helps Explain and Evaluate Vaccine Denialism." *Social Theory and Practice*, May 1, 2013. https://doi.org/10.5840/soctheorpract201339214.

———. *Values and Vaccine Refusal: Hard Questions in Ethics, Epistemology, and Health Care*, 2016. http://cmich.idm.oclc.org/login?url=http://lib.myilibrary.com/detail.asp?ID=830618.

NeJaime, Douglas, and Reva B. Siegel. "Conscience Wars: Complicity-Based Conscience Claims in Religion and Politics." *The Yale Law Journal* 124, no. 7 (2015): 2516–91.

Nekvasil, Nader. "Uninsured Down Since Obamacare; Cost, Quality Still Concerns." Gallup.com. August 29, 2016. http://www.gallup.com/poll/195086/uninsured-down-obamacare-cost-quality-concerns.aspx.

Nelson, J. Lee. "HLA Relationships of Pregnancy, Microchimerism and Autoimmune Disease." *Journal of Reproductive Immunology* 52, no. 1 (October 1, 2001): 77–84. https://doi.org/10.1016/S0165-0378(01)00116-4.

"New NWLC Report: Discriminatory Health Insurance Practices Cost Women $1 Billion a Year." *NWLC* (blog), March 19, 2012. https://nwlc.org/press-releases/new-nwlc-report-discriminatory-health-insurance-practices-cost-women-1-billion-year/.

"New Report Reveals Rampant Discrimination against Transgender People by Health Providers, High HIV Rates and Widespread Lack of Access to Necessary Care." *National LGBTQ Task Force* (blog), October 13, 2010. http://www.thetaskforce.org/new-report-reveals-rampant-discrimination-against-transgender-people-by-health-providers-high-hiv-rates-and-widespread-lack-of-access-to-necessary-care-2/.

Ngo, S. T., F. J. Steyn, and P. A. McCombe. "Gender Differences in Autoimmune Disease." *Frontiers in Neuroendocrinology, Sex Differences in Neurological and Psychiatric Disorders*, 35, no. 3 (August 1, 2014): 347–69. https://doi.org/10.1016/j.yfrne.2014.04.004.

Norlock, Kathryn J. "Can't Complain." *Journal of Moral Philosophy* 15, no. 2 (2018): 117–135. https://doi.org/10.1163/17455243-20170004.

———. Miscarriage, Pregnancy Loss, and Death. Interview by Matthews Beth. 3CR Community Radio, July 19, 2018. https://drive.google.com/file/d/1DM6mhrJS-LXJ3RCKGVdcVNKOG5okjHEV/view.

Norman, Abby. *Ask Me About My Uterus: A Quest to Make Doctors Believe in Women's Pain*. New York: Nation Books, 2018.

Norrell, Laura L., Miriam Kuppermann, Michelle N. Moghadassi, and George F. Sawaya. "Women's Beliefs about the Purpose and Value of Routine Pelvic Examinations." *American Journal of Obstetrics and Gynecology* 217, no. 1 (July 1, 2017): 86.e1-86.e6. https://doi.org/10.1016/j.ajog.2016.12.031.

NSVRC. "National Sexual Violence Resource Center Info & Stats for Journalists Statistics about Sexual Vioelnce," 2015. https://www.nsvrc.org/sites/default/files/publications_nsvrc_factsheet_media-packet_statistics-about-sexual-violence_0.pdf.

Nussbaum, Martha C. "Capabilities and Human Rights." In *Global Justice and Transnational Politics: Essays on the Moral and Political Challenges of Globalization*, edited by Pablo De Greiff and Ciaran Cronin. Studies in Contemporary German Social Thought. Cambridge, Mass: MIT Press, 2002.

———. "Capabilities and Social Justice." *International Studies Review* 4, no. 2 (2002): 123–135.

———. "Judging Other Cultures: The Case of Genital Mutilation." In *Sex & Social Justice*, 118–29. New York: Oxford University Press, 1999.

———. *Sex and Social Justice*. Oxford New York Athens: Oxford University Press, 2000.

Oaklander, Mandy. "Women Doctors Are Paid $20,000 Less Than Male Doctors." *Time*, July 11, 2016. http://time.com/4398888/doctors-gender-wage-gap/.

Obama, Barack. "Read Obama's Full Remarks on Supreme Court Ruling." *US News & World Report*, June 25, 2015. https://www.usnews.com/news/articles/2015/06/25/president-barack-obamas-full-statement-on-supreme-court-affordable-care-act-ruling.

Obed, Aiman, Steffen Stern, Anwar Jarrad, and Thomas Lorf. "Six Month Abstinence Rule for Liver Transplantation in Severe Alcoholic Liver Disease Patients." *World Journal of Gastroenterology: WJG* 21, no. 14 (April 14, 2015): 4423–26. https://doi.org/10.3748/wjg.v21.i14.4423.

O'Brien, Elizabeth, and Pratheek Rebala. "Find Out How Much It Costs to Give Birth in Every State." *Time*, October 30, 2017. http://time.com/money/4995922/how-much-costs-give-birth-state/.

"Obstetrician/Gynecologist Average Salary: Medscape Compensation Report 2014." 2014. http://www.medscape.com/features/slideshow/compensation/2014/womenshealth#17.

O'Connor. Planned Parenthood of Southeastern Pennsylvania, Et Al., Petitioners 91-744 v. Robert P. Casey, Et Al., Etc. Robert P. Casey, Et Al., Etc., Petitioners 91-902, U.S. (U.S. Supreme Court 1992).

OCs OTC Working Group. "Global Oral Contraception Availability." August 1, 2019. http://ocsotc.org/wp-content/uploads/worldmap/worldmap.html.

Office for Civil Rights. "Conscience Protections for Health Care Providers." Text. HHS.gov, October 14, 2010. https://www.hhs.gov/conscience/conscience-protections/index.html.

Office of the Surgeon Genreal (US), Centers for Disease Control and Prevention (US), and Office on Women's Health (US). *Barriers to Breastfeeding in the United States*. 2011. https://www.ncbi.nlm.nih.gov/books/NBK52688/.

Ojanuga, D. "The Medical Ethics of the 'Father of Gynaecology', Dr J. Marion Sims." *Journal of Medical Ethics* 19, no. 1 (March 1993): 28–31.

Ojo, Akinlolu, and Friedrich K. Port. "Influence of Race and Gender on Related Donor Renal Transplantation Rates." *American Journal of Kidney Diseases* 22, no. 6 (December 1, 1993): 835–41. https://doi.org/10.1016/S0272-6386(12)70343-8.

O'Neill, Onora. *Autonomy and Trust in Bioethics*. Cambridge University Press, 2002. http://www.mlegal.fmed.edu.uy/archivos/be/bcc1/trust_and_autonomy.pdf.

———. "Constructivism VS. Contractualism." *Ratio* 16, no. 4 (December 2003): 319–31. https://doi.org/10.1046/j.1467-9329.2003.00226.x.

———. "Paternalism and Partial Autonomy." *Journal of Medical Ethics* 10 (1984): 173–78.

Oniscu, Gabriel C., Helen Brown, and John L. R. Forsythe. "How Great Is the Survival Advantage of Transplantation over Dialysis in Elderly Patients?" *Nephrology Dialysis Transplantation* 19, no. 4 (April 1, 2004): 945–51. https://doi.org/10.1093/ndt/gfh022.

Oreskes, Naomi, and Erik M. Conway. *Merchants of Doubt: How a Handful of Scientists Obscured the Truth on Issues from Tobacco Smoke to Global Warming*. Reprint edition. New York, NY: Bloomsbury Press, 2011.

Organ Procurement and Transplantation Network. "National Data: Transplants in the U.S. by Recipient Gender, January 1, 1988–June 30, 2018." June 30, 2018. https://optn.transplant.hrsa.gov/data/view-data-reports/national-data/#.

Organ Procurement and Transplantation Network Minority Affairs Committee. "Educational Guidance on Patient Referral to Kidney Transplantation." September 2015. https://optn.transplant.hrsa.gov/resources/guidance/educational-guidance-on-patient-referral-to-kidney-transplantation/.

Ortberg, Daniel Mallory. "Help! My Idiot Husband Gave My Heirloom Jewelry to His Mistress." *Slate*, July 24, 2018. https://slate.com/human-interest/2018/07/my-husband-gave-his-mistress-my-jewelry-and-more-advice-from-dear-prudence.html.

Oster, Emily. *Expecting Better: Why the Conventional Pregnancy Wisdom Is Wrong—and What You Really Need to Know*. Penguin Books, 2016.

Osterweil, Neil. "Experts Continue to Scale Back Annual Pap Smear." *WebMD*, 2015. https://www.webmd.com/cancer/cervical-cancer/news/20150501/pap-smear-cervical-cancer.

Ott, Mary A., Gina S. Sucato, and Committee On Adolescence. "Contraception for Adolescents." Pediatrics 134, no. 4 (October 1, 2014): e1257–81. https://doi.org/10.1542/peds.2014-2300.

Overall, Christine. *Why Have Children?: The Ethical Debate. (Basic Bioethics)*. Cambridge, Mass: MIT Press, 2012.

Owens, Deirdre Cooper. *Medical Bondage: Race, Gender, and the Origins of American Gynecology*. 1 edition. Athens, GA: University of Georgia Press, 2017.

Pabst, Selma, Anna Bertram, Tanja Zimmermann, Mario Schiffer, and Martina de Zwaan. "Physician Reported Adherence to Immunosuppressants in Renal Transplant Patients: Prevalence, Agreement, and Correlates." *Journal of Psychosomatic Research* 79 (September 1, 2015): 364–71. https://doi.org/10.1016/j.jpsychores.2015.09.001.

Packham, Analisa. "Family Planning Funding Cuts and Teen Childbearing." *Journal of Health Economics* 55 (2017): 163–85. https://doi.org/10.1016/j.jhealeco.2017.07.002.

Pammer, Kristen, Stephanie Sabadas, and Stephanie Lentern. "Allocating Attention to Detect Motorcycles: The Role of Inattentional Blindness." *Human Factors* 60, no. 1 (February 1, 2018): 5–19. https://doi.org/10.1177/0018720817733901.

"Parental Involvement in Minors' Abortions." Guttmacher Institute, March 14, 2016. https://www.guttmacher.org/state-policy/explore/parental-involvement-minors-abortions.

Parks, Anna L., and Rita F. Redberg. "Women in Medicine and Patient Outcomes: Equal Rights for Better Work?" *JAMA Internal Medicine* 177, no. 2 (February 1, 2017): 161–161. https://doi.org/10.1001/jamainternmed.2016.7883.

Pateman, Carole. *The Disorder of Women: Democracy, Feminism, and Political Theory*. Stanford University Press, 1989.

Patzer, Rachel E., Laura C. Plantinga, Sudeshna Paul, Jennifer Gander, Jenna Krisher, Leighann Sauls, Eric M. Gibney, Laura Mulloy, and Stephen O. Pastan. "Variation in Dialysis Facility Referral for Kidney Transplantation Among Patients With End-Stage Renal Disease in Georgia." *JAMA* 314, no. 6 (August 11, 2015): 582–94. https://doi.org/10.1001/jama.2015.8897.

Pear, Robert. "Women Still Pay More for Health Insurance, Data Shows." *The New York Times*, March 19, 2012, sec. Money & Policy. https://www.nytimes.com/2012/03/19/health/policy/women-still-pay-more-for-health-insurance-data-shows.html.

Pearson, Thomas A., Irene Laurora, Henry Chu, and Stephanie Kafonek. "The Lipid Treatment Assessment Project (L-TAP): A Multicenter Survey to Evaluate the Percentages of Dyslipidemic Patients Receiving Lipid-Lowering Therapy and Achieving Low-Density Lipoprotein Cholesterol Goals." *Archives of Internal Medicine* 160, no. 4 (February 28, 2000): 459–67. https://doi.org/10.1001/archinte.160.4.459.

Peck, Bethany. "No Pro-Life American Advocates Punishment for Abortion." *March For Life* (blog), March 30, 2016. http://marchforlife.org/no-pro-life-american/.

Pellegrino, Edmund D. "Professing Medicine, Virtue Based Ethics, and the Retrieval of Professionalism." *In Working Virtue: Virtue Ethics and Contemporary Moral Problems*, edited by Rebecca L. Walker and Philip J. Ivanhoe. Clarendon Press, 2007.

Pemberton v. TALLAHASSEE MEMORIAL REGIONAL MEDICAL, 66 F. Supp. 2d 1247 (N.D. Fla. 1999), No. ID09-1958 (United States District Court, N.D. Florida, Tallahassee Division October 13, 1999).

"Permissible Medical Experiments." Trials of War Criminals before the Nuremberg Military Tribunals under Countrol Council Law. Washington, D.C.: U.S. Government Printing Office, 1949. https://history.nih.gov/research/downloads/nuremberg.pdf.

Pernick, Martin S. *The Black Stork: Eugenics and the Death of "Defective" Babies in American Medicine and Motion Pictures since 1915*. 1 edition. New York: Oxford University Press, 1999.

Pessach, Itai M., and Luigi D. Notarangelo. "X-Linked Primary Immunodeficiencies as a Bridge to Better Understanding X-Chromosome Related Autoimmunity." *Journal of Autoimmunity* 33, no. 1 (August 1, 2009): 17–24. https://doi.org/10.1016/j.jaut.2009.03.003.

Pew Reasearch Center. "Religious Landscape Study." *Pew Research Center's Religion & Public Life Project* (blog), May 11, 2015. http://www.pewforum.org/religious-landscape-study/.

Pew Research Center. "What Americans Know and Don't Know about Science." *Pew Research Center Science & Society* (blog), September 10, 2015. https://

www.pewresearch.org/science/2015/09/10/what-the-public-knows-and-does-not-know-about-science/.

Picard, Andre. "Time to End Pelvic Exams Done without Consent." *The Globe and Mail*, January 28, 2010. https://www.theglobeandmail.com/life/health-and-fitness/time-to-end-pelvic-exams-done-without-consent/article4325965/.

PICHON and SAJOUS v. FRANCE, No. App. No. 49853/99 (European Court of Human Rights February 10, 2001).

Pitkin, Hanna. "Obligation and Consent—I." *The American Political Science Review* 59, no. 4 (December 1, 1965): 990–99. https://doi.org/10.2307/1953218.

Plato. *Five Dialogues*. Hackett Publishing Company, Inc., 1981.

Plato, and John M. Cooper. *Complete Works*. Edited by D. S. Hutchinson. Hackett Publishing Company, Inc., 1997.

Plotkin, David. "Good News and Bad News About Breast Cancer." *The Atlantic*, June 1, 1998. https://www.theatlantic.com/magazine/archive/1998/06/good-news-and-bad-news-about-breast-cancer/305504/.

Poorman, Elisabeth. "Why Does America Still Have so Few Female Doctors?" *The Guardian*, January 14, 2018, sec. Opinion. http://www.theguardian.com/commentisfree/2018/jan/14/why-are-there-still-so-few-female-doctors.

"Pope Says Church Is Making 'Profound' Birth Control Study." *The New York Times*, June 24, 1964, sec. Archives. https://www.nytimes.com/1964/06/24/archives/pope-says-church-is-making-profound-birth-control-study.html.

"Popularity Disparity: Attitudes About the IUD in Europe and the United States." Guttmacher Institute, November 12, 2007. https://www.guttmacher.org/gpr/2007/11/popularity-disparity-attitudes-about-iud-europe-and-united-states.

"Practice Advisory; Screening Pelvic Examination - ACOG." https://www.acog.org/Clinical-Guidance-and-Publications/Practice-Advisories/Practice-Advisory-Screening-Pelvic-Examination.

"Practice Bulletin No. 168: Cervical Cancer Screening and Prevention." *Obstetrics & Gynecology* 128, no. 4 (October 2016): e111. https://doi.org/10.1097/AOG.0000000000001708.

Prasad, Vinay, Andrae Vandross, Caitlin Toomey, Michael Cheung, Jason Rho, Steven Quinn, Satish Jacob Chacko, et al. "A Decade of Reversal: An Analysis of 146 Contradicted Medical Practices." *Mayo Clinic Proceedings* 88, no. 8 (August 1, 2013): 790–98. https://doi.org/10.1016/j.mayocp.2013.05.012.

"Prevention and Elimination of Disrespect and Abuse during Childbirth." World Health Organization, 2015. http://www.who.int/reproductivehealth/topics/maternal_perinatal/statement-childbirth-govnts-support/en/.

"Preventive Care Benefits." HealthCare.gov. Accessed May 28, 2015. https://www.healthcare.gov/preventive-care-benefits/.

"Preventive Care Benefits for Women." HealthCare.gov. Accessed June 18, 2019. https://www.healthcare.gov/preventive-care-women/.

"Professionally Active Physicians by Gender." *The Henry J. Kaiser Family Foundation* (blog), May 31, 2018. https://www.kff.org/other/state-indicator/physicians-by-gender/.

Promislow, Joanne H. E., Irva Hertz-Picciotto, Margaret Schramm, Margaret Watt-Morse, and John J. B. Anderson. "Bed Rest and Other Determinants of Bone Loss during Pregnancy." *American Journal of Obstetrics and Gynecology* 191, no. 4 (October 1, 2004): 1077–83. https://doi.org/10.1016/j.ajog.2004.05.058.

"Public Funding for Abortion." *American Civil Liberties Union*. Accessed August 19, 2018. https://www.aclu.org/other/public-funding-abortion.

"Publicly Funded Contraceptive Services at U.S. Clinics, 2015." Guttmacher Institute, April 21, 2017. https://www.guttmacher.org/report/publicly-funded-contraceptive-services-us-clinics-2015.

Puoti, Francesca, Andrea Ricci, Alessandro Nanni-Costa, Walter Ricciardi, Walter Malorni, and Elena Ortona. "Organ Transplantation and Gender Differences: A Paradigmatic Example of Intertwining between Biological and Sociocultural Determinants." *Biology of Sex Differences* 7 (July 28, 2016). https://doi.org/10.1186/s13293-016-0088-4.

Purdy, Laura M. *Reproducing Persons: Issues in Feminist Bioethics*. Cornell University Press, 1996.

Qaseem, Amir, Linda L. Humphrey, Russell Harris, Melissa Starkey, and Thomas D. Denberg. "Screening Pelvic Examination in Adult Women: A Clinical Practice Guideline From the American College of Physicians." *Annals of Internal Medicine* 161, no. 1 (July 1, 2014): 67–72. https://doi.org/10.7326/M14-0701.

Rabin, Roni Caryn. "Health Researchers Will Get $10.1 Million to Counter Gender Bias in Studies." *The New York Times*, December 21, 2017, sec. Health. https://www.nytimes.com/2014/09/23/health/23gender.html.

Rachels, James. "Active and Passive Euthanasia." *Bioethics: An Introduction to the History, Methods, and Practice*, 1975, 77–82.

"Radical Attempts to Ban Abortion Dominate State Policy Trends in the First Quarter of 2019." Guttmacher Institute, April 2, 2019. https://www.guttmacher.org/article/2019/04/radical-attempts-ban-abortion-dominate-state-policy-trends-first-quarter-2019.

Rafie, Sally, Sanaz Kelly, Erika K. Gray, Megan Wong, Susannah Gibbs, and Cynthia C. Harper. "Provider Opinions Regarding Expanding Access to Hormonal Contraception in Pharmacies." *Women's Health Issues: Official Publication of the Jacobs Institute of Women's Health* 26, no. 2 (April 2016): 153–60. https://doi.org/10.1016/j.whi.2015.09.006.

Rafie, Sally, Jennifer McIntosh, Kayce M. Shealy, Laura M. Borgelt, Alicia Forinash, Sarah P. Shrader, Erin R. Koepf, et al. "Roles of the Pharmacist in the Use of Safe and Highly Effective Long-Acting Reversible Contraception: An Opinion of the Women's Health Practice and Research Network of the American College of Clinical Pharmacy." *Pharmacotherapy: The Journal of Human Pharmacology and Drug Therapy* 34, no. 9 (September 1, 2014): 991–99. https://doi.org/10.1002/phar.1457.

Rancic, Nemanja, Viktorija Dragojevic-Simic, Neven Vavic, Aleksandra Kovacevic, Zoran Segrt, and Natasa Djordjevic. "Economic Evaluation of Pharmacogenetic Tests in Patients Subjected to Renal Transplantation: A Review of Literature." *Frontiers in Public Health* 4 (August 31, 2016). https://doi.org/10.3389/fpubh.2016.00189.

Rasmussen, Sarah, Pragya Paneru, Kalpana Shrestha, and Pukar C Shrestha. "Gender Bias and Organ Transplantation in Nepal," 2016, 15.

Ravin, Amy J., Mary B. Mahowald, and Carol B. Stocking. "Genes or Gestation? Attitudes of Women and Men about Biologic Ties to Children." *Journal of Women's Health* 6, no. 6 (December 1, 1997): 639–47. https://doi.org/10.1089/jwh.1997.6.639.

Rawls, John. *A Theory of Justice*. Rev. ed. Cambridge, Mass: Belknap Press of Harvard University Press, 1999.

Raymond, Nate. "Opioid Manufacturer Insys Files for Bankruptcy after Kickback Probe." *Reuters*, June 10, 2019. https://www.reuters.com/article/us-insys-opioids-bankruptcy-idUSKCN1TB15Q.

Reagan, Leslie J. *When Abortion Was a Crime: Women, Medicine, and Law in the United States*, 1867–1973. University of California Press, 1996.

"Reasons For Bed Rest During Pregnancy & More." *Cleveland Clinic*. September 24, 2018. https://my.clevelandclinic.org/health/articles/9757-pregnancy-bed-rest.

Redden, Molly. "New York Hospital's Secret Policy Led to Woman Being given C-Section against Her Will." *The Guardian*, October 5, 2017, sec. US news. http://www.theguardian.com/us-news/2017/oct/05/new-york-staten-island-university-hospital-c-section-ethics-medicine.

Reddy, Sumathi. "A Type of Childbirth Some Women Will Fight For." *The Wall Street Journal*, December 8, 2014, sec. Health and Wellness. http://www.wsj.com/articles/a-type-of-childbirth-some-women-will-fight-for-1418081344.

Reindl, Erin K., Bradley M. Wright, and Kurt A. Wargo. "Alternate-Day Statin Therapy for the Treatment of Hyperlipidemia." *The Annals of Pharmacotherapy* 44, no. 9 (September 2010): 1459–70. https://doi.org/10.1345/aph.1M571.

"Requirements for Ultrasound." Guttmacher Institute, March 14, 2016. https://www.guttmacher.org/state-policy/explore/requirements-ultrasound.

Resident Rights. Vol. 483.10. https://www.law.cornell.edu/cfr/text/42/483.10: Legal Information Institute.

Resnick, Brian. "The Weird Power of the Placebo Effect, Explained." *Vox*, July 7, 2017. https://www.vox.com/science-and-health/2017/7/7/15792188/placebo-effect-explained.

Rettner, Rachel. "Women Feel Pain More Intensely Than Men Do." *Scientific American*. January 23, 2012. https://www.scientificamerican.com/article/women-feel-pain-more-intensely/.

Roland, James. "Do You Need to Take the Last Week of Birth Control Pills?" *Healthline*, March 21, 2016. https://www.healthline.com/health/birth-control/last-week-of-birth-control-pills.

"Rifampin: MedlinePlus Drug Information." April 15, 2019. https://medlineplus.gov/druginfo/meds/a682403.html.

———. "HHS Proposes to Revise ACA Section 1557 Rule to Enforce Civil Rights in Healthcare, Conform to Law, and Eliminate Billions in Unnecessary Costs." Text. HHS.gov, May 23, 2019. https://www.hhs.gov/about/news/2019/05/24/hhs-proposes-to-revise-aca-section-1557-rule.html.

———. "Section 1557 of the Patient Protection and Affordable Care Act." Text. HHS.gov, July 22, 2010. https://www.hhs.gov/civil-rights/for-individuals/section-1557/index.html.

Robbins, Alexandra. "The Problem With Satisfied Patients." *The Atlantic*, April 17, 2015. https://www.theatlantic.com/health/archive/2015/04/the-problem-with-satisfied-patients/390684/.

Roberts, Dorothy. *Killing the Black Body: Race, Reproduction, and the Meaning of Liberty*. Vintage, 2014.

———. "Reproductive Justice, Not Just Rights." *Dissent* 62, no. 4 (September 29, 2015): 79–82. https://doi.org/10.1353/dss.2015.0073.

Roe v. Wade, 410 United States 113 (Supreme Court 1973).

Rogers, Katharine M. *The Troublesome Helpmate: A History of Misogyny in Literature*. University of Washington Press, 1968.

Romo, Vanessa. "DNA Test Reveals Fertility Doctor Used His Own Sperm To Impregnate Patient." NPR.org, April 4, 2018. https://www.npr.org/sections/thetwo-way/2018/04/04/599531061/dna-test-reveals-fertility-doctor-used-his-own-sperm-to-impregnate-patient.

Rosenberg, Eli. "He's pro-Incest, Pedophilia, and Rape. He's Also Running for Congress from His Parents' House." *The Washington Post*, June 2, 2018, sec. Local. https://www.washingtonpost.com/news/local/wp/2018/06/01/hes-pro-incest-pedophilia-and-rape-hes-also-running-for-congress-from-his-parents-house/.

Rosin, Hanna. "The Case Against Breast-Feeding." *The Atlantic*, April 1, 2009. https://www.theatlantic.com/magazine/archive/2009/04/the-case-against-breast-feeding/307311/.

Ross, Loretta, and Rickie Solinger. *Reproductive Justice: An Introduction*. First edition. Oakland, California: University of California Press, 2017.

Rothman, Kenneth J. "Fetal Loss, Twinning and Birth Weight after Oral-Contraceptive Use." *New England Journal of Medicine* 297, no. 9 (September 1, 1977): 468–71. https://doi.org/10.1056/NEJM197709012970903.

Roura, Esther, Noémie Travier, Tim Waterboer, Silvia de Sanjosé, F. Xavier Bosch, Michael Pawlita, Valeria Pala, et al. "The Influence of Hormonal Factors on the Risk of Developing Cervical Cancer and Pre-Cancer: Results from the EPIC Cohort." *PLOS ONE* 11, no. 1 (2016): e0147029. https://doi.org/10.1371/journal.pone.0147029.

Rupe, Heather. "An OB Weighs in on the 'Husband Stitch.'" *WebMD* (blog), March 16, 2018, sec. Women's Health. https://blogs.webmd.com/womens-health/2018/03/an-ob-weighs-in-on-the-husband-stitch.html.

Rutecki, Gregory W. "Forced Sterilization of Native Americans: Late Twentieth Century Physician Cooperation with National Eugenic Policies," October 8, 2010. https://cbhd.org/content/forced-sterilization-native-americans-late-twentieth-century-physician-cooperation-national-.

Sachan, Pushp Lata, Meenakshi Singh, Munna Lal Patel, and Rekha Sachan. "A Study on Cervical Cancer Screening Using Pap Smear Test and Clinical Correlation." *Asia-Pacific Journal of Oncology Nursing* 5, no. 3 (September 2018): 337–41. https://doi.org/10.4103/apjon.apjon_15_18.

Safer, Joshua D., Eli Coleman, Jamie Feldman, Robert Garofalo, Wylie Hembree, Asa Radix, and Jae Sevelius. "Barriers to Health Care for Transgender Individuals." *Current Opinion in Endocrinology, Diabetes, and Obesity* 23, no. 2 (April 1, 2016): 168–71. https://doi.org/10.1097/MED.0000000000000227.

Sagan, Dorion. "Special Section: Gender Specifics: Why Women Aren't Men." *The New York Times*, June 21, 1998, sec. Special Edition: Women's Health. https://archive.nytimes.com/www.nytimes.com/specials/women/nyt98/21saga.html.

Saini, Angela. *Inferior: How Science Got Women Wrong—and the New Research That's Rewriting the Story*. Boston: Beacon Press, 2017.

Saint, Mona, Ginny Gildengorin, and George F. Sawaya. "Current Cervical Neoplasia Screening Practices of Obstetrician/Gynecologists in the US." *American Journal of Obstetrics and Gynecology* 192, no. 2 (February 2005): 414–21. https://doi.org/10.1016/j.ajog.2004.09.026.

Sakhuja, A., A. Naik, H. Amer, D. Cibrik, R. Eikstadt, J. D. Schold, and M. D. Stegall. "Underutilization of Timely Kidney Transplants in Those With Living Donors." *American Journal of Transplantation* 16, no. 3 (2016): 1007–14. https://doi.org/10.1111/ajt.13592.

Salam, Muhammad T., Helene G. Margolis, Rob McConnell, James A. McGregor, Edward L. Avol, and Frank D. Gilliland. "Mode of Delivery Is Associated with Asthma and Allergy Occurrences in Children." *Annals of Epidemiology* 16, no. 5 (May 2006): 341–46. https://doi.org/10.1016/j.annepidem.2005.06.054.

Salamon, Maureen. "Half of U.S. Counties Have No Ob-Gyn: Study." *Consumer HealthDay*. May 8, 2012. https://consumer.healthday.com/sexual-health-information-32/childbirth-health-news-126/half-of-u-s-counties-have-no-ob-gyn-study-664462.html.

Samantha Burton, Appellant, v. State of Florida, Appellee, No. 1DO9-1958 (FL Dist. Ct. App. August 12, 2010).

Sanchez, Nelson F., John P. Sanchez, and Ann Danoff. "Health Care Utilization, Barriers to Care, and Hormone Usage among Male-to-Female Transgender Persons in New York City." *American Journal of Public Health* 99, no. 4 (April 2009): 713–19. https://doi.org/10.2105/AJPH.2007.132035.

Sanger, Margaret. *The Autobiography of Margaret Sanger*. Dover Ed edition. Mineola, New York: Dover Publications, 2004.

Sanghani, Radhika. "'It's Just Lady Pains': Are Doctors Not Taking Women's Agony Seriously Enough?" *The Telegraph*. October 22, 2015, sec. Women. https://www.telegraph.co.uk/women/womens-life/11948057/Lady-pains-Are-doctors-not-taking-womens-pain-seriously-enough.html.

———. "Period Pain Can Feel 'as Bad as a Heart Attack' - So Why Is It Being Ignored?" *The Telegraph*, September 6, 2017. https://www.telegraph.co.uk/women/life/period-pain-can-feel-bad-heart-attack-ignored/.

Saraiya, Mona, Gladys Martinez, Katherine Glaser, and Shalini Kulasingam. "Pap Testing and Sexual Activity Among Young Women in the United States:" *Obstetrics & Gynecology* 114, no. 6 (December 2009): 1213–19. https://doi.org/10.1097/AOG.0b013e3181be3db4.

Saslow, Debbie. "American Cancer Society Expert Voices Blog: Is a Pap Test Necessary Every Year?" Cancer.org, March 14, 2012. http://www.cancer.org/Cancer/News/Expert-Voices/.

Saslow, Debbie, Diane Solomon, Herschel W. Lawson, Maureen Killackey, Shalini Kulasingam, Joanna Cain, Francisco A. R. Garcia, et al. "American Cancer Society, American Society for Colposcopy and Cervical Pathology, and American Society for Clinical Pathology Screening Guidelines for the Prevention and Early Detection of Cervical Cancer." *CA: A Cancer Journal for Clinicians* 62, no. 3 (2012): 147–72. https://doi.org/10.3322/caac.21139.

Savulescu, Julian, and Udo Schuklenk. "Doctors Have No Right to Refuse Medical Assistance in Dying, Abortion or Contraception." *Bioethics* 31, no. 3 (2017): 162–70. https://doi.org/10.1111/bioe.12288.

Sawaya, George F., Karen K. Smith-McCune, Steven E. Gregorich, Michelle Moghadassi, and Miriam Kuppermann. "Effect of Professional Society Recommendations on Women's Desire for a Routine Pelvic Examination." *American Journal of Obstetrics and Gynecolo-*

gy 217, no. 3 (September 1, 2017): 338.e1-338.e7. https://doi.org/10.1016/j.ajog.2017.05.003.
Scanlon, Thomas, Alford Professor of Natural Religion, Moral Philosophy, and Civil Polity. *What We Owe to Each Other*. Harvard University Press, 1998.
Schattner, Elaine. "The Placebo Debate: Is It Unethical to Prescribe Them to Patients?" *The Atlantic*, December 19, 2011. https://www.theatlantic.com/health/archive/2011/12/the-placebo-debate-is-it-unethical-to-prescribe-them-to-patients/250161/.
Schechter, Susan. *Women and Male Violence: The Visions and Struggles of the Battered Women's Movement*. Boston: South End Press, 1982.
Schloendorff v. Society of New York Hosp., No. 105 N.E. 92, 93 (1914).
Schmidt, Jennifer. "The Gentle Cesarean: More Like A Birth Than An Operation." NPR.org. March 9, 2015, sec. Shots Health News. https://www.npr.org/sections/health-shots/2015/03/09/390977656/the-gentle-cesarean-more-like-a-birth-than-an-operation.
Schroeder, J. Natanson v. Kline (Supreme Court of Kansas 1960).
Schuklenk, Udo. "Accommodating Conscientious Objection in Medicine-Private Ideological Convictions Must Not Trump Professional Obligations." *The Journal of Clinical Ethics* 27, no. 3 (2016): 227–32.
———. "Conscientious Objection in Medicine: Accommodation versus Professionalism and the Public Good." *British Medical Bulletin* 126, no. 1 (June 1, 2018): 47–56. https://doi.org/10.1093/bmb/ldy007.
Schulte, Brigid. "More U.S. Hospitals Adopting 'Baby-Friendly' Policies." *The Washington Post*. September 10, 2014. https://www.washingtonpost.com/local/more-us-hospitals-adopting-baby-friendly-policies/2014/09/10/49a86998-34c4-11e4-a723-fa3895a25d02_story.html.
Schuman, Rebecca. "Formula Advertising Has Always Gone Straight for the New-Mother Jugular." *Slate*, June 4, 2015. https://slate.com/human-interest/2015/06/a-century-of-formula-advertising-its-always-gone-straight-for-the-new-mother-jugular.html.
———. "Is a Kid Who's 'Old Enough to Ask for It' Too Old to Breast-Feed?" *Slate*, July 18, 2016. https://slate.com/human-interest/2016/07/how-old-is-too-old-to-breast-feed.html.
Schwarz, Eleanor Bimla, Mona Saint, Ginny Gildengorin, Tracy A. Weitz, Felicia H. Stewart, and George F. Sawaya. "Cervical Cancer Screening Continues to Limit Provision of Contraception." *Contraception* 72, no. 3 (September 2005): 179–81. https://doi.org/10.1016/j.contraception.2005.04.009.
"Screening Guidelines." asccp.org, 2012. http://www.asccp.org/guidelines/screening-guidelines.
Scutti, Susan. "'Gentle' C-Sections Are Growing in Popularity." CNN, June 13, 2017. https://www.cnn.com/2017/06/13/health/gentle-natural-c-section/index.html.
"Second Annual Physician Compensation Report: March 2018." Doximity. March, 2018. https://www.doximity.com.
Secura, Gina M., Jenifer E. Allsworth, Tessa Madden, Jennifer L. Mullersman, and Jeffrey F. Peipert. "The Contraceptive CHOICE Project: Reducing Barriers to Long-Acting Reversible Contraception." *American Journal of Obstetrics and Gynecology* 203, no. 2 (August 2010): 115.e1-115.e7. https://doi.org/10.1016/j.ajog.2010.04.017.
Segev, Dorry L., Lauren M. Kucirka, Pooja C. Oberai, Rulan S. Parekh, L. Ebony Boulware, Neil R. Powe, and Robert A. Montgomery. "Age and Comorbidities Are Effect Modifiers of Gender Disparities in Renal Transplantation." *Journal of the American Society of Nephrology* 20, no. 3 (March 1, 2009): 621–28. https://doi.org/10.1681/ASN.2008060591.
Sen, Amartya Kumar. "Democracy as a Universal Value." *Journal of Democracy* 10, no. 3 (1999): 3–17. https://doi.org/10.1353/jod.1999.0055.
———. "Development as Capability Expansion." *The Community Development Reader*, 2nd Ed.; DeFilippis, J., Saeger, S., Eds, 1990, 319–327.
Sensenbrenner, F. James, Henry J. Hyde, Howard Coble, Lamar Smith, Elton Gallegly, Bob Goodlattee, Steve Chabot, et al. "Committee on the Judiciary," November 1, 2005, 101.
Sepper, Elizabeth. "Not Only the Doctor's Dilemma: The Complexity of Conscience in Medicine." *Faulkner Law Review* 4, no. 2 (Spring 2013): 385–410.

———. "Taking Conscience Seriously." SSRN Scholarly Paper. Rochester, NY: Social Science Research Network, September 21, 2012. https://papers.ssrn.com/abstract=1888375.

———. "The Role of Religion in State Public Accommodations Laws." SSRN Scholarly Paper. Rochester, NY: Social Science Research Network, February 1, 2017. https://papers.ssrn.com/abstract=2832866.

———. "Zombie Religious Institutions." SSRN Scholarly Paper. Rochester, NY: Social Science Research Network, March 13, 2017. https://papers.ssrn.com/abstract=2932235.

Sepper, Elizabeth, and Alisha Johnson. "Rhetoric Versus Reality: The Contraception Benefit and Religious Freedom." *Religion and Politics*, April 9, 2013. http://religionandpolitics.org/2013/04/09/rhetoric-versus-reality-the-contraception-benefit-and-religious-freedom/.

Serano, Julia. *Excluded: Making Feminist and Queer Movements More Inclusive*. 10.8.2013 edition. Berkeley, California: Seal Press, 2013.

———. "Trans-Misogyny Primer," https://www.juliaserano.com/av/TransmisogynyPrimer-Serano.pdf.

———. *Whipping Girl: A Transsexual Woman on Sexism and the Scapegoating of Femininity*. Emeryville, CA: Seal Press, 2007.

Kibbe, Melina R. "Sex Bias in Surgical Research." *Physicians Weekly*, June 29, 2017. https://www.physiciansweekly.com/sex-bias-in-surgical-research/.

"Sexual Offense Prevention Policy (SOPP) & Title IX." *Antioch College* (blog). 1991. https://antiochcollege.edu/campus-life/sexual-offense-prevention-policy-title-ix.

Shapiro, Devora. "Should Pregnancy Be Considered a (Temporary) Disability?" *IJFAB: International Journal of Feminist Approaches to Bioethics* 11, no. 1 (February 2018): 91–105. https://doi.org/10.3138/ijfab.11.1.91.

Shapiro, Devora, and Marilea Bramer. "Gender Issues in Corporate Leadership." In *Handbook of the Philosophical Foundations of Business Ethics*, edited by Christoph Luetge, 1177–89. Dordrecht: Springer Netherlands, 2013. https://doi.org/10.1007/978-94-007-1494-6_74.

Sharman, Jon. "Bill to Outlaw Marital Rape Gets No Support from Ohio Republicans." *The Independent*, February 27, 2017. http://www.independent.co.uk/news/world/americas/us-politics/ohio-marital-rape-bill-illegal-wives-husbands-drug-republicans-state-greta-johnson-a7601411.html.

Sharp, Linda, Seonaidh Cotton, Anne-Elie Carsin, Nicola Gray, Alison Thornton, Margaret Cruickshank, Julian Little, and TOMBOLA Group. "Factors Associated with Psychological Distress Following Colposcopy among Women with Low-Grade Abnormal Cervical Cytology: A Prospective Study within the Trial Of Management of Borderline and Other Low-Grade Abnormal Smears (TOMBOLA)." *Psycho-Oncology* 22, no. 2 (February 2013): 368–80. https://doi.org/10.1002/pon.2097.

Sherwin, Susan. "A Relational Approach to Autonomy in Health Care." In *Politics Of Women's Health: Exploring Agency and Autonomy*. Philadelphia: Temple University Press, 1998.

———. *No Longer Patient: Feminist Ethics and Health Care*. Temple University Press, 1992.

Shetterly, Margot Lee. *Hidden Figures: The American Dream and the Untold Story of the Black Women Mathematicians Who Helped Win the Space Race*. Media Tie In edition. William Morrow Paperbacks, 2016.

Shinkman, Ron. "The Big Business of Dialysis Care." *NEJM Catalyst*, June 9, 2016. https://catalyst.nejm.org/the-big-business-of-dialysis-care/.

Shotorbani, Solmaz, Leslie Miller, David K. Blough, and Jacqueline Gardner. "Agreement between Women's and Providers' Assessment of Hormonal Contraceptive Risk Factors." *Contraception* 73, no. 5 (May 2006): 501–6. https://doi.org/10.1016/j.contraception.2005.12.001.

Shoupe, Donna. "LARC Methods: Entering a New Age of Contraception and Reproductive Health." *Contraception and Reproductive Medicine* 1 (2016): 4. https://doi.org/10.1186/s40834-016-0011-8.

Shue, Henry. *Basic Rights: Subsistence, Affluence, and U.S. Foreign Policy*. Princeton University Press, 1996.

Singer, Isaac Bashevis, and Antonio Frasconi. *Yentl the Yeshiva Boy*. 1st ed. New York: Farrar, Straus and Giroux, 1983.

Singer, Peter. *Animal Liberation*. Random House, 2015.

———. "Famine, Affluence, and Morality." *Philosophy and Public Affairs* 1, no. 1 (Spring 1972): 229–43.

———. *Practical Ethics*. 2nd ed. Cambridge: Cambridge University Press, 1993.

———. *The Life You Can Save: Acting Now to End World Poverty*. Random House Publishing Group, 2009.

———. "Why We Must Ration Health Care." *The New York Times*, July 19, 2009. http://www.nytimes.com/2009/07/19/magazine/19healthcare-t.html?pagewanted=all.

Sirovich, Brenda E, and H Gilbert Welch. "The Frequency of Pap Smear Screening in the United States." *Journal of General Internal Medicine* 19, no. 3 (March 2004): 243–50. https://doi.org/10.1111/j.1525-1497.2004.21107.x.

Skloot, Rebecca. *The Immortal Life of Henrietta Lacks*. New York: Broadway Books, 2011.

Smith, Barbara. "Racism and Women's Studies." In *The Truth That Never Hurts: Writings on Race, Gender, and Freedom*. Rutgers University Press, 2000.

Smith, Cedric M. "Origin and Uses of Primum Non Nocere—Above All, Do No Harm!" *The Journal of Clinical Pharmacology* 45, no. 4 (2005): 371–77. https://doi.org/10.1177/0091270004273680.

Smith, J., F. Plaat, and N. M. Fisk. "The Natural Caesarean: A Woman-Centred Technique." *BJOG: An International Journal of Obstetrics & Gynecology* 115, no. 8 (July 2008): 1037–42. https://doi.org/10.1111/j.1471-0528.2008.01777.x.

Smith, Jennifer S., Jane Green, Amy Berrington de Gonzalez, Paul Appleby, Julian Peto, Martyn Plummer, Silvia Franceschi, and Valerie Beral. "Cervical Cancer and Use of Hormonal Contraceptives: A Systematic Review." *The Lancet* (London, England) 361, no. 9364 (April 5, 2003): 1159–67.

Smith, Lesley A., Natalia Price, Vanessa Simonite, and Ethel E. Burns. "Incidence of and Risk Factors for Perineal Trauma: A Prospective Observational Study." *BMC Pregnancy and Childbirth* 13 (March 7, 2013): 59. https://doi.org/10.1186/1471-2393-13-59.

Sonfield, Adam, Kinsey Hasstedt, Megan L. Kavanaugh, and Ragnar Anderson. *The Social and Economic Benefits of Women's Ability to Determine Whether and When to Have Children*. New York: Guttmacher Institute, 2013. https://editor.guttmacher.org/sites/default/files/report_pdf/social-economic-benefits.pdf.

Sosa, C., F. Althabe, J. Belizán, and E. Bergel. "Bed Rest in Singleton Pregnancies for Preventing Preterm Birth." *The Cochrane Database of Systematic Reviews*, no. 1 (2004): CD003581. https://doi.org/10.1002/14651858.CD003581.pub2.

Sparano, Joseph A., Robert J. Gray, Della F. Makower, Kathleen I. Pritchard, Kathy S. Albain, Daniel F. Hayes, Charles E. Geyer, et al. "Adjuvant Chemotherapy Guided by a 21-Gene Expression Assay in Breast Cancer." *New England Journal of Medicine* 0, no. 0 (June 3, 2018). https://doi.org/10.1056/NEJMoa1804710.

Specter, Michael. "Planned Parenthood Means Fewer Abortions," August 20, 2015. https://www.newyorker.com/news/daily-comment/planned-parenthood-means-fewer-abortions.

Stack, Liam. "A Brief History of Deadly Attacks on Abortion Providers." *The New York Times*, November 29, 2015, sec. U.S. https://www.nytimes.com/interactive/2015/11/29/us/30abortion-clinic-violence.html.

"Contract." LII / Legal Information Institute, August 6, 2007. https://www.law.cornell.edu/wex/contract.

Stanger-Hall, Kathrin F., and David W. Hall. "Abstinence-Only Education and Teen Pregnancy Rates: Why We Need Comprehensive Sex Education in the U.S." *PLOS ONE* 6, no. 10 (October 14, 2011). https://doi.org/10.1371/journal.pone.0024658.

"State Bans on Abortion Throughout Pregnancy." Guttmacher Institute, May 1, 2019. https://www.guttmacher.org/state-policy/explore/state-policies-later-abortions.

"States Enact Record Number of Abortion Restrictions in First Half of 2011." Guttmacher Institute, July 13, 2011. https://www.guttmacher.org/article/2011/07/states-enact-record-number-abortion-restrictions-first-half-2011.

Stein, Rob. "U.S. Campaign to Promote Abstinence Begins," June 1, 2008. http://www.washingtonpost.com/wp-dyn/content/article/2008/05/31/AR2008053101742.html.

Steinbock, Bonnie. "The Intentional Termination of Life." *Ethics in Science & Medicine* 6, no. 1 (1979): 59–64.

Steinem, Gloria. "If Hitler Were Alive, Whose Side Would He Be On?" In *Outrageous Acts and Everyday Rebellions*. Second Edition. New York: Holt Paperbacks, 1995.

———. *Outrageous Acts and Everyday Rebellions*. Second Edition. New York: Holt Paperbacks, 1995.

Stern, Alexandra Minna. "That Time The United States Sterilized 60,000 Of Its Citizens." *Huffington Post*, January 8, 2016, sec. Politics. https://www.huffingtonpost.com/entry/sterilization-united-states_us_568f35f2e4b0c8beacf68713.

Stewart, Felicia H., Cynthia C. Harper, Charlotte E. Ellertson, David A. Grimes, George F. Sawaya, and James Trussell. "Clinical Breast and Pelvic Examination Requirements for Hormonal Contraception: Current Practice vs Evidence." *JAMA* 285, no. 17 (May 2, 2001): 2232. https://doi.org/10.1001/jama.285.17.2232.

Stokes, John B. "Consequences of Frequent Hemodialysis: Comparison to Conventional Hemodialysis and Transplantation." *Transactions of the American Clinical and Climatological Association* 122 (2011): 124–36.

Strandberg, Katherine and Kristine Hopkins. "New Title X Birth Control Rules Heed Conservatives, Ignore Women." *USA Today*. June 7, 2016, sec. Opinions. https://www.usatoday.com/story/opinion/2018/06/07/trump-birth-control-plan-ignores-what-women-want-column/670722002/.

Strasser, Annie-Rose. "Despite Growing Number Of Female Doctors And Lawyers, Women's Pay Still Lags Behind." *ThinkProgress*, December 5, 2012. https://thinkprogress.org/despite-growing-number-of-female-doctors-and-lawyers-womens-pay-still-lags-behind-9b43f25c0335/.

Strauss, Elissa, and Jean-Marie Pottier. "Baby-Friendly Hospitals May Not Be So Baby-Friendly After All." *Slate*, February 25, 2016. http://www.slate.com/blogs/xx_factor/2016/02/25/baby_friendly_hospitals_may_not_be_so_baby_friendly_after_all.html.

Sueta, Carla A., Mridul Chowdhury, Stephen J. Boccuzzi, Sidney C. Smith, Charles M. Alexander, Anil Londhe, Ash Lulla, and Ross J. Simpson. "Analysis of the Degree of Undertreatment of Hyperlipidemia and Congestive Heart Failure Secondary to Coronary Artery Disease." *American Journal of Cardiology* 83, no. 9 (May 1, 1999): 1303–7. https://doi.org/10.1016/S0002-9149(99)00117-4.

Sullivan, Andrew. "Unnatural Law." *The New Republic*, March 26, 2003. https://newrepublic.com/article/64542/unnatural-law.

Sullivan, E. Ginger. "Lupus: The Silent Killer." In *African-American Women's Health and Social Issues*, edited by Catherine Fisher Collins. Westport, Conn: Auburn House, 1996.

Sullivan, G. R. "Intent, Subjective Recklessness and Culpability." *Oxford Journal of Legal Studies* 12, no. 3 (1992): 380–91.

Swim, Janet K., and Laurie L. Cohen. "Overt, Covert, And Subtle Sexism: A Comparison Between the Attitudes Toward Women and Modern Sexism Scales." *Psychology of Women Quarterly* 21, no. 1 (March 1, 1997): 103–18. https://doi.org/10.1111/j.1471-6402.1997.tb00103.x.

Tamesha Means, Plaintiff–Appellant, v. United States Conference of Catholic Bishops; Stanley Urban; Robert Ladenburger; Mary Mollison, Defendants–Appellees., No. 15-1779 (United States Court of Appeals, Sixth Circuit September 8, 2016).

Tang, Jennifer, Rie Maurer, and Deborah Bartz. "Intrauterine Device Knowledge and Practices: A National Survey of Obstetrics and Gynecology Residents." *Southern Medical Journal* 106, no. 9 (September 2013): 500–505. https://doi.org/10.1097/SMJ.0b013e3182a5ef0a.

"Targeted Regulation of Abortion Providers." Guttmacher Institute, March 14, 2016. https://www.guttmacher.org/state-policy/explore/targeted-regulation-abortion-providers.

Tasca, Cecilia, Mariangela Rapetti, Mauro Giovanni Carta, and Bianca Fadda. "Women And Hysteria In The History Of Mental Health." *Clinical Practice and Epidemiology in Mental Health: CP & EMH* 8 (October 19, 2012): 110–19. https://doi.org/10.2174/1745017901208010110.

Tavernise, Sabrina. "Maternal Mortality Rate in U.S. Rises, Defying Global Trend, Study Finds." *The New York Times*, September 21, 2016. http://www.nytimes.com/2016/09/22/health/maternal-mortality.html.

Tavernise, Sabrina, and Adeel Hassan. "Missouri Lawmakers Pass Bill Criminalizing Abortion at About 8 Weeks of Pregnancy." *The New York Times*, May 18, 2019, sec. U.S. https://www.nytimes.com/2019/05/17/us/missouri-abortion-law.html.

Teal, Stephanie B., and S. Elizabeth Romer. "Awareness of Long-Acting Reversible Contraception among Teens and Young Adults." *The Journal of Adolescent Health: Official Publication of the Society for Adolescent Medicine* 52, no. 4 Suppl (April 2013): S35-39. https://doi.org/10.1016/j.jadohealth.2013.01.013.

Tello, Monique. "Racism and Discrimination in Health Care: Providers and Patients." *Harvard Health Blog*, January 16, 2017. https://www.health.harvard.edu/blog/racism-discrimination-health-care-providers-patients-2017011611015.

"Text of S. 1 (103rd): National Institutes of Health Revitalization Act of 1993 (Passed Congress Version)." GovTrack.us. 1993. https://www.govtrack.us/congress/bills/103/s1/text.

The American College of Obstetricians and Gynecologists. "ACOG Practice Bulletin Number 106: Intrapartum Fetal Heart Rate Monitoring: Nomenclature, Interpretation, and General Management Principles," July 2009. https://www.mnhospitals.org/Portals/0/Documents/patientsafety/Perinatal/3a_ACOG%20Bulletin%20106.pdf.

———. "Committee Opinion, Number 544 Over-the-Counter Access to Oral Contraceptives." Committee on Gynecologic Practice, December 2012. https://www.acog.org/-/media/Committee-Opinions/Committee-on-Gynecologic-Practice/co544.pdf?dmc=1&ts=20150125T0334021611.

The American College of Obstetricians and Gynecologists Committee on Obstetric Practice. "ACOG Committee Opinion Number 650: Physical Activity and Exercise During Pregnancy and the Postpartum Period." *Obstet Gynecol* 126 (December 2015): 135–42.

"The Choice Project." Accessed October 17, 2016. http://www.choiceproject.wustl.edu/#MISSION.

Neighmond, Patti. "The Hidden Cost Of Mammograms: More Testing And Overtreatment." NPR.org. April 13, 2015, sec. Morning Edition. http://www.npr.org/sections/health-shots/2015/04/13/398818949/the-hidden-cost-of-mammograms-more-testing-and-overtreatment.

"The 'Husband Stitch' Is Real, And It's Horrifying." *Scary Mommy* (blog), July 8, 2016. https://www.scarymommy.com/husband-stitch/.

"The National Intimate Partner and Sexual Violence Survey: 2015 Data Brief — Updated Release," 2015, 32.

"The Project Gutenberg EBook of On Liberty, by John Stuart Mill." Accessed July 18, 2017. https://www.gutenberg.org/files/34901/34901-h/34901-h.htm#Page_103.

Caldwell, Patrick. "The Supreme Court Just Made the Hobby Lobby Ruling Even Worse." *Mother Jones*. July 3, 2014. http://www.motherjones.com/politics/2014/07/supreme-court-scotus-hobby-lobby-all-forms-contraception.

"Think Before You Pink: About Us." http://thinkbeforeyoupink.org/about-us/.

Thomas, Carolyn. "Heart Disease – Not Just a Man's Disease Anymore." *Heart Sisters* (blog), January 11, 2010. https://myheartsisters.org/2010/01/11/not-just-a-mans-disease/.

Thomason, Krista K. "Shame and Contempt in Kant's Moral Theory." *Kantian Review* 18, no. 2 (July 2013): 221–40. https://doi.org/10.1017/S136941541300006X.

Thomas Reuters Foundation. "Study: Transgender People Face Health Challenges Worldwide." NBC News. June 17, 2016. https://www.nbcnews.com/feature/nbc-out/study-transgender-people-face-challenges-adequate-health-care-n594331.

Thompson, Teresa L., James D. Robinson, and R. Wade Kenny. "Gender Differences in Family Communication About Organ Donation." *Sex Roles* 49, no. 11–12 (December 1, 2003): 587–96. https://doi.org/10.1023/B:SERS.0000003129.25173.ad.

Thomson, Judith Jarvis. "A Defense of Abortion." *Philosophy & Public Affairs* 1, no. 1 (Fall 1997): 47–66.

"To Pap or Not to Pap: What the New Cervical Cancer Screening Guidelines Mean for Women." ascp.org, March 14, 2012. http://www.ascp.org/Newsroom/To-Pap-or-Not-to-Pap-What-the-New-Cervical-Cancer-Screening-Guidelines-Mean-for-Women.html.

Tooley, Michael. "Abortion and Infanticide." *Philosophy & Public Affairs* 2, no. 1 (October 1, 1972): 37–65.

Trott, Adriel M. "Women in Philosophy: Trans Philosophers and The Politics of Bathrooms." *Blog of the APA* (blog), August 15, 2018. https://blog.apaonline.org/2018/08/15/women-in-philosophy-trans-philosophers-and-the-politics-of-bathrooms/.

Trussell, James, Germán Rodríguez, and Charlotte Ellertson. "New Estimates of the Effectiveness of the Yuzpe Regimen of Emergency Contraception." *Contraception* 57, no. 6 (June 1, 1998): 363–69. https://doi.org/10.1016/S0010-7824(98)00042-0.

Tsugawa, Yusuke, Anupam B. Jena, Jose F. Figueroa, E. John Orav, Daniel M. Blumenthal, and Ashish K. Jha. "Comparison of Hospital Mortality and Readmission Rates for Medicare Patients Treated by Male vs Female Physicians." *JAMA Internal Medicine* 177, no. 2 (February 1, 2017): 206–13. https://doi.org/10.1001/jamainternmed.2016.7875.

Tucker, Eleanor, "I Had A Natural C-Section." *HuffPost UK*, August 14, 2014. http://www.huffingtonpost.co.uk/2014/08/14/i-had-a-natural-c-section_n_7367200.html.

Tucker, Sarah Yahr. "There Is a Hidden Epidemic of Doctors Abusing Women in Labor, Doulas Say." *Broadly*, May 8, 2018. https://broadly.vice.com/en_us/article/evqew7/obstetric-violence-doulas-abuse-giving-birth?utm_campaign=interest&utm_source=broadlyfbusads.

Tunks, E., Bellissimo, A., and Roy, R. (Eds.). (1990). *Chronic pain: Psychosocial factors in rehabilitation* (2nd ed.). Melbourne, FL, US: Robert E Krieger Publishing Co.

Tuttle, Alexander H., Sarasa Tohyama, Tim Ramsay, Jonathan Kimmelman, Petra Schweinhardt, Gary J. Bennett, and Jeffrey S. Mogil. "Increasing Placebo Responses over Time in U.S. Clinical Trials of Neuropathic Pain." *Pain* 156, no. 12 (December 2015): 2616–26. https://doi.org/10.1097/j.pain.0000000000000333.

UC Hastings College of the Law. "Pregnancy-Related Conditions as Disabilities under the ADA." Accessed March 15, 2017. http://worklifelaw.org/pubs/Preg-Accomm-Disabilities.pdf.

UN General Assembly. "Convention on the Elimination of All Forms of Discrimination Against Women." *Treaty Series*, December 18, 1979.

———. "Universal Declaration of Human Rights," December 10, 1948. http://www.unhcr.org/refworld/docid/3ae6b3712c.html.

"Understanding 'Abstinence': Implications for Individuals, Programs and Policies." Guttmacher Institute, September 22, 2004. https://www.guttmacher.org/gpr/2003/12/understanding-abstinence-implications-individuals-programs-and-policies.

Unger, Cecile A. "Caring for the Transgender Patient: The Role of the Gynecologist." *OBG Management* 29, no. 6 (June 2017): 30–38.

UNICEF. "The Baby-Friendly Hospital Initiative." https://www.unicef.org/programme/breastfeeding/baby.htm#10.

"Unintended Pregnancies and Abortions Averted by Planned Parenthood, 2015." Guttmacher Institute, June 13, 2017. https://www.guttmacher.org/infographic/2017/unintended-pregnancies-and-abortions-averted-planned-parenthood-2015.

Union Pacific R. Co. v. Botsford, 141 United States (Supreme Court 1891).

United Nations Human Rights Office of the High Commissioner. "International Covenant on Economic, Social and Cultural Rights." January 3, 1976. http://www.ohchr.org/EN/ProfessionalInterest/Pages/CESCR.aspx.

———. "International Convention on the Elimination of All Forms of Racial Discrimination." January 4, 1969. http://www.ohchr.org/EN/ProfessionalInterest/Pages/CERD.aspx.

"United Nations Office on Genocide Prevention and the Responsibility to Protect." http://www.un.org/en/genocideprevention/crimes-against-humanity.html.

United Nations Population Fund. *State of World Population 2019: Unfinished Business—The Pursuit of Rights and Choices . . . For All.* United Nations Publications, 2019.

United States Conference of Catholic Bishops. "Ethical and Religious Directives for Catholic Health Care Services, Fifth Edition," November 17, 2009. http://www.usccb.org/issues-and-action/human-life-and-dignity/health-care/upload/Ethical-Religious-Directives-Catholic-Health-Care-Services-fifth-edition-2009.pdf.

United States Department of Labor Occupational Safety and Health Administration Education Center. "Restroom Break Laws." 2019. https://www.oshaeducationcenter.com/articles/restroom-breaks.aspx.

United States Supreme Court. Zubik v. Burwell, No. No. 14-1418 (May 16, 2016).

Urquhart, Evan. "Gatekeepers vs. Informed Consent: Who Decides When a Trans Person Can Medically Transition?" *Slate*, March 11, 2016. http://www.slate.com/blogs/outward/2016/03/11/transgen-der_patients_and_informed_consent_who_decides_when_transition_treatment.html.

US Department of Health and Human Services. "Conscience and Religious Freedom." Text. HHS.gov, January 17, 2018. https://www.hhs.gov/conscience/index.html.

US Department of Health and Human Services, Centers for Disease Control and Prevention, and National Center for Health Statistics. "Health, United States, 2015: With Special Feature on Racial and Ethnic Health Disparities," 2015, 461.

US Department of Veterans Affairs Veterans Health Administration. "Provider Fact Sheet: Cervical Cancer Screening," June 2013. https://www.prevention.va.gov/docs/CervicalC-Provider.pdf.

Martin, Nina, and Renee Montagne. "US Has The Worst Rate Of Maternal Deaths In The Developed World." NPR.org, May 12, 2017. http://www.npr.org/2017/05/12/528098789/u-s-has-the-worst-rate-of-maternal-deaths-in-the-developed-world.

US Preventative Services Task Force. "Cervical Cancer: Screening." uspreventiveservicetaskforce.org, March 2012.

———. "Final Update Summary: Cervical Cancer: Screening," August 2018. https://www.uspreventiveservicestaskforce.org/Page/Document/UpdateSummaryFinal/cervical-cancer-screening2.

———. Screening for Cervical Cancer. Williams & Wilkins, 1996. https://www.ncbi.nlm.nih.gov/books/NBK15479/.

Scheer, Roddy and Doug Moss. "Use It and Lose It: The Outsize Effect of U.S. Consumption on the Environment." *Scientific American*. September 14, 2012. https://www.scientificamerican.com/article/american-consumption-habits/.

Uttley, Christine Khaikin and Lois. "State Oversight of Hospital Consolidation: Inadequate to Protect Patients' Rights and Community Access to Care." *AMA Journal of Ethics* 18, no. 3 (March 1, 2016): 272. https://doi.org/10.1001/journalofethics.2016.18.3.pfor3-1603.

Vääräsmäki, Marja, and Tytti Raudaskoski. "Pregnancy and Delivery after a Cesarean Section." *Duodecim; Laaketieteellinen Aikakauskirja* 133, no. 4 (2017): 345–52.

Vaccarino, V., L. Parsons, N. R. Every, H. V. Barron, and H. M. Krumholz. "Sex-Based Differences in Early Mortality after Myocardial Infarction. National Registry of Myocardial Infarction 2 Participants." *The New England Journal of Medicine* 341, no. 4 (July 22, 1999): 217–25. https://doi.org/10.1056/NEJM199907223410401.

Vaccarino, Viola, Lori Parsons, Eric D. Peterson, William J. Rogers, Catarina I. Kiefe, and John Canto. "Sex Differences in Mortality After Acute Myocardial Infarction: Changes From 1994 to 2006." *Archives of Internal Medicine* 169, no. 19 (October 26, 2009): 1767–74. https://doi.org/10.1001/archinternmed.2009.332.

"Vaginal Birth After Cesarean: New Insights." *Evidence Report/Technology Assessment*, No. 191, March, 2010, 397.

Valdes, Marcela. "When Doctors Took 'Family Planning' Into Their Own Hands." *The New York Times*, December 21, 2017, sec. Magazine. https://www.nytimes.com/2016/02/01/magazine/when-doctors-took-family-planning-into-their-own-hands.html.

Vanakankovit, Natthakan, and Surasak Taneepanichskul. "Effect of Oral Contraceptives on Risk of Cervical Cancer." *Journal of the Medical Association of Thailand = Chotmaihet Thangphaet* 91, no. 1 (January 2008): 7–12.

Varney, Sarah. "Testosterone, The Biggest Men's Health Craze Since Viagra, May Be Risky." NPR.org, April 28, 2014. https://www.npr.org/sections/health-shots/2014/04/28/

305658501/prescription-testosterone-the-biggest-men-s-health-craze-since-viagra-may-be-ris.

Velleman, J. David. "A Right of Self-Termination?" *Ethics* 109, no. 3 (1999): 606–28. https://doi.org/10.1086/233924.

"Victim Issues: Mistrust of Professionals: Responding to Transgender Victims of Sexual Assault," 2014. https://www.ovc.gov/pubs/forge/tips_pro.html.

Villar, José, Guillermo Carroli, Nelly Zavaleta, Allan Donner, Daniel Wojdyla, Anibal Faundes, Alejandro Velazco, et al. "Maternal and Neonatal Individual Risks and Benefits Associated with Caesarean Delivery: Multicentre Prospective Study." *BMJ* (Clinical Research Ed.) 335, no. 7628 (November 17, 2007): 1025. https://doi.org/10.1136/bmj.39363.706956.55.

Vinekar, Kavita S., Anjel Vahratian, Kelli S. Hall, Brady T. West, Amy Caldwell, Jason D. Bell, and Vanessa K. Dalton. "Cervical Cancer Screening, Pelvic Examinations, and Contraceptive Use Among Adolescent and Young Adult Females." *Journal of Adolescent Health* 57, no. 2 (August 1, 2015): 169–73. https://doi.org/10.1016/j.jadohealth.2015.04.001.

Vohr, Eric. "Older Women Less Likely than Men to Be Listed For Kidney Transplants." *Johns Hopkins Medicine*, January 12, 2009. https://www.hopkinsmedicine.org/news/media/releases/Older_Women_Less_Likely_than_Men_to_be_Listed_For_Kidney_Transplants.

Vos, R., K. De Vusser, V. Schaevers, A. Schoonis, V. Lemaigre, F. Dobbels, K. Desmet, et al. "Smoking Resumption after Lung Transplantation: A Sobering Truth." *European Respiratory Journal* 35, no. 6 (June 1, 2010): 1411–13. https://doi.org/10.1183/09031936.00183509.

Wainberg, Sara, Heather Wrigley, Justine Fair, and Sue Ross. "Teaching Pelvic Examinations Under Anaesthesia: What Do Women Think?" *Journal of Obstetrics and Gynaecology Canada* 32, no. 1 (January 1, 2010): 49–53. https://doi.org/10.1016/S1701-2163(16)34404-8.

Walker, Alice. "What Can the White Man Say to the Black Woman?" *The Nation*, May 22, 1989. https://www.thenation.com/wp-content/uploads/2015/05/whitemanblackwoman.pdf.

Walker, Joan L., C. Bethan Powell, Lee-may Chen, Jeanne Carter, Victoria L. Bae Jump, Lynn P. Parker, Mark E. Borowsky, and Randall K. Gibb. "Society of Gynecologic Oncology Recommendations for the Prevention of Ovarian Cancer." *Cancer* 121, no. 13 (July 1, 2015): 2108–20. https://doi.org/10.1002/cncr.29321.

Wang, Amy X. "For the First Time Ever, More Women than Men Are Going to Med School." *Quartz at Work*, December 20, 2017. https://work.qz.com/1161347/medical-school-is-more-female-than-male-for-the-first-time-in-history/.

Warren, Mary Anne. "On the Moral and Legal Status of Abortion." *The Monist* 57, no. 1 (January 1, 1973): 43–61.

Washington, Harriet A. *Medical Apartheid: The Dark History of Medical Experimentation on Black Americans from Colonial Times to the Present*. New York: Harlem Moon, 2006.

Waterman, Amy D., Marie Morgievich, David J. Cohen, Zeeshan Butt, Harini A. Chakkera, Carrie Lindower, Rebecca E. Hays, et al. "Living Donor Kidney Transplantation: Improving Education Outside of Transplant Centers about Live Donor Transplantation—Recommendations from a Consensus Conference." *Clinical Journal of the American Society of Nephrology: CJASN* 10, no. 9 (September 4, 2015): 1659–69. https://doi.org/10.2215/CJN.00950115.

Waterman, Amy D., John D. Peipert, Christina J. Goalby, Katrina M. Dinkel, Huiling Xiao, and Krista L. Lentine. "Assessing Transplant Education Practices in Dialysis Centers: Comparing Educator Reported and Medicare Data." *Clinical Journal of the American Society of Nephrology: CJASN* 10, no. 9 (September 4, 2015): 1617–25. https://doi.org/10.2215/CJN.09851014.

Watt, Helen. *The Ethics of Pregnancy, Abortion and Childbirth: Exploring Moral Choices in Childbearing*. Routledge, 2016.

Wax-Thibodeaux, Emily, and Ariana Eunjung Cha. "Georgia Governor Signs 'Heartbeat Bill,' Giving the State One of the Most Restrictive Abortion Laws in the Nation." *The Washington Post*, May 7, 2019, sec. Health & Science. https://www.washingtonpost.com/national/health-science/georgia-governor-signs-heartbeat-bill-giving-the-state-one-of-the-most-restrictive-abortion-laws-in-the-nation/2019/05/07/d53b2f8a-70cf-11e9-8be0-ca575670e91c_story.html.

WebMD. "Multiple Pregnancy: Twins or More-Topic Overview." January 16, 2019. http://www.webmd.com/baby/guide/multiple-pregnancy-twins-or-more-topic-overview.

Weiner, Jocelyn. "Episiotomies Still Common During Childbirth Despite Advice To Do Fewer." NPR.org. Accessed July 4, 2016. https://www.npr.org/sections/health-shots/2016/07/04/483945168/episiotomies-still-common-during-childbirth-despite-advice-to-do-fewer.

Welch, H. Gilbert, and Brittney A. Frankel. "Likelihood That a Woman with Screen-Detected Breast Cancer Has Had Her 'Life Saved' by That Screening." *Archives of Internal Medicine* 171, no. 22 (December 12, 2011): 2043–46. https://doi.org/10.1001/archinternmed.2011.476.

Welch, H. Gilbert, Lisa Schwartz, and Steve Woloshin. *Overdiagnosed: Making People Sick in the Pursuit of Health*. 1 edition. Boston, Massachusetts: Beacon Press, 2012.

Welch, Shay. *Existential Eroticism: A Feminist Approach to Understanding Women's Oppression-Perpetuating Choices*. Lexington Books, 2017.

Wells, Charlie. "The Good and Bad Statistics on Women in Medicine." *WSJ* (blog), October 29, 2015. https://blogs.wsj.com/experts/2015/10/29/the-good-and-bad-statistics-on-women-in-medicine/.

Wernli, Karen J., Nora B. Henrikson, Caitlin C. Morrison, Matthew Nguyen, Gaia Pocobelli, and Paula R. Blasi. "Screening for Skin Cancer in Adults: Updated Evidence Report and Systematic Review for the US Preventive Services Task Force." *JAMA* 316, no. 4 (July 26, 2016): 436. https://doi.org/10.1001/jama.2016.5415.

"What Are the Recommendations for Breastfeeding?" http://www.nichd.nih.gov/. January 31, 2017. http://www.nichd.nih.gov/health/topics/breastfeeding/conditioninfo/recommendations.

"What Is the Effectiveness of Abstinence and Outercourse?" https://www.plannedparenthood.org/learn/birth-control/abstinence-and-outercourse/how-effective-are-abstinence-and-outercourse.

"What Is the Effectiveness of Birth Control Pills?" https://www.plannedparenthood.org/learn/birth-control/birth-control-pill/how-effective-is-the-birth-control-pill.

"What Is the Effectiveness of Condoms?" January 31, 2017. https://www.plannedparenthood.org/learn/birth-control/condom/how-effective-are-condoms.

White Hughto, Jaclyn M., Adam J. Rose, John E. Pachankis, and Sari L. Reisner. "Barriers to Gender Transition-Related Healthcare: Identifying Underserved Transgender Adults in Massachusetts." *Transgender Health* 2, no. 1 (July 1, 2017): 107–18. https://doi.org/10.1089/trgh.2017.0014.

Whole Woman's Health et al. v. Hellerstedt, Commissioner, Texas Department of State Health Services, et al. 2016, 15 274. Supreme Court of the United States.

Wilhelmson, Anna S., Marta Lantero Rodriguez, Alexandra Stubelius, Per Fogelstrand, Inger Johansson, Matthew B. Buechler, Steve Lianoglou, et al. "Testosterone Is an Endogenous Regulator of BAFF and Splenic B Cell Number." *Nature Communications* 9, no. 1 (May 25, 2018): 2067. https://doi.org/10.1038/s41467-018-04408-0.

Wille, Keith M., Kathy F. Harrington, Joao A. deAndrade, Sonia V. Compton, Robert A. Oster, and Richard A. Kaslow. "Disparities In Lung Transplantation Before And After Introduction Of The Lung Allocation Score." *The Journal of Heart and Lung Transplantation: The Official Publication of the International Society for Heart Transplantation* 32, no. 7 (July 2013): 684–92. https://doi.org/10.1016/j.healun.2013.03.005.

Wills, Matthew. "When Forced Sterilization Was Legal in the U.S." *JSTOR Daily*, August 3, 2017. https://daily.jstor.org/when-forced-sterilization-was-legal-in-the-u-s/.

Wilper, Andrew P., Steffie Woolhandler, Karen E. Lasser, Danny McCormick, David H. Bor, and David U. Himmelstein. "Health Insurance and Mortality in US Adults." *Research and Practice* 99, no. 12 (December 2009): 2289–95.

Wilson, Sarah. "Doctors, Stop Gaslighting Women In Pain." *Thrive Global* (blog), August 24, 2017. https://medium.com/thrive-global/doctors-stop-gaslighting-women-in-pain-3934a2fdc1b.

Wind, Rebecca. "Many American Women Use Birth Control Pills for Noncontraceptive Reasons." Guttmacher Institute, November 15, 2011. https://www.guttmacher.org/news-release/2011/many-american-women-use-birth-control-pills-noncontraceptive-reasons.

Wolf, Jacqueline H. "Risk and Reputation: Obstetricians, Cesareans, and Consent." *Journal of the History of Medicine and Allied Sciences* 73, no. 1 (January 5, 2018): 7–28.

Wolf, Susan M. "Gender, Feminism, and Death: Physician-Assisted Suicide and Euthanasia." in *Feminism and Bioethics: Beyond Reproduction*, edited by Susan M. Wolf. Oxford University Press, 1996. https://papers.ssrn.com/abstract=1737888.

World Health Organization. "WHO Recommendations: Intrapartum Care for a Positive Childbirth Experience." 2018. http://apps.who.int/iris/bitstream/handle/10665/260178/9789241550215-eng.pdf;jsessionid=BE701325C5A41B3C92634F86E2E2BD46?sequence=1.

Yang, Y. Tony, Paul L. Delamater, Timothy F. Leslie, and Michelle M. Mello. "Sociodemographic Predictors of Vaccination Exemptions on the Basis of Personal Belief in California." *American Journal of Public Health* 106, no. 1 (November 12, 2015): 172–77. https://doi.org/10.2105/AJPH.2015.302926.

Yarrow, Allison. "Why Do We Understand so Little about Breast-Feeding?" *The Washington Post*. February 21, 2018, sec. Perspective. https://www.washingtonpost.com/news/posteverything/wp/2018/02/21/why-do-we-understand-so-little-about-breastfeeding/.

Yaver, Miranda. "Analysis: States with More Planned Parenthood Clinics Have Fewer Teen Births and Sexually Transmitted Diseases." *Washington Post*, March 27, 2017, sec. Monkey Cage Analysis. https://www.washingtonpost.com/news/monkey-cage/wp/2017/03/27/states-with-more-planned-parenthood-clinics-have-fewer-teen-births-and-sexually-transmitted-diseases/.

Ye, J., J. Zhang, R. Mikolajczyk, M. R. Torloni, A. M. Gülmezoglu, and A. P. Betran. "Association between Rates of Caesarean Section and Maternal and Neonatal Mortality in the 21st Century: A Worldwide Population-Based Ecological Study with Longitudinal Data." *BJOG: An International Journal of Obstetrics & Gynaecology* 123, no. 5 (August 24, 2015): 745–53. https://doi.org/10.1111/1471-0528.13592.

Young, Alison, and John Kelly. "Episiotomies Are Painful, Risky and Not Routinely Recommended. Dozens of Hospitals Are Doing Too Many." *USA Today*, May 21, 2019. https://www.usatoday.com/in-depth/news/investigations/deadly-deliveries/2019/05/21/episiotomy-vs-tearing-moms-cut-in-childbirth-despite-guidelines/3668035002/.

Young, Iris Marion. *Justice and the Politics of Difference*. Princeton University Press, 1990.

———. *On Female Body Experience: "Throwing Like a Girl" and Other Essays*. New York: Oxford University Press, 2005.

Young, Lynne, and Maureen Little. "Women and Heart Transplantation: An Issue of Gender Equity?" *Health Care for Women International* 25, no. 5 (May 2004): 436–53. https://doi.org/10.1080/07399330490272778.

Yu, Jean M., Jillian T. Henderson, Cynthia C. Harper, and George F. Sawaya. "Obstetrician-Gynecologists' Beliefs on the Importance of Pelvic Examinations in Assessing Hormonal Contraception Eligibility." *Contraception* 90, no. 6 (December 1, 2014): 612–14. https://doi.org/10.1016/j.contraception.2014.06.038.

Zack, Naomi. *Philosophy of Science and Race*. 1st ed. Routledge, 2002.

Zaveri, Mihir. "Mother of Dead Woman Says Medics Told Her She Could Not Afford Ambulance." *The New York Times*, August 7, 2018, sec. U.S. https://www.nytimes.com/2018/07/29/us/black-woman-ambulance-cost-florida.html.

Zeuner, Rachel, Dominick L. Frosch, Marie D. Kuzemchak, and Mary C. Politi. "Physicians' Perceptions of Shared Decision-making Behaviours: A Qualitative Study Demonstrating the Continued Chasm between Aspirations and Clinical Practice." *Health Expectations:*

An International Journal of Public Participation in Health Care and Health Policy 18, no. 6 (December 2015): 2465–76. https://doi.org/10.1111/hex.12216.
Zhang, Sarah. "The Surgeon Who Experimented on Slaves." *The Atlantic*, April 18, 2018. http://www.theatlantic.com/health/archive/2018/04/j-marion-sims/558248/.
Zillman, Claire. "Who Makes Less than $15 per Hour, in 3 Charts." *Fortune* (blog), April 13, 2015. http://fortune.com/2015/04/13/who-makes-15-per-hour/.

INDEX

ABOUT THE AUTHOR

Jill B. Delston is associate teaching professor of philosophy at the University of Missouri–St. Louis.

www.ingramcontent.com/pod-product-compliance
Ingram Content Group UK Ltd.
Pitfield, Milton Keynes, MK11 3LW, UK
UKHW041127071026
15587UKWH00009B/279

9 781498 558211